University Success

WRITING

ADVANCED

Charl Norloff and Ruth Moore

Series Editor: Maggie Sokolik

Authentic Content Contributor: Victoria Solomon

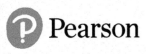

University Success Writing, Advanced Level

Copyright © 2018 by Pearson Education, Inc.

All rights reserved.

Pearson Education, 221 River Street, Hoboken, NJ 07030

Staff credits: The people who made up the *University Success* team, representing content development, design, manufacturing, marketing, multimedia, project management, publishing, rights management, and testing, are Pietro Alongi, Stephanie Callahan, Kimberly Casey, Tracey Cataldo, Sara Davila, Dave Dickey, Gina DiLillo, Warren Fischbach, Nancy Flaggman, Lucy Hart, Sarah Henrich, Gosia Jaros-White, Niki Lee, Amy McCormick, Jennifer Raspiller, Robert Ruvo, Katarzyna Skiba, Kristina Skof, Katarzyna Starzynska-Kosciuszko, Joanna Szyszynska, John Thompson, Paula Van Ells, Joseph Vella, Rebecca Wicker, and Natalia Zaremba.

Project coordination: Robyn Brinks Lockwood

Project supervision: Debbie Sistino

Contributing editors: Lida Baker, Eleanor Barnes, Andrea Bryant, Barbara Lyons, Leigh Stolle, and Sarah Wales-McGrath

Cover image: Oleksandr Prykhodko / Alamy Stock Photo

Video research: Constance Rylance

Video production: Kristine Stolakis, assisted by Melissa Langer

Text composition: EMC Design Ltd

Library of Congress Cataloging-in-Publication Data

A catalog record for the print edition is available from the Library of Congress.

Printed in the United States of America

ISBN-10: 0-13-465269-X

ISBN-13: 978-0-13-465269-6

Contents

PART 1: FUNDAMENTAL WRITING SKILLS

PART 2: CRITICAL THINKING SKILLS

PART 3: EXTENDED WRITING

Welcome to *University Success*

INTRODUCTION

University Success is a new academic skills series designed to equip intermediate- to transition-level English learners with the reading, writing, and oral communication skills necessary to succeed in courses in an English-speaking university setting. The blended instructional model provides students with an inspiring collection of extensive authentic content, expertly developed in cooperation with five subject matter experts, all "thought leaders" in their fields. By utilizing both online and in-class instructional materials, *University Success* models the type of "real life" learning expected of students studying for a degree. *University Success* recognizes the unique linguistic needs of English language learners and carefully scaffolds skill development to help students successfully work with challenging and engaging authentic content.

SERIES ORGANIZATION: *THREE STRANDS*

This three-strand series, **Reading**, **Writing**, and **Oral Communication**, includes five distinct content areas: The Human Experience, Money and Commerce, The Science of Nature, Arts and Letters, and Structural Science, all popular fields of study among English language learners. The three strands are fully aligned across content areas and skills, allowing teachers to utilize material from different strands to support learning. Teachers can delve deeply into skill development in a single area, or provide additional support materials from other areas for richer development across the four skills.

THE *UNIVERSITY SUCCESS* APPROACH: *AN AUTHENTIC EXPERIENCE*

This blended program combines the utility of an interactive student book, online learner lab, and print course to create a flexible approach that adjusts to the needs of teachers and learners. Its skill-based and step-by-step instruction enables students to master essential skills and become confident in their ability to perform successfully in academic degree courses taught in English. Students at this level need to engage with content that provides them with the same challenges native speakers face in a university setting. Many English language learners are not prepared for the quantity of reading and writing required in college-level courses, nor are they properly prepared to listen to full-length lectures that have not been scaffolded for them. These learners, away from the safety of an ESL classroom, must keep up with the rigors of a class led by a professor who may be unaware of the challenges a second-language learner faces. Strategies for academic success, delivered via online videos, help increase students' confidence and ability to cope with the challenges of academic student and college culture. *University Success* steps up to the podium to represent academic content realistically with the appropriate skill development and scaffolding essential for English language learners to be successful.

PUTTING STUDENTS ON THE PATH TO *UNIVERSITY SUCCESS*

Intensive skill development and extended application—tied to specific learning outcomes—provide the scaffolding English language learners need to become confident and successful in a university setting.

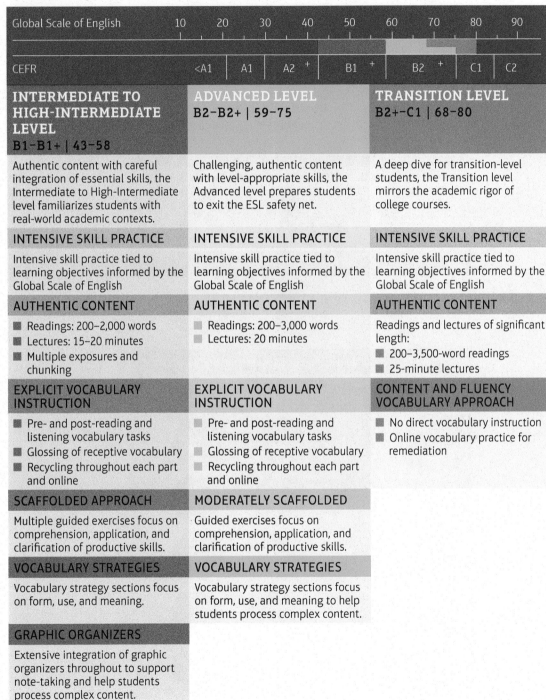

Global Scale of English	10 20 30 40 50 60 70 80 90
CEFR	<A1 | A1 | A2 + | B1 + | B2 + | C1 | C2

INTERMEDIATE TO HIGH-INTERMEDIATE LEVEL B1–B1+ | 43–58	ADVANCED LEVEL B2–B2+ | 59–75	TRANSITION LEVEL B2+–C1 | 68–80
Authentic content with careful integration of essential skills, the Intermediate to High-Intermediate level familiarizes students with real-world academic contexts.	Challenging, authentic content with level-appropriate skills, the Advanced level prepares students to exit the ESL safety net.	A deep dive for transition-level students, the Transition level mirrors the academic rigor of college courses.
INTENSIVE SKILL PRACTICE	**INTENSIVE SKILL PRACTICE**	**INTENSIVE SKILL PRACTICE**
Intensive skill practice tied to learning objectives informed by the Global Scale of English	Intensive skill practice tied to learning objectives informed by the Global Scale of English	Intensive skill practice tied to learning objectives informed by the Global Scale of English
AUTHENTIC CONTENT	**AUTHENTIC CONTENT**	**AUTHENTIC CONTENT**
■ Readings: 200–2,000 words ■ Lectures: 15–20 minutes ■ Multiple exposures and chunking	■ Readings: 200–3,000 words ■ Lectures: 20 minutes	Readings and lectures of significant length: ■ 200–3,500-word readings ■ 25-minute lectures
EXPLICIT VOCABULARY INSTRUCTION	**EXPLICIT VOCABULARY INSTRUCTION**	**CONTENT AND FLUENCY VOCABULARY APPROACH**
■ Pre- and post-reading and listening vocabulary tasks ■ Glossing of receptive vocabulary ■ Recycling throughout each part and online	■ Pre- and post-reading and listening vocabulary tasks ■ Glossing of receptive vocabulary ■ Recycling throughout each part and online	■ No direct vocabulary instruction ■ Online vocabulary practice for remediation
SCAFFOLDED APPROACH	**MODERATELY SCAFFOLDED**	
Multiple guided exercises focus on comprehension, application, and clarification of productive skills.	Guided exercises focus on comprehension, application, and clarification of productive skills.	
VOCABULARY STRATEGIES	**VOCABULARY STRATEGIES**	
Vocabulary strategy sections focus on form, use, and meaning.	Vocabulary strategy sections focus on form, use, and meaning to help students process complex content.	
GRAPHIC ORGANIZERS		
Extensive integration of graphic organizers throughout to support note-taking and help students process complex content.		

Key Features

UNIQUE PART STRUCTURE

University Success employs a unique three-part structure, providing maximum flexibility and multiple opportunities to customize the content. The series is "horizontally" aligned to teach across a specific content area and "vertically" aligned to allow a teacher to gradually build skills.

Each part is a self-contained module allowing teachers to customize a non-linear program that will best address the needs of students. Parts are aligned around science, technology, engineering, arts, and mathematics (STEAM) content relevant to mainstream academic areas of study.

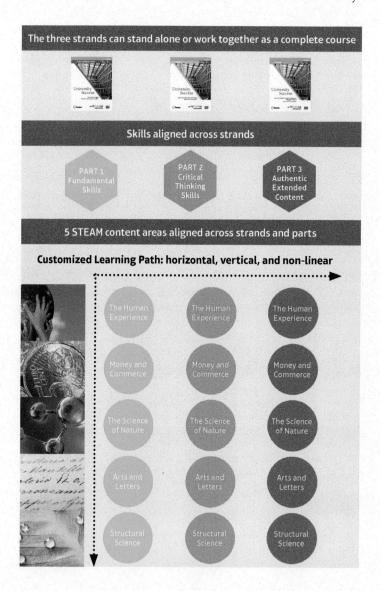

The three strands can stand alone or work together as a complete course

Skills aligned across strands

PART 1
Fundamental
Skills

PART 2
Critical
Thinking
Skills

PART 3
Authentic
Extended
Content

5 STEAM content areas aligned across strands and parts

Customized Learning Path: horizontal, vertical, and non-linear

The Human Experience
Money and Commerce
The Science of Nature
Arts and Letters
Structural Science

THE THREE PARTS AT A GLANCE

 Parts 1 and 2 focus on the fundamental writing and critical thinking skills most relevant for students preparing for university degrees. In Part 1 and Part 2, students work with comprehensive skills that include:

- Understanding the research writing process
- Identifying reliable sources of information
- Developing and organizing ideas
- Revising, editing, and proofreading text
- Organizing and supporting a process

 Part 3 introduces students to extended practice with the skills. Content created by top university professors provides students with a challenging experience that replicates the authentic experience of studying in a mainstream university class.

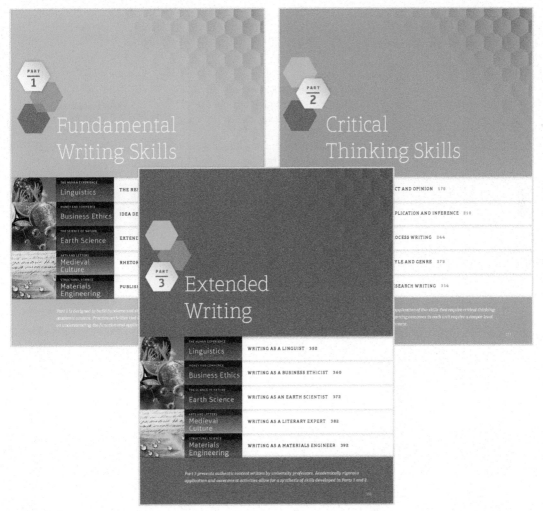

Student Book

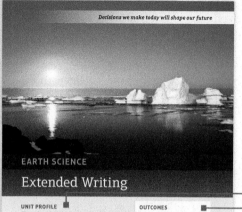

MyEnglishLab

A **unit profile** outlines the content.

Outcomes aligned with the Global Scale of English (GSE) are clearly stated to ensure student awareness of skills.

Self-assessments provide opportunities for students to identify skill areas for improvement and provide teachers with information that can inform lesson planning.

Professors provide a **preview** and a **summary** of the content.

Why It's Useful sections highlight the need for developing skills and support transfer of skills to mainstream class content.

A **detailed presentation** facilitates intensive development of the skills. Follow-up exercises enhance skill understanding and conclude with an authentic academic writing task.

Additional **practice online** encourages the application of skills.

Student Book

MyEnglishLab

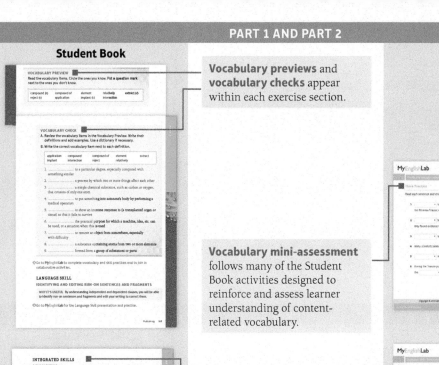

Vocabulary previews and **vocabulary checks** appear within each exercise section.

Vocabulary mini-assessment follows many of the Student Book activities designed to reinforce and assess learner understanding of content-related vocabulary.

Integrated skills provide practice with high-level authentic academic content in reading as well as writing and teaches strategies that apply across language skills.

Additional **MEL exercises** are designed to have learners apply the information presented.

Language skill study provides support for syntactic and grammatical skills.

Vocabulary strategies offer valuable means for recognizing and retaining vocabulary, such as understanding connotations, recognizing in-text definitions, and using a corpus to expand word knowledge.

Student Book

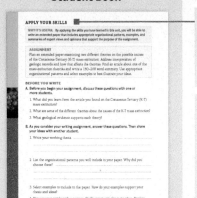

Parts 1 and 2 end with an extended **Apply Your Skills** section that functions as a diagnostic or formative assessment.

A final **Apply Your Skills** section asks students to watch a concluding video, then record their thoughts about related questions. A final **Skill Self-Assessment** enables students to assess their improvement in unit skill areas.

Student Book

MyEnglishLab

Students use **critical thinking** skills to engage at a deeper level, consider a situation related to the content, and record their thoughts.

The Interview sections allow students to view professors discussing how they get their ideas, carry out research, and develop their own writing. Follow-up includes comprehension and **critical thinking** activities.

A culminating **writing assignment** includes **research** and encourages in-class and online project collaboration.

A thematically relevant **reading** written by the professor who has been interviewed promotes further exploration of the content and informs the writing task.

STRATEGIES FOR ACADEMIC SUCCESS AND SOFT SKILLS

Strategies for academic success and soft skills, delivered via online videos, help increase students' confidence and ability to cope with the challenges of academic study and college culture. Study skills include how to talk to professors during office hours and time management techniques.

TEACHER SUPPORT

Each of the three strands is supported with:

- Comprehensive **downloadable teaching notes** in MyEnglishLab that detail key points for all of the specialized, academic content in addition to tips and suggestions for how to teach skills and strategies.
- **An easy-to-use online learning management system** offering a flexible gradebook and tools for monitoring student progress
- Essential tools, such as **video scripts** and **course planners**, to help in lesson planning and follow-up.

ASSESSMENT

University Success provides a package of assessments that can be used as precourse diagnostics, midcourse assessments, and final summative assessments. The flexible nature of these assessments allows teachers to choose which assessments will be most appropriate at various stages of the program. These assessments are embedded in the student book and are available online in MyEnglishLab.

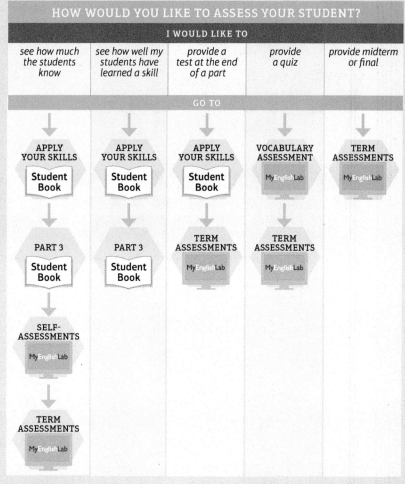

HOW WOULD YOU LIKE TO ASSESS YOUR STUDENT?				
I WOULD LIKE TO				
see how much the students know	see how well my students have learned a skill	provide a test at the end of a part	provide a quiz	provide midterm or final
GO TO				
APPLY YOUR SKILLS **Student Book**	APPLY YOUR SKILLS **Student Book**	APPLY YOUR SKILLS **Student Book**	VOCABULARY ASSESSMENT MyEnglishLab	TERM ASSESSMENTS MyEnglishLab
PART 3 **Student Book**	PART 3 **Student Book**	TERM ASSESSMENTS MyEnglishLab	TERM ASSESSMENTS MyEnglishLab	
SELF-ASSESSMENTS MyEnglishLab				
TERM ASSESSMENTS MyEnglishLab				

Scope and Sequence

 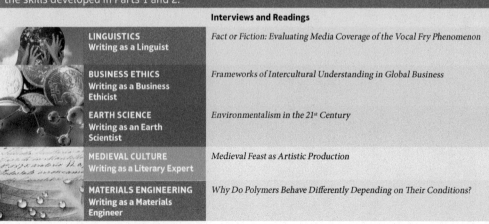

Integrated Skills	Language Skills	Vocabulary Strategy	Apply Your Skills
Annotate research	Identify phrases in academic text	Use a dictionary to expand vocabulary	Plan a paper analyzing how and why words borrowed from other languages enter the English language
Paraphrase	Use direct quotations and reported speech	Recognize in-text definitions	Plan a paper comparing the advantages and disadvantages of putting the interests of shareholders or stakeholders first
Summarize	Use adverbials of cause and effect	Learn root words	Plan an extended paper examining two different theories on the possible causes of the Cretaceous-Tertiary (K-T) mass extinction
Analyze text for style and tone	Use cohesive devices for reference and agreement	Understand connotations	Write an essay of 800–1000 words that analyzes the role of poetry in medieval times and the role of modern music today
Analyze text	Identify and edit run-on sentences and fragments	Understand prefixes	Write a discussion post of 500–600 words about the use of regenerative treatment for one specific injury or illness

Integrated Skills	Language Skills	Vocabulary Strategy	Apply Your Skills
Recognize author bias	Use language of disagreement	Use a dictionary to learn collocations	Write an argumentative essay of 500–800 words taking a position on whether learning a second language has impacted or changed your identity
Understand and respond to implication and inference	Use modals to express degrees of certainty	Use a thesaurus	Write a paper of 800–1000 words that addresses one aspect of culture that influences economies and draw a conclusion about what the effect of that influence is
Synthesize information from sources	Use passive voice in scientific writing	Build discipline-specific vocabulary	Write a process paper of 800–1000 words explaining one way to lessen food insecurity
Analyze descriptive writing	Vary description	Use a corpus to expand word knowledge	Research a folklore story that ends with a moral or lesson. Identify the genre, briefly summarize the story, and write an essay of 500–800 words analyzing the style and appeal
Present a research paper	Use parallel structure	Understand suffixes	Write a 1000–1200 word section of a Materials Engineering research paper on polymeric materials

Research / Assignment

Write an academic paper of 4–6 pages about the way a particular social group uses language.

Write an academic paper of 4–6 pages comparing global business practices of two different countries.

Write an academic paper of 4–6 pages on an environmental issue that is of concern to a region of the world, a specific country, or a particular community.

Write an academic paper of 4–6 pages describing a celebration in a local community you are familiar with.

Write research summaries of 250–500 words each for two peer-reviewed articles based on your research on an innovative technology that uses polymers to address a particular need or problem.

A Note from Maggie Sokolik

Series Editor for *University Success Writing*

Advanced-level EAP students are often planning, or at least contemplating, a move from ELT courses to content-based study in a university or college. Although they have reached a level of success and proficiency in their English language studies, they may lack the academic skills or vocabulary to continue to grow as academic writers. To help students with this continued development as they prepare for more advanced study, *University Success Writing, Advanced Level* features writing instruction and assignments in a way that is more attuned to how writing is taught in higher education and across disciplines. The focus of writing instruction is on inquiry-based and research writing, writing in specific subject areas, and developing critical and creative thinking resulting in strong content development. *University Success Writing, Advanced Level* breaks down and systematically explains the processes involved in various writing tasks. Students see how they can address writing assignments in different disciplines and build essays they can be proud of. The advanced level of *University Success* provides appropriate and authentic content while preparing students to meet their academic goals, making it the ideal resource for students at this stage of their education. In addition, it provides moderate scaffolding needed by students moving from advanced-level English skills towards true academic English skills.

PART 1—FUNDAMENTAL WRITING SKILLS

In the first five units of *University Success Writing Advanced Level*, each of the five main subject areas, Linguistics, Business Ethics, Earth Science, Medieval Culture, and Materials Engineering, is used to provide authentic content for skill-based learning and practice of inquiry and research-based writing. While students have most likely been taught steps in the writing process, they may not have had adequate practice using those skills. The advanced level allows for additional practice, provides some scaffolding for students to understand the demands of different content areas, and encourages students to develop their own ideas in ways that are arguable, supported, and interesting. It also focuses on vocabulary development as a key component of successful writing.

PART 2—CRITICAL THINKING SKILLS

The next five units continue the exploration of the topics from Part 1 from a new angle. With the focus on critical thinking, Part 2 challenges advanced-level students to engage in high-level academic tasks, such as: distinguishing between fact and opinion and learning how to integrate them to develop an argument; reading critically to understand implications and draw inferences; effectively describing a process so that all the steps are clear to the reader; using rhetorical devices to best fit a text's style and genre; and learning how incorporating research informs all types of academic writing.

PART 3—EXTENDED WRITING

Part 3 includes interviews with five professors from Stanford University about their specific writing processes and habits. These interviews provide students with a unique opportunity to hear professors describe how they get their ideas, carry out research, and develop their writing. Students will also hear about what professors expect from them when writing in different disciplines. These interviews are followed by opportunities for students to engage in critical thinking, analysis, and discussion of authentic situations based on assignments in the subject areas. After additional review of the language skills from Parts 1 and 2, students complete a culminating writing task that is preceded by extensive guided research. The writing task builds upon a thematically relevant reading written by the professor who has been interviewed and uses the featured language skills, giving students the opportunity for practice that will help them participate in inquiry-based research and writing.

SUBJECT MATTER EXPERTS

Marisa Galvez specializes in the literature of the Middle Ages in France and Western Europe, especially literature written in Occitan and Old French. Her courses at Stanford focus on medieval and Renaissance French literature and the medieval imaginary in modern literature, film, and art. Her recent book, *Songbook: How Lyrics Became Poetry in Medieval Europe*, is the first comparative study of songbooks and was awarded the John Nicholas Brown Prize from the Medieval Academy of America.

Sarah Heilshorn is an Associate Professor in the Department of Materials Science and Engineering and, by courtesy, of Bioengineering and Chemical Engineering at Stanford University. She completed her PhD and MS degrees in Chemical Engineering at California Institute of Technology. She earned a BS in Chemical Engineering at Georgia Institute of Technology. She is an expert in the design of new materials that mimic those found in our own bodies.

Scotty McLennan is a Lecturer in Political Economy at the Stanford Graduate School of Business (GSB), where he teaches in the areas of business ethics and business and spirituality. He taught business ethics at the Harvard Business School from 1988 to 2000, and from 2000 to 2014 he was the Stanford University Dean for Religious Life as well as Lecturer at the GSB. He is the author of four books and a number of book chapters and articles.

Michael Osborne is a climate scientist turned multimedia producer for Worldview Stanford who teaches science communication classes at Stanford. He co-founded and produces the award-winning *Generation Anthropocene* podcast, a partnership between Stanford and Smithsonian.com featuring stories and conversations about planetary change. "Through the podcasts, we want to capture stories about the changing environmental and cultural landscapes from diverse perspectives...to help guide strategic, editorial, and partnership decisions that bolster Worldview's mission of creating unique learning experiences."

Robert Podesva is an Assistant Professor of Linguistics at Stanford University. He holds degrees from Stanford University (PhD, MA) and Cornell University (BA) and has been an Assistant Professor at Georgetown University. His research examines the social significance of phonetic variation and its role in the construction of identity, most notably gender, sexuality, and race. His most recent projects focus on the interrelation between linguistic variation and embodiment in the expression of affect. He has co-edited *Research Methods in Linguistics, Language and Sexuality*, and the forthcoming *Social Meaning and Linguistic Variation*.

SERIES EDITORS

Robyn Brinks Lockwood teaches courses in spoken and written English at Stanford University in the English for Foreign Students graduate program and is the program education coordinator of the American Language and Culture undergraduate summer program. She is an active member of the international TESOL organization, serves as Chairperson of the Publishing Professional Council, and is a past chair of the Materials Writers Interest Section. She is a frequent presenter at TESOL regional and international conferences. Robyn has edited and written numerous textbooks, online courses, and ancillary components for ESL courses and TOEFL preparation.

Maggie Sokolik holds a BA in Anthropology from Reed College, and an MA in Romance Linguistics and Ph.D. in Applied Linguistics from UCLA. She is the author of over 20 ESL and composition textbooks. She has taught at MIT, Harvard, Texas A&M, and currently UC Berkeley, where she is Director of College Writing Programs. She has developed and taught several popular MOOC courses in English language writing and literature. She is the founding editor of *TESL-EJ*, a peer-reviewed journal for ESL / EFL professionals, one of the first online journals. Maggie travels frequently to speak about grammar, writing, and instructor education. She lives in the San Francisco Bay area, where she and her husband play bluegrass music.

Lawrence J. Zwier is an Associate Director of the English Language Center, Michigan State University. He holds a bachelor's degree in English Literature from Aquinas College, Grand Rapids, MI, and an MA in TESL from the University of Minnesota. He has taught ESL / EFL at universities in Saudi Arabia, Malaysia, Japan, Singapore, and the US. He is the author of numerous ELT textbooks, mostly about reading and vocabulary, and also writes nonfiction books about history and geography for middle school and high school students. He is married with two children and lives in Okemos, Michigan.

Acknowledgments

The authors feel fortunate to have worked with such a strong team. We thank Amy McCormick for taking a great idea from its inception to reality in a series we are proud to be a part of, Debbie Sistino for her oversight of a complex project, guidance and support, Sara Davila for invaluable research, and Niki Cunnion for supporting all of us. We also want to thank Barbara Sihombing, our Pearson specialist and friend, for her faith in us and the hard work to get books, including ours, into the hands of teachers and students who need them.

We thank Maggie Sokolik for development of the writing strand, Victoria Solomon for invaluable content contributions, and give special thanks to Andrea Bryant, our Development Editor. Her expertise, insight, and sharp eye helped shape the manuscript. A good editor helps authors become better writers. We are grateful to Andrea who did that for us.

We thank our students for all they have taught us about language learning and our many colleagues for collaborations resulting in a collective understanding, and respect for the challenges of teaching language, and writing in particular.

Charl Norloff is grateful for the opportunity to work with her talented co-author, Ruth Williams Moore. She appreciated the creative ideas that resulted from collaboration. She thanks Ruth for her steadfastness and tireless efforts. She thanks her husband Richard, sons Jonathan and Joshua, daughters-in-law Amy and Allie, and grandchildren Anna and Christopher for their love and support of her desire to write.

Ruth Williams Moore would like to thank Charl Norloff for sharing her knowledge from many years of writing books. It has been such a rewarding experience having Charl as a co-author, colleague, and friend. Ruth is also thankful for the support of her mother, Lina, who introduced her to the ESL field many years ago. She is deeply grateful to her husband David, and her children Zack and Jessie, for their love and encouragement. —*Charl Norloff* and *Ruth Williams Moore*

Reviewers

We would like to thank the following reviewers for their many helpful comments and suggestions:

Jamila Barton, North Seattle Community College, Seattle, WA; **Joan Chamberlin**, Iowa State University, Ames IA; **Lyam Christopher**, Palm Beach State College, Boynton Beach, FL; **Robin Corcos**, University of California, Santa Barbara, Goleta, CA; **Tanya Davis**, University of California, San Diego, CA; **Brendan DeCoster**, University of Oregon, Eugene, OR; **Thomas Dougherty**, University of St. Mary of the Lake, Mundelein, IL; **Bina Dugan**, Bergen County Community College, Hackensack, NJ; **Priscilla Faucette**, University of Hawaii at Manoa, Honolulu, HI; **Lisa Fischer**, St. Louis University, St. Louis, MO; **Kathleen Flynn**, Glendale Community College, Glendale, CA; **Mary Gawienowski**, William Rainey Harper College, Palatine, IL; **Sally Gearhart**, Santa Rosa Junior College, Santa Rosa, CA; **Carl Guerriere**, Capital Community College, Hartford, CT; **Vera Guillen**, Eastfield College, Mesquite, TX; **Angela Hakim**, St. Louis University, St. Louis, MO; **Pamela Hartmann**, Evans Community Adult School, Los Angeles Unified School District, Los Angeles, CA; **Shelly Hedstrom**, Palm Beach State University, Lake Worth, FL; **Sherie Henderson**, University of Oregon, Eugene, OR; **Lisse Hildebrandt**, English Language Program, Virginia Commonwealth University, Richmond, VA; **Barbara Inerfeld**, Rutgers University, Piscataway, NJ; **Zaimah Khan**, Northern Virginia Community College, Loudon Campus, Sterling, VA; **Tricia Kinman**, St. Louis University, St. Louis, MO; **Kathleen Klaiber**, Genesee Community College, Batavia, NY; **Kevin Lamkins**, Capital Community College, Hartford, CT; **Mayetta Lee**, Palm Beach State College, Lake Worth, FL; **Kirsten Lillegard**, English Language Institute, Divine Word College, Epworth, IA; **Craig Machado**, Norwalk Community College, Norwalk, CT; **Cheryl Madrid**, Spring International Language Center, Denver, CO; **Ann Meechai**, St. Louis University, St. Louis, MO; **Melissa Mendelson**, Department of Linguistics, University of Utah, Salt Lake City, UT; **Tamara Milbourn**, University of Colorado, Boulder, CO; **Debbie Ockey**, Fresno City College, Fresno, CA; **Diana Pascoe-Chavez**, St. Louis University, St. Louis, MO; **Kathleen Reynolds**, William Rainey Harper College, Palatine, IL; **Linda Roth**, Vanderbilt University ELC, Greensboro, NC; **Minati Roychoudhuri**, Capital Community College, Hartford, CT; **Bruce Rubin**, California State University, Fullerton, CA; **Margo Sampson**, Syracuse University, Syracuse, NY; **Sarah Saxer**, Howard Community College, Ellicott City, MD; **Anne-Marie Schlender**, Austin Community College, Austin, TX; **Susan Shields**, Santa Barbara Community College, Santa Barbara, CA; **Barbara Smith-Palinkas**, Hillsborough Community College, Dale Mabry Campus, Tampa, FL; **Sara Stapleton**, North Seattle Community College, Seattle, WA; **Lisa Stelle**, Northern Virginia Community College Loudon, Sterling, VA; **Jamie Tanzman**, Northern Kentucky University, Highland Heights, KY; **Jeffrey Welliver**, Soka University of America, Aliso Viejo, CA; **Mark Wolfersberger**, Brigham Young University, Hawaii, Laie, HI; **May Youn**, California State University, Fullerton, CA

Fundamental Writing Skills

Part 1 is designed to build fundamental skills step by step through exploration of rigorous, academic content. Practice activities tied to specific learning outcomes in each unit focus on understanding the function and application of the skills.

LINGUISTICS

The Research Writing Process

UNIT PROFILE

Many factors result in change in a language. New words are entering the English language each year at a faster pace than ever before. In this unit, you will read and write about topics related to linguistics, aspects of language, the difference between prescriptive and descriptive grammar, and how and why new words enter a language.

Plan a paper analyzing how and why words borrowed from other languages enter the English language. What factors influence which words become part of the language and which do not? Research words that have come into English from your first language or another language or language group that you are familiar with.

OUTCOMES

• Brainstorm topics
• Create an outline
• Annotate research
• Identify phrases in academic text
• Use a dictionary to expand vocabulary

For more about **LINGUISTICS**, see ②③. See also ⓡ and [OC] **LINGUISTICS** ①②③.

GETTING STARTED

Go to MyEnglishLab to watch Professor Podesva's introductory video and to complete a self-assessment.

Discuss these questions with a partner or group.

1. New words are constantly entering English. Where do you think these words come from? How do they get into the dictionary?

2. What is the role of grammar rules in learning a language? How important is it to say something in "the right way" in a language? How does grammar affect communication?

3. Professor Podesva suggests that the distinction between prescriptive and descriptive grammar has to do with who gets to decide what correct language is. Who do you think should decide what is correct? Linguists? The speakers of the language? A governing body that controls the rules?

FUNDAMENTAL SKILL

THE RESEARCH WRITING PROCESS

WHY IT'S USEFUL By understanding and following the research writing process, you will be able to write academic papers that incorporate research to support your ideas and enhance the credibility of your claims.

Good academic writing is the result of carefully following a process to complete a well-organized paper. In assignments where research is required, you need to follow additional steps, which are illustrated in **the research writing process** on page 4. This process requires finding appropriate sources and choosing relevant ideas in those sources to incorporate into your writing to develop and support the points or claims you are making.

To choose an appropriate topic for an academic paper, **brainstorming topics** is an essential first step in planning and pre-writing. In order to successfully brainstorm, you must first fully understand the assignment and consider purpose and audience. Narrowing the topic and choosing a focus or approach to the topic are also essential steps.

The next step in planning and pre-writing is **creating an outline** to organize your ideas. There are many ways to do this—both formal and informal. Outlining helps organize your thoughts and ideas and creates a plan for your paper.

Research occurs more than once in the writing process. In the planning and pre-writing steps, research helps in identifying key words and also in determining what the important issues of the topic are. **Annotating research** is one way to start to gather ideas, focus on an approach to a topic, and narrow the topic. Research also plays a role in outlining as you gather and read sources and identify ideas to develop and support your main points. The information that you have annotated supports your claims in the paper.

With an outline and ideas, it's time to move to the writing step and begin composing the first draft. Research comes in again as you use your annotations and notes to incorporate support from sources. In the final step, the paper is prepared for submission—revising for content and organization, formatting, and finally editing and proofreading to achieve the end result—as a well-written and accurate final paper.

Look at the three steps in the research writing process and notice the highlighted substeps that are unique to research writing.

Step 1: Planning and Prewriting
Brainstorming topics
Understanding the assignment
Researching—finding and reviewing sources for topics and issues
Narrowing the topic
Finalizing the topic and choosing an approach or focus
Creating an outline
Writing a preliminary thesis statement
Researching—gathering and reading appropriate sources; annotating for ideas related to the topic and focus
Choosing main points and supporting ideas
Researching—identifying supporting ideas, annotating sources, and taking notes
Organizing points into a working outline

Step 2: Writing
Drafting
Composing body paragraphs for main points
Writing an introduction and conclusion
Researching
Using annotations and notes to incorporate source information
Creating a works-cited page

Step 3: Preparing for Submission
Revising
Getting feedback
Revising for clarity

Editing and proofreading to arrive at a final draft

Formatting

Editing for grammar, vocabulary, spelling, and punctuation

Proofreading

Now look at the steps another way. We see here that the process is not always linear. For example, if the writer has trouble narrowing the topic, he or she will need to go back and look at the assignment again.

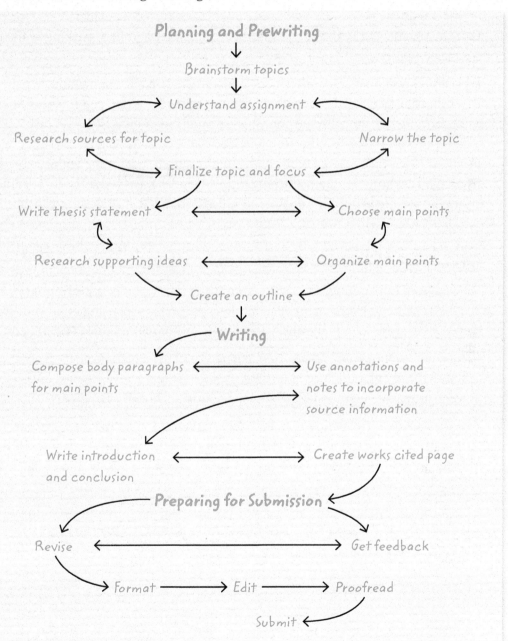

Step 1: Planning and Prewriting

When **brainstorming** topics, it is important to fully understand the assignment. First, consider the purpose of the assignment, the reason(s) for writing, and the audience—the people who will read your paper and what their knowledge about and interest in the topic is.

What are some reasons for writing a research paper? To learn something new? To explore a topic more deeply? To develop new ideas? To share ideas with others or to convince them of a view on an issue? Who is most likely to read a paper assigned in an undergraduate class? The professor, your classmates? Who is most likely to read a paper in a graduate class? The professor, your classmates, others working in the field? A broader audience?

Typically, expectations are different for undergraduate papers and graduate papers. Usually, assignments give a broad topic or area of study. When you first start to brainstorm topics, you will draw on your personal experience. It is also helpful to collaborate with others to generate more ideas. However, in academic writing, you will also need to learn about topics by conducting **research**, beginning with the broad topic given in an assignment. Brainstorming topics includes **narrowing** the topic sufficiently to suit the requirements and the time allowed to complete it. **Research** can also be a part of this step, helping you to identify key words, formulate an approach, or choose an issue to address. Using a graphic organizer to generate or organize ideas can help you focus on a more specific topic.

The final step in planning is to **create an outline** that includes **a preliminary thesis**. The thesis expresses your opinion about the issue you are focusing on in your paper. Here is an example of a preliminary thesis with the narrowed topic underlined:

> An analysis of <u>new words that have entered the English language in the last decade</u> shows the strong influence of technology with its rapid advancement and global reach as major factors, especially among young, tech-savvy people.

Your thesis frames the structure of and helps guide and organize your paper by stating your main points in the order you will present them. It indicates the approach the paper is taking, in this case an analysis. What are the main points in the thesis statement?

With your annotations and notes from your research and your thesis, you can begin to organize your main points and supporting ideas in an outline. Your outline can also show you where you don't have sufficient support for your points so that you can find additional information to provide the support you need.

Step 2: Writing

With a topic, thesis statement, and outline, you are ready to write the paper, **drafting and integrating source information**. The effort put into planning and pre-writing will make the writing step easier. Your first draft will introduce your topic, present your thesis, and identify and develop your main ideas. Compose body paragraphs that support your points, including information and examples that you integrate from your sources. Conclude by reminding your reader of your important ideas and encouraging your reader to think further about your topic.

> For more on developing your ideas and integrating examples into a research paper, see Earth Science, Part 1.

Step 3: Preparing for Submission

After completing your first draft, read it carefully and think about ways to **revise** it. Focus on how to more fully and effectively develop and organize the content. Where could you add more support? Would your points or support be clearer or more effective in a different order? This is the time to think about the "big picture"; do not worry about grammar and vocabulary unless they have a major impact on the content.

Getting feedback is an essential part of the revision process. Feedback can come from a professor, a peer, or even yourself. Instructors often provide feedback prior to submission of a final assignment. If you are offered **instructor feedback**, take advantage of it.

Peer feedback can identify areas where additional support or clarification is needed. Often others question or notice things you can't see in your own writing. Using a peer feedback form can help you revise. Here is an example of a peer feedback form. Notice that feedback and revisions address content and organization only.

	Yes	No	Notes
Does the paper respond appropriately to the assignment?	☐	☐	
Does the paper have a purpose?	☐	☐	
Is there a clear audience?	☐	☐	
Is the topic narrow enough?	☐	☐	
Does the organization help the reader?	☐	☐	
Is there a thesis statement?	☐	☐	
Does the thesis state exactly what the paper is about?	☐	☐	
Are the main points clear?	☐	☐	
Is there support to develop the main points?	☐	☐	
Is there information from sources included to support the main points?	☐	☐	
Do you have questions about the paper's ideas?	☐	☐	

Finally, always read and reread your own drafts. Using **self-feedback** helps you see that you have followed the process and covered the steps. Here is an example of a self-feedback form.

Based on the assignment, what is expected of me? ....

What is my purpose? ....

How does my paper address it? ....

Who is my audience? ....

How am I addressing the needs of my audience? ....

How does my organization help my reader? ....

Does my thesis statement tell the reader exactly what my paper is about? How?

....

What are my main points? ....

What support have I offered to develop my main points? ....

What support from sources have I included to develop my main points? ....

What questions might my reader still have about my ideas? ....

Consider all feedback as you revise. You may need more than one additional draft or you may need to revise some parts of your paper several times while other parts may require little or no revision.

> **TIP**
>
> An effective strategy to revise your paper is to set it aside for a few days. This helps you look at your writing more objectively and more clearly see ways to improve it.

The final step in the research writing process is **formatting**, **editing**, and **proofreading** to arrive at a final draft. Reread your paper for grammar, vocabulary, spelling, and punctuation errors. Get feedback from others reading your work for content at this stage. If you have not already done so, format your paper following any instructions you were given. The goal is an error-free paper that is clear and easy to read.

For more on revising, see Medieval Culture, Part 1.

For more on editing and proofreading, see Materials Engineering, Part 1.

VOCABULARY PREVIEW

Read the vocabulary items. Circle the ones you know. Put a question mark next to the ones you don't know.

factor (n)	evolve	impact (n)	usage
widespread	approach (n)	coin (v)	inclusion

EXERCISE 1

A. Read the writing prompt and the beginning of an essay in response to it.

> How and why do languages change? Identify and research a factor that has had a significant impact on a language. How has this factor impacted a language that you are familiar with?

1 Languages evolve because they are at the center of communication, and the ideas and thoughts we want to communicate are constantly changing. The way we express meaning through grammar, the words and expressions that we use in our everyday lives, and even the way we pronounce those words, change over time. What factors influence these language changes? Where, when, and by whom are the greatest impacts felt? One way to explore language change is by analyzing the entry of words into the language. An important factor that has impacted the English language is new words—where they come from and how they have become commonly used, who uses them, and why they are considered necessary.

2 So how do new words make it into English? Usage is the best answer! New words come from everywhere. We hear them, read them, and find them online, but they have to be used by enough people, in a wide geographic area, and have enough staying power over time to remain in the language. Lexicographers, people who compile dictionaries, know that new words are always being invented. In fact, according to the *Global Language Monitor* which tracks word usage in English, there were an estimated 1,036,000 words in English as of January 1, 2016.[1]

3 In English, when considering whether to include a new word in a dictionary, lexicographers think about words people would actually look up. Two factors are how widespread the usage is and whether the word will continue to be used or will disappear quickly. Lexicographers who take this approach might be called descriptivist. They observe how a word is being used, even if it breaks accepted rules of grammar, and write definitions based on their research. There is also a prescriptivist approach. Those taking this approach, like the French, would be more likely to say a word was not a "real" word if it breaks the rules and, therefore, decide against its inclusion in a dictionary.

4 Who can get a new word into the dictionary? Anyone can coin and use a new word, but being famous, well known, or published can help with inclusion of a new word into a dictionary. William Shakespeare, the famous playwright, coined about 1700 new words. Politicians have coined new words that have been accepted into dictionaries, such as *neologize*, first used by Thomas Jefferson, and *shovel-ready* by Barack Obama. Inventing something new is another way to get a word into the dictionary. Scientific terms such as *Higgs boson* particle, and even culinary terms such as *cronut*, a croissant-doughnut pastry, have become entries in the dictionary. There is even a term for new words, *neologisms*. While looking at the etymology of this word reveals it has been used for a while and has other meanings, it is still a good example of addressing a new idea with a new word.

[1] *The Global Language Monitor* (November 24, 2016) http://www.languagemonitor.com/global-english/no-of-words/

Glossary

Neologize: to coin new words or create new meanings for existing words

Particle: a very small piece of something

Culinary: related to cooking

CULTURE NOTE

Shovel-ready is a political term used to describe construction projects (usually larger-scale infrastructure) where planning and engineering is advanced enough that with sufficient funding construction can begin within a very short time.

A *Washington Post* writer suggested that the phrase did not exist and had not been used until President Barack Obama used it during a television interview in December 2008. Obama used the phrase to describe infrastructure projects that were ready to immediately receive stimulus funding from the American Recovery and Reinvestment Act of 2009.

TIP

An *etymology* is the history of a word. A dictionary etymology reports what is known about an English word before it entered that dictionary. If it was created in English, it shows how it was formed and if the word was borrowed into English, it traces the origin of the word. It also tracks changes in meaning or how a word is used.

The etymology of the word *etymology* is complex, as follows:
- "facts of the origin and development of a word,"
- from Old French *etimologie, ethimologie* (14c., Modern French *étymologie*)
- from Greek *etymologia,* "analysis of a word to find its true origin," properly "study of the true sense (of a word)"

B. Answer the questions.

1. Why do languages change? ....

....

2. What changes in a language? ....

....

3. How do new words enter a language? ....

....

4. Whose words are considered as new dictionary entries? ....

....

5. Give an example from the essay of a famous person who coined a new word.

....

....

6. What are neologisms? Give an example from the essay. ....

....

C. Answer the questions about the writer's process. Discuss your answers with a partner.

1. What is the writer's narrowed topic? What topics do you think the writer considered when brainstorming topics? ....

....

2. What is the approach to the topic? Where did the approach come from? What is the writer's thesis? Underline it. What are the main points that you would expect to see in the writer's outline? ....

....

3. What are some key words? Circle them.

4. What main points did the writer use? Can you think of others the writer might have used? ....

....

5. What source did the writer cite? What idea was this supporting? ....

....

6. Based on the thesis statement and outline, what do you expect to be the topic of the writer's next paragraph? ....

....

D. Find two sources for how new words enter a language. List three new English words and provide a definition, where they come from, who uses them, and any other relevant information about them.

....

....

....

....

....

....

E. Share your sources and words with a partner.

VOCABULARY CHECK

A. Review the vocabulary items in the Vocabulary Preview. Write their definitions and add examples. Use a dictionary if necessary.

B. Choose the sentence that correctly describes the underlined item.

1. Technology is a <u>factor</u> that affects how quickly new words enter a language.
   a. Computers, especially, influence how easily we communicate.
   b. Technology is expensive but it helps us communicate.

2. Languages <u>evolve</u> more quickly than ever now.
   a. Many linguists think that languages are easier to learn now.
   b. Many linguists think it's good that languages change with the times.

3. Learning a second language will have a positive <u>impact</u> on your life.
   a. You will see how difficult it is when you travel and meet new people.
   b. You will see the effects when you travel and meet new people.

4. Marina is writing a paper about the <u>usage</u> of language that comes from technology.
   a. A few years ago, nobody knew the word "selfie"; now almost everybody says it.
   b. A few years ago, nobody knew the word "selfie"; now almost everybody takes selfies.

5. Meeting new people online is <u>widespread</u>.
   a. Most of my friends are in contact with people living in different countries.
   b. Most of my friends aren't sure how to contact people living in different countries.

6. One <u>approach</u> to learning a language is to live among native speakers of that language.
   a. My English teacher says it will be a lot of fun.
   b. My English teacher says it is the best method.

7. Bruno is so excited about his <u>inclusion</u> in the French honors club.
   a. He has wanted to learn more about it for two years.
   b. He has wanted to be a part of it for two years.

8. It feels like a new expression is <u>coined</u> on the internet every day.
   a. And the next day, everybody seems to be saying it.
   b. And the next day, everybody thinks it's funny.

◐ Go to MyEnglishLab to complete vocabulary and skill practices and to join in collaborative activities.

SUPPORTING SKILL 1

BRAINSTORMING TOPICS

WHY IT'S USEFUL   By brainstorming topics, you will take the necessary first steps for planning a successful paper. It is a good investment of your time because you will be able to narrow your topic and focus, generate ideas, and consider different points of view before you begin to write.

Brainstorming is the creative process in which you quickly generate ideas as you begin thinking about and planning for a writing assignment. When **brainstorming topics**, you do not need to write complete sentences or worry about grammar. It's important not to judge your thoughts or be concerned about being specific because you want to stimulate as many ideas as possible. By writing down your ideas, you can better understand what you know and don't know about a topic.

There are many ways to brainstorm. You may want to use more than one brainstorming technique so that you can gather a variety of perspectives on a given topic. Look at the brainstorming techniques. Check any you have used and add others you know.

– listing	– questioning
– cluster diagrams	– preliminary research investigations
– collaborating	

> **TIP**
>
> Brainstorming topics can help you understand what you don't know about the topic and suggest areas of research. You can brainstorm at any point during the research writing process, especially if you get stuck or notice that you don't have enough support for your ideas.

Consider this assignment in a linguistics class:

> Write a paper in which you analyze new words that have entered the English language since 2000. Where do they come from? When were they first used? Who uses them? What factors influenced their use? Are they included in a dictionary? When were they adopted? What criteria were used for their inclusion in the dictionary?

Where do you begin? You might start by **listing**.

A first step might be to think about categories of new words and then identify some new words in those categories. For the assignment, the writer listed these categories. Can you think of others?

technology	politics	music
computers	media	fashion
video games	business	words borrowed from other languages
social media	health and sports	major events (e.g., 9/11)

After examining the categories, the writer added a few new words. Collaborating with other students helped get a few more. Finally, after searching for new words online, the writer decided to use an organizing technique and produced a chart listing new words organized by category. Note that the writer eliminated some of the original categories and added some new categories that resulted from brainstorming.

Category	New words	Additional information
Technology	Web 2.0, texting, World Wide Web, cloud computing, smartwatch, tech-savvy, clickbait, fast follower, geocache, tweet	
Business	social media, sustainability, offline, seamless	These were on a 2013 list of top new business words.
Borrowed words	Jai Ho, anime, manga	
Major events	9/11	
Video gaming	N00b, gamer	
Environment	greenwashing, carbon neutral	
Social media	unfriend, hashtag, emoji, photo bomb	
Music	hip hop, chillwave, electronica, new wave	Chillwave is a new genre influenced by 1980's electronic music.
Fashion	jegging, recessionista, hipster	

After listing, the writer noticed that many ideas were related to each other, in this case technology, and decided that the approach to the topic would be factors that contributed to the new words entering the language. The writer narrowed the topic to *the influence that technology has had on the English language.*

Creating a **cluster diagram**, also known as **mapping**, is a useful technique if visual representations help you understand ideas better. When you think of a topic, what words or phrases come to mind? Write them down and circle them. When you can't think of any more ideas related to the topic, draw lines to show connections between ideas. Seeing visual connections can help you think about other perspectives, or points of view, and generate additional ideas. The visual connections will also help you plan how to organize the ideas when you begin writing. Here, the writer used a cluster diagram to generate main ideas and to start to connect those ideas.

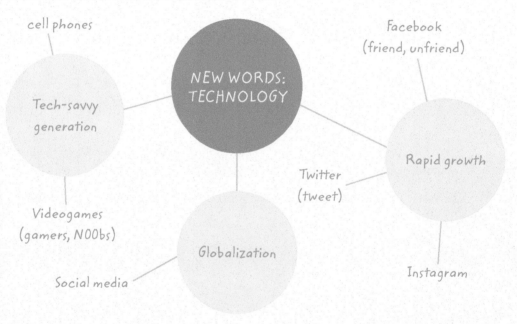

By **collaborating** with friends, classmates, instructors, or professors, you can gain new insights about the topic that you might not have considered or been aware of. Asking *Wh*-questions will help you as you exchange ideas with others. It can also help you narrow the topic.

- What are some new English words that are related to technology?
- When did you first hear or use these words?
- What do you think of the words? How useful are they?
- Why do you think these words have been adopted into the English language?
- Which factors do you think have had the most impact? Why?

Successful academic writing requires that you think critically, so it is important to examine the topic from different points of view. **Asking higher-order critical thinking questions** will help you gain additional insight so you can further narrow your topic and develop an approach or focus for your thesis. It will also identify gaps that need to be further researched. Use the Four A's to brainstorm more critically:

- **Associate: How does the topic relate or compare to something else you already know about?**

  In my country, we are using many of the same English words for technology. Young people in my country are much more adept at using technology than older generations. They are using these new words often to communicate with each other. For example, we don't translate words like 'Facebook' or 'internet'.

- **Analyze: What are the different parts or issues that make up this topic?**

  The rapid growth of new technology has created a need for new words to give names to things that didn't exist before, for example, Facebook and Instagram.

- **Apply: How is it used? By whom? Who would be interested in this information?**

  A young, tech-savvy generation has created many of these new words (unfriend, gamer, n00b). Modern technologies are used to communicate (cell phones, video games), buy products (online stores), and search for information (e.g., 'google' is used as a verb—'Did you google it?') Marketers, writers, and sociologists are interested in how words are used.

- **Argue: What is your opinion about this topic? What are arguments for and against this topic?**

  I think we will continue to create new words as technology changes. It's necessary to do this because there will always be new products and innovation. I don't think a new word should be adopted in a language until it is used by many people and for at least a few years.

By this point, with a sufficiently narrowed topic and approach, you can begin **preliminary research** to help you choose your main ideas and gather appropriate sources. As you conduct online searches or skim articles, identify key words and other ideas. For instance, while researching, you might discover that the rapid advancement and global reach of technology have had an impact on the number of new words entering the language. With these ideas, you can put together a working thesis:

An analysis of <u>new words that have entered the English language in the last decade</u> shows the strong influence of technology with its rapid advancement and global reach as major factors, especially among young, tech-savvy people.

EXERCISE 2

A. Read the writing assignment for a university linguistics course. Then take two minutes to brainstorm factors that can make a language change. List words or phrases related to the topic. Compare your list with a partner's.

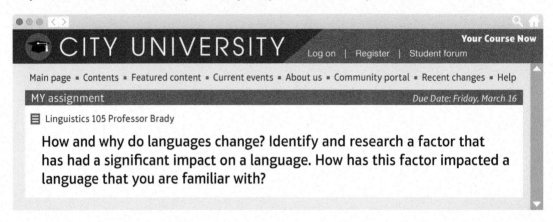

B. Choose two or more of the words or phrases that you listed above and create a cluster diagram to generate additional ideas related to the topic. Draw lines to show relationships and connections between the ideas.

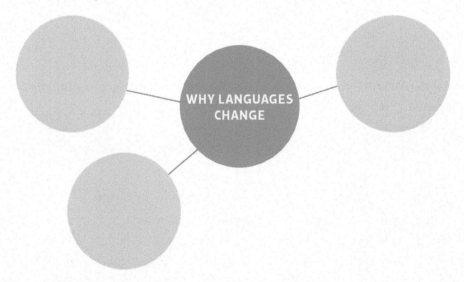

C. Write some *Wh*-questions about the topic. Ask your classmates questions and exchange ideas.

1. ....

2. ....

3. ....

4. ....

D. Explore the topic using critical thinking questions. With a partner, discuss the questions and write down important ideas. When you are finished, write a preliminary thesis for an academic essay on this topic. Share your thesis with your partner.

Associate: How does the topic relate or compare to something else you already know about?

Analyze: What are the different parts or issues that make up this topic?

Apply: How is it used? By whom? Who would be interested in this information?

Argue: What is your opinion about this topic? What are arguments for and against this topic?

Preliminary Thesis

 Go to MyEnglishLab to complete a skill practice and to join in collaborative activities.

SUPPORTING SKILL 2
CREATING AN OUTLINE

WHY IT'S USEFUL By organizing the ideas that you have brainstormed and researched, you will be able to create a plan that will make it easier to begin writing. Later in the writing process, your outline will serve as a framework that will guide you as you revise.

Once you have finished brainstorming and have a preliminary thesis, you are ready to **create an outline**. You may need to conduct additional research now to learn more about the topic and to fill any knowledge gaps you identified earlier while brainstorming. It is critical to carefully read your sources to find evidence to support your main points. Annotating your sources and taking good notes will provide the ideas you need to complete your outline. As you complete these steps, you may need to modify your thesis.

At this point, you will have many notes and ideas, but they will likely not be well organized. An outline is an organized plan for a piece of writing in which ideas are written down in the order you plan to present them. By showing logical relationships between these ideas, you will be able to present them in a way that is clear to your reader. Your thesis will often suggest how you should organize the ideas in the outline.

Here are the steps for creating an outline:

1. Write down your preliminary thesis.

2. Rearrange your notes into categories that group similar ideas together.

3. From these categories, identify a few main ideas that support your thesis. Keep these ideas to include in your outline. Discard ideas that you don't want to use.

4. Write the main ideas in the order you want to present them. Leave spaces under each main idea.

5. Look at your notes again and decide which specific points, or supporting ideas, you want to keep for each main idea.

6. List specific points below each main idea. You should have at least two supporting ideas for each main idea. If you don't, then you will not have enough information to adequately support your main idea and will need to reconsider your main idea or do more research to find additional support.

Just as your thesis may change, your outline may also change as you begin the writing stage and begin to develop your ideas.

An **informal outline** is a quick way to organize your notes. When you create an informal outline, you can use short phrases instead of writing complete sentences for your main and supporting ideas:

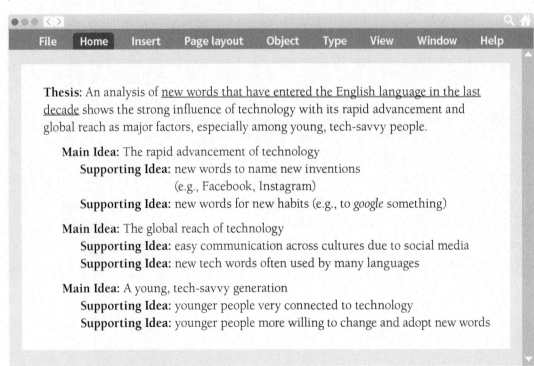

File   Home   Insert   Page layout   Object   Type   View   Window   Help

Thesis: An analysis of new words that have entered the English language in the last decade shows the strong influence of technology with its rapid advancement and global reach as major factors, especially among young, tech-savvy people.

   Main Idea: The rapid advancement of technology
      Supporting Idea: new words to name new inventions
               (e.g., Facebook, Instagram)
      Supporting Idea: new words for new habits (e.g., to *google* something)

   Main Idea: The global reach of technology
      Supporting Idea: easy communication across cultures due to social media
      Supporting Idea: new tech words often used by many languages

   Main Idea: A young, tech-savvy generation
      Supporting Idea: younger people very connected to technology
      Supporting Idea: younger people more willing to change and adopt new words

Some writers, however, prefer using a **formal outline**, especially when the topic is complicated. In a formal outline, the main and supporting ideas are often written in complete sentences. The main ideas can be used as topic sentences for different paragraphs in the paper. Which type of outline do you prefer to use?

Thesis: An analysis of <u>new words that have entered the English language in the last decade</u> shows the strong influence of technology with its rapid advancement and global reach as major factors, especially among young, tech-savvy people

1. **Main Idea:** The rapid advancement of technology has created a need for new words to name new inventions and new habits.
   a. **Supporting Idea:** New types of social media and online platforms have their own vocabulary for new inventions (e.g., Facebook, Instagram).
   b. **Supporting Idea:** New words are regularly being created for how people are applying and using these new inventions (e.g. to *google* something).

2. **Main Idea:** The global reach of technology has made it significantly easier for people to use the new words to communicate with each other.
   a. **Supporting Idea:** With social media, people can communicate anywhere and at any time.
   b. **Supporting Idea:** People who speak different languages are using new words to communicate about their use of technology.

3. **Main Idea:** The young tech-savvy generation has had an impact on how quickly the words have spread and been adopted into English.
   a. **Supporting Idea:** Younger people are very connected to technology and this impacts so many areas of their lives.
   b. **Supporting Idea:** Younger people are adopting these new words at a rapid pace, encouraging an older generation to use these new words as well.

After **creating an outline**, you will be ready to begin writing your first draft. Remember, you will add ideas and might modify the outline as you continue to research your topic. You can refer back to your outline at any point in the writing process to make sure that your ideas are presented clearly.

TIP

You can use index cards for notetaking and organizing. While this system may seem old-fashioned, it remains an easy and effective way to arrange your notes in different categories.

EXERCISE 3

A. Look again at the writing assignment and a possible preliminary thesis. Answer the questions.

> Writing Assignment: How and why do languages change? Identify and research a factor that has had a significant impact on a language. How has this factor impacted a language that you are familiar with?
>
> Preliminary Thesis: Social media is one factor that has had significant impact on how quickly the English language is evolving.

1. What is the purpose of the writing assignment? ....

....

2. Who is the audience? ....

....

3. What is the topic of the paper? ....

....

4. What is the focus of the paper? ....

....

B. Read the points and ideas to support your topic. Using the thesis in Part A, decide whether each point is a main idea or a supporting idea or if the point or idea should be discarded.

Points and Ideas	MI or SI	Discard
The language of social media has changed the level of formality when we communicate.		
It's easy for people to communicate their ideas on different online platforms (Facebook, blogs).		
Old words now have new meanings (e.g., *to like, wall, pin it*).		
People use acronyms as words (e.g. *LOL, TMI, OMG*).		
We don't know how big the impact of social media will be on the English language.		

Points and Ideas	MI or SI	Discard
The English language has evolved rapidly because of our interactions on social media.		
Instead of using words to express emotions, people use emoticons and emojis.		
People use hashtags in written communication.		
People are communicating more personal information than before.		
New words get adopted quickly because of social media's global reach.		
New words have been created for new innovations (e.g., emoticons).		

C. Create an outline. Write the thesis in Part A. Put the main ideas and supporting ideas from Part B in an order that will be clear to your audience. Add one original supporting idea for each main idea.

Thesis: ....

Main Idea: ....

    a. Supporting Idea: ....

    b. Supporting Idea: ....

    c. Supporting Idea: ....

    d. Supporting Idea: ....

Main Idea: ....

    a. Supporting Idea: ....

    b. Supporting Idea: ....

    c. Supporting Idea: ....

    d. Supporting Idea: ....

D. Compare your outline with a partner. Discuss your answers to these questions about your partner's outline.

    1. Are the ideas in a logical order? Why or why not?

    2. Which ideas were discarded? Are there any others that don't belong? Why?

    3. What other information would you include? Why?

🔵 Go to MyEnglishLab to complete a skill practice.

INTEGRATED SKILLS

ANNOTATING RESEARCH

WHY IT'S USEFUL By annotating research, you will engage actively with material to gain a deeper understanding of the content. This will allow you to later explain ideas clearly and support them in your writing with credible sources and evidence.

Conducting research is a critical part of writing an academic paper. Reading articles, books, or other scholarly sources gives you a solid understanding of the topic and helps you identify reliable and credible sources to support your claims and ideas.

While finding and reading relevant material is important, it is especially useful to **annotate research**. The information and ideas you annotate to support claims can later be used for in-text citations in your paper. You can annotate text by highlighting, underlining, circling, and writing short notes and comments in the text or margins.

When you annotate a reading, you engage actively with a text by analyzing the author's ideas. Think of annotating as having a conversation with the author in which you discuss the ideas. You can evaluate an author's argument or question an idea. You can agree, disagree, or note when ideas are contradictory or confusing. Annotating will help you connect the ideas in the reading to what you already know about the topic.

There is more than one way to annotate. Here are some recommendations for how and what to annotate:

Underline or highlight:	Use [brackets] or (parentheses) to:
Main ideas	Indicate evidence that supports your claim
Important details	Note ideas to include in your paper
Circle:	Write short notes and comments in the margin to:
Key words	Agree or disagree
New vocabulary related to the topic	Ask questions that you want to investigate further
References to other sources that you want to research	Summarize complicated discussions and explanations
	Analyze visual descriptions
	Add information to headings and subheadings

VOCABULARY PREVIEW

Read the vocabulary items. Circle the ones you know. Put a question mark next to the ones you don't know.

feature (n)	aspect	distinguish	relate to	acquire
refer to	confirmation	target (v)	precise	

Here is an example of how a writer has annotated a selection from a linguistics textbook. Which techniques did the writer use to annotate? For what purpose?

1   All languages have complex structures and rule systems. A single phrase in any language contains multiple linguistic features, including sound, word order, and meaning. Linguists categorize these features, or aspects, of a language in order to focus more thoroughly on each area. These aspects are known as Phonology, Phonetics, Morphology, Syntax, and Semantics. Each aspect is different, but together they function as a cohesive whole. Phonetics, the study of speech sounds, represents the smallest aspect of spoken language because it focuses on individual sounds in a word. [Semantics, the study of meaning in language, represents a larger aspect of language] because it considers the meaning of whole sentences and paragraphs. In applied linguistics, language teachers often distinguish between the aspects of language to highlight different features in a language. Instructors may focus on one area, such as syntax, which is the structure of sentences, while focusing on a different area, such as vocabulary, on another day. Linguists and teachers understand that languages are comprehended only in their entirety, however, and all linguistic aspects are interconnected.

People who study languages?

Is this grammar?

all the different language features connect together to create the "whole" of a language

THE ASPECTS OF LANGUAGE
Phonology

2   Phonology is the study of sound systems in languages. Phonology focuses on the organization of speech sounds in a language and how they relate to other sounds, particularly in different languages. Phonetics, which is distinguished from phonology, is the study of how human speech sounds are produced and received. An example of phonetics is how we can break down the word *bat* into a first consonant *b*, a middle vowel *a*, and final consonant *t*.

I'm not sure how these two terms are different

The Aspects of Language

Semantics	Meaning	I'm cold. Close the window!
↑		
Syntax	Sentences	Don't you think it's cold?
↑		
Morphology	Words	cold (adj.)
↑		
Phonology	Sounds	/k/ /əʊ/ /l/ /d/

Shows hierarchy of the aspects of language. ↑ Highest level = how words and sentences combine to create meaning.

Morphology

3   Once sounds are combined, they become words. <u>The study of words or parts of words is known as morphology.</u> Morphology focuses on how a given word is put together. Once an individual acquires words, that collection of words is known as the person's lexicon. A language itself also contains a lexicon, which includes all the words used in a language. The lexicon of languages is always changing as older words pass out of usage and new words take root.

does this mean dictionary?

neologisms?

Syntax

4   The language aspect known as syntax refers to the way words are arranged in sentences to create meaning. Sentences in English contain a specific syntactic structure that must be followed. For example, the sentence *I'm going to study tonight* would be ungrammatical if spoken with a different syntactic structure, such as *Tonight study I'm going to.*

Is syntax a synonym for grammar?

Other languages?

Semantics

5   Semantics is the study of meaning in words, phrases, and sentences. <u>Pragmatics, which is related to semantics, is the study of the meaning of words in context.</u> An example of pragmatics can be found in the question, *Don't you think it's a bit cold in here?* In the question, the speaker might be looking for confirmation about the temperature. However, if the speaker asks this question to a person sitting beside a window, the speaker may be making an implied request to close the window.

how we communicate socially? Like polite language

6   Language aspects are all equally important. <u>Separating language into these categories is simply an organization system to help target specific parts of language,</u> similar in some ways to how a music director separates and focuses on different instruments in an orchestra. The language aspects give linguists and teachers more precise ways of studying and teaching.

VOCABULARY CHECK

A. Review the vocabulary items in the Vocabulary Preview. Write their definitions and add examples. Use a dictionary if necessary.

B. Complete each sentence with the correct vocabulary item.

acquire	aspect	confirmation	distinguish	feature
precise	referred to	relate to	target	

1. Many studies say that children .... language much more easily than adults.

2. She .... semantics, the study of the meaning of words, phrases, and sentences, in her lecture on new words.

3. Many students find that working in a study group helps them to .... problems they are having in class.

4. The best .... of my Linguistics book is the part that focuses on the history of one word.

5. One difficult .... of working full-time and going to school is the problem of finding the time to see my family.

6. Professor Lee has such a .... way of speaking. It's very easy to understand what she is saying.

7. Children who spend too much time on a computer might find it hard to .... between online games and online homework.

8. I can .... my classmates who are nervous about living in a new country. Like them, I was scared when I first moved to a new place.

9. My professor always asks for .... that we understand exactly what she is saying.

VOCABULARY PREVIEW

Read the vocabulary items. Circle the ones you know. Put a question mark next to the ones you don't know.

customary	dismiss	perspective	apparent	modified	alternative

EXERCISE 4

A. Read the article *The Prescriptive and Descriptive Divide*.

The Prescriptive and Descriptive Divide

1 Prescriptive linguistics is an approach to language usage that emphasizes the rules of how language ought to be used. Descriptive linguistics, in contrast, aims to describe how a language is actually used. The idea of "prescribing," or creating rules about language use became important in Western society in the 18th century when grammar books became customary in education. The popular book *A Short Introduction to English Grammar*, written by Robert Lowth in 1762, was the first of many successful grammar books that teachers and writers used for more than a century. Lowth's book includes prescriptivist commands, such as the rule that you should never put an adverb or an adverbial phrase in the middle of an infinitive. According to this rule, the famous phrase from *Star Trek*, "To boldly go where no man has gone before," is technically incorrect. The correct version, according to a prescriptivist, would be "To go boldly where no man has gone before." In practice, writers often break this rule for stylistic purposes.

2 There has always been a divide between the prescriptivist approach and the descriptivist approach (Mackay, 1980[1]; Drake, 1977[2]). Descriptive grammarians have accused prescriptivists of being rule-focused and judgmental, while prescriptivists have warned that descriptive grammarians dismiss standards and water down culture. The debate about the two approaches is recorded even in Lowth's era (Drake, 1977). The descriptivist grammarian Joseph Priestley, who authored *Rudiments of English Grammar* in 1772, argued that grammar should be discovered, not invented or prescribed. "The custom of speaking is the original and only just standard of any language," Priestly writes. His position is similar to the perspective of many modern linguists. Indeed, the divide between this type of descriptivist argument and a more prescriptivist view is still apparent today both in academia and popular culture. People humorously refer to grammar-focused individuals as "grammar police." On the opposite side, people with prescriptivist beliefs make fun of nonstandard grammar usage.

3 The reality is that different situations call for either a prescriptivist approach or a descriptivist approach. Linguists, for example, are descriptive grammarians. They study the way language varieties are actually spoken and written, and they do not attempt to correct any aspect of language. Journalists and copy editors, on the other hand, take a prescriptivist approach because they must report information in a way that is most easily understood by everyone. Likewise, teachers also use a prescriptivist approach to grammar because students must learn the standard rules of English. Many teachers, however, practice a modified prescriptivism by offering acceptable alternatives to standard grammar and respecting nonstandard language varieties.

1. Mackay, D. (1980). On the goals, principles, and procedures for prescriptive grammar: Singular *they*. *Language in Society*, Vol. 9, No. 3, pp. 349–367.

2. Drake, G. (1977). American Linguistic Prescriptivism: Its Decline and Revival in the 19th Century. *Language in Society*, Vol. 6, No. 3, pp. 323–340.

Glossary

Water down: to make something less forceful by changing or removing parts of it.

CULTURE NOTE

Star Trek is an American science fiction TV series that originated in the late 1960's. It became so popular that 4 additional TV series, 13 movies, and numerous books and toys have been created since that time. The phrase "To boldly go where no man has gone before" is part of the spoken introduction at the beginning of each show.

B. Answer the questions.

1. What is prescriptive linguistics? ....

....

2. How is descriptive linguistics different from prescriptive linguistics?

....

....

3. What example does the author give for a prescriptive rule of grammar? Can you think of others? ....

....

4. What is the main idea of the article? ....

....

5. What are some examples that the author gives supporting a prescriptive approach?

....

....

....

C. Read the article again and annotate it by highlighting, underlining, circling, bracketing, and writing notes in the margin. Write at least two questions and two comments. Circle key words and vocabulary you aren't familiar with.

D. When you are finished annotating the article, look up any words that you circled. Discuss your annotations with a partner. See if your partner can answer questions that you have written in the margin.

E. Use your annotations to write a paragraph about one key idea that you have learned from this article.

VOCABULARY CHECK

A. Review the vocabulary items in the Vocabulary Preview. Write their definitions and add examples. Use a dictionary if necessary.

B. Complete each sentence with the correct vocabulary item.

alternative	apparent	customary	dismiss	modified	perspective

1. Professor Lee .... the assignment, changing it to include interviews with people who moved from their home countries as adults.

2. In my country, it's .... to bring a gift when visiting somebody for the first time. Most people bring flowers or a small gift.

3. I don't have the time to go to school this year, so taking an online course is a good .... I guess I will be spending a lot of time at my computer instead of going to classes.

4. Linguists cannot .... or fail to consider the impact that technology has had on language learning.

5. It is easy to see that there is an .... connection between age and language learning.

6. Living in another country gave me a different .... on the world. I thought about everything differently after that.

○ Go to MyEnglishLab to complete vocabulary and skill practices and to join in collaborative activities.

LANGUAGE SKILL

IDENTIFYING PHRASES IN ACADEMIC TEXT

WHY IT'S USEFUL By understanding the use of phrases in sentence structure, including embedded phrases, you will be able to comprehend complex academic texts and use more varied and complex sentences in your writing.

○ Go to MyEnglishLab for the Language Skill presentation and practice.

VOCABULARY STRATEGY
USING A DICTIONARY TO EXPAND VOCABULARY

WHY IT'S USEFUL By using a dictionary, you can learn other parts of speech associated with a particular word to increase your vocabulary, which will help you vary your writing.

In academic writing, it's important to be precise and accurate with your words. Dictionaries can help you better understand a word by providing definitions, contexts in which it is used, and specific examples and sentences with its usage. Dictionaries also identify words that have different parts of speech. Having a solid understanding of a word will help you expand your vocabulary and vary your writing.

Notice how the underlined words are used to express ideas on a similar topic.

- One factor affecting how a language <u>evolves</u> is change in a society's culture.
- The <u>evolution</u> of a language can be confusing because of the many factors involved.
- <u>Evolutionary</u> linguists study cultural and social factors that cause languages to change.

Use the dictionary entries to identify the part of speech for *evolve*, *evolution*, and *evolutionary*. What else can you learn about the words from the dictionary entry? Analyze the sentences. How does using different parts of speech help a writer?

TIP

Use an English language learner's dictionary to deepen your understanding of a word. It is an essential resource because it uses clear, easy to understand language to show word use, parts of speech, grammatical information, collocations, and much more.

---

evolve

e·volve /ɪˈvɒlv ɪˈvɑːlv/ ••○ [AWL] *verb* [intransitive, transitive]

1 if an animal or plant evolves, it changes gradually over a long period of time → evolution

🔊 *evolve from Fish evolved from prehistoric sea creatures. Animals have evolved camouflage to protect themselves from predators.*

2 to develop and change gradually over a long period of time

🔊 *The school has evolved its own style of teaching.*

🔊 *Businesses need to evolve rapidly.*

🔊 *evolve out of The idea evolved out of work done by British scientists.*

🔊 *evolve into The group gradually evolved into a political party.*

---

evolution

ev·o·lu·tion /ˌiːvəˈluːʃən, ˌevə-ˌevə-/ ●○○ AWL *noun* [uncountable]

1 the scientific idea that plants and animals develop and change gradually over a long period of time

🔊 *evolution of* the evolution of mammals; the theory of evolution

2 the gradual change and development of an idea, situation, or object

🔊 *evolution of* the evolution of the computer

evolutionary

ev·o·lu·tion·a·ry /ˌiːvəˈluːʃənəri◂,ˌevə-ˌevəˈluːʃənəri◂/ ●○○ AWL *adjective*

1 relating to the way in which plants and animals develop and change gradually over a long period of time

🔊 *the evolutionary development of birds*

🔊 *Some scientists have rejected evolutionary theory.*

2 relating to the way in which ideas or situations gradually change and develop over a long period of time

🔊 *He is in favor of gradual, evolutionary social change.*

TIP

The Longman Advanced American Dictionary highlights the 9000 most important words to learn in English and Academic Word List words.

EXERCISE 5

A. Use a dictionary to complete the chart. Find different parts of speech for each word.

Noun	Verb	Adjective	Adverb
impact			
		precise	
approach			
	target		
inclusion			

B. Choose three nouns from Part A and write a sentence for each about a topic from the unit or a topic familiar to you. Then choose a related part of speech for each noun and write a sentence about the same topic. Underline the word.

1. ....

....

2. ....

....

3. ....

....

4. ....

....

5. ....

....

6. ....

....

C. Discuss with a partner how the word is used in each sentence. What is the meaning of the word?

Go to MyEnglishLab to complete a skill practice.

APPLY YOUR SKILLS

WHY IT'S USEFUL By applying the skills you have learned in this unit, you can successfully use the research writing process to brainstorm ideas, arrive at a narrowed topic and approach, create an outline that includes a preliminary thesis, and main and supporting ideas, and annotate research to inform your ideas.

ASSIGNMENT
Plan a paper analyzing how and why words borrowed from other languages enter the English language. What factors influence which words become part of the language and which do not? Research words that have come into English from your first language or another language or language group that you are familiar with. Brainstorm topics, write a preliminary thesis, and create an outline for your paper.

BEFORE YOU WRITE

A. Before you begin your assignment, discuss these questions with one or more students.

1. What words have come into English from your first language or another language you know?

2. What information did you learn about the words in your research? When, how, or why were they adopted?

3. What factors influenced their use in English? Do they have the same meaning as they do in English?

B. As you consider your assignment, complete the tasks. Then share your ideas with another student. Get feedback and revise your ideas if necessary.

1. List and define the words you have chosen from your research.

   ....

   ....

   ....

   a. What brainstorming techniques will you use to generate ideas about factors that influence the words' inclusion in English? ....

      ....

      ....

   b. What graphic organizers will help you organize your ideas? Why? ....

      ....

2. Write a preliminary thesis and two or three main ideas. Conduct additional research on these ideas. ....

   ....

   ....

   ....

3. Create an outline to organize the information from your research. Include at least two supporting ideas for each main idea.

C. Review the Unit Skills Summary. As you begin the writing task on page 37, apply the skills you learned in this unit.

UNIT SKILLS SUMMARY

Brainstorm topics

- Understand the assignment, including purpose and audience.
- Research by finding and reviewing sources for key words and ideas.
- Narrow the topic.
- Research by finding and reviewing sources for approaches or focus for narrowed topic.
- Finalize topic and choose an approach or focus.

Create an outline

- Write a preliminary thesis statement.
- Research by gathering and reading appropriate sources for ideas related to the topic and focus.
- Write an informal or formal outline.

Annotate research

- Research a topic by reading articles, books, or other scholarly sources.
- Underline main ideas and important details.
- Circle key words, new vocabulary, and references to other sources.
- Use brackets to note ideas and evidence that support your claim.
- Write short notes and comments in the margin to agree or disagree, ask questions, summarize or analyze information.

Identify phrases in academic text

- Identify phrases to understand their structure, function, and meaning in sentences.

Use a dictionary to expand vocabulary

- Look up words to identify part(s) of speech.
- Analyze how words are used in sentences.

THINKING CRITICALLY

As you consider your writing assignment, discuss the questions with another student. Get feedback and revise your ideas if necessary.

1. Do you think that the English language should be so open to adopting words from other languages? Why or why not?

2. Are the words from the language you chose to write about commonly used in English today? What determines whether an adopted word continues to be used?

3. How has the adoption of words from the language you chose to write about affected English-speaking cultures?

THINKING VISUALLY

A. Look at the infographic with statistics about English as a world language. Discuss the questions with a partner.

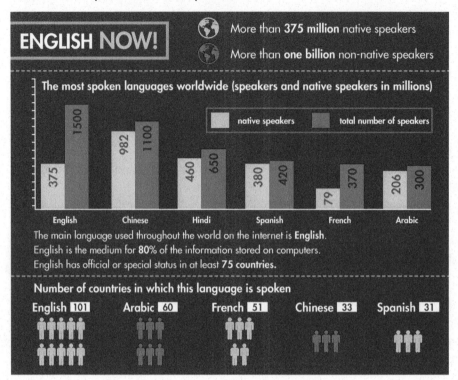

1. What information does the infographic give you?

2. What is the most surprising information?

3. What information that you would like to have is missing from the infographic?

4. How effective is the infographic at presenting the information? Can you suggest a better way to show the data?

B. Find statistics on a language you are interested in and create an infographic with some of the information.

THINKING ABOUT LANGUAGE

Rewrite the bracketed phrases in the correct order to make a complete sentence. Some phrases may need to be embedded in another.

1. The divide [since the first grammar book was written] [to grammar] [between the prescriptivist approach and the descriptivist approach] [[has been going on].

2. Some situations [call for] [to the problem] [only a prescriptive approach].

....

3. Linguists [study] [the way languages are [actually] spoken and written] [typically].

....

4. Editors [in a way] [must report] [by everyone] [information] [that is easily understood]. ....

....

5. Teachers [to grammar] [might use] [a prescriptivist approach] [to teach rules].

....

6. Some teachers [by accepting alternatives] [practice] [a modified prescriptivism] [to standard grammar]. ....

....

WRITE

A. Revisit the writing assignment and your answers to the questions in Before You Write Part B. Were you surprised at your findings? Why?

....

....

....

B. Review your preliminary thesis. Make sure it reflects the audience and purpose of the assignment.

C. Create an outline that includes your preliminary thesis, main ideas, and supporting ideas. Make sure there is enough research to support each idea.

BEYOND THE ASSIGNMENT

Write a paper of 800–1000 words analyzing how and why words borrowed from other languages enter the English language. What factors influence which words make it and which don't? Research words that have come into English from your first language or another language or language group you are familiar with.

◐ Go to MyEnglishLab to watch Professor Podesva's concluding video and to complete a self-assessment.

How cultural and ethical values define a successful business

BUSINESS ETHICS

Idea Development

UNIT PROFILE

There are important differences between private and public companies, but both must consider the individual interests of a range of people, including employees, customers, and investors, in their day-to-day operations. In this unit, you will read and write about topics related to business ethics, the moral principles and values affecting decisions, including who business leaders need to consider when making business decisions.

OUTCOMES

- Develop and organize ideas
- Identify reliable sources of information
- Paraphrase
- Use direct quotations and reported speech
- Recognize in-text definitions

Plan a paper comparing the advantages and disadvantages of putting the interests of shareholders or stakeholders first in decision-making. Develop and organize ideas for one advantage or disadvantage of each side of the issue. Use three or more reliable sources of information. Include two or more paraphrased ideas from each source and one quotation from a source.

For more about **BUSINESS ETHICS**, see ❷❸. See also ⌐R⌐ and ⌐OC⌐ **BUSINESS ETHICS** ❶❷❸.

GETTING STARTED

⊙ Go to MyEnglishLab to watch Dr. McLennan's introductory video and to complete a self-assessment.

Discuss these questions with a partner or group.

1. What are some of the goals of a business? How do businesses decide on their goals? What makes a business successful? What qualities make a business a good one? Give an example of a business you admire and give reasons why you admire it.

2. Who are the people affected by a business? What are the responsibilities of a company to its employees, its customers, and the community where it does business? Are some responsibilities more important than others?

3. Dr. McLennan suggests that we need to consider the difference between stockholders, owners of the company, and stakeholders – all the people the company relates to – when we analyze a company. Why is it important to consider all stakeholders in analyzing a business? Are some stakeholders more important to the success of a business? Whose interests come first?

FUNDAMENTAL SKILL

IDEA DEVELOPMENT

WHY IT'S USEFUL By developing ideas, you increase your knowledge of a topic and will be able to write a more effective paper that provides strong support for your points and connects your topic and research. Spending time developing ideas throughout the writing process will result in a stronger, more credible paper.

Idea development is essential to good writing. **Developing and organizing** your ideas with strong and valid support and presenting them in an effective and organized way are at the core of the entire writing process.

Idea development begins during planning and prewriting as you brainstorm topics to arrive at a narrowed topic, a focus, main and supporting ideas, and a preliminary thesis. You will continue to develop ideas during the writing stage. Using the topic and focus in your thesis statement and the main ideas in your outline, you will add relevant supporting ideas, including evidence from sources, explanations, examples, definitions, and facts. Depending on the type of paper, you will offer opinions—your own and from other sources. Even in the final stage when you are revising for submission, you are further developing and refining your ideas.

As you are drafting, always keep in mind the purpose and audience of the paper as you did when brainstorming and choosing the narrowed topic and focus for the paper. How you develop your ideas will also depend on the genre of the paper, the approach you will take, and the organizational patterns you will use.

For more on brainstorming topics and creating an outline, see Linguistics, Part 1.

For more on understanding an assignment, see Earth Science, Part 1.

Before you begin to develop your ideas, it is important to fully understand the assignment and what is expected from you in choosing an appropriately narrowed topic, a focus, and an approach. For example, a student in a business course narrowed the topic, and then chose a focus, an approach, and decided on main ideas for a writing assignment:

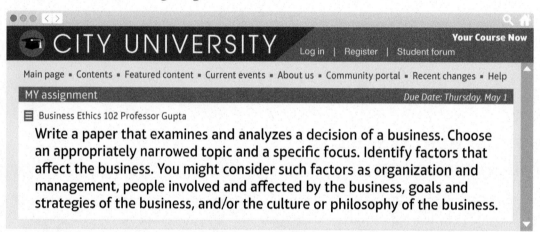

CITY UNIVERSITY
Log in | Register | Student forum
Your Course Now

Main page ▪ Contents ▪ Featured content ▪ Current events ▪ About us ▪ Community portal ▪ Recent changes ▪ Help

MY assignment
Due Date: Thursday, May 1

Business Ethics 102 Professor Gupta

Write a paper that examines and analyzes a decision of a business. Choose an appropriately narrowed topic and a specific focus. Identify factors that affect the business. You might consider such factors as organization and management, people involved and affected by the business, goals and strategies of the business, and/or the culture or philosophy of the business.

Look at how the student addressed the assignment.

Topic: Private companies

Focus: Factors that affect the decision of a private company to go public

Approach: Analysis, compare/contrast

Main ideas: Organization and structure of the business
People involved in the business
Business strategies and goals

With a topic, focus, approach, and an outline of main ideas, you are ready to develop your ideas. As you move out of the planning stage into drafting the paper, it can be difficult to know where to begin, but it is also exciting to embark on the journey to learn more about a topic that interests you. A good starting point is to explore what you already know about the topic. Some of the techniques that were useful in brainstorming topics during the planning stage can be utilized to develop the ideas that will be used to support that topic. Here, the writer used a prewriting task, listing, to identify key words and generate ideas that would be useful in both researching the topic for evidence and supporting the main ideas.

Organization and structure – CEO (boss), management, employees, policies, products/services, employee benefits, regulations

Strategies/goals – grow, promote brand, sell product or service, make a profit, satisfy customers, make employees happy, increase profit, raise capital, pay dividends to stockholders, control costs/losses, maintain liquidity, invest, compensate employees, have ethics, honesty, passion

People – stakeholders, CEO (boss), managers, directors, employees, customers, investors/shareholders, neighbors, community, government

Glossary

Dividend: a part of a company's profit that is paid to people who have shares in the company [A share is one of the equal parts into which the ownership of a company is divided.]

Capital: money or property, especially when it is used to start a business or produce more wealth

Creating a **cluster diagram**, also known as **mapping**, can be used to generate and organize ideas to best develop the support for your main ideas. Another useful technique for developing ideas is **freewriting**. Set a time limit and write as many ideas as you can about your topic and focus. Do not worry about organizing your ideas, being specific, or even writing complete sentences. The purpose is to write down as many ideas and their connections as possible.

For more on cluster diagrams, see Linguistics, Part 1.

Our writer decided to freewrite about what affects a private company's decision to go public. Can you add other ideas?

> What affects the decision of a private company to go public?
> I think maybe size matters in the decision of a company – number of
> employees, etc. The people who run the business; how about the product or
> service? How much money the company makes? Are they in debt? Do they
> need more capital to grow the business? Are there government rules and
> regulations?; passion; ethics; quality service – I want a business that does what
> it says – honest in promoting its product or service. It seems like it matters if
> it's run well and has good employees. What is the goal of the business? Improve
> brand awareness? Grow?

Once you have explored what you know about the topic, review your ideas and consider where there are gaps in your knowledge. You may still be lacking key words and specific information. Another good brainstorming technique to use at this point in the process is to write questions that you need to answer to fully develop the support for your main ideas. Our writer asked these questions. Can you add other questions?

1. What are the differences between public and private companies?
2. What and who most affects the decision of a private company to go public?
3. What additional factors might affect a company's decision?
4. What are the advantages of going public? The disadvantages?

In order to answer your questions, you will want to research your topic and begin to gather ideas from sources, which requires you to **identify reliable sources of information** and evaluate them for inclusion in your paper. Choosing ideas from appropriate sources will help you support your own ideas as you develop them.

TIP

Keeping a writing journal with all your ideas in one place is a good way to organize and have what you need at hand when you draft your paper.

VOCABULARY PREVIEW

Read the vocabulary items. Circle the ones you know. Put a question mark next to the ones you don't know.

regulations	strategy	promote	brand	liquidity
invest	compensate	ethics	passion	investor

EXERCISE 1

A. Read the narrowed topic and focus for the assignment and the list of ideas that the writer generated. Complete the cluster diagram on public and private companies. Draw lines to connect ideas to public or private businesses or to both.

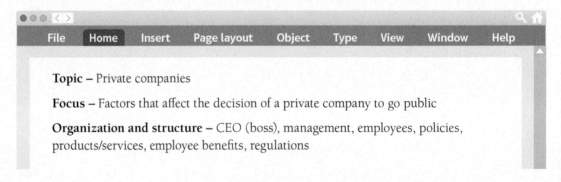

Topic – Private companies

Focus – Factors that affect the decision of a private company to go public

Organization and structure – CEO (boss), management, employees, policies, products/services, employee benefits, regulations

Strategies/goals – grow, promote brand, sell product or service, make a profit, satisfy customers, make employees happy, increase profit, raise capital, pay dividends to stockholders, control costs/losses, maintain liquidity, invest, compensate employees, have ethics, honesty, passion

People – stakeholders, CEO (boss), managers, directors, employees, customers, investors/shareholders, neighbors, community, government

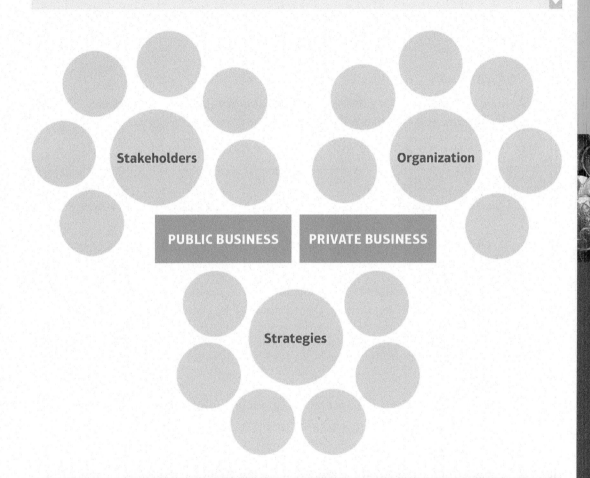

Stakeholders

Organization

PUBLIC BUSINESS

PRIVATE BUSINESS

Strategies

CULTURE NOTE

Private businesses range in size from a single owner/employee to corporations with tens of thousands of employees. In the United States, 86.4% of businesses with more than 500 employees are privately held. While public businesses often get more attention because they are traded on the stock market, in 2013, according to Forbes, less than 1% of the estimated 27 million US businesses were traded on a major stock exchange. Moreover, the number of public businesses also fell between 2000 and 2012 while the number of private businesses is growing, making them important contributors to the global economy.

B. Discuss your cluster diagram with a partner.

C. Freewrite for three minutes on the questions. Don't worry about using complete sentences or about accuracy.

> How do public and private companies differ? Do they have different stakeholders?
> Do they have different practices? Are they organized differently?
> Do they treat their customers differently?

D. Share your freewriting with a partner. Discuss comparisons that will be useful in writing about public and private businesses.

VOCABULARY CHECK

A. Review the vocabulary items in the Vocabulary Preview. Write their definitions and add examples. Use a dictionary if necessary.

B. Complete each sentence with the correct vocabulary item.

brand	compensate	ethics	invest	investor
liquidity	passion	promote	regulations	strategy

1. The company president has a new .... for selling more products; he plans to send new customers a gift card on their birthdays.

2. My business professor was an early .... in that computer company. She gave $1,000 ten years ago, and now she has over $50,000.

3. She has a great .... for inventing products for older people. After seeing her grandfather's struggles with simple tasks, she really wants to help others.

4. Most people, given a chance, will choose one product over another because they know the company and are familiar with the ....

5. It is important to have .... with some of your money in case you need to pay for something or give someone money right away.

6. Our company reviews its .... every year. We keep all of the rules that are good and change the ones that have problems.

7. My sister is going to .... money in my new business. I need about $10,000 to rent an office and hire an assistant.

8. Mr. Lee wants to .... workers with a higher salary next year, but his company is doing badly.

9. All new employees have to take a class on business .... The president wants everyone to work hard, be honest, and do the right thing for the company.

10. Movie studios spend a lot of money to send actors all over the world to .... new movies.

🔵 Go to MyEnglishLab to complete vocabulary and skill practices and to join in collaborative activities.

SUPPORTING SKILL 1
DEVELOPING AND ORGANIZING IDEAS

WHY IT'S USEFUL By developing and organizing your ideas, you will be able to support your ideas appropriately and fully, and in ways that make them clear and understandable to your reader.

Developing and organizing your ideas requires careful thought and planning, whether you are knowledgeable about your topic or new to it. It is important to have your **purpose** and **audience** clearly in mind as you begin the drafting stage to guide your choice of supporting ideas. Whether these were stated directly in your **assignment** or left up to you, they will affect the **approach** you take to developing your ideas and how you organize them. For example, if your purpose is to persuade your reader of a position, you will develop strong arguments in favor of your position and address counterarguments. If your purpose is to explain the issues of a topic, you will use facts and opinions that present a more neutral and balanced view of the topic. In both cases, examples may be good support, but the choice of examples and how they are developed may differ. The **rhetorical mode,** the way in which you communicate the information, should be clear to your reader by the organizational patterns you choose to develop and organize your ideas. Often more than one rhetorical mode is used in a paper, and even within a paragraph, to effectively develop and support your ideas. For example, the main rhetorical mode in a paper on factors in the decision of a private company to become public is analysis. However, comparison of public and private companies is likely, and the paper will also use cause and effect to examine the decision.

During this stage, be open to ideas you may not have considered, but also evaluate and even challenge ideas you are considering for inclusion. Discuss your ideas with peers, classmates, your professors, or others to get different viewpoints. Write down as many ideas as possible. The very process of writing down your ideas often generates new ones or reveals new connections.

For more on organizational patterns and selecting examples, see Earth Science, Part 1.

Begin by reviewing your **thesis statement,** which states your topic and your focus. Just as it guides your reader by stating your intention, it can guide you in developing and organizing ideas which fit your point of view and support your thesis. Keeping your thesis in mind may also suggest ways to improve and refine it as your ideas about it come together. For example, here is our writer's preliminary thesis:

> To analyze and evaluate a private company's decision to become a public company, it is important to consider such factors as its organization and structure, stakeholders, and business strategies and goals.

Using your **outline** from the planning stage, key words you listed, and the ideas you generated, develop each main idea in one or more paragraphs that relate to your thesis. Develop each of your points in its own paragraph with sufficient support to make that point convincing. For example, what main ideas would you expect the writer to include in an outline and further develop based on the thesis statement above?

For more on outlining and thesis statements, see Linguistics, Part 1.

TIP

Overgeneralized statements do little to convince the reader. Support should be specific and detailed and as complete as possible. For example, in developing the main point of stakeholders being included in the decision of a private business to go public, it is not enough to say that all stakeholders are important and must be considered. To fully develop the idea, specific stakeholders and reasons why they are important must be included and details or detailed support must be provided to convince the reader.

As you consider **developing your ideas**, take each main idea and consider how to best support it. There are many ways to do this:

- Define a concept in order for your reader to understand.
- Explain the idea or its importance to your thesis.
- Give an example to help your reader see its value.
- State facts and include data to support ideas.
- Compare one idea to another idea.
- Offer reasons.
- Suggest causes or effects.
- Discuss advantages or disadvantages.
- Classify or in some way show a relationship to the bigger picture.
- Provide evidence backed by a source.

Look at the paragraph developing one of the main ideas in the outline about a private company's decision to become public.

In analyzing the decision of a private company to go public, it is beneficial to understand how the organization and structure of each type of company affects how it is run. First, private companies are most often run by an owner, whereas a public company is typically controlled by a board of directors. Private companies can have investors, people who give money to the business, but unlike a large group of shareholders who own stock in the company, they may have closer ties to the business and be far more involved in the day-to-day business. This gives both the owner(s) and investors of private companies greater control over the operation of their business. In going public, a private business must answer to a much larger group of shareholders and must submit to stricter government regulations in reporting on its business activities. Therefore, in making this major decision to become a public company, a private business must determine if it is willing to give up this control.

topic

focus

supporting ideas

comparison

explanation

definition

fact

It isn't enough to develop your ideas well. You need to consider **ways to organize** them. You want to arrange your ideas in ways that fit your purpose. As a reminder, the language used in an assignment may indicate the organization or structure of your paper. For example, an assignment to analyze might be organized by presenting each factor in the analysis with support, whereas an assignment to compare might be organized by developing the reasons for each factor in a separate paragraph. The ideas presented are the same, but the order is different. There are many ways to organize ideas both within the paragraphs you develop and between them.

As in developing your ideas, start with your thesis and outline. These may help you decide on the overall structure of the paper and the order in which you present your ideas:

- How you will introduce your topic? What background information is needed?
- What order will you use to present your main ideas? Most important first? Last?
- What you will say in your conclusion?

During the drafting stage, expect to add or delete ideas as well as move them from one part of your paper to another. Ideas can be presented in several orders:

- Chronological –first, second, next, then, finally, last
- Spatial – next to, between, near, far
- Logical progression – before, after, most/least important
- General to specific – in general, overall
- Specific to general – for example, for instance, specifically
- Block
- Point-by-point

This chart explains the difference between block and point-by-point.

Block	Point-by-Point

I. Introduction
Thesis:
II. Body
  A. Reasons to stay a private company
    1. Supporting detail
    2. Supporting detail
    3. Supporting detail
  B. Reasons to become a public company
    1. Supporting detail
    2. Supporting detail
    3. Supporting detail
III. Conclusion
	I. Introduction
	Thesis:
	II. Body (stay private vs go public)
	  A. Organization
	    1. Supporting detail
	    2. Supporting detail
	    3. Supporting detail
	  B. Stakeholders
	    1. Supporting detail
	    2. Supporting detail
	    3. Supporting detail
	  C. Strategies and goals
	    1. Supporting detail
	    2. Supporting detail
	    3. Supporting detail
	III. Conclusion

TIP

It is important to use good transitions both within paragraphs and between them that help your reader see the connections between ideas. This improves the flow of the paper and its readability.

A good way to organize your ideas before writing is to put them into a graphic organizer. A **graphic organizer** is helpful in organizing the supporting (specific) ideas that you will use in the paragraphs that develop main ideas. It isn't necessary to write the ideas in complete sentences or to punctuate carefully. Our writer organized ideas about public and private companies in the table using a point-by-point order.

	PUBLIC	PRIVATE
Organization	run by board of directors; traded on stock market – has shareholders	can be a corporation, a partnership, or a sole owner, as long as shares are not traded publicly
Decision-making	pressure from, and reporting to, shareholders can slow down the pace at which decisions get made	decisions made by owner and/or investors; overlap of management and investors = aligned goals
Quality of financial information accessible to (potential) investors and risk factors	stricter legal obligations – has to comply with government rules and submit required quarterly financial reports; more known, so less risk	fewer legal obligations – doesn't have to disclose financial information, so less known about ; lower valuation and higher risk due to less transparency
Quality of management	easier to raise capital for expansion and projects – less risk and more potential for large rewards	can focus on long-term growth instead of quarterly dividends to shareholders
		growth prospects are lower but more sensitive and responsive to opportunities for capital
	can attract high quality management = strong, experienced = lower risk	theoretically less able to attract high-quality management candidates – can't match the salary or benefits of a larger business = higher risk; have less management depth

Stakeholders	Shareholders	Investors
Business strategies/ goals	seek to increase shareholder value as a long-term strategy	less focused on increasing value
	under pressure to have consistent growth rates and earnings as it directly relates to its stock price performance	doesn't need shareholder approval for operational and growth strategy decisions made by company
	trying to meet short term goals – rather than look to future	increased flexibility in short- and long-term business decisions.
	can raise more capital in the stock market	seek to minimize taxes

EXERCISE 2

A. Read the paragraph from a first draft of the paper for the assignment on page 40. Answer the questions about how the writer developed the ideas.

Business strategies always influence the way a business decides to make a major change. When considering a transition from private to public, strategies and goals may be the most important factors. There are clear differences in the goals of a private company versus a public one. A public company naturally must always have as a major strategy increasing shareholder value. It is under pressure to have consistent growth rates, and its stock must perform well in the market. This may result in its constantly trying to meet short-term goals rather than looking to the future. A private company, in contrast, can be less focused on increasing value and growing as it makes decisions. Because it doesn't have shareholders whose approval may be required in decisions, it has more flexibility in both short- and long-term decisions. This may be one of the main reasons a private company decides against going public.

1. What is the topic of the paragraph? ....

....

2. What is the focus? ....

....

3. What organizational patterns are used? ....

....

4. How is it organized? ....

....

5. What other ways to develop ideas might help the writer develop the topic of business strategies? ....

....

6. What ideas in the graphic organizer on page 49 were not included in the paragraph?

....

....

7. In organizing the essay, where should the writer put this paragraph about strategies in relation to the other main ideas of organization and stakeholders? Why? ....

....

B. Discuss your answers to the questions in Part A with a partner.

C. Look back at the chart on page 49. See how supporting details were added for the main points of organization and business strategies/goals. With a partner, complete a graphic organizer for the main idea of stakeholders. Include details about the different stakeholders—their importance and/or impact on the business.

	Public	Private
Stakeholders	Shareholders	Investors

D. Use the ideas in your graphic organizer to write a paragraph about stakeholders in both private and public companies.

◐ Go to MyEnglishLab to complete skill practices.

SUPPORTING SKILL 2

IDENTIFYING RELIABLE SOURCES OF INFORMATION

WHY IT'S USEFUL By identifying reliable sources of information, you will be able to find and evaluate expert ideas and opinions to include in your own writing. Using reliable and credible sources will make your arguments stronger and more well-supported.

Once you have established a thesis and considered ways to develop and organize your ideas, it is important to conduct research to first expand your knowledge on the topic and then support your ideas in your paper. **Identifying reliable sources of information** is a challenging, but critical skill because it will help you become an accomplished writer in a university setting. You must be able to not only find reliable sources, but also evaluate them and determine if the source material will be appropriate for use in your paper. Your professors will expect you to integrate trustworthy and reliable scholarly sources in your writing to demonstrate your understanding of a topic.

You will likely use different types of sources of information for different fields of study. A combination of both primary and secondary sources is common in university research. If you are writing a paper for a sociology class, for example, **primary sources** like interviews or photographs give first-hand information. In the hard sciences, results from experiments or observations can be used as evidence to support a claim.

Secondary sources, such as scholarly books, journals, and articles which interpret and evaluate other sources, are commonly used to introduce ideas, explain concepts, or provide evidence or counterarguments for your paper. Secondary sources can include information from reputable newspapers and magazines as well as audio and visual information from your courses, lectures, and the internet. In business classes, students often use industry and market reports, professional trade journals, business publications, and government reports.

Knowing how to find and identify reliable sources efficiently can save you a lot of time during the research process. For an unfamiliar topic, you can begin your research online with general reference materials like encyclopedias or specialized dictionaries which can give you a good overview.

Once you have a general understanding of the topic, you can begin your search for reliable sources of information. Follow these steps:

1. Identify key or subject terms for use in online searches.

2. Use scholarly search engines, databases, and websites to find appropriate sources for academic work.

   • **Online Databases:** As part of a university community, you most likely will have access to scholarly databases like EBSCOhost or ProQuest. Often universities will have online tutorials to help you get started with your search.

   • **The Internet:** Avoid using general search engines like Yahoo® or Google® because they will include both reliable and unreliable sources of information. Instead, go directly to scholarly search engines like Google Scholar, iSeek Education, or Microsoft® Academic Search for access to trustworthy information without a subscription.

   • **Websites:** Websites can be unreliable and highly biased because anyone can create a website. For this reason, choose university, government, or library websites, like the Public Library of Science or the Library of Congress, which are considered reputable. The URLs for these websites end in *.gov* or *.edu*.

3. Visit a library to find sources in print, such as books or newspapers, or other audio or visual materials that may not be available online. Libraries are also excellent resources for finding primary research such as interviews, photos, or letters.

4. Evaluate the credibility and reliability of published source material. As you scan a text, ask questions to determine if the information is scholarly.

   • Is the author an expert in the discipline? How do you know?

   • Does the author present both sides of an issue?

   • Does the text include discipline-specific language?

   • Are other sources cited in the text?

   • Is the text peer-reviewed (evaluated by experts in the same discipline)?

   • Is the source from a reputable publisher?

   • What is the date of publication? If the information is dated, is it still relevant?

5. Consider the purpose of your assignment as you evaluate source information. Read actively to understand and evaluate the information. Asking questions can help you decide if information is appropriate to include in your paper.

   • Is it relevant to your topic and thesis?

   • Is it accurate and comprehensive?

   • Does it provide evidence or examples to support your ideas?

   • Does it provide visuals that support your ideas?

   • Can it be used to enhance your arguments if the source is a well-known expert in the field?

   • Does it help you build a strong argument?

   • Does it offer a unique perspective on the topic?

6. Keep a list of the credible and reliable sources that are relevant to your topic. Include the title of the text, date, name of author(s), and a one-sentence summary for each source. This list will save you time later in the research process when you begin selecting your sources.

> **TIP**
>
> Wikipedia can be a good resource to begin your research because it provides background information on a topic and usually lists academic sources that you can refer to, evaluate, and potentially use later. However, do not use Wikipedia as a source in academic settings. Because it is collaboratively written and edited by its users, it is not reliable for supporting ideas.

EXERCISE 3

A. Review the sources from an online search. Which are most likely to provide reliable and relevant information? Rank the sources from the most relevant (1) to least relevant (6). Compare and discuss your rankings with a partner.

.... "Public and Private Companies: What's the Difference?" 2015 *Journal of Management Today* article

.... "Privately Held Company" webpage in Wikipedia

.... "The Basics of Corporate Structure" www.investopedia.com (financial education website) article

.... "The World's Largest Public Companies in 2016" www.forbes.com online business magazine article

.... "Create the Winning Advantage: Public vs Private Companies" http://www.jobvine.co.za/blog/2015/10

.... "Should my Company Go Public?" 2016 www.sec.gov (U.S. Securities and Exchange Commission) guidelines

B. Look back at the topic, focus, and ideas for the student writing assignment in Exercise 1, Part A. Identify keywords you could use for an online search for why private companies go public. List them under Original Keywords. Then type your keywords into a scholarly database. Look at two or three of the results and find the subject or descriptor field. Are subject terms listed? If so, list them under Subject Terms and use these terms to continue your online search. List three possible sources from your search for this paper.

Original Keywords	Subject Terms	Possible Sources

C. Choose a source from the results in Part B. Evaluate its credibility and reliability by answering the questions.

1. Is the author an expert in the discipline? How do you know? ....

....

2. Does the author present both sides of an issue? ....

....

3. Does the text include discipline-specific language? ....

....

4. Are other sources cited in the text? ....

....

5. Is the text peer-reviewed? ....

....

6. Is the source from a reputable publisher? ....

....

7. What is the date of publication? If the information is dated, is it still relevant?

....

D. Write a brief paragraph about how this source could be used in a paper discussing why private companies decide to go public. Consider the purpose of the assignment and address the relevance and the reliability of the source.

⬆ Go to MyEnglishLab to complete a skill practice.

INTEGRATED SKILLS

PARAPHRASING

> **WHY IT'S USEFUL** By paraphrasing, you can integrate credible sources into your paper to support your own ideas. When you integrate source material in your own words, your ideas flow smoothly and without abrupt shifts in style that can be distracting to the reader.

At the university level, you will be expected to develop and support your ideas with expert opinion and evidence from reliable sources. The primary way to do this is by **paraphrasing**. A paraphrase is a statement that expresses something that someone has said or written, but in a different way. Like summaries, paraphrases must be written *in your own words*. Unlike summaries, paraphrases are approximately the same length as the original text and often include details. Including paraphrases from credible and reliable sources in your papers makes your argument or ideas stronger and more credible.

What does a good paraphrase do?

- accurately reports what a source says
- uses your own style and language (written in your own words)
- cites the source

When do you paraphrase?

- when you don't need to report exact language from a source
- when you want to include a complete idea, including details, from a source
- when you want to simplify technical or abstract language for your reader
- when you need to demonstrate that you have understood a source's idea

Paraphrasing is challenging, even for native speakers. Here are some guidelines:

DO
✓ Read the original text several times to make sure you fully understand it.
✓ Annotate the text by underlining each key point and writing keywords and phrases in the margin.
✓ Use your margin notes to orally paraphrase the text.
✓ Paraphrase the entire idea, including details.
✓ Include a signal phrase to introduce the paraphrase and/or an in-text citation to make it clear to your reader that the material is paraphrased. *According to [author]…, [Author] states…*
✓ Include the source's tone and/or opinion.
✓ Check your paraphrase with the original text when you are finished to make sure it is accurate and complete, and not plagiarized.
✓ Include an in-text citation.

DON'T

✗ Don't add or delete ideas.

✗ Don't change the original meaning.

✗ Don't copy sentences or parts of sentences from the original.

✗ Don't replace all words in a sentence with synonyms.

✗ Don't use more than three original words in a row.

✗ Don't include your own opinion.

TIP

After reading the original text carefully, put it away so you are not tempted to use the same wording. It is helpful to let some time pass before writing your paraphrase using your notes.

Changing the structure and words of the original text will help you paraphrase using your own words. Here are some effective strategies:

Language Strategies for Paraphrasing	Examples
Change word form	To **acquire** other businesses with the public company's stock …like **acquiring** a new business…
Change verb tense or voice (active to passive and vice versa)	Companies **go** public for a number of reasons. Companies **have gone** public for many reasons. Companies attract and **compensate employees** with public company stock and stock-option compensation. … **employees can be compensated** with company stock and stock-options.
Reduce clauses to phrases	**Employees can be compensated** with company stock and stock-options. **Compensating employees** with company stock and stock options is a way to attract them.
Move clauses to different parts of a sentence	Companies may go public to increase liquidity for a company's stock, **which may allow owners and employees to more easily sell stock.** **It may be easier for stakeholders to sell their stock** in a company when the company goes public.
Use synonyms or word substitutions when they don't change the original meaning	Companies may go public to **create publicity, brand awareness,** and **status** for a company. …some companies believe that going public is a good way to **promote their brand** and **build their reputation**.
Other strategies for paraphrasing?	

Read the passage from a government website on why private companies choose to go public. Then review the student paraphrase that follows the passage.

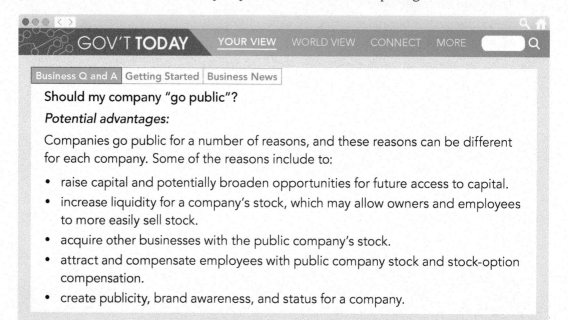

Business Q and A | Getting Started | Business News

Should my company "go public"?

Potential advantages:

Companies go public for a number of reasons, and these reasons can be different for each company. Some of the reasons include to:

- raise capital and potentially broaden opportunities for future access to capital.
- increase liquidity for a company's stock, which may allow owners and employees to more easily sell stock.
- acquire other businesses with the public company's stock.
- attract and compensate employees with public company stock and stock-option compensation.
- create publicity, brand awareness, and status for a company.

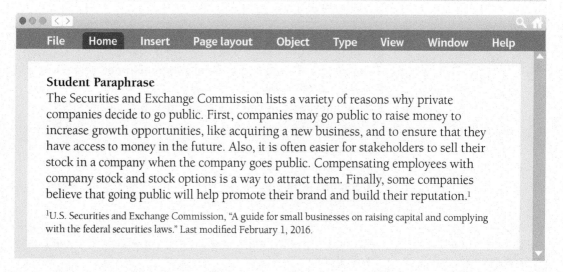

Student Paraphrase

The Securities and Exchange Commission lists a variety of reasons why private companies decide to go public. First, companies may go public to raise money to increase growth opportunities, like acquiring a new business, and to ensure that they have access to money in the future. Also, it is often easier for stakeholders to sell their stock in a company when the company goes public. Compensating employees with company stock and stock options is a way to attract them. Finally, some companies believe that going public will help promote their brand and build their reputation.[1]

[1]U.S. Securities and Exchange Commission, "A guide for small businesses on raising capital and complying with the federal securities laws." Last modified February 1, 2016.

Notice how the student incorporated different strategies to paraphrase the passage. What other strategies did the student use that are not listed? How could the paraphrase be improved? Look at the guidelines on pages 56–57. Does the paraphrase follow these guidelines?

VOCABULARY PREVIEW

Read the vocabulary items. Circle the ones you know. Put a question mark next to the ones you don't know.

corporate	interference	criticism	unethical	extensive
critic	wealth	overseas	maximize	adjust

EXERCISE 4

A. Read the article in *Business Strategy* magazine (January 2017) which examines US shareholder and stakeholder business theories.

Stakeholder or Shareholders: Who Comes First?

By Jessie Lu

1   The question of who business leaders should think about when they make decisions is the focus of many business ethics discussions. Should the priority of a company be to satisfy its employees and customers, or those who own stock in the company? This is a question in discussions about corporate social responsibility as well. Corporate social responsibility, often abbreviated CSR, is an approach to business behavior that encourages leaders to make decisions with the greater community and environment in mind. Many business leaders today argue that a model business is one in which "value creation"—or increasing the value of goods, services, and stocks—occurs when a company makes decisions in the best interest of everyone.

2   There are two commonly held views of whose interests companies should serve: shareholder theory and stakeholder theory. The first, shareholder theory, is the more traditional view of business and model of corporate responsibility. It is taught in business schools and widely accepted in the business world. The basis of shareholder theory—also called stockholder theory—is the idea that for-profit businesses should be focused on creating wealth for their shareholders, or the owners of shares of stock in the company. Under this theory, business leaders, who are representatives of the shareholders, should make business decisions with a focus on providing wealth to shareholders. The economist Milton Friedman is

(Continued)

known for creating the shareholder theory in 1970. Friedman argued that the purpose of the business is to maximize profits to owners, and that businesses should be free from government interference.

3   Many business ethicists warn, however, that shareholder theory creates an unethical corporate environment in which it is easy—or even preferable—for the corporation to ignore its moral responsibility to interests outside its shareholders. Focusing on creating wealth can lead to a loss in trust from the community, and this can affect the company in the long run. Take the case of Nike, Inc. as a classic example of how shareholder-focused management may have harmed the company. Nike faced wide criticism from customers in the 1990s for its low-cost but unethical labor standards in overseas factories. When managers realized Nike needed to win back trust from customers and rescue the reputation of its brand name, it released an extensive report that evaluated its factories. Feedback from many stakeholders such as suppliers, employees, and consumers, was critical for shifting the company's business practices. Today, Nike is known as a good example of a socially responsible company that succeeds at value creation and benefitting the community. Nike's business practices now follow stakeholder theory.

4   Stakeholder theory, in contrast to shareholder theory, proposes that a corporation should have an equal responsibility to all "stakeholders," that is, those who are affected by the corporation's practices and policies. Stakeholders could include employees, customers, the outside community, and even the environment. Many business leaders today argue that corporations must have more of a stakeholder approach in order to be successful and to avoid scandals. Critics of stakeholder theory argue, however, that stakeholders are not always clearly identifiable, nor do corporations have any reason to put the interests of stakeholders above that of shareholders. Moreover, business leaders making decisions on behalf of stakeholders may be making decisions about matters in which they are not experts. There are also cases of businesses that fail in today's economy because they choose to focus too much on stakeholders and not enough on maximizing shareholder wealth. A company's solvency, the ability to produce enough wealth to stay in business, is at the heart of why business leaders try to make decisions with shareholders in mind. The case of Malden Mills is a good example of this.

5   Malden Mills Industries, which produced Polartec® fabric, was located in the small town of Lawrence, Massachusetts, and employed several thousand residents of the area. After a fire burned down the factory in 1995, owner Aaron Feuerstein decided to rebuild on the same site instead of moving the factory overseas, as many other companies were doing in the 1990s. Malden Mills also agreed to pay unemployed workers during the rebuilding process, which cost millions. His decisions made him into an American hero, and the company into a golden example of prioritizing people over profit. However, the decisions also contributed to the company's financial ruin.

6   While ignoring shareholder interests is not good practice, many business leaders today recognize that companies cannot maximize value for shareholders without investing—to varying degrees—in important stakeholders. Many successful companies today have solid stakeholder relationships that help maximize wealth for shareholders in the long run. Many of these companies enthusiastically embrace a corporate social responsibility approach by developing programs that benefit the community and environment. Accepting a strong stakeholder management style in many ways is simply adjusting to a changing society—shareholder theory was much stronger in the past than it is today. Social media has played an important role in shifting attitudes about corporate responsibility by highlighting companies that improve environmental and social conditions and exposing those who don't. These companies often attract talented employees and make work environments more innovative and healthier, which goes a long way in driving up both satisfaction among stakeholders and wealth in shareholders.

Glossary

For-profit organization: a company whose primary goal is to make a profit

B. Answer the questions.

1. What is the basis of shareholder theory? ....

....

....

2. What concerns do business ethicists have with shareholder theory? Why?

....

....

3. Why did many customers criticize the company Nike in the 1990s? How did Nike respond? ....

....

....

4. What is the basis of stakeholder theory? ....

....

....

5. Why do many business leaders believe that a stakeholder approach is better than a shareholder approach? ....

....

....

6. What are some arguments that critics of stakeholder theory have?

....

....

7. Why did the author include the example of Malden Mills Industries?

....

....

C. **Read the excerpts from the article and annotate them. Underline key points and write keywords and phrases in the margin. Use your margin notes to orally paraphrase the excerpt to a partner. Listen to your partner's paraphrase and give feedback using the paraphrasing guidelines on pages 56–57.**

1. Many business ethicists warn, however, that shareholder theory creates an unethical corporate environment in which it is easy—or even preferable—for the corporation to ignore its moral responsibility to interests outside its shareholders. Focusing on creating wealth can lead to a loss in trust from the community, and this can affect the company in the long run.

2. Take the case of Nike, Inc. as a classic example of how shareholder-focused management may have harmed the company. Nike faced wide criticism from customers in the 1990s for its low-cost but unethical labor standards in overseas factories. When managers realized Nike needed to win back trust from customers and rescue the reputation of its brand name, it released an extensive report that evaluated its factories. Feedback from many stakeholders such as suppliers, employees, and consumers, was critical for shifting the company's business practices.

3. Critics of stakeholder theory argue, however, that stakeholders are not always clearly identifiable, nor do corporations have any reason to put the interests of stakeholders above that of shareholders. Moreover, business leaders making decisions on behalf of stakeholders may be making decisions about matters of which they are not experts.

D. Write your paraphrases from Part C. Make sure you include a signal phrase and cite the source. Refer to the guidelines on pages 56–57 for writing a good paraphrase.

E. PEER REVIEW. Exchange one or more paraphrases with a partner. Respond to the questions to evaluate each other's work. For responses marked No, give feedback in the Notes column to help your partner revise.

	Yes	No	Notes
Is the paraphrase comprehensive?	☐	☐	
Is the paraphrase accurate?	☐	☐	
Are keywords from the original text included?	☐	☐	
Is the paraphrase written in the writer's own words?	☐	☐	
Does the writer change the original sentence structure?	☐	☐	
Does the paraphrase include an in-text citation?	☐	☐	

CULTURE NOTE

Corporate social responsibility (CSR) began to take hold in the 1960s when people started to express ethical concerns about how companies should behave. Organizations around the world began to implement initiatives to address sustainable economic development, conservation, and the influence of stakeholders in business decisions. Today, many international governments, companies, and organizations have adopted CSR standards to address growing social and global environmental concerns.

VOCABULARY CHECK

A. Review the vocabulary items in the Vocabulary Preview. Write their definitions and add examples. Use a dictionary if necessary.

B. Write the correct vocabulary item next to each definition.

adjust	corporate	critic	criticism	extensive	interference
maximize	overseas	reputation	unethical	wealth	

.... 1. belonging to or relating to a large company or group of companies acting together as a single organization

.... 2. the act of deliberately getting involved in a situation where you may not be wanted or needed

.... 3. remarks that say what you think is bad about someone

.... 4. not obeying rules of moral behavior, especially those concerning a profession

.... 5. containing or dealing with a lot of information and details

.... 6. someone who makes judgments about a person, organization, or idea

.... 7. a large amount of money and possessions

.... 8. to or in a foreign country that is across the ocean

.... 9. to increase something such as profit or income as much as possible

.... 10. to gradually become familiar with a new situation

.... 11. the opinion that people have about someone or something because of what has happened in the past

🔾 Go to MyEnglishLab to complete vocabulary and skill practices and to join in collaborative activities.

LANGUAGE SKILL

USING DIRECT QUOTATIONS AND REPORTED SPEECH

WHY IT'S USEFUL Knowing how to use both direct quotations and reported speech correctly will help you effectively introduce the ideas of others as support in your writing. Reporting verbs can indicate point of view of the author and reflect your opinion of the ideas.

🔾 Go to MyEnglishLab for the Language Skill presentation and practice.

VOCABULARY STRATEGY
RECOGNIZING IN-TEXT DEFINITIONS

WHY IT'S USEFUL By recognizing in-text definitions, you will be able to build your vocabulary without having to interrupt your reading to look up key terms and concepts.

University textbooks frequently identify and define discipline-specific vocabulary and key concepts that students are expected to understand. Key terms and concepts may be defined in the margin, or listed in a glossary at the end of a unit or in a section review.

In some cases, new words will appear in **bold** or *italics* in the text, with a definition or descriptive details included within the text to help students understand the subject content. These definitions are introduced with **context clues** that include punctuation, verbs, and/or other words and phrases. **Recognizing in-text definitions** helps you to build your vocabulary in a more natural way by looking for information as you read rather than having you check a dictionary or glossary.

Punctuation
Definitions can follow or be enclosed by commas, dashes, or parentheses.

Clues	
commas	Private companies can have <u>investors</u>, **people who give money to the company in order to get a profit,** who may be involved in the day-to-day management of the business.
dashes	Private companies may go public to raise <u>capital</u>—**money**—for new business opportunities.
parentheses	A <u>shareholder</u> **(stockholder)** of a public company is usually not involved in making major business decisions for the company.

Verbs
Key terms are often followed by specific verbs that introduce definitions.

Clues	
is/are (was/were)	A <u>critic</u> **is someone who makes judgments about a person, organization, or idea.**
means/meaning	A corporation focused on shareholders may make <u>unethical choices</u>, **meaning they are morally unacceptable.**
include/ including	A person's <u>wealth</u> **includes money, property, and stocks owned in a company.**

Examples

Key terms can be followed by words and phrases that introduce examples. Examples are used to make word meanings clear.

Clues	
such as/like	<u>Unethical business practices</u> could include actions **such as dumping waste into rivers, mistreating employees, or cheating on government taxes**.
for instance/ for example	Many business leaders think that companies should be free from government <u>interference</u>. **For instance, regulations, policies, and laws** can make it more difficult for companies to conduct business.

Synonyms and Restatements

Key terms and concepts can be followed by synonyms or restatements that help the reader understand the meaning. These are introduced by specific words or phrases.

Clues	
also known as/ also called	Public companies sell <u>stocks</u>, **also known as shares**, in a company.
or	Business leaders must consider the interests of <u>shareholders</u>, **or the owners of shares of stock in the company**.
that is	Companies may choose to go public to increase their <u>prestige</u>, **that is, reputation**, in an industry.

TIP
Research shows that it is easier to learn new words when you learn them by topics. List words by topics in a vocabulary journal. For example, group all new business terms in the same list and review them together.

EXERCISE 5

A. Circle the definition clue in each sentence from the reading in this unit. Then underline the key term and the words or phrases that define the term.

1. Corporate social responsibility is an approach to business behavior that encourages leaders to make decisions with the greater community and environment in mind.

2. Many business leaders today argue that a model business is one in which "value creation", or increasing the value of goods, services, and stocks, occurs when a company makes decisions in the best interest of everyone.

3. The basis of shareholder theory—also called stockholder theory—is the idea that for-profit businesses should be focused on creating wealth for their shareholders.

4. Stakeholder theory, in contrast to shareholder theory, proposes that a corporation should have an equal responsibility to all "stakeholders," that is, those who are affected by the corporation's practices and policies.

5. Stakeholders could include employees, customers, the outside community, and even the environment.

6. A company's solvency, the ability to produce enough wealth to stay in business, is at the heart of why business leaders try to make decisions with shareholders in mind.

B. **Choose six new words from this unit and write sentences in which you define the words. Use definition clues in your sentences.**

C. **Share your sentences with a partner. Have your partner circle the definition clue in each sentence and then underline the key term and the words or phrases that define the term.**

⬤ Go to MyEnglishLab to complete a skill practice.

APPLY YOUR SKILLS

WHY IT'S USEFUL By applying the skills you have learned in this unit, you can successfully develop and organize ideas, identify reliable sources of information, paraphrase, use direct quotations and reported speech, and recognize in-text definitions to develop discipline-specific vocabulary.

ASSIGNMENT

Plan a paper comparing the advantages and disadvantages of putting the interests of shareholders or stakeholders first in decision-making. Develop and organize ideas for one advantage or disadvantage of each side of the issue. Use three or more reliable sources of information. Include two or more paraphrased ideas from each source and one quotation from a source.

BEFORE YOU WRITE

A. **Before you begin your assignment, discuss these questions with one or more students.**

1. What are the advantages and disadvantages of putting the interests of shareholders over stakeholders? Stakeholders over shareholders?

2. What do business leaders take into account when making decisions that involve the interests of shareholders and/or stakeholders?

3. Is it ever acceptable to ignore the interests of a stakeholder? Shareholders? Why or why not?

B. As you consider your writing assignment, complete the tasks. Then share your ideas with another student. Get feedback and revise your ideas if necessary.

1. List the advantages or disadvantages you will focus on. What techniques do you plan to use to develop and organize your ideas? ....

   ....

2. List the sources you will use. What types of online searches will you do and what types of sources will you look for? How will you verify their credibility and reliability? ....

   ....

3. Which techniques will you use to paraphrase ideas in your own words? What will you do to make sure you paraphrase source information accurately? ....

   ....

C. Review the Unit Skills Summary. As you begin on the writing task on page 71, apply the skills you learned in this unit.

UNIT SKILLS SUMMARY

Develop and organize ideas

- Use your thesis statement to guide you in developing and organizing your ideas.
- Choose the best way to develop and support each main idea.
- Choose the best way to organize ideas within paragraphs and the best order for the paragraphs in the paper.

Identify reliable sources of information

- Identify key terms for online searches.
- Use scholarly search engines.
- Visit a library to find sources in print.
- Evaluate the credibility and reliability of published source material.
- Create a list of all relevant credible and reliable sources.

Paraphrase

- Integrate credible sources into your paper.
- Accurately report what a source says.
- Use your own style and language.

Use direct quotations and reported speech

- When quoting directly, introduce the quotation, quote exactly, punctuate carefully, and explain the reason for the quote.
- Use reporting verbs that help the reader understand the meaning of the ideas and your opinion.

Recognize in-text definitions

- Look for context clues that signal a definition.
- Keep a list of word definitions by topic.

THINKING CRITICALLY

As you consider your writing assignment, discuss the questions with another student. Get feedback and revise your ideas if necessary.

1. What responsibilities does a company have to the community where its business is located? What about responsibility to the global community?

2. What does it look like when a company is socially and environmentally responsible? Should governments require companies to practice social and environmental business responsibility? Why or why not?

3. What would you do if you found out that a company you support engages in unethical practices? Would it ever be acceptable to continue supporting the company? Why or why not?

THINKING VISUALLY

A. Look at the bar graph showing the average survival rate of small companies in the United States over 10 years. Answer the questions.

1. What do you think are the biggest factors in a company's survival?

2. What does the graph tell you about the survival rate of small companies in the United States?

3. Who might the information be useful for? Who might be interested in this data?

4. What other types of information would be useful in a graph like this?

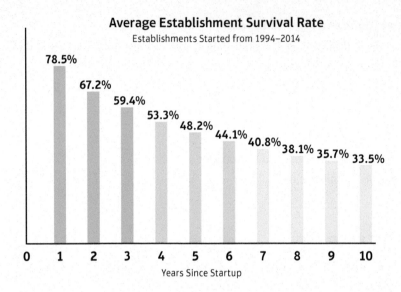

Average Establishment Survival Rate
Establishments Started from 1994–2014

78.5%
67.2%
59.4%
53.3%
48.2%
44.1%
40.8%
38.1%
35.7%
33.5%

0 1 2 3 4 5 6 7 8 9 10

Years Since Startup

B. Go online and research information to create a visual that depicts data about public and/or private companies in a specific industry. Write a few sentences about the bar graph. Discuss the bar graph with a partner.

THINKING ABOUT LANGUAGE

Find a quotation in one of your sources for the assignment that you could use in planning the paper. Write a brief paragraph that introduces the quote, presents the quote using exact wording and correct punctuation, and explains the quote. Use reported speech at least once in the introduction. Cite your source accurately.

WRITE

A. Revisit the writing assignment and your answers to the questions in Before You Write, Part B. Take notes about how you will organize your information.

B. Write a thesis statement for your paper.

....

....

C. Plan your paper. Make sure that you are clear about which material is quoted and which material is paraphrased.

> ### BEYOND THE ASSIGNMENT
> Write a paper of 800–1000 words analyzing the responsibilities stakeholders have in companies that implement business practices that benefit society such as corporate social responsibility (CSR). Develop and organize your ideas. Include three or more reliable sources of information. Include one or more paraphrased ideas from each source and one quotation from a source.

◎ Go to MyEnglishLab to watch Dr. McLennan's concluding video and to complete a self-assessment.

EARTH SCIENCE

Extended Writing

UNIT PROFILE

Climate change has led to significant loss of life on Earth both in the distant past and in the present. In this unit, you will read and write about topics related to climate change and its impact on plant and animal species. Specifically, you will learn about Earth's sensitive regions that are experiencing loss of species. You will also learn about the periods of time, called the five mass extinctions, when many species disappeared, and about the potential causes of these events. Finally, you will examine the role that humankind may be playing in what some scientists believe is Earth's sixth mass extinction.

Plan an extended paper examining two different theories on the possible causes of the Cretaceous Tertiary (K-T) mass extinction. Address interpretation of geologic records and how that affects the theories. Find an article about one of the mass extinction theories and write a 150–200 word summary.

OUTCOMES

• Use organizational patterns
• Select examples
• Summarize
• Use adverbials of cause and effect
• Learn root words

For more about **EARTH SCIENCE**, see ② ③. See also [R] and [OC] **EARTH SCIENCE** ① ② ③.

GETTING STARTED

Go to MyEnglishLab to watch Dr. Osborne's introductory video and to complete a self-assessment.

Discuss these questions with a partner or group.

1. What issues do you think of when you hear the term *climate change*? What concerns you most about climate change?

2. Are there species that are endangered in your country or in a region you are familiar with? How important is it to save these species?

3. Dr. Osborne suggests that some scientists believe we might have entered a new geologic age, the Anthropocene, based on the global footprint of humankind. One of the markers of the Anthropocene is that we are about to experience the sixth mass extinction. What evidence do you think scientists are basing this opinion on? Do you agree? Are you concerned about this? Why or why not?

FUNDAMENTAL SKILL

EXTENDED WRITING

WHY IT'S USEFUL By completing an extended writing assignment, you will be able to explore a topic more deeply and use critical and creative thinking skills to develop your ideas and produce a paper that uses appropriate organizational patterns and examples.

Extended writing means writing a longer paper. The paper's length will vary depending on the purpose, audience, resources available, and the writer's interests and aptitude. Extended writing also means exploring and thinking about a topic more deeply and gaining new knowledge that will be passed on to the reader. It requires reading critically to gather ideas from sources, **summarizing** key ideas, developing and organizing ideas, and integrating relevant evidence to support a thesis.

Fully developing ideas in extended writing usually requires using more than a single approach. **Organizational patterns**—also known as rhetorical modes—are ways to organize and present ideas, and it is common to use a variety of these patterns in extended writing. Argumentation, cause and effect, classification, compare and contrast, description, exemplification, extended definition, narration, and process are typical patterns used to organize, develop, and support main ideas.

Extended writing helps students develop strong reasoning and creative thinking skills. It requires analysis, synthesis, and interpretation to understand the interrelationships of evidence and successfully integrate these into an extended paper. **Selecting examples** and other evidence to support main ideas is essential in an extended assignment.

Extended writing assignments often require collaboration with others through discussion and peer review while brainstorming ideas during the drafting stage and when revising and editing. Extended writing helps students develop problem-solving skills and encourages them to work independently to complete a complex, multitask assignment that effectively conveys ideas in a way that is appropriate to a particular discipline. An extended writing assignment results in a piece that demonstrates the writer's ability to effectively convey ideas in a way appropriate to a particular discipline.

TIP

Extended writing takes place over time, so it requires good time-management skills and use of resources to meet a deadline. Planning is an essential part of successfully completing a paper over an extended period of time. A common problem is misjudging how much time to spend on each aspect of an extended assignment. Creating and following a plan for researching, writing, revising, and editing will help you successfully complete the assignment by the deadline.

Successfully completing an extended writing assignment begins with **understanding the assignment.** In order to meet the requirements, read the assignment carefully and be able to answer the following questions:

What type of paper will it be? Extended writing is common in academic settings in most disciplines, though the types of assignments can vary greatly. The chart shows some types of papers assigned in various fields and disciplines. While there is overlap, some assignments are more common than others in each discipline. Can you think of others?

Discipline	Types of assignments
The Human Experience (Linguistics)	term papers, research papers; reflection journals; expository essays, argument essays; critical response papers; summaries; online discussion posts
Money and Commerce (Business Ethics)	business reports; research papers; case studies; business letters and email; promotional materials
The Science of Nature (Earth Science)	research papers and reports; lab reports; journal articles
Arts and Letters (Medieval Culture)	literary criticism; essays (analysis, argument/persuasion, narrative, description); short stories; poetry; bibliographies; online discussions; essay exams
Structural Science (Materials Engineering)	research papers; journal articles; lab reports; summaries; project reports or write-ups; online discussion posts

The type of paper typically dictates how the paper is formatted and structured. Most extended writing assignments involve several tasks. Some assignments are broken down into specific tasks that have their own instructions and may have their own deadlines. Other assignments may leave managing the various tasks up to the writer.

What is the purpose of the paper? Before beginning an extended assignment, it is essential to know the reason for writing—to learn something new, to explore a topic more deeply, to convince others of a view, or to add to the body of knowledge on a topic. Often, the purpose is clearly stated in the assignment. When it is not, you as the writer must determine what the purpose is and convey that to your reader.

Who is the audience? How you express your ideas and how much information you provide depends on who will read your paper and how much knowledge they have of the topic. For a general audience, you might need to define more terms, give more explanations, and avoid complex statistical data. However, if you are addressing experts in the field (such as your professor), you will not need to explain simple concepts as much, but you might need to provide much more specific and complex data and ideas. While not typically stated in the assignment, it is important to think about audience in any writing task—from an email to your professor to a research paper.

What is the topic? Usually, assignments give a broad topic or area of study. You are then expected to narrow the topic sufficiently to suit the requirements of the assignment, your interests, and the time allowed to complete it.

> For more on brainstorming and narrowing topics, see Linguistics, Part 1.

What will the paper focus on? Just as the topic in an extended assignment might be broad, the issue about the topic may be broad and complex, too, or it may be left entirely up to the writer. Whether the issue is directly stated, given in broad terms, or not stated at all, it will be necessary to narrow the focus to a specific issue about the topic. Writing a **preliminary thesis** can guide you in choosing a specific issue that reflects your interest and opinion, can help you in identifying main points, and can suggest a suitable approach for the paper.

> For more on focus and approach, see Linguistics, Part 1.

> For more on thesis statements, see Linguistics, Part 1.

What organizational patterns will you use?

Next, you need to consider how you will develop and organize your paper. Assignments may include guidelines, instructions, or questions that help you choose an appropriate organizational pattern. The language used to explain the assignment usually suggests the approach and offers guidance on organizational patterns that would best develop and support the main points.

Look for these verbs: *argue, persuade, analyze, explain, describe, compare, contrast, summarize, paraphrase, integrate, synthesize, classify, exemplify, define.*

You can also look for these nouns: *reasons, problems, solutions, causes, effects, results, consequences, examples, definitions, comparisons, processes, narratives, descriptions, arguments, analysis.*

Consider this assignment on climate change from an Earth Science course:

TIP

Rubrics as grading criteria are common tools in academic settings today. When you are given an assignment, read the rubric carefully and refer to it as you write and revise your paper. You may find additional information in the grading criteria or rubric that can help you choose appropriate organizational patterns. For example, if the rubric says, "The paper effectively compares the topic to …," or "The paper addresses the causes of …," you know that you will need to use comparison in the first instance and cause/effect in the second as organizational patterns.

● ● ● ‹ ›

CITY UNIVERSITY　　　　**Your Course Now**

Log on | Register | Student forum

MY assignment – Earth Science 104 Professor Rao

Write an 8–10 page research paper analyzing the impact of the Arctic ice melt on biodiversity. Include the causes of the ice melt and the consequences for biodiversity. Take a position on the impact and state it clearly in a strong thesis statement. Include facts and data from research to support your ideas. Give examples and explain their relevance to the issue.

Cite at least three sources on climate change in your paper, including a journal article and a government publication. Synthesize the information from the sources you use. Summarize and paraphrase carefully and use proper citation form to avoid plagiarizing.

Find a peer review partner among your classmates. Plan to exchange papers at least twice before the due date and use the peer feedback form each time. Submit these forms with your final paper.

Revise your paper using the feedback you received and the grading rubric you used to help you. Proofread and edit your paper before you submit the final draft.

Grading Rubric

4	The paper is comprehensive and focused around a specific and clearly stated thesis and uses a variety of sources, including at least one journal article and one government publication. The paper contains original analysis and synthesizes information. References are cited correctly. Writing is excellent.
3	The thesis or problem is clearly stated. There are some gaps in information and a narrow range of sources, though at least one journal article or one government publication has been used. The paper has some original thinking but is not well focused. References are cited correctly. Writing is good.
2	The focus of the paper is unclear. There is an overdependence on a single source and inadequate detail on important parts of subject. Writing is adequate.
1	The focus of the paper is unclear. There is an overdependence on a single source and inadequate detail with no analysis. Writing is poor.

Glossary

Biodiversity: the variety of plants and animals in a particular place

How would you begin to analyze the assignment? Using a chart is an effective visual way to make sure you fully understand an assignment. It provides a quick and easy-to-read checklist that is a good way to begin any (extended) writing assignment. Look at the completed chart. What information was not directly stated in the assignment? What additional questions might a writer have? If you cannot answer any of the questions, or have concerns about an extended writing assignment, ask the professor to clarify before getting too far into the assignment.

Earth Science Assignment	
Type of paper	*research*
Purpose	*analysis—analyze impact of Arctic ice melt on biodiversity*
Audience	*not stated—professor and classmates?*
Topic	*Arctic ice melt*
Focus or issue	*impact on biodiversity*
Organizational patterns	*primary—cause and effect* *other—extended definition, example, compare and contrast*
Key words to understand assignment	*analyze, explain, synthesize* *causes, consequences* *data, examples*
Additional information	*8–10 pages* *Instructor, peer, and self-feedback required (forms available)* *Grading criteria available* *3 sources required—proper citation form*
Questions I have	

VOCABULARY PREVIEW

Read the vocabulary items. Circle the ones you know. Put a question mark next to the ones you don't know.

publication	pertain to	ambitious	concise	articulated
transparent	substantially	consideration	innovative	earnest

EXERCISE 1

A. Read the two extended writing assignments. How are the assignments similar to and different from each other?

PART 1

Main page ▪ Contents ▪ Featured content ▪ Current events ▪ About us ▪ Community portal ▪ Recent changes ▪ Help

| File | Home | Insert | Page layout | Object | Type | View | Window | Help |

Sociology assignment

The Service-Learning Project reflection journal provides an opportunity to think about your service-learning activities and integrate ideas from the classroom into your real-world experiences.

Write reflections about your experience. You may write informally, but your writing should be clear and easy to understand. Write a single page each week, for a total of about 10 pages. Feel free to write more.

CULTURE NOTE

Service-learning activities, such as volunteering at a senior center, tutoring at a local school, participating in the cleanup of a park, and many other activities to help others in the community, are commonly integrated into academic courses. Also called community engagement, they combine learning and community service goals through a strategy that integrates meaningful community service with reflection to enhance learning, teach civic responsibility, and strengthen communities.

The goal of this assignment is reflection. You will have many experiences in your service-learning time. Reflection involves recounting experiences and observations. However, reflection also implies thoughtful consideration. What did you infer from those experiences and observations? How did they make you (or others) feel? How do they fit with, or depart from, the ideas and expectations you came with or discussed in class? What have you learned from those experiences? How have they changed your thinking?

In each weekly reflection, describe your activities or the people you work with, write a narrative about a particularly memorable interaction with a coworker, or analyze a problem or conflict in the setting. Explain how the interaction reflects the goals of your service-learning organization and analyze its effectiveness in meeting them. Compare your service-learning organization to another.

You may also be creative and choose an innovative approach such as a dialogue or conversation. Or you might focus on a particular topic, such as the people being served by the organization. You can include additional materials (visuals or documents).

Evaluation of reflection journals

I want to see evidence of earnest effort and some thought. I assign grades of "check minus," "check," or "check plus." A "check" indicates that you are doing work of the quality I expect. "Check plus" indicates that you have done an outstanding job. "Check minus" indicates that your reflection journal is substantially below the expected quality standards.

Economics assignment

Submit a final 10–15 page typed report that involves the economic analysis of an issue dealing with international trade. The assignment is in four parts and needs to be turned in on the dates indicated.

Objectives:

1. Apply the analytical skills you learned in your economics course to examine an economic issue in which you have a special interest.
2. Learn how to write a formal report.

The target audience for your report is your peers; i.e., educated college students. Before turning in your assignment, you must have it reviewed by a classmate. Turn in a brief, but specific, assessment on the usefulness of the comments.

You are required to read at least one academic article from an economics publication. The purpose of that is to become familiar with the structure and format of writing in economics. Submit a complete reference of the article. Do not use popular publications such as magazines and newspapers.

All assignments are to be turned in on or before the due dates.

If at any time you have a problem understanding what you are being asked to do or how you should go about completing the assignment successfully, please contact me.

Parts:

1. **Report topic**—Submit a one-page paper explaining the topic you chose, which must pertain to international trade. Start with one sentence clearly describing the question or topic you want to analyze and explaining its importance. Your project should not be too general or too ambitious. Narrow the topic to a specific aspect of a more general question. Well-defined, clear, and concise topics are easier to complete successfully.

2. **Report outline**—Submit a 2–3 page outline that includes:
   - A clear introduction describing the topic and how you will analyze it
   - A summary of your essential ideas; limit yourself to three main ideas/points, presented in three different and concise paragraphs
   - A conclusion that restates the question you are analyzing and includes a summary of the main points and a presentation of the results of the analysis
   - A reference section
   - An appendix for graphs or other data

3. **First Draft**—Submit a 10–15 page paper containing the main ideas/points you will develop. If your first draft is good, you will only have to make minor revisions to your final report and will not need to include additional material. The first draft should contain the elements in the outline, but each main idea/point should be fully developed and articulated. Your paper should be coherent and your logic transparent.

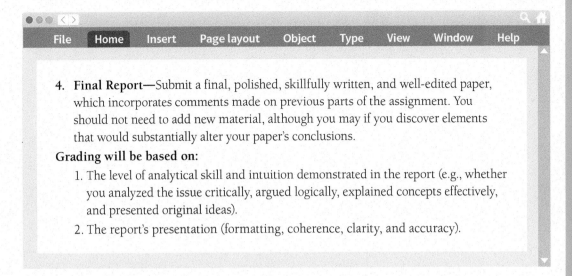

4. **Final Report**—Submit a final, polished, skillfully written, and well-edited paper, which incorporates comments made on previous parts of the assignment. You should not need to add new material, although you may if you discover elements that would substantially alter your paper's conclusions.

Grading will be based on:

1. The level of analytical skill and intuition demonstrated in the report (e.g., whether you analyzed the issue critically, argued logically, explained concepts effectively, and presented original ideas).
2. The report's presentation (formatting, coherence, clarity, and accuracy).

B. Complete the charts for each assignment.

Sociology	
Type of paper	
Purpose	
Audience	
Topic	
Focus or issue	
Organizational patterns	
Key words to understand the assignment	
Additional information	

Economics	
Type of paper	
Purpose	
Audience	
Topic	
Focus or issue	
Organizational patterns	
Key words to understand the assignment	
Additional information	

C. Compare your charts with a partner and discuss the questions.

1. Which assignment provided more comprehensive guidelines? ....

....

2. Which assignment broke the process into specific tasks? How might this help
the writer? ....

....

3. Which assignment used questions to help the writer? Are they helpful to
the writer? ....

....

4. Considering your answers to the first three questions, which assignment is the
easiest to understand? Give specific reasons for your answer. ....

....

....

5. Compare the grading criteria of the two assignments. Which grading criteria seem
easier? Harder? More complete? Easier to understand? More helpful? ....

....

....

6. What question(s) would you need to ask in order to fully understand each
assignment? ....

....

....

7. Pick one assignment. How would you begin the assignment? ....

....

....

D. Find an extended writing assignment in your discipline or a discipline you are interested in. Complete the chart.

Discipline:	
Type of paper	
Purpose	
Audience	
Topic	
Focus or issue	
Organizational patterns	
Key words to understand the assignment	
Additional information	

E. Share the assignment you found and discuss your chart with a partner.

VOCABULARY CHECK

A. Review the vocabulary items in the Vocabulary Preview. Write their definitions and add examples. Use a dictionary if necessary.

B. Complete each sentence with the correct vocabulary item.

ambitious	articulated	concise	consideration	earnest
innovative	pertain to	publication	substantially	transparent

1. The article clearly .... all of the reasons countries need to work together to stop climate change.

2. Next week's class will be a discussion on global government policies as they relate or .... climate change.

3. Professor Brady's article about climate change is the lead story in a new .... called *Everyday Science*.

4. Professor Hobson's lectures are always so .... ; he truly believes that every person plays a role in the future of this planet.

5. The conference featured two days of meetings focusing on .... research about new and creative ways to combat climate change.

6. Her writing is always very .... ; she names her sources and clearly notes which opinions are hers.

(Continued)

7. Setting new policies on climate change his first month as president is .... and will not be easy, but he believes it is critical for the future.

8. After a lot of serious .... and thought, Oscar decided to major in Environmental Science.

9. Dr. Rio's presentations are always informative but .... ; today she spoke for only 15 minutes, but I learned so much.

10. Many scientists believe that using clean energy will .... slow down climate change.

Go to MyEnglishLab to complete vocabulary and skill practices and to join in collaborative activities.

SUPPORTING SKILL 1

USING ORGANIZATIONAL PATTERNS

WHY IT'S USEFUL By using a variety of organizational patterns in extended writing, you will be able to organize your ideas in a way that makes sense and most effectively expresses your intent, making it easier for the reader to understand and remember the information being presented.

Writers use different **organizational patterns**, or **rhetorical modes**, to help them communicate ideas logically and effectively. The patterns you use will depend on the topic and purpose of your writing assignment. You may be asked to examine or analyze a situation, synthesize and interpret ideas, discuss causes and effects, or compare and contrast events for an extended writing assignment, such as an argumentative essay, a report, a research paper, or a case study. Even though you might use one predominant organizational pattern to write your paper, you will most likely include other patterns to help you develop and analyze ideas more logically and clearly. In extended writing, organizational patterns often change from one paragraph to the next, and even within the same paragraph.

Types of Common Organizational Patterns	
Argumentation	Supports writer's opinion and tries to persuade using facts and expert opinion
Cause and effect	Describes the reasons for something and/or the results
Classification	Organizes something into parts, categories, or classes
Comparison and / or contrast	Describes the way in which two or more things are similar and/or different
Description	Provides details, characteristics, features, or functions of something
Exemplification	Uses examples to explain abstract or complex ideas
Extended definition	Defines a concept and provides more details than a standard dictionary
Narration	Tells a story of specific events that happened
Process	Presents a sequence of actions or steps that lead to a result

By combining organizational patterns, you will have greater flexibility in writing a logical and interesting paper. For example, if you are writing an extended paper that analyzes the effects of climate change on biodiversity, you might begin with a paragraph that gives an **extended definition** of *climate change* so the reader can understand how this term differs from *weather* or *climate*. In your paper, you can use **cause and effect** to show reasons for biodiversity loss and the results, and **comparison and contrast** to show similarities and differences of areas affected by climate change. You might also include **exemplification**, or specific examples, to explain, clarify, and develop ideas.

VOCABULARY PREVIEW

Read the vocabulary items. Circle the ones you know. Put a question mark next to the ones you don't know.

precipitation	extreme	severe	consensus	rapid
ecosystem	mass (adj)	extinction	habitat	

Notice the different organizational patterns used in the excerpt from a student paper.

While climate is the typical weather condition of a particular area, climate change is a permanent change in Earth's weather conditions. Climate change refers to changes in precipitation or typical temperature patterns in specific areas or regions, as well as to long-term changes to global temperatures and weather patterns. The Earth has always experienced climate change, but it has usually happened over the course of hundreds, thousands, or even millions of years. Regions undergoing climate change experience extreme weather events such as hurricanes, or severe droughts and heat waves. These weather events are becoming increasingly more common, creating consensus among climatologists that Earth is experiencing the most rapid climate change ever. The Earth's surface temperature has increased 1.8°F (1°C) in the last century, with all but one of the 15 warmest years occurring since the year 2001 (NASA 2016). Most scientists agree that this rise in global temperature is having and will continue to have a significant impact on the environment and biodiversity. Sea levels are rising, glaciers are melting, and plant life cycles and ranges are shifting, impacting complex ecosystems.

Extended definition with Exemplification

The impact of climate change on the biodiversity of species varies in different parts of the world but is having a negative impact on the most sensitive ecosystems. These areas are affected by the smallest temperature changes, meaning that they have already experienced a loss in biodiversity due to both rapid and high rates of warming. For instance, warmer sea surface temperatures in tropical regions have resulted in significant die-off of coral reefs, which are home to 25% of marine species. Scientists estimate that by the year 2050, most coral reefs will no longer exist, contributing to a mass extinction of tropical marine species. Similarly, warming ocean waters have had a significant impact on Arctic regions. A wide number of species in this region are at risk of losing their habitat due to the loss of arctic ice under which algae grows. With the melting of ice, small marine animals that feed off algae have a decreasing food supply, which results in a loss of food supply up the food chain for larger fish, birds, and other mammals.

Cause and Effect with Exemplification

Comparison and Contrast and Exemplification

Cause and Effect

Species must either evolve to survive temperature changes to their habitat or migrate to other areas. However, most species cannot adapt rapidly to these changes, leading scientists to predict that climate change will result in the next mass extinction of many species. In fact, many experts believe that we are now entering the sixth mass extinction on Earth...

Cause and Effect

> **TIP**
>
> When you write an extended definition, you can include different organizational patterns that will give your reader a more comprehensive definition, as demonstrated by the extended definition with exemplification in the text example.

When you write an extended paper, it is important to use **signal words and phrases** that identify organizational patterns or reflect changes in patterns. These words help your reader understand the connections and relationships between ideas.

> **TIP**
>
> To divide extended text, writers often use headers that suggest organizational patterns such as classification. These headers help the reader understand the purpose of a passage.

Organizational Pattern	Signal Words and Phrases
Argumentation	first, second, third; in addition; however; for instance, for these reasons; nevertheless; therefore; still; yet
Cause	because; because of; one cause is; another cause is; one reason is; due to…
Classification	the first category; another category; different varieties of; classified as; is composed of; consists of; first, second, third
Comparison	like; likewise; similarly; in comparison…
Contrast	although; even though; despite; in contrast; whereas; unlike…
Description	described as; appears; has; includes; large, excessive, cold, etc. (adjectives)…
Effect	as a result; results in; consequently; the effect of…
Exemplification	for example; an example of; for instance; specifically; such as…
Extended definition	is; is known as; is defined as; is the state of; refers to…
Narrative	when; before; next; meanwhile; during; first, second, third; later; finally
Process	first; next; meanwhile; at the same time; after; finally

VOCABULARY CHECK

A. Review the vocabulary items in the Vocabulary Preview. Write their definitions and add examples. Use a dictionary if necessary.

B. Choose the sentence that correctly describes the underlined item.

1. There have been many changes in <u>precipitation</u> patterns over the last few years.

   a. It has been raining and snowing more often than ever.
   b. It has been hotter and colder than ever.

2. Scientists are very concerned with <u>extreme</u> weather.

   a. When we have unusual rain, snow, and wind, people have to prepare for the worst.
   b. When the weather does not change, scientists stop studying it.

3. Farmers do their best to prepare for <u>severe</u> storms.

   a. They need a lot of rain to help their crops grow.
   b. They will lose a lot of money if their crops are destroyed by bad weather.

4. There is growing <u>consensus</u> that countries need to work together to combat climate change.

   a. World leaders agree that something needs to be done.
   b. World leaders are asking scientists to do more research before agreeing that something needs to be done.

5. <u>Rapid</u> weather changes have been happening a lot more recently.

   a. In the past, weather also changed quickly.
   b. In the past, weather changed more slowly.

6. Climate change has a major impact on delicate <u>ecosystems</u>.

   a. It can be difficult for animals and plants to adjust to new ways to deal with climate change.
   b. It can be difficult for animals and plants to adjust to new weather patterns in their environment.

7. Major weather changes can cause <u>mass</u> destruction in a short amount of time.

   a. A few people were injured, but most people left town and weren't hurt.
   b. Almost 2,000 people died and thousands more were injured during the hurricane.

8. The <u>extinction</u> of one species often affects other species.

    a. When a species is gone forever, the food chain is broken.

    b. When there are fewer of a species, the food chain is disrupted.

9. Many species find it difficult to adjust to a new <u>habitat</u>.

    a. It is important to keep the natural homes of plants and animals safe.

    b. It it is important to keep the weather comfortable around plants and animals.

EXERCISE 2

A. Read the informal plan for an extended paper analyzing the impact of the Arctic ice melt on biodiversity. The paper will address causes of this ice melt and the consequences for biodiversity. For each section, write which organizational patterns you would expect the writer to include. Share your ideas with the class.

Introduction:

How the Arctic region looked 30 years ago ....

How the Arctic region looks today ....

What global warming is ....

What biodiversity is ....

Thesis: The declining Arctic ice pack is having a significant impact on the biodiversity of the Arctic ecosystem.

Body paragraphs:

The characteristics of the Arctic ice pack (sea ice) and ecosystem

....

Why the sea ice is melting ....

The sea ice melt cycle (how the sea ice melts) ....

Ice algae and the related food web ....

      Ice-dependent seals ....

      Seabirds such as the ivory gull ....

Conclusion:

Restatement of thesis ....

How the Arctic region might look 30 years from now ....

B. Choose three of the ideas listed in Part A and write several sentences about each, using appropriate organizational patterns. Use words and phrases that identify the organizational patterns and show relationships and connections between the ideas. Conduct research if necessary. (See the chart on p. 67 for a list of signal words and phrases.)

C. Share your sentences with a partner. Discuss why you used specific organizational patterns. What additional information could you discuss for each idea? What other organizational patterns could you use?

D. Expand on one of the ideas above and write a paragraph using two or more organizational patterns. Circle the words and phrases that identify the organizational patterns. Conduct additional research on the topic if necessary.

○ Go to MyEnglishLab to complete vocabulary and skill practices and to join in collaborative activities.

SUPPORTING SKILL 2
SELECTING EXAMPLES

WHY IT'S USEFUL   By selecting and incorporating relevant and appropriate examples, you strengthen the support of your ideas, making your writing more precise and avoiding too many generalizations.

Examples are used in academic writing in all disciplines. Regardless of the topic, issue, or predominant organizational pattern being used, exemplification, as a means to fully develop supporting ideas, is very common.

Good examples give readers information that helps them fully understand the point being made. Examples are concrete, specific, and more interesting and memorable than generalizations. They connect ideas to real-life situations, minimizing the chance that an idea is misunderstood or applied incorrectly.

Examples are representative members of a class or category. Examples can also be a specific case or instance of something used to show what is typical of a larger group.

Look at the chart. What other categories, representative members, and specific cases could be added? Introduce examples with expressions such as: *For example, for instance, …is one example of, as an example, this is exemplified by…, such as…, as…, to name/mention a few.*

Class or Category	Representative Member	Specific Case or Instance
Climate change	polar ice melt	**For instance**, in July of 2017, <u>sea ice area in the Arctic</u> was lower than its lowest point during the 1980s.
Severe weather	hurricanes	Hurricanes, **such as** <u>Hurricane Katrina</u>, clearly show the devastation that severe weather can cause.

To support a point effectively, it is essential to **select relevant examples** that fit your topic and the issue you are addressing. Start by looking at your thesis statement. A specific thesis statement often points to appropriate examples. Providing examples that are familiar to the reader helps the reader relate to the points being made. You can engage and persuade the reader by providing new or unfamiliar examples as well.

In selecting examples, consider how many to include and where and how to include them. Examples can be organized by time, if that is relevant to the issue. They can also be organized by importance. Give enough examples to support each point. Listing examples without explaining them is sometimes sufficient to support a point.

> Regions undergoing climate change experience extreme weather events such as hurricanes, severe droughts, or heat waves.

Other times, it is best to provide an extended example that is fully developed. When using examples, especially in extended writing, it is more effective to fully **develop an example** rather than to simply list it. The information in the example must be complete, and it must have factual data that is related to the main point it is supporting and to the broader issue.

A fully developed example gives readers enough description to help them imagine what a situation is like and experience it as if they were there. The example can be a narrative that readers can relate to and easily understand even if they have no personal experience with the situation. A well-written example evokes an emotion in readers that makes it memorable.

> **TIP**
>
> A common problem in academic papers is the use of general statements that are unsupported or weakly supported, resulting in a paper that is overgeneralized and thin. One way to avoid this is by including fully developed examples as part of the support structure for your ideas.

For instance, warmer sea surface temperatures in tropical regions have resulted in significant die-off of coral reefs, which are home to 25% of marine species. Snorkeling on a colorful, vibrant, and healthy coral reef was the highlight of a trip to Australia. Now seeing pictures of completely white coral that has been bleached by warming seas is shocking. Scientists estimate that by the year 2050, most coral reefs will no longer exist, contributing to a mass extinction of tropical marine species. It is unimaginable to think that future generations won't experience the beauty of a living coral reef.

description and narrative

evoking emotion

factual data that is related to the main point of climate change and its impact on diversity

Visuals, including photographs or illustrations, are often used as examples to help readers visualize an idea or concept.

Healthy coral reef

Bleached coral reef

EXERCISE 3

A. Read the extended example for the paper on the effects of Arctic ice melt on biodiversity and answer the questions.

Warming ocean waters have had a significant impact on Arctic regions. A wide number of species in this region are at risk of losing their habitat due to the loss of Arctic ice.

With the melting of Arctic ice, small marine animals that feed off algae have a decreasing food supply, resulting in a domino effect up the food chain for larger fish, birds, and other mammals. One of the most well-known species affected by polar ice melt is the polar bear. We have all seen photographs of pure white polar bear mothers and their fluffy, coal-eyed cubs on a floating sheet of bluish-white ice. Polar bears were put on the Endangered Species list in 2008 due to the loss of their Arctic ice habitat. Loss of habitat means loss of food source. The iconic polar bear photo we associate with polar bears is being replaced by one of a clearly starving, thin polar bear wandering on land.

1. What point is the example supporting? ....

....

2. Is the example relevant? Support your answer with reasons. ....

....

3. What factual data is provided? ....

....

4. What descriptive language is used? ....

....

5. What visual would enhance the example? ....

....

6. Is the example memorable? (How likely are you to remember it?) Justify your response. ....

....

A polar bear and cub crossing an ice floe.

B. Select relevant examples to support these points about climate change. Do research if necessary and list at least three examples to support each point.

Point 1: A species affected in another ecosystem ....

....

....

Point 2: Human impact on rain forests ....

....

....

Point 3: Loss of biodiversity in rain forests ....

....

....

C. Share your list and discuss the relevance of the examples with a partner.

D. Choose one example from Part B. Develop the example in a well-written paragraph.

E. PEER REVIEW. Exchange paragraphs with a partner and complete the peer review form. Respond to the questions to evaluate each other's work. For responses marked No, give feedback in the Notes column to help your partner revise.

	Yes	No	Notes
Is the information in the example complete?	☐	☐	
Does the example present factual data related to the main point?	☐	☐	
Does the example have enough description to help the reader experience it?	☐	☐	
Does the example evoke an emotion in the reader that makes it memorable?	☐	☐	
Does the writer use other organizational patterns to develop the example?	☐	☐	
Is the example fully developed?	☐	☐	

⬆ Go to MyEnglishLab to complete a skill practice.

INTEGRATED SKILLS

SUMMARIZING

WHY IT'S USEFUL By summarizing, you demonstrate how well you understand a text. You can use summary in extended writing to connect ideas and support your points with an expert's view or opinion about a topic.

A **summary** states the main ideas of a text without giving all the details and should be written *in your own words*. Summaries are always shorter than the original text because they include only the most important points. They do not include your opinion or analysis of the text. Depending on the purpose, summaries will vary in length from one sentence to several or more paragraphs.

At the university level, professors and instructors frequently ask students to summarize texts in discussion boards, essays, and final exams to check students' understanding of a topic. In extended writing, students summarize expert opinions and ideas to support the points they are making in a paper.

When you write a summary, you must use your own words so that you do not plagiarize. If your language or sentence structure is too similar to the original text, it will be considered plagiarism. Here are some steps to help you **summarize** without plagiarizing:

- Read the original text several times to make sure you understand it well.

- Annotate the text. Underline or highlight the main ideas and supporting ideas of each paragraph. Write key words and brief paraphrases in the margin.

- Use your margin notes to write a brief outline on a separate sheet of paper.

  For more on annotating research, see Linguistics, Part 1.

- Write your summary from your outline. Do not look at the original text.

- Begin your summary with the author's name, title of the source material, and main idea in your introduction.

- Check your summary with the original text once you are finished to make sure the ideas are accurate.

Notice how the excerpt from the paper *Climate Change and the Impacts on Biodiversity* has been annotated to prepare for writing a summary:

Main Points

1   While climate is the typical weather condition of a particular area, climate change is a permanent change in Earth's weather conditions. Climate change refers to changes in precipitation or typical temperature patterns in specific areas or regions, as well as to long-term changes to global temperatures and weather patterns. The Earth has always experienced climate change, but it has usually happened over the course of hundreds, thousands, or even millions of years. Regions undergoing climate change experience extreme weather events such as hurricanes, or severe droughts and heat waves. These weather events are becoming increasingly more common, creating consensus among climatologists that Earth is experiencing the most rapid climate change ever. The Earth's surface temperature has increased 1.8°F (1°C) in the last century, with all but one of the 15 warmest years occurring since the year 2001 (NASA 2016). Most scientists agree that this rise in global temperature is having and will continue to have a significant impact on the environment and biodiversity. Sea levels are rising, glaciers are melting, and plant life cycles and ranges are shifting, impacting complex ecosystems.

climate change: accelerating faster than any other time

scientific consensus: ↑ increase global temp. will lead to biodiversity loss

2   The impact of climate change on the biodiversity of species varies in different parts of the world but is having a negative impact on the most sensitive ecosystems. These areas are affected by the smallest temperature changes, meaning that they have already experienced a loss in biodiversity due to both rapid and high rates of warming. For instance, warmer sea surface temperatures in tropical regions have resulted in significant die-off of coral reefs, which are home to 25% of marine species. Scientists estimate that by the year 2050, most coral reefs will no longer exist, contributing to a mass extinction of tropical marine species. Similarly, warming ocean waters have had a significant impact on Arctic regions. A wide number of species in this region are at risk of losing their habitat due to the loss of Arctic ice under which algae grows. With the melting of ice, small marine animals that feed off algae have a decreasing food supply, which results in a loss of food supply up the food chain for larger fish, birds, and other mammals.

sensitive ecosystems experiencing loss of species

3 Species must either evolve to survive temperature changes to their habitat or migrate to other areas. However, <u>most species cannot adapt rapidly to these changes, leading scientists to predict that climate change will result in the next mass extinction of many species.</u> In fact, many experts believe that we are now entering the sixth mass extinction on Earth …

scientists – mass extinction

difficult to adapt to rapid changes

Language for summarizing

Summaries typically have a similar structure and use similar language. Include an introductory sentence that identifies the author, source, and main idea of the text. The introductory sentence helps your reader understand the author's point of view and acknowledges that the ideas belong to the author. Here are some ways you could begin a summary of the paper *Climate Change and the Impacts on Biodiversity*. Notice the boldfaced words to show summarizing

In his paper *Climate Change and the Impacts on Biodiversity*, author **Jan Kumler** (2016) **analyzes** the negative effects that climate change is having on the biodiversity of species.

Kumler (2016) **notes** in his article *Climate Change and the Impacts on Biodiversity* that climate change is having a negative effect on the biodiversity of species.

According to Kumler (2016), author of *Climate Change and the Impacts on Biodiversity*, climate change is having a negative effect on the biodiversity of species.

Throughout the summary, use reporting verbs to signal that you are summarizing someone else's ideas. These verbs are frequently used in a summary to refer back to the author of the source. Note how reporting verbs are chosen based on how strongly speakers feel about what they are saying.

Neutral	Tentative	Strong
explain	claim	agree
report	question	argue
say	suggest	believe
state		emphasize

Kumler **states** that climate change is accelerating faster than any other time on Earth.

Kumler **emphasizes** that scientists believe we may be experiencing the beginning of the sixth mass extinction because many species are not able to adapt to rapid climate changes.

Read the summary written in the writer's own words. The beginning of the summary includes a signal phrase that introduces the title of the paper, the name of the author, the year of publication, and the main idea of the original text. In the body of the summary, the writer accurately restates important ideas using key words and phrases as necessary. Notice how the writer uses other reporting verbs to paraphrase the author's ideas and refer back to the source.

> In his paper *Climate Change and the Impacts on Biodiversity*, author Jan Kumler (2016) analyzes the negative effects that climate change is having on the biodiversity of species. Kumler states that climate change is accelerating faster than any other time on Earth. There is scientific consensus that the rapid rise in global temperatures is negatively impacting the environment. Losses in biodiversity are currently visible in the most sensitive ecosystems on Earth—the tropical coral reefs and the Arctic. Kumler emphasizes that scientists believe we may be experiencing the beginning of the sixth mass extinction because many species are not able to adapt to rapid climate changes.

Look at the summarizing guidelines. Does the summary follow the guidelines?

Summarizing Guidelines	
DO	**DON'T**
✓ Restate the author's ideas in your own words.	✗ Don't include your opinion or analysis.
✓ Include only main ideas and supporting ideas.	✗ Don't include details or unessential examples from the original text.
✓ Use keywords from the original text.	✗ Don't include additional information or change the meaning.
✓ Be concise and accurate.	✗ Don't copy sentences or parts of sentences from the original.
✓ Include an in-text citation.	
✓ Keep ideas in the same order.	
✓ Be comprehensive–summarize the entire text.	

VOCABULARY PREVIEW

Read the vocabulary items. Circle the ones you know. Put a question mark next to the ones you don't know.

prime (adj)	as a consequence of	abundant	hypothesis	catastrophic
impact (n)	flourish (v)	roam	speculate	

EXERCISE 4

A. Read the excerpt from an article in *Earth Science Magazine* (June 2016) describing Earth's five mass extinctions.

Mysteries of Earth's Mass Extinctions

By Joaquin Soria

1 Earth's geologic history is full of dramatic twists and turns. The planet has undergone startling changes in its climate, from freezing ice ages to global warming. Species have evolved, dominated Earth, and then disappeared. Scientists know through fossil records that Earth has had five distinct periods in time when most life on the planet disappeared. These events, known as mass extinctions, occurred many millions of years ago.

Ordovician-Silurian Mass Extinction

2 The first mass extinction took place 444 million years ago, in the Ordovician period, long before the time of the dinosaurs. Life on Earth during this time was marine based, and the seas were full with animals such as brachiopods, a type of shellfish. Geologists believe that an ice age was the prime cause of extinction during this period. During the Ordovician period, continental landmass slowly drifted to the southern polar regions of the planet. Geologists have found evidence of glacial deposits in the Sahara Desert, which was located in the South Pole during the Ordovician period, to support this hypothesis. As a consequence of ice formation, sea levels dropped and resulted in the loss, or mass extinction, of 85 percent of all species.

(Continued)

Devonian Mass Extinction

3   Sometimes referred to in the plural as the Devonian mass extinctions, these events occurred in several phases that began approximately 375 million years ago and destroyed between 70 to 80 percent of the world's species. Most life on Earth was still found in the oceans, and fish were particularly abundant. Land-crawling creatures like wingless insects and arachnids like spiders had also evolved. Scientists do not credit a single cause to the Devonian mass extinctions. Some paleobotanists speculate that the development of plants with extensive root systems caused nutrient runoff, which polluted the seas. Scientists have found evidence of such conditions in black shale—a type of rock—deposits dated to the Devonian age. Black shale is a sign of low-oxygen marine conditions.

Permian-Triassic Mass Extinction

4   The single deadliest mass extinction in history took place 250 million years ago. Nicknamed "The Great Dying," the Permian-Triassic extinction resulted in the loss of 90 percent of all living species. Marine species were abundant during the Permian period, as were land animals like synapsids, which were mammal-like reptiles. Some geologists point to a catastrophic event, like an asteroid impact, as a cause for such a huge loss of species. To support the theory, geologists offer evidence: "shocked" quartz crystal, which is defined as quartz with microscopic fractures caused by powerful explosions, such as asteroid impacts. Geologists discovered an enormous crater in Antarctica in 2006 that they say may be the footprint of such an impact. If such an explosion took place, carbon dioxide levels would spike, contributing to a warming of the planet.

5   Other possible causes for extinction during the Permian period include volcanism, possibly caused by an asteroid impact. Paleontologists have evidence of this hypothesis in fossil records of volcanic rock. Volcanic eruptions may have released toxic gases into the atmosphere and, like an asteroid impact, greatly affected the climate of Earth. Yet another possibility for what pushed life to extinction is an unexpected suspect: microbes. Sediments—solid substances that settle at the bottom of liquids—from this period reveal a surprising growth of a microbe known as *Methanosarcina*. This microbe releases methane—a potent greenhouse gas—into the atmosphere. Paleobiologists believe this microbe may have contributed to, or even caused, unstable conditions.

Triassic-Jurassic Mass Extinction

6   Following the Great Dying of the Permian era, life began to flourish once again in an era known as the Triassic period. Marine life populated the seas, and mammals, reptiles, and birds roamed the Earth on a supercontinent called Pangaea. Approximately 200 million years ago, at the end of the Triassic period and the beginning of the Jurassic period, approximately 50 percent of all living species died out. Paleontologists speculate that intense volcanic eruptions at the site of the Central Atlantic magmatic province—an enormous area that once lay in the center of the supercontinent—may have caused the extinction event. The eruptions may have triggered high levels of carbon dioxide in the atmosphere and acid in the oceans.

Cretaceous-Tertiary Mass Extinction

7 The Cretaceous-Tertiary mass extinction, known as the "K-T event," occurred 65 million years ago. The popularity of dinosaurs makes the K-T mass extinction a well-known mystery. Whatever caused the fall of the mighty dinosaurs affected other life on the planet, as well. Approximately 80 percent of all animal species died, and marine and plant life also suffered greatly. Some geologists speculate that an enormous asteroid impact may have been the force behind the extinction. The evidence lies in the Yucatan Peninsula in Mexico, where there is a 112-mile crater that dates back to the extinction period. In addition, geologists claim that iridium, a metal, may be a clue. In layers of rock in multiple locations on the planet, there is a layer of iridium-rich clay that dates back to the extinction of the dinosaurs. Iridium is rare on Earth but common on asteroids. The presence of this layer of iridium, along with shocked quartz dated to the same period, point to an asteroid as the likely cause of the extinction of life during this period.

8 Mystery surrounds these mass extinction periods, and scientists acknowledge that it may not be a single cause, but many causes, that finally extinguished so much of life on Earth.

Eras and points of mass extinction

Phanerozoic (542mya present)

Phanerozoic Era (542 mya to the present)

  Cenozoic Era (65.5 mya to the present)

  Mesozoic Era (251 to 65.5 mya)

    Cretaceous Period (146 to 66 mya)

    Jurassic Period (200 to 146 mya)

    Triassic Period (251 to 200 mya)

  Paleozoic Era (542 to 251 mya)

    Permian Period (299 to 251 mya)

    Carboniferous Period (359 to 299 mya)

    Devonian Period (419 to 359 mya)

    Silurian Period (444 to 416 mya)

    Ordovician Period (488 to 444 mya)

    Cambrian Period (542 to 488 mya)

  Precambrian (4600 to 542 mya)]

mya = million years ago

Glossary

Asteroid: one of the many small, rocky objects that move around the Sun, especially between Mars and Jupiter

Microbe: an extremely small living organism that you can only see if you use a microscope

CULTURE NOTE

American children have long been fascinated by dinosaurs, perhaps because many were huge and powerful, and learning about these animals is part of their childhood experience. The popularity of dinosaurs in American culture is undeniable—they are featured in movies, toys, books, games, museums, and much more.

B. Answer the questions.

1. What is the predominant organizational pattern the writer uses to organize the information? Why did the writer choose this pattern? ....
....

2. Describe the Ordovician-Silurian period. What do geologists believe caused the Ordovician-Silurian extinction? What evidence supports this theory?
....
....
....

3. What type of species lived during the Devonian period? Describe one theory that paleobotanists believe caused the Devonian extinction. ....
....
....
....

4. What is most notable about the Permian-Triassic mass extinction? What different theories have scientists found as possible causes of this extinction?
....
....
....

5. Describe the Triassic-Jurassic period. What do paleontologists believe caused the extinction of 50% of all living species? Why? ....
....
....

6. Why do geologists believe that an asteroid caused the Cretaceous-Tertiary extinction?
....
....
....

C. Read the article again and annotate it by highlighting or underlining the main and supporting ideas of each paragraph. Write key words and brief paraphrases in the margin.

D. When you are finished annotating the article, use your notes to write an informal outline. Use your outline to orally summarize the text to a partner. Clarify any questions you or your partner may have about the text.

E. Use your outline to write a 200–250 word summary about the article. Refer to the steps and guidelines on pages 95–98 for writing a summary.

VOCABULARY CHECK

A. Review the vocabulary items in the Vocabulary Preview. Write their definitions and add examples. Use a dictionary if necessary.

B. Write the correct vocabulary item next to each definition.

abundant	as a consequence of	catastrophic	flourish	hypothesis
impact	prime		roam	speculate

1. .... an idea that is suggested as an explanation for something, but has not yet been proved to be true

2. .... to guess about the possible cause or effects of something, without knowing all the facts or details

3. .... as a result of something

4. .... to grow well and be very healthy

5. .... most important

6. .... existing or being available in large quantities

7. .... causing a lot of destruction, suffering, or death

8. .... to walk or travel, usually for a long time, with no clear purpose or direction

9. .... the force of one object hitting another

◐ Go to MyEnglishLab to complete vocabulary and skill practices and to join in collaborative activities.

LANGUAGE SKILL

USING ADVERBIALS OF CAUSE AND EFFECT

WHY IT'S USEFUL By using adverbials of cause and effect, you will be able to connect ideas in writing in ways that show or clarify relationships. Showing relationships and connecting ideas makes your writing more cohesive and helps your reader understand your points.

◐ Go to MyEnglishLab for the Language Skill presentation and practice.

VOCABULARY STRATEGY
LEARNING ROOT WORDS

WHY IT'S USEFUL   By learning root words, you can break down a new word to understand its meaning. You can also add prefixes and suffixes to root words to build new words and expand your vocabulary.

English words are often a combination of root words, prefixes, and suffixes. A root word is the basic part of a word that contains its main meaning, to which a prefix or suffix can be added. Many root words in English are of Greek or Latin origin. **Learning root words** will make it easier to understand what a new word means. For example, look at the word *biodiversity*:

bio + **diverse** + **ity**

> **bio** is the Greek root word meaning life or living matter
>
> **diverse** means very different from each other
>
> **-ity** is the suffix that means the state of having a particular quality

By breaking down the word *biodiversity*, you can guess the meaning of the word as "the state of having very different forms of life or living matter (animals and plants)."

Notice how similar this definition is compared to the dictionary definition:

> the variety of plants and animals in a particular place

Root words can be at the beginning, in the middle, or at the end of a word. Some root words are words on their own, such as *sphere*, but many must be combined with other roots, prefixes, or suffixes to make a word.

TIP

Make flash cards to learn root words. Write the root word on one side of the card and the definition with examples on the other. Review the root words regularly to build your vocabulary.

Understanding root words is critical in many scientific fields; this is especially true in the medical field, since standardized terms are used to communicate accurately. Although some new words may seem very difficult when you first encounter them, if you break them down into word parts, they will be much easier to understand.

EXERCISE 5

A. Use combinations of root words, prefixes, and suffixes to create six or more words, including words from the unit and other scientific words. Use the charts to help you define the words on your own. Then look up the words in a dictionary and compare your definition to the one you find.

Root Word	Meaning
astro/aster	stars/space
bio	life/living matter
geo	Earth/Earth's surface
micro	extremely small
paleo	ancient
sphere	ball-shaped

Suffix	Meaning
-oid	similar to or shaped like something
-ology	the study of something, especially scientific
-ist	someone who studies a particular subject

....
....
....
....
....
....

B. Write original sentences that demonstrate your understanding of the words from Part A.

....
....
....
....
....

C. Identify three root words of your own that relate to a field you are interested in. Create two words for each root word. Explain what the words mean to a partner.

....
....
....
....

⊗ Go to MyEnglishLab to complete a skill practice.

APPLY YOUR SKILLS

WHY IT'S USEFUL By applying the skills you have learned in this unit, you will be able to write an extended paper that includes appropriate organizational patterns, examples, and summaries of expert views and opinions that support the purpose of the assignment.

ASSIGNMENT

Plan an extended paper examining two different theories on the possible causes of the Cretaceous-Tertiary (K-T) mass extinction. Address interpretation of geologic records and how that affects the theories. Find an article about one of the mass extinction theories and write a 150–200 word summary. Use appropriate organizational patterns and select examples to best illustrate your ideas.

BEFORE YOU WRITE

A. Before you begin your assignment, discuss these questions with one or more students.

1. What did you learn from the article you found on the Cretaceous-Tertiary (K-T) mass extinction?

2. What are some of the different theories about the causes of the K-T mass extinction?

3. What geological evidence supports each theory?

B. As you consider your writing assignment, answer these questions. Then share your ideas with another student.

1. Write your working thesis. ....

....

....

2. List the organizational patterns you will include in your paper. Why did you choose these? ....

....

....

3. Select examples to include in the paper. How do your examples support your thesis and ideas?

4. Discuss your article with a partner. Orally summarize the main ideas. Explain how this article supports the topic of your writing assignment.

C. Review the Unit Skills Summary. As you begin the writing task on page 109, apply the skills you learned in this unit.

UNIT SKILLS SUMMARY

Use organizational patterns
- Choose an organizational pattern to organize and express ideas.
- Use signal words and phrases that identify organizational patterns or reflect changes in patterns.

Select examples
- Select relevant appropriate examples.
- Develop extended examples to support points with facts, description, and narrative.

Summarize
- Follow specific steps to summarize a text accurately and concisely.
- Include an introductory sentence that identifies the author, source, and main idea of the text.
- Use reporting verbs and phrases to signal that you are summarizing someone else's ideas.
- Review the summary guidelines when you are finished writing.

Use adverbials of cause and effect
- Use adverb clauses and phrases to express reasons why something happened.
- Use transitions to connect results to the preceding idea.

Learn root words
- Identify the root, the basic part of a word that contains its meaning.
- Break down words into roots, prefixes, and suffixes to better understand them.

THINKING CRITICALLY

As you consider your writing assignment, discuss the questions with another student. Get feedback and revise your ideas if necessary.

1. How important is biodiversity? Why? Are you concerned that many species are in danger of becoming extinct?

2. What might be some of the challenges that scientists face in trying to solve the mysteries of mass extinctions? Can advances in technology help scientists, or will they create new problems? Given that this is a global issue, are policy differences among countries a hindrance to solving the mystery?

3. With the changes in global warming, do you think we may be at the beginning of a sixth mass extinction? Why or why not?

THINKING VISUALLY

A. Look at the graph that tracks Earth's temperatures for the past 545 million years. Write two or three sentences describing Earth's temperatures during the Cretaceous-Tertiary (K-T) mass extinction. What is the connection between the geologic events during that time and Earth's temperatures? What does this graph tell you about other mass extinctions and Earth's temperatures? How do those temperatures compare to present day?

B. Go online and research another graph that depicts data for one or more geological time periods (e.g., biodiversity, carbon dioxide levels, sea levels, etc.). Write a few sentences about the graph. How could it be used as an example in an extended writing assignment? Discuss the graph with a partner.

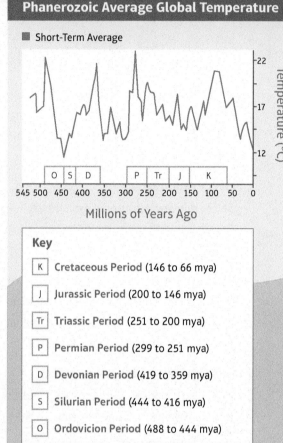

Phanerozoic Average Global Temperature

■ Short-Term Average

Temperature (°C)

Millions of Years Ago

Key

K Cretaceous Period (146 to 66 mya)

J Jurassic Period (200 to 146 mya)

Tr Triassic Period (251 to 200 mya)

P Permian Period (299 to 251 mya)

D Devonian Period (419 to 359 mya)

S Silurian Period (444 to 416 mya)

O Ordovicion Period (488 to 444 mya)

THINKING ABOUT LANGUAGE

Combine the sentences. Use an appropriate adverbial for cause or effect. Punctuate correctly.

1. Scientists are examining evidence. Scientists don't agree on why dinosaurs disappeared during the K-T event.

2. There are two theories. There is no consensus of opinion, with each theory having its proponents.

3. One theory points to volcanism on the Indian continent. It is important to have data on when the eruptions occurred.

4. Scientists have used a new dating technique. They have dates for the eruptions.

5. Scientists estimated lava flows. They were able to determine the size and strength of each major eruption.

6. One scientist who studies the asteroid impact says there is evidence that the impact had little effect on volcanic activity. He doesn't agree with the commonly held theory.

7. There are not many dinosaur fossils in rocks laid down just before the K-T event. It is hard to know whether dinosaurs were thriving right up until the asteroid impact.

8. Phytoplankton show no die off coinciding with volcanism in the lengthy period before the impact. Some micropaleontologists said they are not convinced that volcanism triggered the mass extinctions.

WRITE

A. Revisit the writing assignment and your answers to the questions in Before You Write Part B. Which two theories will you discuss in your extended paper?

....

....

B. What examples will you include in your paper? Will you include a visual? If so, describe it. If not, why not? ....

....

....

....

....

C. Write a summary of the article you found on the K-T mass extinction. Make sure you use your own words and do not plagiarize.

BEYOND THE ASSIGNMENT

Write an extended paper of 1000–1200 words examining two different theories on the possible causes of the Cretaceous-Tertiary (K-T) mass extinction. Address interpretation of geologic records and how that affects the theories. In your paper, include a brief summary about one of the mass extinction theories using an article from a reliable source.

⬆ Go to MyEnglishLab to watch Dr. Osborne's concluding video and to complete a self-assessment.

Present times are connected to the past

MEDIEVAL CULTURE

Rhetorical Context

UNIT PROFILE

Poetry evolved in medieval times (500–1500 CE) from an oral to a written art form to tell stories about religion, war, love, and politics. In this unit, you will read and write about topics related to the poetry of western European medieval culture and its celebration of human emotions, which was new for that time. Specifically, you will learn about the popular troubadour poets who entertained their audiences through poetry and song.

Write an essay of 800–1000 words that analyzes the role of poetry in medieval times and the role of modern music lyrics today. Analyze rhetorical contexts (purpose, audience, and types of poetry and lyrics). Compare the themes and the different aspects of style and tone of medieval poetry with the modern music lyrics. Include selections of medieval poetry and modern music lyrics to support your ideas.

For more about **MEDIEVAL CULTURE**, see ❷ ❸.
See also ⓡ and [OC] **MEDIEVAL CULTURE** ❶ ❷ ❸.

OUTCOMES

- Make stylistic choices
- Revise
- Analyze text for style and tone
- Use cohesive devices for reference and agreement
- Understand connotations

GETTING STARTED

⊙ Go to MyEnglishLab to watch Professor Galvez's introductory video and to complete a self-assessment.

Discuss these questions with a partner or group.

1. What do you know about the Middle Ages? What images come to mind when you think about medieval culture? There have been many televisions shows and movies set in medieval times. Discuss any you are familiar with. Why do people seem fascinated by the Middle Ages?

2. What is poetry? What features distinguish poetry from other types of writing? Are song lyrics poetry? Why does poetry appeal to people? Do you have a favorite poem? Have you written a poem?

3. Professor Galvez suggests that poetry was of a musical nature in the Middle Ages, which made it easy to remember. She says everyone knows a song by heart. Can you think of a song you know by heart or know at least some of the lyrics for? When did you first hear the song? Why do you remember the lyrics?

FUNDAMENTAL SKILL

RHETORICAL CONTEXT

WHY IT'S USEFUL By understanding rhetorical context and becoming aware of types of writing for different situations, you will make appropriate decisions about style and format in your own writing.

Rhetoric is the art of speaking or writing to persuade or influence people. To communicate effectively, we are constantly making rhetorical choices, whether or not we realize it. For example, an email to a professor will be written differently than a text to a friend, just as a research paper is different from a personal essay. Whatever the writing context, or situation, you must think carefully about what you are writing, for whom, and why.

Rhetorical context is a combination of purpose (reason for writing), audience (the reader), and genre (the form or type of text). The three are interrelated and each one influences the others. It is critical to consider each of these in any writing situation.

To understand rhetorical context, begin with **rhetorical purpose**. Rhetorical purpose includes your reason for writing, or personal motivation. In school, the broad answer to why you are writing is to fulfill an assignment, but rhetorical purpose goes beyond that. It requires you to think about what your writing is intended to do and how you want the reader to understand the topic. The text will be different depending on whether the writer's purpose is to describe, to explain, to analyze, to persuade, or to entertain.

What is the rhetorical purpose of a research study on effective polymers? A business case study? An editorial on dying languages? An analysis of the effects of Arctic ice melt? A medieval poem?

Knowing your **audience** is also an important factor. Even when your audience is just your professor, considering a wider audience can help make your writing more effective as you decide how much background information to provide. If your audience is your professor or your classmates, you probably need less background information. For a more general audience, you may need to provide more information to successfully convey your message. You must also determine what style is appropriate and **make stylistic choices** to ensure the language, structure, voice, and tone suit that audience. An academic paper that is written in an informal style may not be taken seriously. In contrast, when writing for a general audience, sounding too formal may put off or annoy your audience.

The final element in rhetorical context is **genre**. Types of writing that have a similar approach, structure, and style are known as genres. Examples of nonfiction genres are essays, case studies, laboratory reports, research studies, and articles ranging from scholarly to news reports and blogs. Fiction or literary genres include novels, short stories, music lyrics, and poetry. Can you think of others?

When you write in a genre, you must follow its conventions, or agreed upon rules or practices, to meet the expectations of the readers. For example, the reader of a novel expects dialogs between characters that develop the story while the reader of an academic article expects citations from other sources that support a thesis.

As you work through multiple drafts and **revise** your work, keeping the rhetorical context, your purpose, the audience, and genre in mind as you write will help you communicate your ideas effectively.

Consider the relationship between rhetorical purpose, audience, and genre in writing in this rhetorical context and analyze the task.

You want to write to thank a professor, an expert on medieval culture, for meeting with you to answer your questions about poets and singers for a research assignment.	Rhetorical purpose – Personal desire to express thanks and to show an appropriate level of politeness
	Audience – a professor you met once
	Genre – letter or email

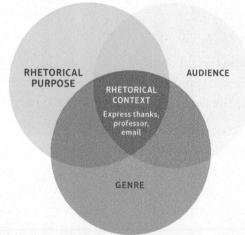

A good way to analyze the rhetorical context of an assignment or writing task is to answer questions about how purpose, audience, and genre are interrelated and influence the text. This checklist can be used with any assignment or writing task.

☐	How does your reason for writing and the rhetorical purpose influence the content?
☐	How does your audience influence the style of writing? Should the tone be formal or informal? Should the sentences be concise, avoiding unnecessary words for greater clarity, or descriptive, creating mental images for the reader? A combination of both?
☐	How does the genre affect the style of writing? Are there conventions or rules that dictate the content and development? The organization? The amount of information you provide or the length of the text that is acceptable?

TIP

Write down the rhetorical purpose, audience, and genre before you begin an assignment and refer to it as you write. This can help you keep the rhetorical context in mind and guide your writing.

VOCABULARY PREVIEW

Read the vocabulary items. Circle the ones you know. Put a question mark next to the ones you don't know.

noblemen/noblewomen	devotional	secular	composed
melodic accompanied	manuscript	concept	immensely

EXERCISE 1

A. Read the assignment for a research paper on medieval culture and an excerpt from the paper. Is the topic sufficiently narrowed? Is the style appropriate?

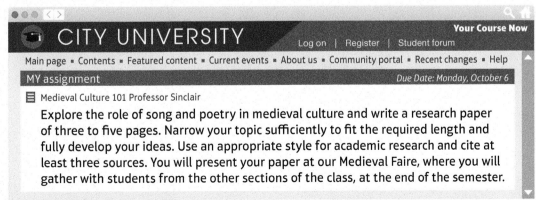

CITY UNIVERSITY

Your Course Now

Log on | Register | Student forum

Main page ▪ Contents ▪ Featured content ▪ Current events ▪ About us ▪ Community portal ▪ Recent changes ▪ Help

MY assignment   Due Date: Monday, October 6

Medieval Culture 101 Professor Sinclair

Explore the role of song and poetry in medieval culture and write a research paper of three to five pages. Narrow your topic sufficiently to fit the required length and fully develop your ideas. Use an appropriate style for academic research and cite at least three sources. You will present your paper at our Medieval Faire, where you will gather with students from the other sections of the class, at the end of the semester.

Medieval Poetry of Troubadours in the Late Medieval Age

1   One of the most famous types of medieval poetry came from the troubadours, who were poets and singers of the 12th and 13th centuries in southern France. Like all traveling singers common in the Middle Ages, troubadours performed for others. The troubadours differed from other singers, however, because they were of higher status in society. Troubadours were noblemen or noblewomen who performed for the upper classes. Troubadour poetry differed significantly from other Middle Age poetry because it was written in the vernacular, or the common language of the people, rather than in Latin and Greek. In addition, while most music of the Middle Ages was for devotional purposes, troubadour poetry was secular, and it was intended only for entertainment.

2   With the focus on entertainment, troubadour songs were sung in front of a crowd, and sometimes two or more troubadours performed as a contest. There were many rules about how the songs should be composed. The poems from the period follow specific forms and themes, and they also use rhyme extensively, which likely made the poems more melodic when performed (Scott, 2014). Some troubadour poets wrote their own music, while others worked with musicians to compose the music that accompanied the poem. In surviving manuscripts of troubadour poetry, the same poems can be found in different texts, implying that some of the songs were well-known and widely performed.

Nobleman with his beloved

3   Troubadour poetry touched on topics like war and politics, but it was most well-known for its focus on love. Troubadours wrote about the emotions of "courtly love," which was a concept that went on to become a theme in other literary works in the Middle Ages and beyond. Courtly love was a type of love between a nobleman and a noblewoman that focused on the ideal of love. The courtly love in troubadour poems was often unrequited, or unfulfilled, love and the poems celebrated the emotions of love, such as the longing, happiness, and doubt. Though the subject of many troubadour songs was often a married woman, the name of the woman was withheld in most poems. Addressing the woman only as "my lady" in the song preserved the secrecy of the person and allowed listeners to speculate about the identity of the love interest of the singer. This appealed to audiences.

4   The celebration of emotion in troubadour poetry was a new concept in the Middle Ages, and troubadour poetry was immensely popular. The poets traveled widely, visiting courts in France and across Europe. Certain forms of troubadour poetry, such as the sestina—a complex verse form invented in the 12th century by the famous troubadour Arnaut Daniel, are still in use today by modern poets. Professor Marisa Galvez in her work on medieval songbooks also compares troubadour poetry to rap songs today, as they are both forms in which performers engage in "insult wars."

CULTURE NOTE

The word *troubadour* comes from the Occitan verb *trobar* which can mean "to explore, to invent, or to disturb." *Trobar* likely derives from the Greek and Arabic words for melody and singing.

Glossary

Longing: a strong feeling of wanting someone or something

B. Answer the questions.

1. How did troubadours differ from other traveling singers in the 12th and 13th centuries? ....

....

2. How did troubadour poetry differ from other medieval poetry? ....

....

3. How was troubadour poetry performed? ....

....

4. What were typical themes of troubadour poetry? ....

....

5. What is courtly love? ....

....

6. What emotions of love did troubadour poetry focus on? ....

....

C. Answer the questions about the rhetorical context of the excerpt in Part A. Use the assignment to help you.

1. What is the rhetorical purpose? Who is the audience? What genre is required?

....

....

2. How does the writer's reason for writing and the rhetorical purpose influence the content? ....

....

....

3. How does the audience influence the style of writing? Should the tone be formal or informal? Should the sentences be descriptive or concise? ....

....

....

4. How does the genre affect the style of writing? Are there conventions or rules that dictate the content and development? The organization? The amount of information you provide or the length of the text that is acceptable?

....

....

D. **Write a brief paragraph analyzing the rhetorical context of the assignment.**

E. **Share your responses to the questions in Part C and your paragraph in Part D with a partner. Are your analyses of the rhetorical context similar? Discuss any differences.**

VOCABULARY CHECK

A. Review the vocabulary items in the Vocabulary Preview. Write their definitions and add examples. Use a dictionary if necessary.

B. Write the correct vocabulary item next to each definition.

accompany	compose	concept	devotional	immensely
manuscript	melodic	noblewoman	secular	

.... 1. to write a piece of music

.... 2. not relating to or controlled by a religious authority; not overtly or specifically religious

.... 3. sounding like music or having a pleasant tune

.... 4. relating to or used in religious services

.... 5. a woman who is a member of the highest social class and has a title such as Duchess

.... 6. very much

.... 7. a book or piece of writing before it is printed

.... 8. an idea of how something is, or how something should be done

.... 9. to be in association with

◐ **Go to MyEnglishLab to complete vocabulary and skill practices and to join in collaborative activities.**

SUPPORTING SKILL 1
MAKING STYLISTIC CHOICES

WHY IT'S USEFUL By making appropriate stylistic choices, you will have the effect you want on your audience, presenting your ideas in a way that fits the rhetorical context and influences how readers perceive and respond to your ideas.

The term **style**, as it applies to writing, focuses on how you express your ideas rather than what the ideas actually mean. Style affects how a reader perceives ideas and must fit the rhetorical context. Writers create style through word choice, sentence structure, and the point of view used (first, second, third person).

Register, or level of formality, required by the context or situation also affects stylistic choice. Register can be achieved through stylistic choices that contribute to the tone and voice of your writing. **Tone** is the attitude you want to convey: personal/impersonal; humorous/serious; objective/subjective; literal/ironic; pleasant/angry; optimistic/pessimistic. **Voice** is your approach, or how you want your reader to see you: As an expert/an amateur? A student/a scholar? An authority/a peer? An optimist/a pessimist? A liberal/a conservative? Can you think of other tones and voices?

Look at these examples and note how each introduces the topic of troubadour poets.

The troubadour poets of the medieval period are some of the most romanticized artists in Western culture today. When I imagine a cast of characters in a wealthy Middle Ages castle, sitting at long tables enjoying a great feast while being entertained, one of the first roles I picture is the troubadour – a colorfully dressed man playing a lute and singing of love. In movies and television shows about medieval times, such a scene, which would take place in a castle's dining hall, is commonplace.

Medieval troubadour playing a lute.

One of the most famous types of medieval poetry came from the troubadours, who were poets and singers of the 12th and 13th centuries in southern France. Like all traveling singers common in the Middle Ages, troubadours performed for others. The troubadours differed from other singers, however, because they were of higher status in society. Troubadours were noblemen or noblewomen who performed for the upper classes.

The first example has an informal style, using a conversational tone and addressing the audience from a first-person point of view. Descriptive language creates an image of the troubadours in the reader's mind, which evokes an emotional response. The reference to movies and TV assumes common knowledge and treats the reader as a peer. In contrast, the second example is more formal and has a more scholarly and impersonal tone. It provides more factual information in clear, concise language, which helps the reader perceive the writer as a neutral observer. Each writer has a different tone and voice, showing how different stylistic choices can affect the reader.

Making stylistic choices is difficult. Answering questions about each element can help you make choices that match the style with the rhetorical context. Here are some elements to consider about style.

Elements that Affect Style

Word Choice	Should I write concisely and provide only necessary information to present my idea or elaborate more fully on ideas and include description and detail?
	What types of words should I choose? academic/descriptive, general/technical, formal/idiomatic, common/unusual?
	Do I want words with positive or negative implied meanings (connotations)? For example, *interest* vs. *obsession*.
Sentence Structure	What types of sentences should I write? simple/complex, active/passive, using many modifiers/few modifiers?
	Should I use parallel structures? Should I use long or short sentences? Vary my sentences?
	Should I use contractions (*I've, she's,* etc.)?
Point of View	What point of view should I use? first person (*I, me, mine, we, us, ours*), second person (*you, yours*), third person (*he, him, his, she, her, it, its, they, them, their*)?

Tone	What attitude do I want to convey? personal/impersonal, humorous/serious, objective/subjective, literal/ironic, pleasant/angry, optimistic/pessimistic?
Voice	How do I want my reader to see me? as an expert/an amateur, a student/a scholar, an authority/a peer, an optimist/a pessimist, a liberal/a conservative? Can you think of other tones and voices?

Academic disciplines use different styles. Style choices are subjective, and there are differences of opinion on what is appropriate, even within a particular field of study, so making choices requires considering many factors. As with all writing, the style should fit the rhetorical context and be consistent throughout the paper. Reading and analyzing journal articles and research papers in your discipline for style conventions and elements that are commonly used will help you notice appropriate style choices. Your professor, a librarian, or your college writing center can help you find model papers to analyze.

Although style may vary from discipline to discipline, there are common elements of style in most academic writing that will help you achieve a tone with the right level of formality and present the content in an academic and authoritative voice. Here are some general stylistic features of academic writing:

- Language is concise to increase clarity.

- Vocabulary is academic and discipline-specific.

- Sentences include:
  - complex noun phrases (e.g., poets and singers *of the 12th and 13th centuries in southern France*)
  - single verbs instead of phrasal verbs (e.g., *consider* instead of *think about*)
  - parallel structure (e.g., create style through word choice, sentence structure, and point of view)
  - few or no contractions (e.g., *it is* instead of *it's*)

- Point of view tends to be in the third person (singular is more common than plural) though first person is used in reflective essays and other genres.

- A more formal register is usually used (e.g., *The troubadours differed from other singers, however, because they were of higher status in society.*).

For more on identifying phrases in academic text, see Linguistics, Part 1.

For more on parallel structure, see Materials Engineering, Part 2.

VOCABULARY PREVIEW

Read the vocabulary items. Circle the ones you know. Put a question mark next to the ones you don't know.

romanticized	socioeconomic	commonplace	appeal
prior to	incredibly	novelty	recognizable

EXERCISE 2

A. Read the blog on troubadours.

Medieval Literature Society

YOUR VIEW   CONNECT

Blog | Comments | Tags

The Appeal of the Troubadours

1   The troubadour poets of the medieval period are some of the most romanticized artists in Western culture today. When I imagine a cast of characters in a wealthy Middle Ages castle, sitting at long tables enjoying a great feast while being entertained, one of the first roles I picture is the troubadour—a colorfully dressed man playing a lute and singing of love. In movies and television shows about medieval times, such a scene, which would take place in a castle's dining hall, is commonplace. There are groups today who perform troubadour-style songs, often using the word troubadour as part of their group's name such as Troubadour Art Ensemble.

2   The appeal of the troubadours today comes from much more than just the modern imagination, however.

3   Troubadour singers existed in the Middle Ages in the 1100s and 1200s and were incredibly popular. Their poetry spread like wildfire all over Europe. In fact, the poetic forms in troubadour poetry and the theme of courtly love remained fashionable well into the Renaissance. The reason for this is because the troubadours did something no one else had done before at court: They appealed to people's emotions in a way that was easy to understand.

4   Prior to the troubadours, most music in the early medieval period was religious. At some point, however, the upper-class audience demanded entertainment that went beyond choral hymns written in Latin and Greek. That's when poetry about love came onto the scene. Most of the individuals who wrote and performed troubadour poems were from the upper class, and, interestingly, some were women. (They're called "trobairitz".) Their audiences, which were primarily from the same socioeconomic group, would gather to listen to the singer, whose songs were written in the vernacular.

5   Such audiences, of course, had no phones or televisions for entertainment. I imagine the troubadours were to a medieval audience what a risqué television show is to us today. After all, singing of forbidden love in front of a court was quite a shocking novelty back then, since the culture of the Middle Ages was so conservative.

6   The songs of the troubadours were wildly popular. In books that have survived from the time period, the same song lyrics can be found in multiple places, which means they were well-known enough to be performed over and over by different troubadours, and they were likely recognizable to audience members, too. It makes me wonder if the audience ever broke into song as they listened to the troubadours perform, as we so often see at concerts today when musicians perform their fans' favorites.

CULTURE NOTE

The Renaissance was a period of European history, from the 15th to the 17th centuries, considered a cultural bridge between the Middle Ages and modern history. *Renaissance*, from French, means "rebirth." During the Renaissance there was a revival of interest in classical art and literature and it was considered as the beginning of modern science.

Glossary

Risqué: **slightly shocking**

B. Answer the questions.

1. How does the writer describe troubadours? ....
   ....

2. What setting did the writer place them in? ....
   ....

3. What reason did the writer give for their appeal to their audiences and their popularity? ....
   ....

4. What was the common type of music before the troubadours and in what languages was it written? ....
   ....

5. What socioeconomic class were troubadours in? Their audiences? ....

....

6. What modern form of entertainment was troubadour poetry compared to?

....

C. Look back at the academic excerpt on troubadours in Exercise 1, Part A and the blog in Exercise 2, Part A. Answer the questions about the stylistic choices each writer made.

1. The blog uses "spread like wildfire" to describe where the troubadour poetry was found.
   Their poetry **spread like wildfire** all over Europe. (Paragraph 3)
   How does the academic piece express this same idea in Paragraph 4?

   ....

2. The academic excerpt uses the adjective *immensely* to describe how popular the troubadour poetry was.
   … and troubadour poetry was **immensely** popular. (Paragraph 4)

   What word does the blog use in Paragraph 3? Which word is more academic? More common? ....

   ....

3. What are some of the differences in word choice and sentence structure in these two sentences? Complete the chart.

   In addition, while most music of the Middle Ages was for devotional purposes, troubadour poetry was secular, and it was intended only for entertainment. (Academic excerpt, Paragraph 1)

   Prior to the troubadours, most music in the early medieval period was religious. At some point, however, the upper-class audience demanded entertainment that went beyond choral hymns written in Latin and Greek. (Blog, Paragraph 4)

	Word Choice	Sentence Structure
Academic excerpt		
Blog		

4. What are some of the differences in word choice and sentence structure in these two sentences?

In surviving manuscripts of troubadour poetry, the same poems can be found in different texts, implying that some of the songs were well-known and widely performed. (Academic excerpt, Paragraph 2)

In books that have survived from the time period, the same song lyrics can be found in multiple places, which means they were well-known, enough to be performed over and over by different troubadours, and they were likely recognizable by audience members, too. (Blog, Paragraph 6)

	Word Choice	Sentence Structure
Academic excerpt		
Blog		

5. Which point of view is used in the academic excerpt? The blog? Find examples in the blog where the point of view makes the piece more informal.

6. In Paragraph 2, the academic excerpt explains the form and themes of troubadour poetry.

The poems from the period follow specific forms and themes, and they also use rhyme extensively, which likely made the poems more melodic when performed.

Does the blog explain the form of the troubadour poetry? The themes? If you answered yes, find the evidence in the text.

7. What are some differences in how each piece is organized? (Hint: Look at where the sentences in questions 4 and 5 are placed in each piece.)

8. Why does the academic excerpt use and define "courtly love" in Paragraph 3? Why does the blog mention women's being troubadours?

D. Compare your answers in Part C with a partner. Discuss the style of the academic excerpt and the blog. What is the tone or approach to the topic in each? What voice is used? How is the audience addressed? Consider the word choice, sentence structure, organization, and register in deciding on the tone and voice of each piece. Include additional examples that weren't used in Part C.

E. Rewrite this paragraph from the blog to make it more academic in tone and voice. Consider the elements in the chart on pages 118–119.

> Such audiences, of course, had no phones or televisions for entertainment. I imagine the troubadours were to a medieval audience what a risqué television show is to us today. After all, singing of forbidden love in front of a court was quite a shocking novelty back then, since the culture of the Middle Ages was so conservative.

....

....

....

....

....

VOCABULARY CHECK

A. Review the vocabulary items in the Vocabulary Preview. Write their definitions and add examples. Use a dictionary if necessary.

B. Complete each sentence with the correct vocabulary item.

appeal	commonplace	incredibly	novelty
prior to	recognizable	romanticize	socioeconomic

1. In the past, most people did not know anyone outside of their own .... group, but today, it is much easier to meet people who are not like you.

2. Learning about medieval history was a .... to me; I really knew very little about it before taking this class.

3. Professor Wallace is .... intelligent. She speaks six languages and has written five books on medieval history.

4. It is easy to .... medieval times, but life was difficult in many ways. Many people were not educated and also died at a young age from illnesses that are now easily cured.

5. Movies and television shows about medieval times .... to a lot of people – even people who don't like to study history!

6. In medieval times, it was .... for education to be overseen by the church. Most children attended religious schools.

7. People like to hear songs that are .... so they can sing along.

8. We learned that .... the Middle Ages, the church did not have as much power as it did later.

⊙ Go to MyEnglishLab to complete vocabulary and skill practices and to join in collaborative activities.

SUPPORTING SKILL 2
REVISING

WHY IT'S USEFUL By revising your paper, you will improve your writing and ensure that your ideas are developed, supported, and organized in the most effective way for your audience.

Revising is a critical step that occurs continually throughout the writing process. Revision requires that you read parts or all of your drafts multiple times and make appropriate changes to achieve the assignment's purpose. When you revise, you must consider how and what you are communicating to your audience. You might delete ideas that are confusing, off-topic, or repetitive; add new information to other parts of the paper; or move ideas and explanations to improve organization. You may also add or change words and phrases or rewrite sentences to improve clarity and readability.

Always give yourself plenty of time to revise. When possible, wait one or two days before revising so you can analyze your writing from your audience's perspective. Revising for content means making sure that your ideas are developed and supported effectively. As you reread your work, confirm that your:

- thesis is clear and connected to the purpose of the assignment.
- thesis accurately reflects the content of your paper.
- main and supporting ideas in body paragraphs support the thesis.
- ideas are fully developed with evidence, examples, and explanations.
- evidence is interpreted correctly.
- conclusion reinforces the thesis or main ideas.

Revising for coherence makes a text easier to read and understand because all of its parts are connected in a clear and reasonable way. A coherent text has unity, meaning that all the sentences in each paragraph relate to and support the topic sentence.

A coherent text is logically organized and includes appropriate organizational patterns to present and develop ideas. Writers also use various cohesive devices to ensure a text has cohesion, or that all the ideas connect within and between sentences. When your writing is coherent, ideas flow smoothly from one idea to the next.

Here are some examples of cohesive devices that can be used to achieve coherence in a text:

For more on organizational patterns, see Earth Science, Part 1.

Cohesive Devices	Using Cohesive Devices
Use transition signals to show logical connections between ideas within paragraphs.	Transition signals introduce: • an additional idea (in addition, also, furthermore) • a contrasting idea (however, instead, in contrast) • a restatement (in fact, indeed, that is) • an example (for instance, for example) • a result (as a result, consequently, accordingly)
Use transitional phrases or sentences to link ideas between paragraphs.	Repeat previous ideas and connect them to new ones: With the focus on entertainment [previous idea], troubadour songs were sung in front of a crowd, and sometimes two or more troubadours performed as a contest [new idea].
Repeat key words and phrases for clarity.	Repeat key nouns or use synonyms when the pronoun could refer to another noun or after using a pronoun several times in a row: The <u>songs</u> of the troubadours were wildly popular. In books that have survived from the time period, the same <u>song</u> lyrics can be found in multiple places, which means <u>they</u> were well-known, enough to be performed over and over by different troubadours, and <u>they</u> were likely recognizable by audience members, too. It makes me wonder if the audience ever broke into <u>song</u> as they listened to the troubadours perform …
Use consistent verb tense.	Use consistent verb tense in one time frame; make it clear when switching to another with a signal word or time phrase: The troubadour poets of the medieval period are some of the most romanticized artists in Western culture <u>today</u> … Troubadour singers existed <u>in the Middle Ages in the 1100s and 1200s</u> and were incredible popular …

TIP

Overusing transitions can be distracting to the reader. Use them selectively to guide the reader from one idea to the next.

TIP

You can find comprehensive lists of transition signals in research writing manuals or grammar reference books.

Read this excerpt from *Medieval Poetry of Troubadours in the Late Medieval Age* before it was revised. While the paragraph includes a topic sentence, main ideas, and support, notice how it lacks coherence:

For more on transitional signals and phrases, see Business Ethics, Part 1.

> Troubadour poetry touched on topics like war and politics. It was most well-known for its focus on love. They wrote about the emotions of "courtly love," which was a concept that went on to become a theme in other literary works in the Middle Ages and beyond. Troubadour poems are often about unrequited, or unfulfilled love, and they celebrate the emotions of love. The subject of many songs was often a married woman. The name of the woman is withheld in most poems. By addressing the woman only as "my lady" in the song, it preserved the secrecy of the person and allowed listeners to speculate about the identity of the love interest of the singer. The celebration of emotion in troubadour poetry was a new concept in the Middle Ages, and troubadour poetry was immensely popular.

The writer revised the paragraph using several techniques to achieve coherence, for better flow of ideas and language. The writer combined sentences, repeated key nouns for better clarity, corrected inconsistent verb tense, and deleted a sentence for better organization and unity. In considering the audience, the writer also included a definition and additional examples to the content. Notice how the paragraph now has better flow.

> Troubadour poetry touched on topics like war and politics, but it was most well-known for its focus on love. Troubadours wrote about the emotions of "courtly love," which was a concept that went on to become a theme in other literary works in the Middle Ages and beyond. Courtly love was a type of love between a nobleman and a noblewoman that focused on the ideal of love. The courtly love in troubadour poems was often about unrequited, or unfulfilled, love and the poems celebrated the emotions of love, such as the longing, happiness, and doubt. Though the subject of many troubadour songs was often a married woman, the name of the woman was withheld in most poems. Addressing the woman only as "my lady" in the song preserved the secrecy of the person and allowed listeners to speculate about the identity of the love interest of the singer. This appealed to audiences. ~~The celebration of emotion in troubadour poetry was a new concept in the Middle Ages, and troubadour poetry was immensely popular.~~

Getting feedback is an important part of revision. You can use different strategies to get feedback as you revise your writing. Peer critiques provide useful feedback on content and organization by identifying areas that are difficult to understand. In some cases, instructors may be willing to review your work, offering a different point of view and revision suggestions. If you are not getting feedback from anyone else, a checklist with specific questions is an excellent tool.

	Revision Checklist
☐	Is the thesis clear?
☐	Is the thesis connected to the purpose of the assignment?
☐	Do the main and supporting ideas in the body paragraphs support the thesis?
☐	Are ideas fully developed with evidence, examples, and explanations?
☐	Is the evidence interpreted correctly?
☐	Does the conclusion reinforce the thesis or main ideas?
☐	Are the ideas presented in a logical order?
☐	Does the paper have unity?
☐	Does the paper use cohesive devices? • transition signals • transitional phrases and sentences • repetition of keywords • consistent verb tense

TIP

Read your paper aloud when revising for coherence. It will be easier to notice places in your paper where ideas are not flowing logically or smoothly when you hear them, rather than just read them.

EXERCISE 3

A. Read the excerpt of the blog post on the troubadour poets of the medieval period from Exercise 2, Part A.

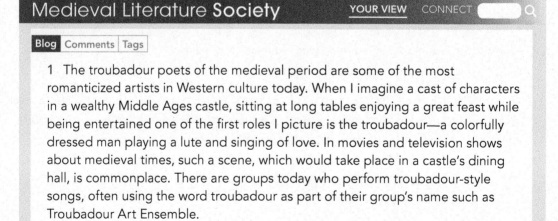

Medieval Literature **Society**   YOUR VIEW   CONNECT

Blog Comments Tags

1 The troubadour poets of the medieval period are some of the most romanticized artists in Western culture today. When I imagine a cast of characters in a wealthy Middle Ages castle, sitting at long tables enjoying a great feast while being entertained one of the first roles I picture is the troubadour—a colorfully dressed man playing a lute and singing of love. In movies and television shows about medieval times, such a scene, which would take place in a castle's dining hall, is commonplace. There are groups today who perform troubadour-style songs, often using the word troubadour as part of their group's name such as Troubadour Art Ensemble.

2 The appeal of the troubadours today comes from much more than just the modern imagination, however.

3 Troubadour singers existed in the Middle Ages in the 1100s and 1200s and were incredible popular. Their poetry spread like wildfire all over Europe. In fact, the poetic forms in troubadour poetry and the theme of courtly love remained fashionable well into the Renaissance. The reason for this is because the troubadours did something no one else had done before at court: they appealed to people's emotions in a way that was easy to understand.

B. Answer the questions.

1. How many times is the key word *troubadour* repeated in this excerpt? ....

....

2. What is the role of Paragraph 2? ....

....

3. What three transitional signals does the writer use in this excerpt? How do they make the writing more coherent? ....

....

4. Classification, comparison, cause and effect, description, exemplification, and extended definition are common organizational patterns in academic papers. Which of these are used in Paragraph 1? Paragraph 3? ....

....

5. Does the writer achieve unity in Paragraph 1? Explain. ....

....

....

....

C. Revise the sentences to improve coherence using the cohesive devices suggested in parentheses.

1. Most music in this early medieval period was religious. This begins to change when nobles demand entertainment that went beyond religious themes. (use consistent verb tense)

2. Students have long been fascinated by the troubadours. They perform troubadour-style songs, and there are many singing groups named after the troubadours. (substitute a noun for a pronoun that is not clear)

3. During medieval times, troubadours sang about forbidden love to large crowds. Students continue this tradition when they sing as troubadours at universities. (add a time phrase)

4. Troubadours were entertainers who traveled from village to village. They often lived in the same area for extended periods of time when they were financially supported by wealthy nobles. (add a transition)

5. In addition to forbidden love, troubadours also sang about brave heroes. One of the most famous poems from medieval times is *Beowulf*. The hero bravely fights and defeats a monster. (add a transitional phrase to refer to *Beowulf*)

6. Troubadours performed poems about honor, bravery, and love. They spread current news. (add a transition)

D. Read the draft conclusion paragraph for the blog article in Exercise 2, Part A. Revise the paragraph for content, coherence, cohesion, and unity. Add more explanation if necessary. Use at least three transitional phrases, consistent verb tense, and repeat keywords for clarity.

So why were the troubadour poems so popular? They were written in the vernacular so that everyone could understand them. They were about love and all its heartbreaking emotions. They were so popular because of the poetry itself. But perhaps the biggest reason is that troubadour poetry is something totally new that makes quite an impression on an audience. Audiences were impressed by the storytelling abilities of the troubadour poets.

E. PEER REVIEW. Exchange paragraphs with a partner. Respond to the questions to evaluate each other's work and to offer suggestions. For responses marked No, give feedback in the Notes column to help your partner revise.

	Yes	No	Notes
Are ideas fully developed?	☐	☐	
Does the conclusion reinforce the thesis or main ideas?	☐	☐	
Are the ideas presented in a logical order?	☐	☐	
Does the paragraph have unity?	☐	☐	
Are transition signals or phrases used effectively?	☐	☐	

	Yes	No	Notes
Are key words repeated?	☐	☐	
Is the verb tense usage consistent?	☐	☐	
Did the writer use other techniques to achieve coherence?	☐	☐	

◐ Go to MyEnglishLab to complete a skill practice.

INTEGRATED SKILLS

ANALYZING TEXT FOR STYLE AND TONE

WHY IT'S USEFUL By analyzing the style and tone of different texts you will not only become a better reader but a better writer as well. As a writer, you will be able to express your own ideas more effectively when you understand how stylistic choices help writers achieve their purpose.

Just as every person has a unique personality, every writer has a unique writing style. In **analyzing a text for style**, you are considering how a writer writes and communicates ideas. As we saw in Supporting Skill 1, a writer's style is determined by the way different elements—such as words, sentence structure, or language features— are used to create meaning. These elements are combined to express **tone**, which is a general feeling or attitude about a topic. The tone of literary texts like novels or poems often conveys emotions and may change throughout the text, depending on context. Literary texts express many tones including humorous, serious, cheerful, or tragic. In non-literary texts, such as academic papers or newspaper articles, tone can be objective, subjective, formal, informal, or persuasive. Active readers look beyond words and consider style and tone to help them understand what the text is conveying, what the writer's purpose is, and how style and tone can influence the reader.

To analyze a text for style and tone, first identify the stylistic elements used and then analyze how those elements work together to create meaning. While there are many different elements that a reader can analyze, they generally fall into three categories: word choice, sentence structure, and language features.

Good writers are careful about the words they use to describe and explain information, or to inform or persuade their audience. Style and tone can be inferred through **word choice.**

- Formal, academic, technical, informal, or even slang vocabulary is used to address a specific audience and achieve a specific purpose.
- Descriptive adjectives are used to create images in a reader's mind that reveal a writer's emotions about a topic. This is common in poetry and storytelling.
- Words with positive or negative connotations are used to imply something that a writer may not want to state directly. They are often used to express opinions or attitudes about a topic.

Clues to a writer's style and tone can be found in a text's **sentence structures.**

- Simple and compound sentences are used when the topic needs to be explained in a simple manner. They are often used in informal writing.

  The songs of the troubadours were wildly popular.

- Complex sentences and embedded phrases are used to explain complicated ideas. They are often used in formal writing and in fiction.

  Troubadours wrote about the emotions of "courtly love," which was a concept that went on to become a theme in other literary works in the Middle Ages and beyond.

- Short sentences can convey a sense of urgency or anger, make an impact, or reinforce a point:

  Their poetry spread like wildfire all over Europe.

- Longer sentences can explain ideas or connections between ideas. They are often used to transition to new ideas.

  The appeal of the troubadours today comes from much more than just the modern imagination, however.

- Rhetorical questions are used to invite the reader into the conversation.

  So why were the troubadour poems so popular?

- Passive voice can communicate a sense of objectivity.

  Troubadour poetry differed significantly from other medieval poetry because it *was written* in the vernacular, or the common language of the people, rather than in Latin and Greek.

Writers use a variety of **language features** to express style and tone.

- The register, or level of formality, contributes to the style and tone of a text.
- Point of view is the perspective used to communicate a message.
  - First person (*I, we*) is used when the writer wants to create a more personal tone in a text. It is common in informal writing and in some academic disciplines.

- Second person (*you*) is used to address the reader directly. It is frequently used in technical writing for giving instructions.
- Third person (*they, she, he, it*) is preferred for most academic and more formal styles. Third person can be used to present objective and subjective arguments.

• Punctuation can reveal information about a writer's tone. For example, in informal writing, exclamation points (!) express strong emotions while ellipses (…) can express hesitation.

Answering questions that focus on style and tone can help you analyze how the writer wants to appear to the reader (voice), the attitude the writer is expressing, and how that attitude might add meaning to a text. Here are some guiding questions to ask to understand different elements of style and tone:

Elements of Style and Tone	Questions
Word choice	• What types of words does the writer use (technical, academic, formal, informal, slang, etc.)? Why does the writer use these words? • When does the writer use descriptive words? For what purpose? • Do any words have positive or negative connotations (implied meanings)? What effect do they have on the reader?
Sentence structure	• What types of sentences does the writer use to explain simple or complex ideas? • Does the writer use active or passive voice? • Does the writer use a variety of sentence structures? • What effect does the sentence structure have on the reader? • Does the writer use long or short sentences for a specific reason? • Does the writer ask questions? For what purpose?
Language features	• What is the register, or level of formality? • What point of view is used in the text? • How would the effect change with a different point of view? • Does the writer use punctuation for a specific purpose?

Think about other stylistic choices that writers make to achieve their purpose or influence their audience. What are the choices and are they effective? Can you think of an example of a writer making a choice that did not work with the material?

VOCABULARY PREVIEW

Read the vocabulary items. Circle the ones you know. Put a question mark next to the ones you don't know.

blast	sorrow	mourn	tender
stem	barren	shrill	tremble

EXERCISE 4

A. Read the medieval poem "Merry It Is While Summer Lasts" (lyrics before 1500) and the poem "Very Early Spring," by Katherine Mansfield (published in 1912) several times. Then read the poems aloud to a partner. Discuss what the poems are about. How do you know? Take notes and share ideas with the whole class.

Poetry   POEMS   POETS   ABOUT   SEARCH

Blog | Comments | Tags

"Merry It Is While Summer Lasts"

Mirie it is while sumer ilast
With fugheles song,
Oc nu necheth windes blast
And weder strong.Ej! Ej!
what this nicht is long,
And ich with wel michel wrong
Soregh and murne and fast.

Merry it is while summer lasts,
With birds in song;
But now there threaten windy blasts
And tempests strong.
Ah! Ah! but the night is long,
And I, being done such wrong,
Sorrow and mourn and fast.

Blog | Comments | Tags

"Very Early Spring" by Katherine Mansfield

The fields are snowbound no longer;
There are little blue lakes and flags of tenderest green.
The snow has been caught up into the sky—
So many white clouds—and the blue of the sky is cold.
Now the sun walks in the forest,
He touches the bows and stems with his golden fingers;
They shiver, and wake from slumber.
Over the barren branches he shakes his yellow curls.
Yet is the forest full of the sound of tears…
A wind dances over the fields.
Shrill and clear the sound of her waking laughter,
Yet the little blue lakes tremble
And the flags of tenderest green bend and quiver.

Glossary

Tempest: a violent storm

Quiver: to shake slightly from cold or
from fear, anger, excitement; to tremble

Slumber: literary word for sleep

B. Answer the questions about style and tone in "Merry It Is While Summer Lasts" and "Very Early Spring." Compare answers with a partner.

Questions about Style and Tone	"Merry It Is While Summer Lasts"	"Very Early Spring"
1. What types of words does the writer use? Do they rhyme? Why does the writer use these words?		
2. When does the writer use descriptive words? For what purpose?		

3. Do any words have positive or negative connotations (implied meanings)? What effect do they have on the reader?		
4. What effect does the sentence structure have on the reader?		
5. Does the writer use long or short sentences for a specific reason?		
6. What point of view is used in the text? How would the effect change with a different point of view?		
7. Does the writer use punctuation for a specific purpose?		
8. What attitude is the writer expressing? How do you know?		

C. Write two or more paragraphs comparing the style and tone of the poems. Use your answers in the chart in Part B to help you. For each poem, what is the poet trying to say? What thoughts or feelings are being expressed? Which lines or words express that meaning? How do the different elements of style help the writer achieve this goal? Quote directly from the poems to support your ideas.

CULTURE NOTE

While many people may think poetry is no longer as popular as it was hundreds of years ago, the reality is that it has evolved into new forms. Poetry is alive in the songs we listen to, and in text messages, online posts, and books that we read. As in the past, poetry brings people together as they search for meaning in life and express their understanding of humanity.

VOCABULARY CHECK

A. Review the vocabulary items in the Vocabulary Preview. Write their definitions and add examples. Use a dictionary if necessary.

B. Choose the sentence that correctly describes the underlined item.

1. The <u>blast</u> of wind was very strong but only a couple of trees were damaged.

   a. People were surprised because earlier, the wind was very warm.

   b. People were surprised because earlier, the wind was very light.

2. Everyone in town felt great <u>sorrow</u> after the storms killed a family of three.

   a. The people were nervous because they were afraid more people could die the next time there is a storm.

   b. The people were sad because they loved the family and there was nothing anyone could do to help.

3. The leaves of the tomato plant are still young and <u>tender</u>.

   a. It's too soon to plant them in the ground outside.

   b. Let's plant them in the ground today.

4. That plant is so unusual. It is very short, but the <u>stems</u> are thick.

   a. There are plenty of stems growing out of the leaves, so I am sure it is healthy.

   b. There are plenty of leaves growing out of the stems, so I am sure it is healthy.

5. He was hoping to plant a garden at his new house, but the ground is <u>barren</u>.

   a. His neighbor never saw any plants or flowers growing there.

   b. His neighbor said there used to be plants and flowers there but the previous owner took them.

6. The whole town <u>mourned</u> the loss of its last movie theater when it closed because it couldn't make enough money to stay open.

   a. People were shocked to learn a popular business was closing.

   b. People were sad as another business failed due to the economy.

(Continued)

7. Cats and dogs sometimes <u>tremble</u> when they are around people they don't know.

   a. The first time I saw my cat shaking, I got nervous because I thought she was sick.

   b. The first time I saw my cat running around, I got nervous because I thought she was sick.

8. My English professor is great, but she has a <u>shrill</u> voice that is sometimes hard to listen to.

   a. It's a shame she sounds so unpleasant because she is an excellent teacher.

   b. It's a shame her voice is so weak and low because she is an excellent teacher.

🔼 Go to MyEnglishLab to complete vocabulary and skill practices and to join in collaborative activities.

LANGUAGE SKILL

USING COHESIVE DEVICES FOR REFERENCE AND AGREEMENT

WHY IT'S USEFUL By using cohesive devices for reference and agreement, you will make clear connections between ideas that help your reader understand how the ideas relate to each other.

🔼 Go to MyEnglishLab for the Language Skill presentation and practice.

VOCABULARY STRATEGY
UNDERSTANDING CONNOTATIONS

WHY IT'S USEFUL By understanding connotations, you will be able to choose words that most effectively express your intended meaning.

When you look up a word in a dictionary, the definition there is the denotation, or literal meaning of that word. However, words can also have an implied, or suggested meaning in addition to the basic dictionary meaning. These additional meanings, known as **connotations**, can be positive, negative, or neutral, and they frequently have an emotional association. For example, why might a poet choose to use the word *home* instead of *house*? Their dictionary definitions are similar: *a building or structure where people live*. What emotional meanings, if any, are attached to these words? For many people, the word *home* is associated with family and feelings of love and belonging, but the word *house* is not. Writers choose words with specific connotations when it is important to create a strong emotional or visual image. Writers will also carefully choose the right words when they want to persuade or influence a reader by appealing to the reader's emotions.

Connotations can reveal social and cultural attitudes as well. People may use words with positive or negative connotations to imply something they do not want to state directly. In the United States, for instance, people describing a coworker as a *politician* may be implying that the coworker attempts to gain power in questionable ways. Because it is socially and culturally acceptable to express distrust and dislike for politicians, this would certainly not be a compliment.

Connotations are well understood by native speakers because they do not have to think about the implied meaning, but connotations can be particularly challenging for nonnative speakers. Be careful when selecting synonyms because while they may have similar dictionary meanings, their connotations could be very different. This is critical to watch in writing when you cannot see a person because you may imply something that was not intended or even communicate the wrong message!

When you learn new vocabulary words, make note of both the denotative and connotative meanings. An English Language Learner's dictionary or thesaurus often provides additional information about a word and includes descriptive adjectives to help you understand its connotation. Any negative or positive associations in a dictionary usually point to how native speakers use that word. Reading all the definitions and example sentences can also help you understand slight nuances in meaning or contexts in which a word may be used.

Look at this dictionary entry for the word *lady*. In medieval culture, a lady was a woman born into a high social class. It was often used as the title of the wife or daughter of a nobleman or the wife of a knight. Today, the word *lady* is used as a title in some royal families, but it can have different connotations depending on the context in which the word is used.

Read the different definitions for *lady*. When is it appropriate to use this word? Would it be acceptable to use this word in an academic paper? Why or why not? What word might be used as a substitute?

---

la·dy /ˈleɪdi/ ••• [S1] [W2] noun (*plural* **ladies**) [countable] ◀))

1 a) a woman of a particular type or age **young/old/elderly, etc., lady**
   b) a word meaning woman, used in order to be polite
   The young lady at reception sent me up here.
   Give your coat to the lady over there.
lady doctor/lawyer, etc. (= a doctor, lawyer, etc., who is a woman. Some women think this use is offensive.)
◀)) see thesaurus at <u>woman</u>

REGISTER

Lady often sounds old-fashioned, especially when it is used about younger women. In everyday English, people usually say woman:
His cousin is a 26-year-old woman who works in a kindergarten.

2 a woman who is polite and behaves very well
3 → **Lady** used as the title of the wife or daughter of a British nobleman or the wife of a knight
4 a woman, especially one with a strong character—used to show approval
   She can be a tough lady to negotiate with.
5 American English *spoken* used when talking directly to a woman you do not know, when you are **angry** with her
   Hey, lady, would you mind getting out of my way?

REGISTER

Addressing a woman directly as **lady** sounds rude. In polite American English, people use **Miss** or **Ma'am** instead: Can I help you, **Miss**?

These definitions show that it is not always appropriate to use the word *lady* because it can have both positive and negative connotations depending on the context. It is often used to politely refer to a woman that we may not know, but if used to directly address that same woman, it would be considered rude. For any academic use outside of referring to a medieval noblewoman, use the word *woman*.

> **TIP**
>
> In your vocabulary journal, write down any positive or negative connotations that a word may have. Include notes about how the word is used or use visual images 😊 ☹ to help you remember the additional meanings.

EXERCISE 5

A. Read the definitions for the noun *blast* and the example sentences for each definition. After each sentence, write down if the word is associated with a positive, neutral, or negative connotation. How do you know? Does the word *blast* have an overall positive, negative, or neutral connotation?

---

blast¹ /blæst/ •○○ noun [countable] ◀))

1 AIR/WIND a sudden strong movement of wind or air
blast of
    A **blast of** cold **air** hit him. ....

2 EXPLOSION an explosion, or the very strong movement of air that it causes
in the blast
    Thirty-six people died **in the blast**. ....

3 LOUD NOISE a sudden very loud noise, especially one made by a whistle or horn
blast on
    The station master **gave** a **blast on** his whistle and
    we were off. ....

4 EMOTION a sudden strong expression of a powerful emotion
blast of
    She was totally unprepared for the **blast of** criticism
    she received. ....

B. Write each word in the column which best describes its connotation. Use a dictionary if necessary.

barren	tender	shrill	tempest	secular	popular
noblewoman	melodic	risqué	forbidden	well-known	conservative

Positive	Neutral	Negative

C. Revise the sentences to be more neutral. Share your sentences with a partner.

1. She was unprepared for the blast of criticism she received. ....
   ....

2. The sports hall was a rather barren building. ....
   ....

3. The remarks that the politician made were slightly risqué. ....
   ....

4. The teacher did not like the shrill demands of the children. ....
   ....

5. I would like to find a lady doctor for my mother. ....
   ....

6. The scientist has become popular for his views on climate change. ....
   ....

🔾 Go to MyEnglishLab to complete a skill practice.

APPLY YOUR SKILLS

WHY IT'S USEFUL By applying the skills you have learned in this unit, you can make stylistic choices, revise a paper, analyze a text for style and tone, improve cohesion, and use a dictionary to understand connotations.

ASSIGNMENT

Write an essay of 800–1000 words that analyzes the role of poetry in medieval times and the role of modern music lyrics today. Analyze rhetorical contexts (purpose, audience, and types of poetry and lyrics). Compare the themes and the different aspects of style and tone of medieval poetry with the modern music lyrics. Include selections of medieval poetry and modern music lyrics to support your ideas.

BEFORE YOU WRITE

A. Before you begin your assignment, discuss these questions with one or more students.

1. Who were the audiences for medieval poetry? Who are the audiences for modern music lyrics? How are they similar? Different?

2. What style(s) and tone(s) were used for medieval poetry? What style(s) and tone(s) are used for modern music lyrics?

3. What are some similarities between medieval poetry and modern music lyrics? Differences?

B. As you consider your writing assignment, complete the tasks. Then share your ideas with another student. Get feedback and revise your ideas if necessary.

1. List two or three things you need to learn about medieval poetry and modern music lyrics. How do you plan to do the research? ....

....

....

2. List some titles of medieval poetry and the modern music lyrics that you will use.

....

....

3. Consider your audience and purpose. What stylistic choices will you make to use the appropriate tone and voice?

....

....

C. Review the Unit Skills Summary. As you begin on the writing task on page 147, apply the skills you learned in this unit.

UNIT SKILLS SUMMARY

Make stylistic choices

- Use word choices, sentence structure, and point of view to contribute to the tone and voice you want to convey.
- Make stylistic choices that match the rhetorical context.
- Match register (level of formality) to the writing situation.

Revise

- Consider how you communicate to your audience.
- Consider how to develop and support ideas more effectively.
- Check for coherence in:
  - logical organization
  - cohesion
  - unity
- Use a checklist to get feedback.

Analyze text for style and tone

- Identify the stylistic elements the writer uses:
  - word choice
  - sentence structure
  - other language features
- Analyze how the elements work together to create meaning.

Use cohesive devices for reference and agreement

- Refer to information using pronouns and determiners to make clear connections and avoid repetition.
- Check that each subject in a sentence agrees with the verb in number and person.

Understand connotations

- Use a dictionary to learn positive and negative associations of words.
- Read all the definitions for a word to understand slight differences in meaning.
- Choose the best word for the writing purpose.

THINKING CRITICALLY

As you consider your writing assignment, discuss the questions with another student. Get feedback and revise your ideas if necessary.

1. What effect can literature, music, or art have on a culture or society? Why?
2. What is the importance of poetry in modern culture? Is it necessary? How will future generations describe the role of poetry in today's society?
3. What role does music play in modern society? What role does music play in your life? Why?

THINKING VISUALLY

A. This graphic shows a comparison of two different styles of medieval poetry in Western Europe. Answer the questions.

1. What were the similarities of these two styles of poetry?
2. What were the differences between these two styles?
3. What might the information be useful for? What are the advantages of this type of visual?

WESTERN EUROPEAN MEDIEVAL POETRY

RELIGIOUS POETRY

- Theme: Religion
- Languages: Latin and Greek
- Genre: Sacred
- Purpose: Devotional for Christians

- Vocal & Instrumental Music
- Written & Oral tradition

TROUBABOUR POETRY

- Theme: Love, War, Politics
- Languages: Vernacular
- Genre: Secular
- Purpose: Entertainment for upper classes

B. Create a similar graphic comparing the role of poetry in medieval times and the role of music lyrics of a particular type of modern music. Consider rhetorical contexts, themes, and different aspects of style and tone that you can use for your writing assignment. Discuss the visual with a partner.

THINKING ABOUT LANGUAGE

Revise the paragraph replacing some of the repeating nouns or phrases with pronouns or determiners for better cohesion. Find and correct four errors in subject-verb agreement.

A canso was a genre of lyrical poetry sung by troubadours. The canso was the most common genre used by early troubadours. There is three parts in a canso. In the first part, the troubadour explains the purpose of the canso. The second part, the main body of the canso, is made of stanzas (groups of lines in a repeated pattern) with the same sequence of verses. The same sequence of verses makes it possible to use the same melody in every stanza. The same melody means the sequence of stanzas can be very simple. The sequence can be very complex, too. Each stanza in a canso has the same internal rhyme pattern, so if the first line rhymes with the third line in the first stanza, the first line rhymes with the third line in every other set of three in the stanza. What varies is the rhyme scheme in different stanzas. Each rhyme scheme are given a different name. The last part of the cansos are called the envoi. The envoi is a shortened stanza that contains only the last part of a body stanza. This lyrical poetry were very popular.

....

....

....

....

....

....

....

....

....

....

WRITE

A. Revisit the writing assignment and your answers to the questions in Before You Write, Part B. Think about medieval poetry and modern song lyrics. How are they similar? How are they different?

B. How do rhetorical contexts help you to better understand the medieval poetry and modern song lyrics? What aspects of tone and style will you address?

....

....

C. Write your essay. Use a checklist to revise your paper. Check your paper for coherence and cohesion. Choose the best words for your purpose.

BEYOND THE ASSIGNMENT

Write a paper of 800–1000 words comparing poetic forms from two different regions of the world. Analyze rhetorical contexts (purpose, audience, and types of poetry). Compare different aspects of style and tone.

◐ Go to MyEnglishLab to watch Professor Galvez's concluding video and to complete a self-assessment.

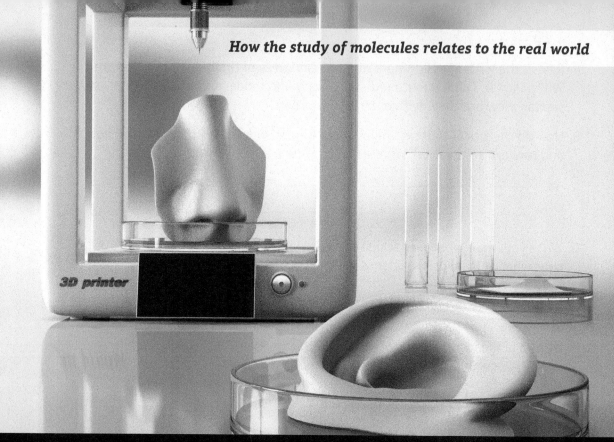

How the study of molecules relates to the real world

3D printer

MATERIALS ENGINEERING

Publishing

UNIT PROFILE

Regenerative medicine is a rapidly evolving interdisciplinary field in which the body uses its own systems along with biological materials to rebuild tissues and organs. In this unit, you will read and write about topics related to materials science including polymers and polymeric scaffolds used in tissue engineering, regenerative medicine, and stem cells.

Write a discussion post of 500–600 words about the use of regenerative treatment for one specific injury or illness. What materials are used? Discuss types of materials and their advantages and disadvantages. What is the role of stem cells? Include at least one cited source. Edit and proofread your post for publication on a course discussion forum.

For more about **MATERIALS ENGINEERING**, see ② ③.

See also ⟨R⟩ and ⟨OC⟩ **MATERIALS ENGINEERING** ① ② ③.

OUTCOMES

- Edit text
- Proofread text
- Analyze text
- Identify and edit run-on sentences and fragments
- Understand prefixes

GETTING STARTED

🔗 Go to MyEnglishLab to watch Professor Heilshorn's introductory video and to complete a self-assessment.

Discuss these questions with a partner or group.

1. What materials are used to make some of the products you use in your everyday life? Be specific. Which materials are natural and which are synthetic (man-made)? Which materials are most important to us today? Why?

2. What types of medical devices are made from man-made materials? How are they used? How have they changed both patients' lives and the practice of medicine?

3. Professor Heilshorn suggests that materials science can aid in getting stem cells inside the body to help regenerate damaged tissue. What damaged tissues might she be talking about? What areas of medicine might use stem cells? How is materials science related to regenerative medicine?

FUNDAMENTAL SKILL

PUBLISHING

WHY IT'S USEFUL By editing and proofreading your writing, you prepare your text for publication and create a polished and professional-looking document that is well-written, correctly formatted, and error free, improving both the quality of your content and the overall look and feel of your work.

When you are ready to submit a text—either as a class assignment or **for publication**—it is critical that your writing be accurate and that you have followed the instructions and guidelines you received.

Your audience may be your instructor, your classmates, readers of online posts, or others in your field. Regardless of who your audience is, you want them to find your work worthy and credible. Your content must be accurate and the writing polished and professional.

> **TIP**
> While many professors say they are primarily interested in the content of writing assignments, most will provide instructions for formatting and will ask that all assignments be error-free when submitted. Some will lower your grade for poor spelling, careless punctuation or formatting, grammar mistakes, and lack of clarity or consistency of expression.

At this stage, you should have revised your content and should be satisfied that you have fully developed and supported your ideas, including incorporating and citing sources appropriately. You should have received feedback from others or used a self-feedback form to help you revise. You are ready to edit only when you are fully satisfied that the content is the way you want it.

For more on revising a paper, see Medieval Culture, Part 1.

Before submitting a final piece of writing, **edit** and **proofread** it carefully to make sure it is well written, formatted appropriately, and free of grammar, vocabulary, spelling, and punctuation errors.

Editing and **proofreading** are closely connected, and many writers treat them as synonyms. However, considering them as separate and sequential tasks will help you achieve the best results in completing a paper.

Look at your document's formatting before you start to edit.

- The appearance of your document should follow the style conventions of the genre and discipline.

- The headings and subheadings should provide a helpful framework for organizing key points.

- The design and layout should present the ideas in a way that enhances clarity and reflects your knowledge of the organizational patterns for the genre and discipline.

- The visuals should be well placed and help the reader understand your ideas.

For more on using visuals, see Earth Science, Part 2.

After formatting, edit the text to improve the quality of your writing, checking for clarity of expression, consistency and conciseness of language use, tone and formality, and overall readability of the text. Correct any grammar, vocabulary, spelling, or punctuation errors you notice, but keep the main focus of your editing on how well you expressed your ideas. It is helpful to think of editing as looking at the big picture.

Consider getting additional feedback or help during the editing process. It is easy to miss things after you have worked on a paper for an extended period of time, and others will often notice problems you have missed. This is especially helpful if you are unsure about language or grammar choices you made to express an idea.

When you are satisfied with your edited paper, it is time to proofread it. Doing a final, careful read of the paper is helpful in finding last minor errors in grammar, vocabulary, spelling, and punctuation, and in ensuring that you have used appropriate academic language and tone. Proofreading is where attention to detail is the key to success.

VOCABULARY PREVIEW

Read the vocabulary items. Circle the ones you know. Put a question mark next to the ones you don't know.

interdisciplinary	tissue	restore	functional	defective
regenerate	synthetic	toxicity	versatility	composition

EXERCISE 1

A. Read the assignment on polymers and the writer's introduction.

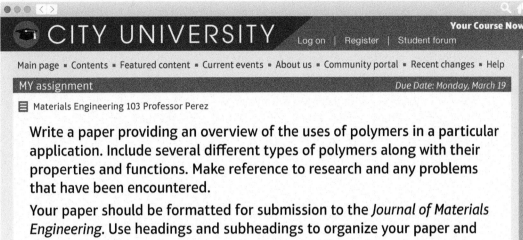

••• ‹ ›

CITY UNIVERSITY   Your Course Now
Log on | Register | Student forum

Main page ▪ Contents ▪ Featured content ▪ Current events ▪ About us ▪ Community portal ▪ Recent changes ▪ Help

MY assignment   *Due Date: Monday, March 19*

Materials Engineering 103 Professor Perez

Write a paper providing an overview of the uses of polymers in a particular application. Include several different types of polymers along with their properties and functions. Make reference to research and any problems that have been encountered.

Your paper should be formatted for submission to the *Journal of Materials Engineering*. Use headings and subheadings to organize your paper and give your paper a title. Cite your sources using the style in the journal. Include appropriate visuals to support your ideas. Proofread your paper for appearance and accuracy of both content and expression.

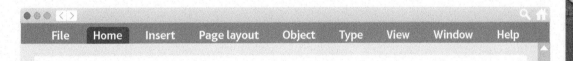

| File | Home | Insert | Page layout | Object | Type | View | Window | Help |

Introduction

1   Regenerative medicine is a rapidly growing interdisciplinary field of medicine that seeks to heal, repair, rebuild, or replace human tissue and organs to restore normal function. Polymers, substances made up of high mass molecules in long chains of repeating units, play a significant role in the context of regenerative medicine. Specifically, these polymers, often referred to as macromolecules due to their large size, are a major area of biomaterial used in tissue engineering. Tissue engineering combines polymer scaffolds, structures on which tissue can be grown, with cells, and also biologically active molecules into functional tissues. Tissue engineering has as its goal restoring or improving the function of living human tissues that are defective, damaged, or have been lost as a result of disease by developing substitutes or by reconstructing tissue. Over the past few decades, extensive research has been done to develop polymeric scaffold materials for these biomedical applications. To regenerate tissue or restore function, a scaffold that can be implanted, placed in the tissue, is necessary as a temporary frame on which to grow living cells.

(Continued)

2   Scaffolds can be biological—derived from human and animal tissue—or synthetic. They can be degradable, able to be broken down, or nondegradable depending on their intended use. They are defined as porous three-dimensional solid biomaterials designed to perform functions such as regeneration of tissue and then to biodegrade with minimal toxicity to the body. Scaffolds need to have certain properties—strength, a reasonable rate of degradation, porosity, solubility, and appropriate shapes and sizes.

3   Polymeric scaffolds are of interest to researchers because they are easily reproducible and can be controlled for the required properties. They are the main types of biomaterials used in tissue engineering and regeneration. They have high porosity with very small pores, they biodegrade, and they have the required mechanical properties. They offer advantages of biocompatibility and versatility of chemistry and biological properties which are important in tissue engineering. Polymeric scaffolds have been used in tissue engineering to grow bone, cartilage, ligament, skin, vascular tissues, neural tissues, skeletal muscle, and other soft tissues.

4   Different types of polymeric scaffolds are being developed based on their structural, chemical, and biological characteristics, each with different properties and functions depending on the composition, structure, and arrangement of their macromolecules.

Glossary

Porous: allowing liquid, air, etc., to pass through

Solubility: the ability of a substance to dissolve in or to mix with and become part of a liquid

Cartilage: strong substance that can bend and stretch that is around the joints in the body in such places as the outer ear and nose

Ligament: a band of strong white tissue that holds bones together at a joint, place where they meet

Vascular: relating to tubes through which liquids flow in the body

Neural: relating to the nerves or nervous system through which the body feels pain, heat, etc.

Skeletal: relating to the skeleton or structure of bones in the body

Muscle: pieces of flesh inside the body that join bones together and make the body move

CULTURE NOTE

Tissue engineering is quickly becoming an alternative or complementary solution to organ transplants, surgery, or mechanical repair for tissue and organ failure. It involves the process of implanting natural or synthetic tissues that are functional or grow into the required functionality. Many tissue types, such as artificial skin and cartilage, are now being engineered along with biomaterials and scaffolds used as delivery systems. As a result of their potential, there is significant interest in this technology.

B. Answer the questions.

1. What does the writer need to do to follow the instructions for formatting the assignment? ....

....

....

2. What is the writer's thesis? ....

....

3. Read the list of subheadings for the paper in the outline. Based on the thesis and the subheadings, what two headings could the writer use to organize the paper?

Introduction

Heading .... **Heading** ....

 Porous Scaffold   Physicochemical Characterization

 Microsphere Scaffold   Surface Properties

 Hydrogel Scaffold   Porosity and Pore Size

 Fibrous Scaffold   Degradation Rates

 Microsphere Scaffold   Mechanical Properties

4. Based on the assignment, what does the writer need to add to finish formatting the paper? ....

....

5. What visuals could the writer include to enhance the paper? Where should they be placed? ....

....

6. What is a good title for this paper? ....

C. Discuss your answers in Part B with a partner.

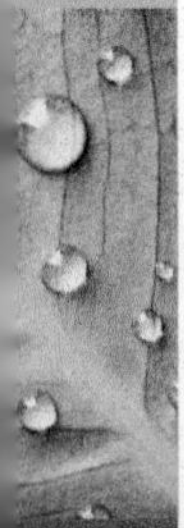

VOCABULARY CHECK

A. Review the vocabulary items in the Vocabulary Preview. Write their definitions and add examples. Use a dictionary if necessary.

B. Complete each sentence with the correct vocabulary item.

composition	defective	functional	interdisciplinary
regenerate	restore	synthetic	tissue
toxicity	versatility		

1. Peter won't be released from the hospital until all of his organs are __________ and working normally again.
2. The __________ of human tissue is complex. The make-up of tissue includes water and proteins.
3. Many professors today teach with an __________ approach. It's useful to learn about how different fields of study affect each other.
4. Janna has been very sick and needs surgery immediately to repair a __________ valve in her heart.
5. Any treatment causing __________, harming a patient, should be changed.
6. Scientists have developed __________ tissues and organs, extending the lives of sick and injured people as artificial replacements are more readily available than natural ones.
7. The fact that some diseased tissue can __________ or grow back is an important step toward curing serious illnesses.
8. Scientists learn a lot about disease preventions and cures by studying human __________ because it combines similar cells with a specific function.
9. It can take a long time to __________ normal functions after a person has been sick or injured.
10. The __________ of some treatments is exciting because the treatments can be used in many medical situations.

Go to MyEnglishLab to complete vocabulary and skill practices and to join in collaborative activities.

SUPPORTING SKILL 1

EDITING TEXT

> **WHY IT'S USEFUL** By editing your writing, you ensure that your text is well written and your ideas clear and understandable. Your ideas are more credible to your reader when your text is readable and presented in a polished and professional-looking document.

Editing is a critical step in the final stage in the writing process after revision. When you are satisfied that you have a strong thesis, fully developed main points, sufficient support from sources, and appropriate visuals, you are ready to edit your work.

Just as in other stages of the writing process, doing more than one pass over your writing will result in a better product. Start with more global issues such as style, tone, flow, conciseness, sentence variety, and word choice, all of which affect the readability of your text. If you find errors in grammar, vocabulary, spelling, and punctuation, correct them, but keep your main focus on expressing your ideas well.

The goal of editing is to achieve:

- Academic style and tone—to ensure the paper has the right level of formality and reflects your purpose.

- Logical flow—to make the text easy to read by connecting ideas within and between paragraphs, using appropriate transitions and adverbials to achieve cohesion.

- Sentence variety—to balance sentence types to avoid monotony and keep the reader's interest.

- Conciseness—to eliminate repeated words, unnecessary modifiers, introductory expressions, or phrases like *It is, There is, At this time,* in order to make the text clearer and more readable.

- Appropriate word choice—to correct words that do not convey the meaning you want, to eliminate or change words that are overused, to correct word form, and to ensure the use of gender-neutral and unbiased language.

Edit separately for:

- Uniform presentation—to be consistent in formatting and concepts.

- Correct use of sources—to check accuracy of facts, figures, spelling of names, and quotations.

For more on style and tone, see Medieval Culture, Part 1.

Most editing is done on a computer using a word-processing program. Printing a hard copy and marking it is another option. Use the method that is best for you. You may find that a combination of both methods helps you edit more effectively. For example, you may find marking a hard copy easier than working on a screen, but you may edit more quickly and easily on a screen. Here are some useful strategies and techniques for editing, whichever method you choose.

- Take your time and read your document carefully.

- Make several passes over the document and edit for one item at a time.

- Mark the document using underlining, highlighting, circling, bracketing, and crossing out, and code errors using abbreviations or symbols, such as *sp* for spelling, *VT* for verb tense, or *agr* for agreement of subject and verb. A good research and writing manual has standard editing symbols that can be helpful in marking your text.

- Use an editing checklist and check off completed items.

- Use tools to find and replace other instances of errors such as wrong or misspelled words.

- Use grammar or spelling checkers carefully as they sometimes miss errors and do not always make corrections in appropriate ways.

- Get feedback from your teacher and peers, or go to a writing center, if one is available.

- Set the document aside if time allows and look at it later with fresh eyes.

- Do a final editing pass keeping your audience in mind. Will a reader find your text easy to understand?

> **TIP**
>
> Most writing teachers give their students a list of symbols they use to edit their students' work. A good research and writing manual typically has common editing symbols, too.

Look at this editing checklist.

Check for errors in:	Notes
Clarity ☐ academic style and tone ☐ logical flow ☐ sentence variety ☐ compound sentences ☐ complex sentences ☐ conciseness	• Clarity is an important consideration when editing. You should strive to present your ideas as clearly as possible so your reader can easily understand them. • Consider changing language that doesn't fit the academic tone and formality the assignment requires. • Combine sentences and add transition words to help the reader see the connection between your ideas. • Shorten lengthy phrases or sentences if they might confuse your reader.

Check for errors in:	Notes
Vocabulary ☐ word choice ☐ discipline-specific and key words ☐ specific words vs. general words ☐ word forms ☐ gender and other biased words	• Vocabulary, especially use of discipline-specific terminology, gives you credibility. • Verify that you have chosen the best words to convey your meaning and that you used the correct word forms. • Correct gender-biased or other biased words or expressions.
Grammar ☐ verb tense and form ☐ subject-verb agreement ☐ connectors, transitions and adverbials ☐ noun phrases ☐ modifiers ☐ pronoun reference ☐ article use	Grammar affects meaning; using correct grammar is essential for your writing to be understood.
Spelling ☐ discipline-specific and key words ☐ proper names	Spelling is noticeable, and while it doesn't affect the reader's ability to understand your text, any errors detract from the quality of your work and may affect how your ideas are perceived.
Punctuation ☐ capitalization ☐ comma use ☐ end punctuation	Punctuation matters, and can affect meaning.

Spelling for all words, as well as punctuation, including capitalization, comma use, and end punctuation, are all checked during the proofreading stage.

TIP

Marking your text while editing and using color-coding or symbols can help you see the errors you frequently make. This can improve your accuracy and overall writing skills.

Read the sentence from the assignment in Exercise 1 and notice the errors the student marked.

Marked text	Corrected sentence
agr art Polymeric scaffold are of interest to the P WC researchers, because they are easily redone and VF WF sp can be control for the requiring propurties. grammar—subject-verb agreement (agr); article use (art), verb form (VF) vocabulary—word choice (WC) and word form (WF) spelling (sp) punctuation—(P) use of commas with subordinating clauses	Polymeric scaffolds are of interest to researchers because they are easily reproducible and can be controlled for the required properties.

EXERCISE 2

A. Read an earlier draft of the writer's first paragraph. Then follow the instructions to make edits.

Regeneritive medicine is a really fast growing interdisciplinary field of medicine that seeks to heal human tissue, repair the tissue, rebuild the tissue, or replace the tissue and organs to get normal function. Polymers are substances. Polymers are made up of high-mass molecules in long chains of repeating units. They play a significant role in context of regenerative medical. Specifically, these polymers, often referred to as macromolecules due to their large size, are a major area of biomaterial that is use in tissue engineering and regeneritive medicine. Tissue engineering has as it's goal restoring or improving the function of tissues that are defect or have been lost as a result of disease by developing substitutes or reconstructing tissue. Over the past few decade, research has been made to develop polymeric scaffold materials for these biomedical applications. To regenerate tissue or restoring function a scaffold that can be implanted, placed in the tissue, is necessary as a temporary frame on which to grow living cells.

Combine two sentences. ....

....

....

....

Rewrite one sentence to make it more concise.

....

Change the formality of one expression to make it sound more academic.

....

Now mark the text for these errors. Note each type of error and show the correction in the chart.

2 word choice errors	
3 grammar mistakes	
2 word form mistakes	
1 spelling mistake (repeated)	
1 punctuation error	

B. Compare your paragraph and notes from Part A with a partner.

C. Write a paragraph about a common polymer. What are the properties of the polymer that make it useful for a specific application? Edit your paragraph using the checklist. Keep your unedited paragraph to note the types of errors you frequently make.

D. Discuss your edited paragraph from Part C with a partner.

🔾 Go to MyEnglishLab to complete a skill practice.

SUPPORTING SKILL 2

PROOFREADING TEXT

WHY IT'S USEFUL By carefully proofreading your text, your final paper will be well written and easy to read, demonstrating the quality of your work and making a positive impression on your reader.

The final step in preparing to publish is to **proofread** your writing carefully to find and correct any errors you may have missed in revising and editing. Proofreading ensures that your final paper is communicating your message in a clear, concise, and polished manner. When your paper is well written, appropriately formatted, and error free, you increase your credibility as a writer and send a message to your reader that you care about the quality of your work.

Use one or more of these techniques to effectively proofread your work:

- Read your work out loud. When you read out loud, you read every word in your paper, making it more likely that you will find errors. Pause between sentences to maintain a slow pace.
- Double-check anything you rewrote in revising or editing.
- Read in reverse. Start at the end of your paper until you reach the beginning of your paper. This helps you focus on each sentence individually.

Give your paper one final check for:

- **Spelling**—Check for commonly confused words such as *their, there* or *affect, effect.*
- **Punctuation and capitalization**—Review each sentence for punctuation. Make sure you have started each sentence with a capital letter, capitalized proper nouns and spelled names consistently, used commas correctly, and ended each sentence with end punctuation.
- **Source information**—Make sure you have cited sources correctly. Double-check statistics or data to make sure the information is accurate. Check formatting and punctuation of titles and direct quotations.
- **Formatting**—Check that you have used the appropriate format for the type of paper. Consider spacing, indentation, font size and style, titles, heads, and margins.
- **Visuals**—Make sure visuals are accurate and close to the text they refer to. Visuals must also be free of grammar, spelling, and punctuation errors, and must look professional.

Recheck your work to make sure you have not missed any of the more substantive changes in the editing process:

- **Grammar**—Review verb tenses, subject-verb agreement, or any other errors you typically make. For example, if you consistently forget to use articles before count nouns, check all your nouns to see if they need an article.
- **Language**—Review your word choices and the conciseness and clarity of your text. Ensure that you are using the appropriate tone and formality for the assignment.

Read a student's paragraph on polymeric scaffolds. Notice the errors the student marked during the proofreading process.

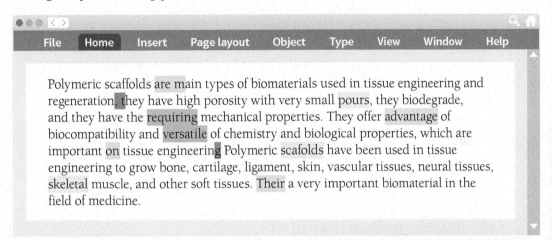

File   Home   Insert   Page layout   Object   Type   View   Window   Help

Polymeric scaffolds are main types of biomaterials used in tissue engineering and regeneration, they have high porosity with very small pours, they biodegrade, and they have the requiring mechanical properties. They offer advantage of biocompatibility and versatile of chemistry and biological properties, which are important on tissue engineering Polymeric scafolds have been used in tissue engineering to grow bone, cartilage, ligament, skin, vascular tissues, neural tissues, skeletal muscle, and other soft tissues. Their a very important biomaterial in the field of medicine.

What are the errors, and how should the student correct them?

> **TIP**
>
> Check a style manual for guidelines on how to format specific texts such as emails, research papers, lab reports, or memos.

EXERCISE 3

A. Read the writing assignment and a student's response. Then read the response slowly and out loud. Proofread to find six errors in spelling, punctuation, capitalization, and formatting. Ignore grammar and language errors that were missed in editing. Use symbols to note your corrections and then correct the errors.

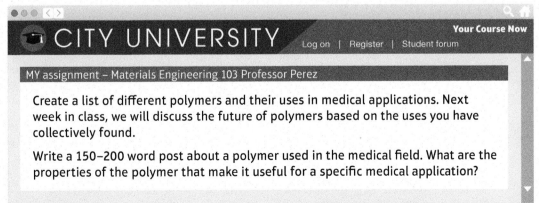

CITY UNIVERSITY   Your Course Now

Log on | Register | Student forum

MY assignment – Materials Engineering 103 Professor Perez

Create a list of different polymers and their uses in medical applications. Next week in class, we will discuss the future of polymers based on the uses you have collectively found.

Write a 150–200 word post about a polymer used in the medical field. What are the properties of the polymer that make it useful for a specific medical application?

Polyether ether ketone, or PEEK, is an organic thermoplastic polymer that has become a preferred material for many orthopedic devices, it is beginning to be used for regenrative medicine for bone tissue.

PEEK is a high-performance plastic with properties that make it an excellent choice for medical implants such as hip and other bone replacements. It is stable at high temperatures, does not weigh much, and is more flexible then the metals that have been traditionally used for these treatments. PEEK is biocompatible, so it will not cause harm to living tissue in the body. it is biostable, which allows it to maintain its chemical properties when it is placed inside the body. One disadvantage of PEEK is that it has a very much higher cost than other polymers used for similar applications.

Recently, researchers have been investigating the use of PEEK in tissue healing and regenerative medicine. When is combined with other materials, it can actually help promote tissue growth. For instance, PEEK has been used to create highly porous scaffolds in which a patients own bone cells can be placed to encourage bone growth.

B. Read the post again, but this time *in reverse*. Proofread to find two errors in sentence structure and two areas to reduce wordiness that were missed during editing. Use symbols to help you proofread and then correct the errors. Compare your answers with a partner's.

C. Discuss the proofreading techniques with a partner. Which technique do you each prefer? Is one technique more effective than the other? Why?

D. Proofread your paragraph from Exercise 2 Part C. Use symbols to mark errors. Have a partner proofread the paragraph and note any additional errors. Note which types of errors you frequently make.

🔿 Go to MyEnglishLab to complete a skill practice.

INTEGRATED SKILLS

ANALYZING TEXT

WHY IT'S USEFUL By analyzing text, you will better understand how important ideas and topics in a text are organized and developed. You can use the same analytical skills when you write to make sure your paper is well written and organized.

Analyzing text helps you read and comprehend more effectively. In higher education classes, you will read a wide range of texts, including journal articles, case studies, lab reports, research studies, and informational readings in textbooks. These texts use a variety of organizational patterns, discipline-specific vocabulary, and grammatical structures. When you analyze a text, you examine the different parts in order to understand the whole. As part of your analysis, you will recognize how information is organized and developed in different fields, allowing you to develop a deeper understanding of the material. Analyzing text also informs your own writing. As a writer, you become better prepared to make appropriate organizational and language choices so you can communicate your ideas clearly and concisely.

Use these guidelines when analyzing text:

Before you read: Survey the text

- Identify the general organization of the text. Notice if the ideas are organized from general-to-specific, or specific-to-general. For some types of text, there are predictable organizational structures. For example, a lab report will have an introduction, a description of the procedure, results, analysis, and a conclusion.

- Read the **title**, the **main headings** (that introduce general topics at the beginning of texts), and the **subheadings** (that introduce more specific topics within a longer piece of writing). In many texts, headings and subheadings are written in a different font or size, or appear in bold. They reveal information about how the text is organized.

- Review the visuals within the text. Visuals are often included to simplify complex processes, provide examples, or present data in an easy-to-understand format.

> **TIP**
>
> For scholarly research articles, always read the abstract (summary) before you begin reading the text. Abstracts contain the most important ideas and conclusions, and often reveal the complexity and formality of a text.

While you read: Analyze development, organizational patterns, and language

- Find the topic and main idea of each paragraph. This will make it easier to follow the writer's discussion. What are the most important ideas in each paragraph? Notice how examples, explanations, facts, expert opinions, or statistics are used to develop and support these ideas.

- Identify organizational patterns within each paragraph. Is the writer describing causes and effects? Or is the writer providing a definition, an example, or a description? Noticing how the writer uses these patterns will help you understand the relationship or connection between ideas.

- Observe how language is used in the text. Are specific grammatical structures and language used for specific types of writing?

> For more on organizational patterns, see Earth Science, Part 1.

- Look for transition words and phrases. These words guide the reader through the text. Closely examining how and where transitions are being used will reveal clues about patterns of organization and relationships among the ideas.

- Skim the text for key words in bold. These are often words the author wants you to remember. They can be discipline-specific vocabulary or key concepts.

- Notice how sources are introduced in the text and in different fields of study.

- Notice the level of formality of the language. Formal texts limit the use of contractions and do not use slang. They also use more complex sentence structures.

TIP

Most course textbooks feature information in text boxes. Text boxes often provide tips, definitions, or real-world application of the subject matter, so be sure to read them. What types of text boxes are used in this book?

After you read: Reflect on your analysis

Write down any information that will help you with your own writing in the future. This could include key vocabulary terms for your field, common organizational patterns, specific transition words or signal phrases that you would like to use, or specific grammatical structures. Taking notes and annotating will make you more likely to incorporate this information in your writing.

For more on annotating a text, see Linguistics, Part 1.

VOCABULARY PREVIEW

Read the vocabulary items. Circle the ones you know. Put a question mark next to the ones you don't know.

compound (n)	composed of	element	relatively	extract (v)
reject (v)	application	implant (v)	interaction	

EXERCISE 4

A. Read the excerpt from a materials engineering textbook. Before you read the content, read the titles, headings, and subheadings. Also, notice the general organizational structure and pay attention to the visuals.

Unit 10 Polymer Structures

10.1 INTRODUCTION TO POLYMERS

1 The study of polymers is important in materials engineering because polymers are used in a wide variety of common objects. From cars to milk cartons to clothing, you can find polymeric material everywhere. Polymers are both synthetic and natural, and can be combined with metals and ceramics to produce composite, or combined, materials that are superior for their light weight and their strength. Chemists discovered the science behind synthetic polymers in the early 20th century, but people have been using natural polymers, such as cotton and silk, for thousands of years. Today, chemically modified polymers make materials that allow us to accomplish great feats, including exploring space, developing digital technology, and improving people's lives with biomedical treatments.

10.1.1 The structure of polymers

2 Polymers are large chemical compounds that have repeating structural units. These repeating units are linked together like rings on a chain, and they form the main chain, or backbone, of the polymer. Because of their size, polymers are termed macromolecules, or large molecules. Most polymers are formed from compounds of carbon and hydrogen (hydrocarbons). One common hydrocarbon polymer is polypropylene, which is found in common plastic packaging products. Polymers can be composed of other elements as well, including nitrogen, oxygen, and silicone. Nylons, for example, have nitrogen atoms in their backbone, and polyesters have oxygen atoms in their backbone.

(Continued)

SPECIAL TOPIC:
How are polymers used in regenerative medicine?

Regenerative medicine

3 The human body's ability to regenerate tissue and heal itself is limited. Salamanders can grow new limbs and organs— humans are not so lucky. While some areas of the body, such as the skin and the liver, are able to grow new tissue, the regenerative capacity of the human body is very limited. Regenerative medicine is a relatively new field of advanced science that aims to change this. Treatments in regenerative medicine use tissue-engineering polymers, and stem cell research to help rejuvenate cells and heal parts of the body. While the origins of regenerative medicine began decades ago with organ and bone marrow transplants, the cutting-edge aspect of regenerative medicine today lies in our newfound understanding of stem cells combined with advances in polymer science.

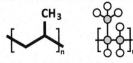

Figure 1: Polypropylene's chemical structure

Stem cells

4 Stem cells, also known as master cells, are cells that can become other cell types in the body, such as bone, blood, or skin cells. Stem cells also replenish the body by self-dividing and producing more cells, which makes them valuable in regenerative medicine. Stem cells can be extracted from both human embryos and from adult tissue. Of the two types, embryonic stem cells are pluripotent, meaning they can be differentiated into any cell type. Compared to adult stem cells, embryonic stem cells have a higher success rate at being grown in a laboratory. Adult stem cells, however, have the benefit of being less likely to be rejected by a patient's body when they are from the patient's own tissue. Scientists are hopeful that someday, stem cells will provide targeted, approved regenerative therapy for many different illnesses, including organ damage, vascular system damage, and brain tissue damage.

Materials used in regenerative medicine

5 In regenerative medicine, stem cells are combined with advanced materials known as biomaterials. Often, these biomaterials are made with polymers. The polymer-based biomaterials support the transplanted cells by acting as a three-dimensional frame, or scaffold, for the cells until the cells stabilize within the body. Biomaterial scaffolds are seeded with stem cells and cell stimulators. The scaffolds are then transplanted into a patient at the site of damage.

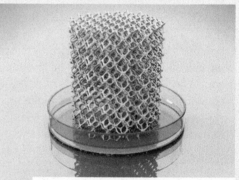

Figure 2: Polymer biomaterial scaffold

In lab studies, polymer-based biomaterials have shown promise in promoting stem-cell survival. In many ways, the synthetic biomaterials mimic the body's tissue. Some polymer-based biomaterials have distinct qualities that make them superior materials to use in tissue engineering, including being biocompatible, highly porous, and flexible. One popular polymeric material can be engineered to biodegrade, or break down inside the body, at specific times.

6 One of the most important applications of stem cells and biomaterials in regenerative medicine is in tissue and organ regeneration. Scientists are working toward stem cells being used to heal tissue in a damaged organ if directed to produce that particular type of tissue. Currently, when a patient experiences organ failure, there is little to do but wait and hope for a donor. In addition, even when a patient receives an organ transplant, there is the risk of the body's rejecting the new organ. Stem cell treatments may be a welcome alternative. Such treatments could use stem cells seeded into a polymer-based biomaterial scaffold that is constructed outside the body. Once implanted, it could restore

organ function, and in doing so, benefit millions of individuals because there would be no need to wait for an organ donor and less risk of organ rejection. The interaction of stem cells and polymer-based biomaterials is likely to continue in the coming years as the field of tissue engineering and regenerative medicine continues to advance.

Glossary

Nitrogen: a gas that is an element, has no color or smell, and is the main part of the Earth's air

Hydrogen: a gas that is an element and that is lighter than air, and that forms water when it combines with oxygen

Carbon: a simple substance that is an element and that exists in a pure form as diamonds, graphite, etc. or in an impure form as coal, gasoline, etc.

Silicon: an element that is often used for making glass, bricks, and parts for computers

Nylon: a strong artificial material that is used for making plastic, clothes, rope etc.

Polyester: a chemical compound used to make cloth and plastics

CULTURE NOTE

In the US, many stem cell treatments are still in the research stage or clinical trials. The US Food and Drug Administration's first—and only—approved stem cell treatment is called Hemacord, and is used in patients with blood forming disorders. The treatment uses the stem cells that create blood cells in the body.

B. Answer the questions.

1. Why is the study of polymers important in materials engineering?

....

....

2. What are polymers? What do they look like? ....

....

....

3. What is regenerative medicine? What materials are commonly used in regenerative treatments? ....

....

4. What are stem cells? Why are they so important in regenerative medicine?

....

....

5. What is a biomaterial scaffold used for in regenerative medicine?

....

....

6. What qualities do biomaterials have that make them so desirable for tissue engineering? ....

....

7. How might stem cells and polymers be used in the future for organ regeneration?

....

....

C. Read the materials engineering textbook sections on polymers again. Analyze the text for organizational structure, development, organizational patterns, and language. Complete the chart as you analyze the text.

	Analysis	Evidence/Examples from Text
Organizational structure and development		
Organizational patterns		
Language		

D. Share your analysis with a partner. Does your partner agree with your analysis?

E. Use your answers in Part C to write a short analysis about idea development, organization, or language of the text. How will you apply what you have learned to your own writing?

VOCABULARY CHECK

A. Review the vocabulary items in the Vocabulary Preview. Write their definitions and add examples. Use a dictionary if necessary.

B. Write the correct vocabulary item next to each definition.

application	compound	composed of	element	extract
implant	interaction	reject	relatively	

1. .... to a particular degree, especially compared with something similar

2. .... a process by which two or more things affect each other

3. .... a simple chemical substance, such as carbon or oxygen, that consists of only one atom

4. .... to put something into someone's body by performing a medical operation

5. .... to show an immune response to (a transplanted organ or tissue) so that it fails to survive

6. .... the practical purpose for which a machine, idea, etc. can be used, or a situation when this is used

7. .... to remove an object from somewhere, especially with difficulty

8. .... a substance containing atoms from two or more elements

9. .... formed from a group of substances or parts

⬆ Go to MyEnglishLab to complete vocabulary and skill practices and to join in collaborative activities.

LANGUAGE SKILL

IDENTIFYING AND EDITING RUN-ON SENTENCES AND FRAGMENTS

WHY IT'S USEFUL By understanding independent and dependent clauses, you will be able to identify run-on sentences and fragments and edit your writing to correct them.

⬆ Go to MyEnglishLab for the Language Skill presentation and practice.

VOCABULARY STRATEGY

UNDERSTANDING PREFIXES

WHY IT'S USEFUL By understanding prefixes, you can analyze words to decode their meaning as you read. You can apply your knowledge of a prefix to understand other words that use the same prefix.

A **prefix** is added to the beginning of a word and changes its core meaning, making it a new word. For example, the prefix *re-* can be added to the root word *read* to make the word *reread*. The prefix *re-* means "again," so if you reread a text, you read it again.

A good way to expand your vocabulary is by **understanding prefixes**. If you understand the meaning of a prefix, you can break down a word into smaller parts, which will help you decipher the meanings of unfamiliar words. For example, you might encounter the word *regenerate* in an academic text. If you know that *re-* means "again," you are more likely to better understand how the word is being used in a given context. If you are still unsure, it will be easier for you to remember the word once you look it up in a dictionary because you already know what part of the word means.

Understanding prefixes will also help you build your vocabulary because you will be able to add prefixes to many words you already know.

> **TIP**
>
> Understanding prefixes is a valuable test-taking strategy for university admission exams like the SAT or GRE. If you understand a prefix, you will be better prepared to guess the meaning of an unfamiliar word in context.

> **TIP**
>
> Many words in the medical and scientific fields contain prefixes. Understanding prefixes in these disciplines will make it easier to learn new words.

English language learners' dictionaries usually list common prefixes as separate entries, followed by a definition, examples, and sometimes synonyms. Look at the dictionary entry for the prefix *re-* and the chart showing words using it.

---

re- /riː/ *prefix*

1 again

◀)) *They're rebroadcasting the play.*

2 again in a better way

◀)) *She asked me to redo the essay.*

3 back to a former state

◀)) *After years of separation they were finally reunited.*

Words you already know	New words with prefix re-	Definition
build (v)	rebuild	to build something again after it has been damaged or destroyed
place (v)	replace	to get something new to put in the place of something that is broken, too old, etc.
store (v)	restore	to repair something so that it is in its original condition

Regenerative medicine is a rapidly growing interdisciplinary field of medicine that seeks to heal, **rebuild**, or **replace** human tissue and organs to **restore** normal function.

EXERCISE 5

A. Use a dictionary to complete the definition of each prefix.

Prefix	Definition	Words from unit
poly-		polymer
		polyester
im-		implant
de-		degrade
		defective
anti-		antibacterial
bio-		biomedical
		biostable
		biocompatible
ex-		extract
macro-		macromolecule
hydro-		hydrogen
		hydrocarbon

B. There are many other words that use these prefixes. List at least two additional words and definitions for each prefix. Use a dictionary if necessary.

Prefix	Word and definition	Word and definition
poly-		
im-		
de-		
anti-		
bio-		
ex-		
macro-		
hydro-		

C. Compare your list with another student and explain what the words mean. How is the prefix related to the definition? Circle any words that you can use in the unit assignment.

⬆ Go to MyEnglishLab to complete a skill practice.

APPLY YOUR SKILLS

WHY IT'S USEFUL By applying the skills you have learned in this unit, you can successfully format, edit, and proofread to complete a polished paper that presents your ideas in a clear and concise way.

ASSIGNMENT
Write a discussion post of 500–600 words about the use of regenerative treatment for one specific injury or illness. What materials are used? Discuss types of materials and their advantages and disadvantages. What is the role of stem cells? Include at least one cited source. Edit and proofread your post for publication on a course discussion forum.

BEFORE YOU WRITE

A. Before you begin your assignment, discuss these questions with one or more students.

1. What illness or injury will you focus on? Which regenerative treatment will you write about? Why?

2. What materials are used? What are advantages and disadvantages of these materials? How are stem cells used?

3. What source did you use to find information on this topic? What are the most important ideas from this source?

B. As you consider your writing assignment, complete the tasks. Then share your ideas with another student. Get feedback and revise your ideas if necessary.

1. Why do university professors use discussion posts? How do they help students understand course content? List ways that posts are different from other types of writing. ....

....

....

2. How will you format your discussion post? What font will you use? Will your post be formal or informal? Why? Will you use headings and subheadings?

3. List the types of errors you will need to focus on when you edit and proofread your work. Which techniques will you use to help you find these errors?

....

....

C. Review the Unit Skills Summary. As you begin the writing task on page 176, apply the skills you learned in this unit.

UNIT SKILLS SUMMARY

Edit text

- Edit your work slowly and carefully, doing several passes to mark errors for correction.
- Edit your work for accuracy, word choice, conciseness and flow, sentence variety, style, and tone.

Proofread text

- Choose an appropriate proofreading technique to find errors.
- Double-check for errors in:
  - spelling
  - punctuation and capitalization
  - grammar
  - language
  - source information
  - formatting
  - visuals

Analyze text

- Survey the text.
- Analyze development, organization, and language.
- Reflect on your analysis.

Identify and edit run-on sentences and fragments

- Identify run-on sentences and fragments by annotating for subjects, verbs, clause type, and punctuation.
- Correct errors by punctuating correctly and connecting fragments to clauses.

Understand prefixes

- Use a dictionary to learn common prefixes.
- Break down words into smaller parts to understand them.

THINKING CRITICALLY

As you consider your writing assignment, discuss the questions with another student. Get feedback and revise your ideas if necessary.

1. What do you think are the biggest obstacles in regenerative medicine? Do you think the benefits outweigh the obstacles? Explain.

2. What do you think are the most promising uses for regenerative medicine? Why?

3. Do you have ethical concerns about regenerative medicine? Why or why not? How do you think ethical concerns are being addressed? Does more need to be done?

THINKING VISUALLY

A. The timeline shows some of the major achievements in regenerative medicine. How does the timeline help you understand the history of regenerative medicine? What do you think will be added to the timeline in the future?

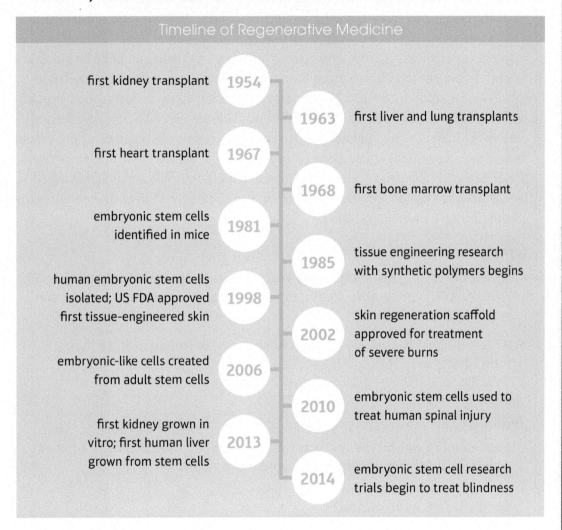

Timeline of Regenerative Medicine

first kidney transplant	**1954**
	1963 first liver and lung transplants
first heart transplant	**1967**
	1968 first bone marrow transplant
embryonic stem cells identified in mice	**1981**
	1985 tissue engineering research with synthetic polymers begins
human embryonic stem cells isolated; US FDA approved first tissue-engineered skin	**1998**
	2002 skin regeneration scaffold approved for treatment of severe burns
embryonic-like cells created from adult stem cells	**2006**
	2010 embryonic stem cells used to treat human spinal injury
first kidney grown in vitro; first human liver grown from stem cells	**2013**
	2014 embryonic stem cell research trials begin to treat blindness

B. Create a brief timeline of polymers in medicine. Which events do you think are the most important? Why? Discuss your ideas with another student.

THINKING ABOUT LANGUAGE

Identify and correct run-on sentences, comma splices, and fragments in the paragraph. Circle the seven errors and then rewrite the paragraph to correct them.

One of the most important applications of stem cells and biomaterials in regenerative medicine is in tissue and organ regeneration. Stem cells could be used to heal tissue in a damaged organ. If directed to produce that particular type of tissue. Currently, when a patient experiences organ failure, there is little to do but wait and hope for a donor. Even if the patient receives an organ transplant. There is risk of the body rejecting the organ. Stem cell treatments may be a welcome alternative. Such treatments could use stem cells. Seeded into a polymer-based biomaterial scaffold that is constructed outside the body. Once implanted, a stem cell could rejuvenate organ function. Would benefit millions of individuals. Because there would be no need to wait for an organ donor. Less risk of organ rejection. The interaction of stem cells and polymer-based biomaterials is likely to continue in the coming years. As the field of tissue engineering and regenerative medicine advances.

WRITE

A. Revisit the writing assignment and your answers to the questions in Before You Write Part B. Regenerative treatment is a quickly changing field so make sure your information is current.

B. Write a discussion post. Use at least one source for research. Write the source here. ....

....

C. Format, edit, and proofread your discussion post. Include a citation for your source. Notice which types of errors you make more often and write a note in your journal to learn about how to avoid these errors.

BEYOND THE ASSIGNMENT

Write a paper of 800–1000 words on how a polymer in a specific application has revolutionized a specific field or industry. What factors influenced its use in this field or industry? What positive and negative impacts has it had on society?

⬤ Go to MyEnglishLab to watch Professor Heilshorn's concluding video and to complete a self-assessment.

PART

2

Critical
Thinking Skills

*Part 2 moves from skill building to application of the skills that require critical thinking.
Practice activities tied to specific learning outcomes in each unit require a deeper level
of understanding of the academic content.*

LINGUISTICS

Fact and Opinion

UNIT PROFILE

Language is a critical aspect of identity. In this unit, you will read and write about topics related to identity, specifically social identity, indigenous languages and language loss, the role language plays in identity, including linguistic style, and the impact of learning English on identity of non-native speakers.

OUTCOMES

• Use expressions of fact and opinion
• Present a counterargument
• Recognize author bias
• Use language of disagreement
• Use a dictionary to learn collocations

Write an argumentative essay of 500–800 words taking a position on whether learning a second language has impacted or changed your identity. Use facts and opinions about how and why or why not to support your claims. Address at least one counterargument.

For more about **LINGUISTICS**, see ❶❸. See also Ⓡ and OC **LINGUISTICS** ❶❷❸.

GETTING STARTED

Go to MyEnglishLab to watch Professor Podesva's introductory video and to complete a self-assessment.

Discuss these questions with a partner or group.

1. How would you respond to the question, "Who are you?" What is the first thing you would think of? What factors have contributed to your identity? How important is your culture to who you are?

2. What role does your first or native language play in your identity? Do you think this changes when you learn a new language?

3. Professor Podesva suggests that we change how we talk depending on who we are talking to or what situation we are in. Do you believe you talk differently at work or school from the way you talk at home? With friends, teachers, parents, or a boss. If so, give examples. If not, explain why not.

CRITICAL THINKING SKILL

FACT AND OPINION

WHY IT'S USEFUL By using facts and opinions in developing an argument, you will be able to more strongly support your claims. Including accurate and relevant facts adds to your readers' understanding of the topic. Opinions that are based on factual evidence and the opinions of experts make your claims stronger.

In academic writing, it is essential to provide support for your ideas. Especially in developing an argument, presenting **facts** and **opinions** is a good way to support the claims you make and convince your reader. Use of facts and opinions is also effective when **presenting a counterargument** and then refuting it.

Facts are pieces of information that are known or generally accepted to be true. Facts can be data, which is raw information about something, or statistics, which are the numerical interpretations of the data. To be accepted as fact, a piece of information must be based on observable evidence that has been collected using sound methods.

Facts can also be the testimony of participants in, or witnesses to, real events or reports of incidents that actually happened. Reports of events from the point of view of a participant or eyewitness create vivid images for the reader.

Facts are strong support of claims in academic writing when they fit the context and are accurate, verifiable, and appropriate. Facts alone are not sufficient support for claims. Look at the different types of facts.

Types of Facts	Examples
Data	While Iran was never under the direct influence of France, there are many French expressions in the Persian language.
Statistics	English is the language spoken by the largest number of non-native speakers. The number of non-native speakers of English is estimated at 250–350 million.
Testimony	Lucila D. Ek said, "My sisters and I never really learned to speak Maya despite hearing it spoken by our parents and adult relatives who spoke it with each other."

Opinions are ideas about a particular subject. Opinions can support claims in academic work, but they must be based on factual evidence or study and analysis. Reasonable or logical conclusions from data, while not always completely verifiable, are supported opinions. The ideas of experts in a given field represent opinions based on knowledge gained through in-depth study over time.

Opinions are changeable and subject to different interpretations, so, like facts, they are not always considered adequate when used alone to support claims. You should show your reader how the opinions you choose are based on evidence or study to support your claims. Look at the different types of opinions.

Types of Opinions	Examples	Explanations
Evidence-based opinion	For example, in a study done in 1980, **maintenance of Portuguese among immigrants in California was found to be low** possibly due to a desire to achieve the greater social mobility that English could offer.	The opinion is based on **factual evidence** from a study. The conclusion drawn from that evidence is a logical one.
Expert opinion	**Dr. Lucila D. Ek, Associate Professor of Bicultural-Bilingual Studies**, said, "The loss of Yucatec Maya in my family both in the US and in Mexico is distressing because identity and culture are inextricably connected to language."	This is the opinion of an **expert** who has studied the topic and has personal experience. This supports the opinion that language is an important aspect of identity.

In academic writing, it is important to present ideas in a balanced way that avoids being overly biased toward a position. It is critical to **recognize bias** in the writing of others and to **avoid bias** in your own writing. **Beliefs** are ideas based on morals, values, and faith. Beliefs are opinions, but they are not based on evidence or expert knowledge. They cannot be proved or disproved or contested in a logical way. While beliefs are used in writing, typically to appeal to a reader's emotions, they are generally considered biased and, therefore, not acceptable support for claims in academic work. Look at the examples of different types of beliefs.

Types of Beliefs	Examples
Based on personal morals	Everyone should speak a foreign language!
Based on cultural value	English is the most important language to learn.
Based on faith	Everyone should believe in a higher power.

Accurate and appropriate facts and evidence or evidence-based or expert opinions, when used together, are valid support for the claims and counterarguments you make in an argument essay and help you avoid bias.

TIP

When supporting your ideas and claims, it is helpful to your reader to clearly indicate which ideas are facts and which are opinions. Using expressions that distinguish them helps your reader to see the connection between fact and opinion and strengthens the support. Use phrases such as, "It's a fact that" or "Data shows that" or "(Name) believes that" or "is of the opinion that" to introduce facts and opinions.

VOCABULARY PREVIEW

Read the vocabulary items. Circle the ones you know. Put a question mark next to the ones you don't know.

comprise	gender	trait	heritage	assert
context	reveal	conferred	maintenance	mobility

EXERCISE 1

A. Read the beginning of an article on language identity.

The Role of Language in Identity

1 Before considering the role of language in identity, it is important to define identity and understand it from different perspectives. Most dictionaries define identity as the qualities and beliefs or attitudes that make a particular person or group different from others. From the perspective of a psychologist, identity is our own sense of who we are. Sociology, concerned with the individuals who comprise a group, seeks to understand social identity, where the focus is on membership in a group based on a shared aspect.

2 Social identity has a historical basis in shared aspects such as ethnicity, gender, social class, and physical or psychological traits. Geography, national and regional identity, is also a factor in social identity. Beliefs and values, both spiritual and political, also play a role in social identity. Even school, work, or leisure activities can be shared aspects of people's lives. Therefore, an individual can be a member of one or more groups based on a shared heritage, belief, or activity.

3 What is the role, then, of language in identity? It can be argued that language is the factor that has the greatest impact on social identity because how we communicate and interact with others shapes our identity in many ways, both as an individual and as a member of one or more groups. Rusi Jaspal, professor of psychology, argues in "Language and social identity: A psychosocial approach," that language, in addition to its function as a means of communication, is a means of asserting identity and one's sameness or distinctiveness, that is, difference, from others. Most linguists believe identity is context specific. We are products of our experiences—historical, social, and political. It is through language that we express ourselves and reveal our identity.

4 Speaking a common language connects people in ways that even ethnicity or beliefs may not. People can gain entry into a group by adopting the language of that group. Linguistic identity can also divide people. Languages are neither good nor bad. Value and meaning are conferred on them by those who speak them and sometimes by those who don't. A group may even consider as part of its identity a language its members don't speak. For example, although only a portion of the Welsh in the United Kingdom speak the Welsh language natively, the language is important as a symbol of the group's identity and distinctiveness from the English and is frequently used on traffic signs in Wales.

Train station in Wales showing the longest place name in the United Kingdom

5 The loss of a language can also affect identity. Dr. Lucila D. Ek, Associate Professor of Bicultural-Bilingual Studies said, "My sisters and I never really learned to speak Maya despite hearing it spoken by our parents and adult relatives who spoke it with each other." She said, "The loss of Yucatec Maya in my family, both in the US and in Mexico, is distressing because identity and culture are inextricably connected to language."

6 People may leave one group and seek entry into another group by learning to speak a second language. If there are negative feelings about the native language, individuals may use the new language to gain entry into a group with a more positive identity. For example, in a study done in 1980, maintenance of Portuguese among immigrants in California was found to be low possibly due to a desire to achieve the greater social mobility that English could offer. Sheila Kohler, an author who grew up in South Africa chose to leave that country and learn languages other than English as a result of her negative feelings about apartheid.

CULTURE NOTE

Apartheid is the former South African political and social system in which only white people had full political rights, and people of other races, especially black people, were forced to go to separate schools, live in separate areas, etc. The term comes from Afrikaans and means *separateness*.

7 From the viewpoint of linguists, social identity based on language must take into consideration attitudes about the language. Most are of the opinion that this can affect the shaping of language. For example, while it's a fact that Iran was never under the direct influence of France, there are many French expressions in the Persian language. It appears that modern Persian was, in actual fact, codified by intellectuals who had studied in Paris and held the opinion that French culture was desirable and that importing French words was a means to improve perceptions of the Persian language.

CULTURE NOTE

An ethnic group is a category of people who identify with each other based on similarities—common ancestors, culture, nationality, and language. Ethnicity is often inherited, unlike social groups (wealth, age, participation in common activities), and usually based on the society in which a person lives. The traditional definition of race is related to biological factors and ethnicity to sociological ones. Race refers to a person's physical characteristics, such as height, weight, skin, hair or eye color. Ethnicity, however, refers to cultural factors, including nationality, regional culture, ancestry, and language.

Glossary

Codify: in Linguistics, to standardize a language, usually by systematizing it; setting up official rules for grammar, writing, pronunciation, and vocabulary

B. Answer the questions.

1. What is the dictionary definition of identity from the article? ....
....

2. How does the view of identity of a psychologist differ from that of a sociologist?
....
....
....

3. What three areas of shared aspects are mentioned in the explanation of social identity? ....
....

4. What life experiences can be part of an individual's social identity?
....
....

5. Why is language the factor that most impacts social identity? ....
....
....

6. What example is given of a language that defines group identity but is not spoken by many members of the group? ....
....

7. Why is the loss of Yucatec Mayan troubling to Dr. Ek? ....
....

8. What was the explanation of why the Persian language contains expressions in French? ....
....

C. Look back at the article in Part A. Complete the chart with examples of each type of fact and opinion. Discuss your answers with a partner.

Facts	
Data	
Statistics	
Testimony	

Opinion	
Evidence-based opinion	
Expert opinion	

D. Find a source on language identity. Write at least two facts and two opinions from that source. Are there beliefs that cannot be proved or disproved?

....

....

....

....

E. Share your facts and opinions on language identity with a partner.

VOCABULARY CHECK

A. Review the vocabulary items in the Vocabulary Preview. Write their definitions and add examples. Use a dictionary if necessary.

B. Choose the sentence that correctly describes the underlined item.

1. Professor Dugan's English class is <u>comprised</u> of students from Poland, South Korea, and Brazil.

   a. His class is very difficult for students from these three countries.
   b. His class is made up of students from these three countries. *(Continued)*

2. For some studies, researchers separate people by <u>gender</u>.

   a. The researchers want to see if men and women answer questions differently.
   b. The researchers want to see if young and old people answer questions differently.

3. My sister and I share many of the same <u>traits</u>.

   a. We both have brown hair and are very shy.
   b. We both live in New York and go to City College.

4. Maria went to Italy last year to learn more about her family <u>heritage</u>.

   a. She had a great time with her cousins and they promised to visit her in California next year.
   b. Her cousins told her about their family's history and she even learned how to make her great-grandmother's fresh pasta.

5. Even though she has lived in many countries, Marisol will always <u>assert</u> her identity as a Filipina.

   a. She is very proud of her native country and her family history.
   b. She wants to learn more about the histories of the other places she has lived.

6. Most people have different writing styles depending on the <u>context</u>.

   a. I prefer writing to friends. I get nervous when I write to teachers.
   b. When I write to friends, it is very casual. When I write to teachers, it's more formal.

7. I only <u>reveal</u> information about my family to my very close friends.

   a. I never talk about my family, even to very close friends.
   b. It takes me a long time to tell people personal things.

8. Respect is <u>conferred</u> to you when you respect other people.

   a. The best way to get respect is to give it.
   b. It is very difficult to respect some people.

9. My mother taught us that <u>maintenance</u> of family traditions is important.

   a. The best way to continue remembering family traditions is by doing little things every day that remind me of my family.
   b. The best way to change family traditions is by doing little things every day that remind me of my family.

10. Feeling a true sense of <u>mobility</u> is difficult when you have family commitments and other obligations.

    a. Not everybody has the desire to move to a new place or change jobs.

    b. Not everybody has the ability to easily move to a new place or change jobs.

⊙ Go to MyEnglishLab to complete vocabulary and skill practices and to join in collaborative activities.

SUPPORTING SKILL 1

USING EXPRESSIONS OF FACT AND OPINION

WHY IT'S USEFUL By using a variety of expressions of fact and opinion, your readers will have a clear understanding of how you are supporting your claims in your writing.

When **using facts and opinions** as supporting ideas in academic work, introduce them using expressions that clearly identify the ideas as either fact or opinion.

Given the fact that sociology is concerned with the individuals that comprise a group, it seeks to understand social identity where the focus is on membership in a group based on a shared aspect.

In the opinion of a psychologist, identity is our own sense of who we are.

Expressions can also add information on the quality and type of fact or opinion. It is common to use adjectives to describe (qualify) the facts and opinions. Adjectives can indicate the strength of evidence to support the facts and opinions but also the degree of bias of the writer.

It is a **well-known** fact (strength of evidence)

She expressed a **strong** opinion. (degree of bias)

Careful reading of the expressions used to present facts and opinions can help you determine whether they will successfully support your ideas.

Commonly used expressions of fact and opinion use a variety of clauses, phrases, adjectives, verbs, idiomatic expressions, and synonyms, as seen in the chart:

	Expressions of fact	Expressions of opinion
Clauses that introduce	It is a fact; I know for a fact that; The fact (of the matter) is	The (general) opinion is that; My (her, etc.) opinion is that; I am (he is, etc.) of the opinion that; I think that; They believe that
Phrases that introduce	Given the fact that; Due to the fact that; In (actual) fact Despite the fact that; In spite of the fact that (counterargument)	In my opinion; Given the opinion that
Adjectives used with	well-known; little-known; widely accepted; basic/key; simple/plain; clear; actual; hard; historical; scientific; bare; evidence-based	general; popular; prevailing; accepted; public; personal; strong; honest; high; good; low; poor; favorable; unfavorable; different; legal; scientific; divided
Verbs that introduce	give; provide; establish; piece together; gather; examine; check; state; stick to; accept; be based on	ask; give; change; hold; express; ask for; form
Idiomatic expressions	get the facts straight/wrong; stick to the facts; the facts speak for themselves; the fact remains that; facts and figures	x is a matter of opinion; opinion maker/shaper
Synonyms	truth; evidence; general knowledge	view; point of view; attitude; feeling; conviction; position; stance; sentiment; perspective

EXERCISE 2

A. Read this excerpt from the article in Exercise 1. Identify the expressions of fact and opinion. Underline expressions that introduce facts and circle those that introduce opinions.

> From the viewpoint of linguists, social identity based on language must take into consideration attitudes about the language. Most are of the opinion that this can affect the shaping of language. For example, while it's a fact that Iran was never under the direct influence of France, there are many French expressions in the Persian language. It appears that modern Persian was, in actual fact, codified by intellectuals who had studied in Paris and held the opinion that French culture was desirable and that importing French words was a means to improve perceptions of the Persian language.

B. Read the sentences and decide whether each states a fact or an opinion. Rewrite each sentence two ways, adding different expressions of fact and opinion. Use an adjective in at least one sentence. Underline the expressions.

1. Speaking a common language connects people in ways that even ethnicity or beliefs may not. ....

....

....

2. People can gain entry into a group by adopting the language of that group.

....

....

3. Linguistic identity can also divide people. ....

....

....

4. Languages are neither good nor bad. ....

....

....

5. A group may consider as part of its identity a language its members don't speak.

....

....

6. Only a fifth of the Welsh in England speak the Welsh language natively.

....

....

7. Even though few speak Welsh, traffic signs in the Welsh areas of England are written in both English and Welsh. ....

....

....

8. The Welsh language is important as a symbol of the group's identity and distinctiveness from the English. ....

....

....

C. **Compare your answers in Part A and share your sentences in Part B with a partner. Discuss any disagreements or differences.**

D. **Rewrite your facts and opinions from Exercise 1 Part C, adding expressions of fact or opinion.**

⬆ Go to MyEnglishLab to complete a skill practice.

SUPPORTING SKILL 2

PRESENTING A COUNTERARGUMENT

WHY IT'S USEFUL By presenting a counterargument, you show the reader that you are informed about the issue you are writing about and understand that different viewpoints exist. Your writing will be more persuasive when you present a differing point of view in an objective and balanced way and then respond to it with evidence and clear reasoning.

When you begin writing an argumentative paper, it is critical to carefully examine who your audience is. Does the audience agree with your argument or position? Does the audience have opinions about the issue? Or, does the audience disagree with you? Thinking about your audience will help you plan the type and amount of evidence you need to support your argument or position. It will also help you anticipate opposing views or **counterarguments** that may be important to include in your paper.

In an argumentative paper, you want to prove that your opinion, theory, or hypothesis about an issue is correct. Your thesis will state what your position is on the issue. To persuade your audience, you must provide enough evidence, including appropriate facts and opinions, to support your thesis and arguments. You should also **present a counterargument** to demonstrate that you have considered the issue from different points of view than your own. University professors, who try to take a neutral approach, often expect or require students to address the opposition in their work. By choosing counterarguments that are logical, reasonable, and well known, you establish your authority and credibility on the issue, and ultimately strengthen your own argument.

After you present a counterargument, you must respond to it. If you **concede**, you acknowledge that all or some parts of the opposing view are valid. However, you will explain why the opposing view is weaker or less relevant than the position you are taking. If you **refute** the counterargument, you will explain why it is wrong or flawed. A strong response includes credible cited research, facts, or expert opinions that support your position and weaken or disprove the counterargument.

You can include counterarguments anywhere that you think your audience might have objections to your argument or assumptions. Sometimes writers will present the strongest counterargument at the beginning of their paper when they introduce the issue and begin developing their argument. They may also address counterarguments point by point within different paragraphs as they present their main or supporting arguments.

Consider these guidelines as you read a counterargument in an essay about language loss and identity. In the essay, the writer discusses the value in preserving traditional languages.

State the counterargument accurately. Include reasoning for this point of view.	Some government officials believe that tax dollars should not be invested in teaching traditional languages of Native Americans. They argue that money is better spent teaching Native American children Chinese or Spanish because these languages are used for many global interactions.
Concede or refute the counterargument and state your argument or position.	While it is true that traditional languages are not used globally, it's critical that we preserve them so that young Native Americans understand who they are. Dr. Lucila Ek claims that identity and
Use credible evidence to support your position. Include quotes, paraphrases, or summaries.	culture cannot be separated from language (2014). Language plays an important role in how people identify with a group or culture. For this reason, if we do not invest money to teach these languages,
Explain the evidence.	then it is likely that many Native Americans will lose their traditional identities, negatively affecting future generations.

When presenting counterarguments, it is important to use clear transitions and phrases so your audience doesn't get confused about which side you support. What words or phrases does the writer use above to present the counterargument? To respond to the counterargument?

Discuss the different meanings and/or functions of the words and phrases in the chart. Can you think of others to include?

Present a Counterargument	Respond to a Counterargument
[Someone] states that ...	Even so,
According to [someone],	Nevertheless,
[Some people] argue (claim, support, insist, believe) that ...	While it's true that ...
	Although ...
Opponents of this position believe ...	What they don't state, however ...
It's a well-known fact that ...	Despite the fact that ...
	It's possible that ... but ...
	It's more likely that ...

TIP

Before you write, brainstorm the most reasonable or popular counterarguments to the issue you are writing about. Responding to these will test your ideas and make your writing more persuasive.

EXERCISE 3

A. Read the assignment.

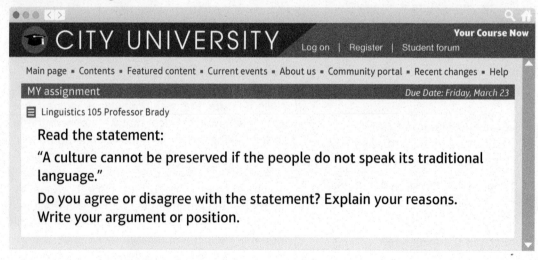

●●● < >

⊕ CITY UNIVERSITY
Your Course Now
Log on | Register | Student forum

Main page ▪ Contents ▪ Featured content ▪ Current events ▪ About us ▪ Community portal ▪ Recent changes ▪ Help

MY assignment   *Due Date: Friday, March 23*

Linguistics 105 Professor Brady

Read the statement:

"A culture cannot be preserved if the people do not speak its traditional language."

Do you agree or disagree with the statement? Explain your reasons.
Write your argument or position.

Your argument or position

B. List evidence to support your position. List possible counterarguments for your evidence.

Evidence to Support Position	Counterarguments

C. Write a short counterargument paragraph in which you refute the claim, or position, in Part A. Use appropriate transitions or phrases to present a counterargument, your position, and evidence supporting your position. Make sure you explain your evidence.

D. PEER REVIEW. Exchange paragraphs with a partner. Respond to the questions to evaluate each other's work.

	Response
What is the counterargument?	
What reasoning did the writer include for the counterargument?	
What is the writer's argument or position?	
What evidence did the writer use to support his or her position?	
How did the writer explain the evidence?	
What transitions or phrases did the writer use to introduce the counterargument and the writer's position?	
How effective is the counterargument?	

⬆ Go to MyEnglishLab to complete a skill practice.

INTEGRATED SKILLS

RECOGNIZING AUTHOR BIAS

WHY IT'S USEFUL By recognizing author bias, you can evaluate the credibility of an author's opinions. This will help you as you analyze your sources to choose appropriate support to include in your writing.

When you read a text, such as an article, newspaper, book, or blog, you will most often find that it includes author **bias**, or an attitude that shows more support for one group, person, or belief than others in a situation where fairness to all people and balanced treatment of all beliefs is important. **Recognizing bias** will help you better understand an author's purpose and allow you to evaluate the validity of the author's arguments.

How can you recognize author bias? You should first consider who the author is and evaluate the author's credentials. For example, if the author is an expert in the field and is known to produce objective, reliable research, then the author will most likely present a balanced and fair argument. It is important to evaluate how an author presents information in developing an argument. Are counterarguments presented? If so, are they presented accurately and fairly? What are the sources for the statistics and facts that are presented? Are the sources credible? You should also evaluate the language that the author uses to express assumptions and opinions. For example, is it neutral and factual? Or does it frequently include words with positive or negative connotations? Finally, you should consider evaluating the overall tone of the text. If the tone is highly emotional, it is likely a sign that bias exists.

Compare these biased sentences with neutral, or unbiased, sentences:

Biased

It's <u>ridiculous</u> for governments to <u>waste</u> money on preserving traditional languages that few people identify with or speak.

<u>Business leaders</u> have been <u>amazingly generous</u> in providing scholarships to support indigenous people who <u>never learned</u> their traditional languages.

Neutral

Several government officials opposed funding to preserve traditional languages because they believe people should learn languages that are frequently used for global interactions.

Many businesses have provided scholarships to support indigenous people who want to learn their traditional languages.

Asking questions that critically evaluate an author's arguments will help you recognize bias. Use the questions in this chart when you are reading and evaluating a text. If you answer *Yes* to any of the questions, you will need to carefully examine the reading to determine how the author is presenting arguments.

	Yes	No
Does the author represent any special interest, political, or religious groups?		
Does the author consider only one side of an issue?		
Is any information missing?		
Does the author only include generalizations?		
Does the author's argument appeal to the reader's emotions?		
Does the author include words that are overly positive or negative?		
Does the author use language that is offensive?		
Does the author exaggerate or create fear?		

When you recognize an author's bias, you will be able to assess the author's credibility and make decisions about whether or not you should use the information as a source in your own writing. If you are not careful about which sources you use to support your argument, your reasoning for or against an issue could be flawed, incorrect, or not logical. If you use sources that are not credible, your own arguments and assumptions will not be considered credible to those who understand the issue well.

You can also use these questions to evaluate your own writing for bias. Remember, if you include language that is overly biased when you present an argument, your reader will most likely not find you to be credible either!

TIP

When you read about an issue, you should evaluate your own bias. This will help you understand your reaction to what you are reading.

TIP

Ask a librarian for help if you are having difficulty determining the credibility of an author or source.

Read the vocabulary items. Circle the ones you know. Put a question mark next to the ones you don't know.

concept	shifts (n)	flawed	unreliable	alternative
broadcast (v)	established (adj)	associate with	sophisticated	appreciation

EXERCISE 4

A. Read the two articles. The first, *Speech Style and Social Identity*, is a scholarly essay, and the second is a blog from a website on language issues.

Speech Style and Social Identity

1 Sociolinguistics is the field of study that examines language in a social context. One of the topics sociolinguists focus on is how language is connected to identity. In sociolinguistics, identity is a flexible, multi-aspect concept. Under this framework of understanding, a person is always shaping his or her identity in relation to a social context, and this influences the person's language use. The way a student speaks to a parent, for example, is likely not the same way she speaks to a friend, nor to an employer. Individual patterns of speech, word choices, and manner of communicating are known as linguistic style, or speech style. Speech style and its connection to identity has been a developing subject of study in sociolinguistics since the mid-20th century (Labov, 1972; Giles, 1973; Bell, 1984; Milroy, 1987).

2 William Labov, whose work helped to establish the field of sociolinguistics, was one of the first linguists to study the shifts that speakers make in their style when they are talking to different individuals. Labov argued that when speakers are not paying attention to how they are speaking, they slip into an informal style. In contrast, when speakers are more aware of their speech style, they tend to shift into a more formal, or standard, style (Labov, 1972). Labov's attention-to-speech model is flawed, however. Many sociolinguists find Labov's model one-dimensional and unreliable, and say that situational context is more important than simply paying attention to the level of formality (Milroy, 1987).

3 Sociolinguists and others in the field of language study have developed several alternative theories for why speakers shift their speaking style. Sociolinguist Allan Bell's "audience design theory," assumes that speakers shift their speaking style in response to their audience (Bell, 1984). According to Bell, style is essentially

"what an individual speaker does with a language in relation to other people" (Eckert, Rickford, 2001; 141). Bell examined two radio stations in New Zealand, one targeting a higher status group in the community, and one a lower status group. The stations were broadcast from the same location, but individual newsreaders often spoke differently depending on who their audience was. In some cases, their speech style even shifted on identically written news items, one way to one group of listeners, and another way to the other group. The only different factor was the audience to whom the newscasters were speaking. Bell's work drew from an established theory developed outside the field of sociolinguistics by social psychologist Howard Giles. Giles's theory, known as "communication accommodation theory," argues that speakers shift their speaking style either to more closely associate themselves with their listeners or to dissociate themselves further from their audience (Giles, 1973).

4　The study of speech style in sociolinguistics is a key to unlocking the mystery of how individuals form social identity. Through shifting their linguistic style in relation to their audience, individuals use their linguistic style—whether they are aware of it or not—to shape their identities. In doing so, speech style takes an active role in a person's construction of identity.

References

Bell, A. (1984, June). Style as audience design. *Language in Society* 13(2): 145–204.

Bell, A. (2001). Back in style: reworking audience design theory. In Eckert, P., & Rickford, J.R. (eds.), Style and sociolinguistic variation. Cambridge, UK: Cambridge University Press.

Giles, Howard. (1973, January). Accent mobility: A model and some data. Anthropological Linguistics. 15: 87–105.

Giles, Howard. Accommodation theory: Some new directions. York Papers in Linguistics. 9: 105–36.

Giles, H. (2009). The process of communication accommodation. In Coupland, N. & Jaworski, A. (eds.), The new sociolinguistics reader. Basingstroke: Palgrave Macmillan.

Labov, W. (1972). *Sociolinguistic patterns*. Philadelphia, PA: University of Pennsylvania Press.

Milroy, L. (1987). *Observing and analysing natural language: a critical account of sociolinguistic method.* Oxford: B. Blackwell.

SpeakNow **YOUR VIEW** WORLD VIEW CONNECT MORE 🔍

Blog Comments Tags

A LANGUAGE IDENTITY STRUGGLE   Lina Scott

1 Lucky to be born to a Spanish mother and a bilingual American father, I have been exposed to Spanish and English my entire life. When I was young, my mother would speak only in Spanish in our home so this was the first language I learned to speak. But I grew up in the US surrounded by English. I spoke in English everywhere in our community, so as I grew older, I spoke more and more English at home.

2 I never gave much thought to how these two languages shaped my identity until I went to Spain in my early 20's to study at a university. I had always been proud of my Hispanic heritage, and wanted to fully experience the culture and become more "Spanish." I had sufficient language skills to talk to my Spanish grandmother, aunts, and cousins, but I lacked the ability to discuss sophisticated ideas. I knew I would learn how to use the language really well. I didn't know at the time how much I would also learn about the profound effect language can have on shaping who we are.

3 It didn't take long for me to notice that when I spoke in Spanish, I felt like a completely different person. I felt weak. I struggled to find the exact words to express my thoughts, and when the words came out of my mouth, I felt childish, stupid, and insecure. In conversations, I wasn't skilled at shifting my speech style. I listened more than I wanted, and when I had opinions to express, I did so quietly and unconvincingly. In a culture where people engaged in spirited discussion on politics and religion, I sat there spiritless, struggling to respond. My words were flat and bland. I didn't know who I was.

4 After a year in Spain, I did significantly improve my Spanish, but I began to have a deeper appreciation for the English language and decided to return "home." I was happy to be surrounded by a language that I could better identify with. When I spoke in English, I never struggled to find the right word. I could be direct and express ideas with nuance. I could use words in playful ways. I was able to adapt my speech depending on who I was talking to. I was confident and powerful again.

New York City

Madrid, Spain

Glossary

Nuance: a very slight, hardly noticeable difference in manner or meaning

B. Answer the questions.

Reading 1: Scholarly Essay

1. What is linguistic style, or speech style? ....
....

2. What is linguist William Labov's theory on language shift? ....
....
....

3. How is the "audience design theory" different from Labov's theory on language shift? ....
....

4. How is the "alternative design theory" similar to the "communication accommodation theory"? ....
....

Reading 2: Blog on Language Identity

1. Describe the writer's language experience growing up. ....
....
....

2. Why did the writer decide to study in Spain? ....
....

3. What happened to the writer's identity in Spain? ....
....

4. What happened to the writer's identity after returning to the US?
....
....

C. Read the articles in Part A again and annotate them by highlighting or underlining words, phrases, or sentences that are biased. Use the chart to identify the type of bias.

Questions for recognizing author bias	Yes	No	Evidence from the reading
Does the author represent any special interest, political, or religious groups?			
Does the author only include generalizations?			
Does the author's argument appeal to the reader's emotions?			
Does the author include words that are overly positive or negative?			
Does the author use language that is offensive?			
Does the author exaggerate or create fear?			

D. Answer these questions and discuss your ideas with a partner or in a small group.

1 Which article shows more bias?

2 When would it be appropriate to use information from each article to support your ideas in an argumentative paper?

3 Is there information that would not be appropriate to include? Explain.

E. Rewrite the sentences so that they no longer are biased.

1. Labov's attention-to-speech model is flawed. ....
....

2. Learning a second language has a huge effect on a person's identity. ....
....

3. We are in grave danger of losing many of the world's languages. ....
....

4. The way women speak says a lot about who they are. ....
....

5. Undoubtedly, the loss of a language can also affect identity. ....
....

VOCABULARY CHECK

A. Review the vocabulary items in the Vocabulary Preview. Write their definitions and add examples. Use a dictionary if necessary.

B. Complete each sentence with the correct vocabulary item.

alternative	appreciation	associate with	broadcast
concept	established	flawed	shifts
sophisticated	unreliable		

1. For our final paper, Professor Washington asked his students to use both .... research and newer studies.

2. My study partner is so .... He misses a lot of classes and he doesn't follow up on assignments.

3. Professor Simon made critical mistakes in his research article, so it is .... It was unusual because his research is usually excellent.

4. Being completely bilingual is such an exciting .... Right now, it is hard to imagine this idea, but I know I can do it!

5. Most of the class wrote papers on the history of linguistics, but I chose the .... : a comparison of language teaching in two countries.

(Continued)

6. People often change their speaking style depending on who they are speaking to. But people make .... in their style when they write to different people, as well.

7. College radio stations often .... music from all over the world.

8. Professors usually like to .... researchers so they can hear about the latest studies in their field.

9. After I began tutoring a high school student, I understood and had a new .... for how hard my professors work.

10. The research started out as a simple idea, but in the end, it was a .... in-depth analysis of the most successful methods of language learning all over the world.

● Go to MyEnglishLab to complete vocabulary and skill practices and to join in collaborative activities.

LANGUAGE SKILL
USING LANGUAGE OF DISAGREEMENT

WHY IT'S USEFUL By using appropriate academic language of disagreement, you will be able to counter arguments or disagree with an opposing view in a way that is fair.

● Go to MyEnglishLab for the Language Skill presentation and practice.

VOCABULARY STRATEGY
USING A DICTIONARY TO LEARN COLLOCATIONS

WHY IT'S USEFUL By using a dictionary to learn collocations, you will be able to choose combinations of words that ensure that your writing sounds natural, is easier to understand, and does not sound translated.

Native English speakers know how words frequently combine together to express an idea. Groups of words that "naturally" go together through common usage are known as **collocations**. A good example of a collocation is the phrase *according to*. Native English speakers know that the word *according* is always followed by the preposition *to*. Here are some other examples:

key fact   opposing view   express an opinion

Understanding which word combinations to use can be difficult for even the most advanced English learners. When you learn new vocabulary words, it is critical to learn their common collocations as well. Understanding how these words work together will help you avoid making errors due to translating from your first language. You will also be able to express your ideas more clearly, and as your ability to use these word combinations increases, your fluency will improve as well.

Think of a collocation as a single unit of language. When you learn a new word, it's helpful to write down typical collocations for that word so you can use them correctly in your writing. A good learner's dictionary will identify collocations by showing the word combinations in **boldface**. It will also include examples which demonstrate how the collocations are used. Often the examples will help you choose the correct collocations for the part of speech that you are using.

Look at the dictionary entry for the verb *disagree*:

---

dis·a·gree /ˌdɪsəˈɡriː/ ●●● S3 verb [intransitive]

1 to have or express a different opinion from someone else OPP **AGREE**
🔊 *disagree with*
   He is tolerant of those who disagree with him.
🔊 *disagree about/on/over*
   Experts disagree on how much the program will cost.

2 if statements, numbers, or reports about the same event or situation disagree, they are different from each other OPP **AGREE**
🔊 *The statements of several witnesses disagree.*

From this entry, notice that the collocation "disagree with" is used when we are expressing a different opinion from someone else. The collocations "disagree on" and "disagree about" are interchangeable, and used when referring to an idea.

TIP

The *Longman Dictionary of Contemporary English Online* is a useful resource for learning common collocations for many English words. Go to http://www.ldoceonline.com and search for the collocation boxes under the dictionary definitions.

EXERCISE 5

A. Use an English learner's dictionary to review typical collocations for disagreeing. For each word, write two collocations that are appropriate for use in an academic paper and a sample sentence for each.

Word	Collocation	Sample sentences
wrong		
mistaken		
dispute		
despite		

B. Use the collocations in Part A to write an original sentence for each.

1. ....
2. ....
3. ....
4. ....
5. ....
6. ....
7. ....
8. ....

C. Share your sentences with a partner and discuss the context in which each collocation is used.

Go to MyEnglishLab to complete a skill practice.

APPLY YOUR SKILLS

WHY IT'S USEFUL By applying the skills you have learned in this unit, you can accurately express fact and opinion, present a counterargument, recognize bias and use language to disagree in writing an argument.

ASSIGNMENT

Write an argumentative essay of 500–800 words taking a position on whether learning a second language has impacted or changed your identity. Use facts and opinions about how and why, or why not, to support your claims. Address at least one counterargument. Use a variety of expressions to introduce facts and opinions and academic language to disagree.

BEFORE YOU WRITE

A. Before you begin your assignment, discuss these questions with one or more students.

1. What are some ways that learning a second language might impact someone's identity?

2. How can learning a second language affect one's awareness of who they are?

3. Can people adopt a new identity depending on what language is being spoken at the time?

B. As you consider your assignment, complete the tasks. Then share your ideas with another student. Get feedback and revise your ideas if necessary.

1. What position have you chosen to take for the assignment? ....

2. List three or more facts and opinions that support your position. ....

3. List two or more of the counterarguments to your position. ....

C. Review the Unit Skills Summary. As you begin on the writing task on page 209, apply the skills you learned in this unit.

UNIT SKILLS SUMMARY

Use expressions of fact and opinion

- Use expressions of fact to present accurate, verifiable and appropriate facts.
- Use expressions of opinion to present evidence-based and expert opinions.
- Use adjectives with expressions of fact and opinion to indicate the strength of evidence to support the facts and opinions.
- Choose expressions that help your reader distinguish facts from opinions and see the connection between them.

Present a counterargument

- State the opposing view, or counterargument.
- Concede or refute the counterargument and state your position clearly.
- Use credible evidence to support your position.
- Explain the evidence.

Recognize author bias

- Evaluate an author's credentials.
- Analyze how counterarguments are presented.
- Evaluate the language the author uses to express assumptions and opinions.
- Consider the overall tone of a text.

Use language of disagreement

- Concede a point but disagree.
- Disagree by offering a contrasting point of view.
- Use adverbials and conjunctions of concession and contrast to disagree.
- Disagree with arguments that are wrong, exaggerated, unsound, or offer solutions that do not work.

Use a dictionary to learn collocations

- Use a dictionary to identify word combinations that often go together.
- Analyze example sentences that show how collocations are used.

THINKING CRITICALLY

As you consider your writing assignment, discuss the questions with another student. Get feedback and revise your ideas if necessary.

1. What would you say about cultural identity to someone who is learning your first language as their second language?

2. What role has your second language classroom environment had on shaping your sense of identity? Have you had opportunities to discuss or notice ways in which you use your second language that may be different from your home culture? For example, do you adopt behaviors that are not part of your home culture? Explain.

3. Do you like who you are when you are speaking a second language? Explain.

THINKING VISUALLY

A. Look at this visual showing the number of learners of these languages. Discuss the questions with a partner.

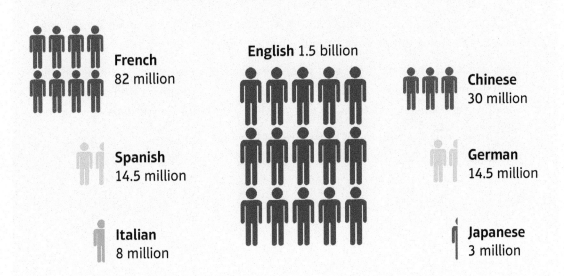

French
82 million

English 1.5 billion

Chinese
30 million

Spanish
14.5 million

German
14.5 million

Italian
8 million

Japanese
3 million

1. What information does this visual give you? Is there any information that is missing that you would like to see? Which language would come next in the graph? Which languages will people want to study in the future?

2. Does the information surprise you? Why or why not?

3. Is the visual effective in presenting the data? Why or why not?

B. Create a pie chart illustrating the languages spoken in a particular region or country.

THINKING ABOUT LANGUAGE

Complete the sentences with an appropriate adverbial or coordinating conjunction. More than one adverbial or conjunction is possible. Use a different adverbial or coordinating conjunction in each sentence.

1. .... the loss of indigenous languages seems inevitable, we should continue to work to preserve as many as possible given their importance as part of the diverse cultural identity of this country.

2. .... the Native American Languages Act of 1990 that recognizes language rights, many languages need additional support in the effort to preserve them.

3. Of the 300 languages that were spoken when Europeans arrived in what is now the US, only 175 remain. .... , many people fail to see the need for additional funding to avoid losing more.

4. There are federal grants that help provide language immersion programs, ... those programs are in danger of being cut.

5. .... immersion programs are proven to work in preserving languages, many in our government wrongly seek to stop funding them.

6. Some claim there is no proof that teaching native languages to the young people will keep the languages alive. .... there is evidence that teaching an indigenous language to a younger generation of speakers can save it.

7. We must keep working to save as many indigenous languages as possible ....

WRITE

A. Revisit the writing assignment and your answers to the questions in Before You Write Part B. Make sure it is clear to the reader which information is fact and which is opinion.

B. What is the most interesting fact? Opinion? Counterargument?

....

....

....

....

....

....

C. Write your argumentative essay. Include facts and opinions. Make sure your essay has the tone you wish to convey.

BEYOND THE ASSIGNMENT
Write a paper of 800–1000 words on the factor that you think is most important in a person's identity. Use facts and opinions to support your position. Address at least one counterargument.

🔺 Go to MyEnglishLab to watch Professor Podesva's concluding video and to complete a self-assessment.

How cultural and ethical values define a successful business

BUSINESS ETHICS

Implication and Inference

UNIT PROFILE

Sociology is the science of society, social institutions, and social relationships. In this unit, you will read and write about topics related to economies from a sociological perspective, focusing on how people's behaviors affect economic structures. Specifically, you will learn about income inequality and the values behind some of the ways business is conducted in the United States.

Write a paper of 800–1000 words that addresses one aspect of culture that influences economies and draw a conclusion about what the effect of that influence is. Support your ideas with evidence from sources. Use boosting as appropriate to strengthen your claims and hedging to avoid overstating or exaggerating them. Use modals to express degrees of certainty about your claims.

OUTCOMES

• Integrate evidence from sources
• Use hedging and boosting language
• Understand and respond to implication and inference
• Use modals to express degrees of certainty
• Use a thesaurus

For more about **BUSINESS ETHICS**, see ❶ ❸. See also ⟦R⟧ and ⟦OC⟧ **BUSINESS ETHICS** ❶❷❸.

GETTING STARTED

⬤ Go to MyEnglishLab to watch Dr. McLennan's introductory video and to complete a self-assessment.

Discuss these questions with a partner or group.

1. How does sociology help us understand economics for individuals, communities, countries, and the world? Why might it be important to learn about economies from a sociological perspective?

2. What is income inequality? What are some causes and effects of income inequality? What are some ethical issues concerning income inequality? What is the impact on society?

3. Dr. McLennan suggests that religion, the way people think about life and their relation to God, affects how they do business. He believes a Protestant Christian work ethic has had a strong influence on capitalism in Western Europe and the United States. How might religion affect how business is conducted in a particular place or culture? What values and behaviors would be affected?

CRITICAL THINKING SKILL

IMPLICATION AND INFERENCE

WHY IT'S USEFUL By reading texts critically, you will be able to understand the implications that a source makes and draw inferences about what you have read. This will ensure that you have correctly understood ideas presented in a text and will allow you to choose the best evidence and support for your own writing.

Reading critically is essential in order to find and integrate evidence from sources into your writing. In particular, you need to understand the main ideas, claims, or arguments that an author presents. Reading a text critically will help you connect ideas within the text or with other texts you have read. It will also help you evaluate and understand **implications**, ideas that are suggested or hinted at but not directly stated by the author, which you are expected to understand on your own. Read this statement:

> **TIP**
> Sources must be read critically to find the implications because authors may purposely not include specific information or details so they are not held accountable, or responsible, for making statements that might anger, embarrass, or cause problems for someone. This is especially true with politics and other controversial topics.

The "American Dream"—the idea that the US is a place where all citizens have the chance of becoming successful if they work hard enough—is deeply rooted in the culture. Many politicians use this as an excuse to oppose funding for government programs that help the poor.

The excerpt implies that the author most likely does not agree with the politicians who do not support funding for government programs. In fact, by using the word *excuse*, the author may show some contempt, or anger, toward the politicians. What else might the author be implying?

When you read a text, you will notice that the author may not always include every detail or explain every relationship between ideas. Instead, the author assumes you already know certain things or that you will draw inferences, or conclusions, about implications and facts in the text. An **inference** is something that a reader thinks is true or logical, based on information that the reader knows about the world, topic, author, or even the language. Our own assumptions, or things we believe are true although we may not have proof, can affect the conclusions that we make about what we have read. Readers with different background knowledge and assumptions are likely to draw different inferences about a statement.

While it may seem more natural to make inferences about statements that are implications, it is common for readers to make inferences about facts. Inferences can be made about causes and effects, the author's purpose, or the author's tone. Look at this factual statement and possible inferences that could be made. Can you think of others?

> The difference in weekly pay in the US between higher and lower earners has grown significantly since 1979.

Possible inferences:

- Lower wage earners can't buy as many things as they did before.
- Lower wage earners have a harder time paying bills than they did before.
- The economy has experienced changes to cause a wider income gap.
- There is more social unrest now than there was in 1979.

TIP

The inferences you make may not always be accurate. Take the time to question your assumptions by discussing topics with classmates and professors. Doing so will improve your ability to make strong inferences as you gain knowledge of a topic or field of study.

After critically reading information from sources, understanding implications, and making inferences, you can more effectively represent ideas and **integrate evidence from sources** to support your claims in your own writing. For academic writing, it is important to use language for **hedging** (showing level of certainty of a claim) or **boosting** (showing level of confidence in a claim) to make sure that you are presenting your ideas as accurately as possible based on the evidence that is available.

> **TIP**
>
> Read critically by annotating the text—underlining important ideas, taking notes, asking questions—and rereading difficult parts.

VOCABULARY PREVIEW

Read the vocabulary items. Circle the ones you know. Put a question mark next to the ones you don't know.

asset	distribution	manufacturing	disproportionate	disparity
attain	pronounced	accessible	pursuing	

EXERCISE 1

A. Read the excerpt from a student paper on the widening gap in income inequality in the United States.

The Widening Gap in Income in the United States

1   Income inequality, or the difference in levels between the rich and the poor, has widened significantly in many developed world economies in the last few decades. This gap, or difference, in income equality has always existed in the United States. However, between the late 1940s and 1970s, income from wages, interest earned, stocks, and profits from selling assets like homes and businesses, grew at fairly equal percentages for all Americans. After this period, income began to grow unequally for Americans at different levels of the income distribution, creating a larger gap in income equality. In fact, since the Great Recession of 2007–2009, income has not grown for the majority of people except for those at the very top of the income distribution. This had a significant impact on family wealth and has created a disparity in American society. The US Congressional Budget Office reports that in 2013, families in the top 10% of the income distribution held 76% of all family wealth, while those families in the bottom 50% held only 1% of the wealth (CBO, 2013). This sizable gap in income distribution makes the US, known for the American Dream, one of the top countries in the developed world for income inequality.

(Continued)

2   While there is some debate as to all the possible causes of income inequality, there is general agreement that technological advancements have without a doubt negatively impacted the American income distribution. Changes in traditional manufacturing have disproportionately affected workers without high school or college degrees. For example, new technologies that improve automation, using computers and machines instead of people to do a job, have increased demand for jobs requiring strong technical skills, but decreased demand for jobs that typically do not require high levels of education. This loss of mid-skilled jobs has become much more pronounced since 2007. Many of these job losses have been permanent, forcing workers to seek out low-skilled jobs that pay much less. The result has been a growing gap in income equality. While there may be hope among mid-skilled workers that new government policies will reverse this trend, the reality is an economy which will probably continue to favor workers who are highly educated and skilled or those who already have wealth.

3   What can we do to lessen income inequality? If one probable cause of income inequality is workers' lack of education, then a possible solution is to provide more opportunities to attain a level of education high enough to find work that will help future workers achieve upward social mobility. According to economic policy analysis specialist Nicholas Parker, research shows that workers with a higher level of education are more likely to earn a higher wage (Parker, 2014). For this reason, it is critical to make education more accessible to those in the lower income distribution levels. One way to lessen the gap is continued efforts to get children off to a good start through early education programs. There is research to suggest that children who receive quality pre-kindergarten education should graduate from high school at higher rates and may frequently go on to attend college. Another effective way to address education and income inequality is to make access to post-secondary education more readily available to everyone. While higher education costs have risen, pursuing a degree is worth the investment. Based on statistics, those with a four-year degree typically make significantly more than those with only a high school diploma. In fact, the Pew Research Center reports that college graduates born after 1980 earn almost $18,000 more per year than their peers who did not go to college (PRC, 2014). Clearly, over a period of an individual's career, the investment in a college degree will pay for itself many times over.

CULTURE NOTE

The Great Recession started with a financial crisis in the United States. Many investment banks had engaged in unethical lending practices that caused the US housing market to crash. The effects were felt throughout the world, and resulted in the worst global economic crisis since World War II, with steep declines in international trade, employment, and housing prices.

B. Answer the questions.

1. What is income inequality? ....

....

2. What are some ways people earn income? ....

....

3. What has happened to income inequality in the United States since the
Great Recession? ....

....

....

4. What is one major cause for the increase in income inequality? ....

....

....

5. Who has been most affected by the changes to the US economy? Why?

....

....

6. What is one possible solution to lessen income inequality in the US?
Why might it be effective? ....

....

....

C. Read the statements. Which are facts and which are implications? List one or more inferences that you can make about each statement. Share your answers with a partner.

1. Income inequality, or the difference in levels between the rich and the poor, has
widened significantly in many developed world economies in the last few decades.

....

2. In fact, since the Great Recession of 2007–2009, income has not grown for the
majority of people except for those at the very top of the income distribution.

....

3. This sizable gap in income distribution makes the US, known for the American
Dream, one of the top countries in the developed world for income inequality.

....

4. While there is some debate as to all the possible causes of income inequality, there is general agreement that technological advancements have without a doubt negatively impacted the American income distribution. ....

....

5. Changes in traditional manufacturing have disproportionately affected workers without high school or college degrees. ....

....

6. While there may be great hope among many mid-skilled workers that new government policies will reverse this trend, the reality is an economy which will probably continue to favor workers who are highly educated and skilled or those who already have wealth. ....

....

D. What inferences can you make about the author's tone in all three paragraphs? Explain.

E. Write a short paragraph about a cause for income inequality in a country you are familiar with. Include at least two implications and underline them. Look back at the material you underlined. What inferences might the reader make about your implications? Why?

VOCABULARY CHECK

A. Review the vocabulary items in the Vocabulary Preview. Write their definitions and add examples. Use a dictionary if necessary.

B. Complete each sentence with the correct vocabulary item.

accessible	assets	attain	disparity	
disproportionate	distribution	manufacturing	pronounced	pursue

1. The company has over $20 million in .... now, but that number will go down after they sell their warehouses.

2. World leaders discussed how to make the .... of money and resources more equal among struggling countries.

3. Over 300 people in the city lost .... jobs because machines can now make the computer parts for a lot less money.

4. There is .... difference in the number of new management jobs and the smaller number of lower-skilled factory jobs.

5. The .... in income is growing wider in many countries, which often leads to problems in housing, education, and other important services.

6. Most people want to .... enough wealth to have a safe and secure life for themselves and their families.

7. There was a .... feeling of worry in the town after a lot people lost their jobs at the factory.

8. The company promised to make training more .... to all their employees, but it is hard to do during normal working hours.

9. He is going to .... a better job so he can make more money and save to buy a house.

⊙ Go to MyEnglishLab to complete vocabulary and skill practices and to join in collaborative activities.

SUPPORTING SKILL 1

INTEGRATING EVIDENCE FROM SOURCES

WHY IT'S USEFUL By integrating evidence from sources, you demonstrate your knowledge about a topic and show that your claims are well supported, adding credibility to your own ideas.

Integrating evidence from sources into a paper can be challenging, but it is required for most scholarly writing. When you combine ideas from sources with your own ideas, your writing becomes much stronger and more effective. Using a variety of relevant and meaningful evidence from different sources ensures that the claims you make are well supported. Evidence can include expert opinion, facts, numerical or statistical data, or visuals from both primary and secondary sources. Make sure that any evidence you include accurately and fairly represents what the source says.

For more on primary and secondary sources, see Business Ethics, Part 1.

There are three basic steps for integrating evidence from sources:

State your claim → Introduce evidence from source(s) → Explain the evidence

First, **state your claim**, which is your position on a topic or a statement of fact. Provide a context for the information you will be using to help the reader follow your reasoning. Before you introduce the evidence, decide how you will integrate it into your writing. There are several ways to do this:

Integrating Evidence	When to Use
<u>Paraphrase</u>: to use your own words to express the same ideas that someone has said or written, but in a different way	to report specific information or details from a short part of a text to support a point
<u>Summary</u>: to use your own words to state the main ideas from a text, without giving all the details	to present background information or a general overview of a topic or argument
<u>Direct quotation</u>: to express the exact words, sentences, or phrases from a text or speech	to report the exact words that a source has said or written when the words are unique or cannot be changed

Use signal phrases to **introduce evidence from sources** and distinguish your ideas from those of the source.

Common signal phrases are:
   According to [author],
   [Author] *states*… (*suggests, explains, argues*, etc.)
   In [title of article], [author] *emphasizes*…

For more on paraphrasing, see Business Ethics, Part 1.

For more on summarizing, see Earth Science, Part 1.

For more on using direct quotations and reported speech, see Business Ethics, Part 1.

After introducing the evidence, it is critical to **explain its significance**. You can do this by analyzing or interpreting the information, explaining how it supports your main claim, or connecting it to other evidence in your paper. Never assume that your reader will understand why you have included specific evidence. A reader may make different assumptions about a topic than you. As a general guideline, for each piece of evidence that you integrate into your paper, you should have approximately the same length of explanation in the text.

For more on using reporting verbs, see Earth Science, Part 1 and Business Ethics, Part 1.

For more on using signal phrases, see Business Ethics, Part 1.

TIP

When checking your work, use different colored highlighters to distinguish between your evidence and explanation throughout the paper. This will help you see if you have introduced evidence accurately and provided sufficient explanation. The more controversial the topic, the more evidence you will need to support your points.

Using another person's words, ideas, or work without stating the source, is considered **plagiarism**. At all US universities and most universities around the world, plagiarism is considered a form of cheating, and often an honor code violation, which can result in anything from a failing grade to academic suspension or even expulsion. Examples of plagiarism include copying a source word-for-word without using quotation marks, replacing just a few words of a text in a paraphrase, and inadequately citing your sources for any material or ideas that come from others. To avoid plagiarizing, make sure you distinguish your ideas from the source using signal phrases and reporting verbs. You must also always include a citation to let the reader know the source of the information. Integrate and cite sources according to the style guidelines your professor requires (e.g., APA [American Psychological Association], MLA [Modern Language Association], CMS [Chicago Manual of Style], IEEE [Institute of Electrical and Electronics Engineers]). Academic disciplines typically have preferred styles, and university departments are usually strict about which style they prefer. Review the style guidelines in the course syllabus or confirm with the instructor before you write your paper.

> **TIP**
>
> Take careful notes when using sources. Never copy and paste text from an online source directly into your paper because you may forget that it has not been paraphrased—keep the material from sources in a separate document and make sure to include the title, author, page number, and date of publication. If you do copy exact phrases or sentences, always put them in quotes so you know which words belong to you and which words belong to the source.

Look at this excerpt from an article in a student paper on income inequality. Notice how the writer has made a claim and introduced the source with a signal phrase. The writer integrates the paraphrased evidence, includes an in-text citation, and then explains the significance of the evidence.

> **TIP**
>
> Writers will often include explanations before making claims and they may not always include evidence for every claim they make.

After this period, income began to grow unequally for Americans at different levels of the income distribution, creating a larger gap in income equality. In fact, since the Great Recession of 2007–2009, income has not grown for the majority of people except for those at the very top of the income distribution. ← writer makes claim

This had a significant impact on family wealth and has created a disparity in American society. The US Congressional Budget Office reports that in 2013, families in the top 10% of the income distribution held 76% of all family wealth, while those families in the bottom 50% held only 1% of the wealth (CBO, 2013). This sizable gap in income distribution makes the US, known for the American Dream, one of the top countries in the developed world for income inequality.

← introduces and cites source material

← signal phrase

← explains significance of source material

EXERCISE 2

A. Read the second paragraph from Exercise 1, Part A. Underline four claims that the writer makes and write possible evidence the writer could include to better support the claims made. Discuss your answers with a partner.

While there is some debate as to all the possible causes of income inequality, there is general agreement that technological advancements have without a doubt negatively impacted the American income distribution. Changes in traditional manufacturing have disproportionately affected workers without high school or college degrees. For example, new technologies that improve automation, using computers and machines instead of people to do a job, have increased demand for jobs requiring strong technical skills, but decreased demand for jobs that typically do not require high levels of education. This loss of mid-skilled jobs has become much more pronounced since 2007. Many of these job losses have been permanent, forcing workers to seek out low-skilled jobs that pay much less. The result has been a growing gap in income equality. While there may be hope among many mid-skilled workers that new government policies will reverse this trend, the reality is an economy which will probably continue to favor workers who are highly educated and skilled or those who already have wealth.

....

....

....

....

B. Read the quoted or paraphrased evidence that the writer is considering including in the paragraph in Part A. Check off two pieces of evidence that will help the writer support two of the claims made. With a partner, discuss why the evidence is appropriate.

Paraphrased and Quoted Evidence	Source Notes
☐ In 2014, the median income in the US was 8% less than in 1999.	*America's Shrinking Middle Class: A Close Look at Changes Within Metropolitan Areas* Pew Research Center, May 11, 2016 http://www.pewsocialtrends. org/2016/05/11/americas-shrinking-middle-class-a-close-look-at-changes-within-metropolitan-areas/
☐ "It is no secret that the past few decades of widening inequality can be summed up as significant income and wealth gains for those at the very top and stagnant living standards for the majority."	US Federal Reserve Chairman Janet Yellen, October 17, 2014

Paraphrased and Quoted Evidence	Source Notes
☐ The loss of mid-skill jobs has resulted in a restructured and divided labor market with opportunities for high-skilled, high-paying jobs on one end, and low-skilled, low-paying jobs on the other.	*Income Inequality in the US (testimony before US Congress), January 2014, p. 3* Melissa Kearney, Associate Professor of Economics, University of Maryland
☐ Employment decreased 16% for people in manufacturing, craft, and repair jobs during the Great Recession.	*The Polarization of Job Opportunities in the US Labor Market, April 2010, p. 4* David Autor, MIT Department of Economics and National Bureau of Economic Research
☐ The increase in gap between those who are highly-skilled and those who are not should be addressed by government policies.	*Income Inequality in the US (testimony before US Congress), January 2014, p. 3* Melissa Kearney, Associate Professor of Economics, University of Maryland

C. Rewrite the paragraph in Part A to include the appropriate evidence from Part B. Introduce the evidence by including a signal phrase or reporting verb and include an in-text citation using the style guide recommended by your professor. Integrate the evidence and explain its significance. Use different color highlighters or text colors to distinguish between the claim, the evidence, and the explanation.

D. PEER REVIEW. Exchange paragraphs with a partner. Respond to the questions to evaluate each other's work. For responses marked No, provide feedback in the Notes column to help your partner revise.

	Yes	No	Notes
Is there a claim with a statement of fact or the writer's position on a topic?	☐	☐	
Does the writer introduce the evidence with a signal phrase?	☐	☐	
Is the evidence paraphrased, summarized, or quoted?	☐	☐	
Is the evidence properly cited?	☐	☐	
Does the writer include an explanation of the evidence?	☐	☐	
Is the explanation sufficient?	☐	☐	

⬥ Go to MyEnglishLab to complete a skill practice.

SUPPORTING SKILL 2

USING HEDGING AND BOOSTING LANGUAGE

WHY IT'S USEFUL By using hedging and boosting language, you soften or strengthen statements in your writing and indicate to your reader how certain and confident you are about your ideas.

In academic writing, there are times you will need to reveal your attitude about your ideas or show your reader how confident you are about the truth of your statements. In order to convince your reader of the credibility of your ideas, you must show that there may be other opinions or points of view, and that you have seriously considered how certain you are about your ideas.

Hedging and **boosting** are communicative strategies for indicating the strength of statements you make in claims or in support of your claims. These two strategies serve the same purpose, but in opposite ways. Hedging reduces the certainty of a claim, while boosting shows the confidence of the writer in the claim. Writers sometimes use both strategies in the same statement to accurately express both an attitude about a statement and their degree of certainty about the point.

> **Hedge**   **Hedge**
> While there is some debate as to all the possible causes of income inequality,
> **Booster**   **Booster**
> there is general agreement that technological advancements have without a doubt
> negatively impacted the American income distribution.

Hedging and boosting can be accomplished in different ways. Adverbs (of frequency, degree of certainty, and generalization), adjectives, nouns, verbs, and modals to express degrees of certainty are commonly used to soften or strengthen statements in academic writing.

Hedging softens a claim and avoids making it seem too strong or direct. Hedging language moderates or tones down assertions and claims and make the writer sound more reasonable. They can be used to lessen the writer's commitment to an idea that may later be proven incorrect or to qualify claims that are not fully supported by evidence and make them more precise. Hedging helps the writer express the validity of a claim in a way that lessens the chance that the reader will dispute or reject the information.

> **TIP**
>
> Hedging and boosting may be used differently depending on the discipline. For example, hedging may be more common in the arts and social sciences than the hard sciences. You may also see cultural differences in their use. For example, in research articles in English, hedging may be more common in the discussion, whereas boosting occurs more often in the conclusion. This may not be true in all cultures.

Hedging Language	Examples
Adverbs of frequency usually, frequently, often, sometimes, occasionally, hardly ever, rarely, seldom	Children who receive quality pre-kindergarten education **usually** graduate from high school at higher rates.
Adverbs of generalization mainly, normally, primarily, generally, typically, fairly, presumably, conceivably, necessarily, roughly, approximately, for the most part, to a great extent, the majority of, except for, apart from	Between the late 1940s and 1970s, income grew at **fairly** equal percentages for all Americans. Since the Great Recession of 2007–2009, income has not grown for **the majority of** people **except for** those at the very top of the income distribution.
Adverbs of certainty arguably, probably, likely, theoretically, possibly, maybe, perhaps, primarily, relatively, roughly, somewhat, less / least (likely), unlikely	… the reality is an economy which will **probably** continue to favor workers who are highly educated and skilled and the people who already have wealth.
Verbs seem, tend, look like, appear (to be). based on, think, believe, doubt, indicate, suggest, claim, assume, speculate, propose, estimate (verb + adverb = seems likely)	The income gap **appears** to be widening. Economists **speculate** the gap will not close any time soon.
Nouns probability, possibility, assumption, estimate, likelihood, (to my) knowledge, (in) most cases	The **likelihood** of an increase in poverty rates due to the widening gap **seems likely based on** research done by the government. The **assumption** that the "American Dream" exists may be in question given the reality of income inequality.
Adjectives likely, probable, possible, difficult, doubtful, less (certain), uncertain, unclear, unconfirmed, unreliable, vague, ambiguous	There is some debate as to all the **possible** causes of income inequality.
Modals may, might, can, could, would	While there **may** be great hope among many unskilled workers that new government policies will reverse this trend, …

Boosting language strengthens a claim. It is used to present a strong point of view and show the writer's confidence and commitment to the ideas by emphasizing or increasing the importance of an idea. Boosting is a persuasive strategy. It is often used to mark a point and show its acceptance among members of a shared community such as an academic discipline.

Boosting Language	Examples
Adverbs of frequency always, often, never, normally	A gap in income equality has **always** existed in the United States.
Adverbs of certainty absolutely, certainly, clearly, conclusively, definitely, easily, especially, evidently, frequently, likely, largely, more/most / much, naturally, notably, obviously, of course, particularly, significantly, undoubtedly, unquestionably	Income inequality has widened **significantly** in many developed world economies in the last few decades.
Verbs show, prove, demonstrate	Research **shows** that workers with a higher level of education are more likely to earn a higher wage.
Nouns certainty, conviction, assurance, proof, evidence, significance, there is no doubt that/without a doubt	There is general agreement that new manufacturing technologies have **without a doubt** negatively impacted the American income distribution.
Adjectives accurate, certain, clear, conclusive, definite, effective, essential, evident, interesting, noteworthy, obvious, positive, significant, true, useful, valid, sure, confident	This had a **significant** impact on family wealth and has created a disparity in American society.
Modals will, must, can, should	... the reality is an economy which **will** probably continue to favor workers who are highly educated and skilled and the people who already have wealth.

EXERCISE 3

A. Read the excerpt from the student paper on income inequality. Circle the six hedges and underline the nine boosters. With a partner, discuss other choices of hedges and boosters to replace those in the text.

What can we do to lessen income inequality? If one probable cause of income inequality is workers' lack of education, then a possible solution is to provide more opportunities to attain a level of education high enough to afford work that will help future workers achieve upward social mobility. According to economic policy analysis specialist Nicholas Parker, research shows that workers with a higher level of education are more likely to earn a higher wage (Parker, 2014). For this reason, it is critical to make education more accessible to those in the lower income distribution levels. One way to lessen the gap is continued efforts to get children off to a good start through early education programs. There is research to suggest that children who receive quality pre-kindergarten education should graduate from high school at higher rates and may frequently go on to attend college. Another effective way to address education and income inequality is to make access to post-secondary education more readily available to everyone. While higher education costs have risen, pursuing a degree is worth the investment. Based on statistics, those with a four-year degree typically make significantly more than those with only a high school diploma. In fact, the Pew Research Center reports that college graduates born after 1980 earn almost $18,000 more per year (PRC, 2014) than their peers who did not go to college. Clearly, over a period of an individual's career, the investment in a college degree will pay for itself many times over.

B. Rewrite each statement about income equality in two ways. Add a booster to strengthen the statement, and then add a hedge to soften the statement.

1. The earnings gap between college and high school graduates has increased over the past three decades. ....

....

....

2. Higher income for the top wage earners has contributed to income inequality.

....

....

3. A decline in income for lower earners has contributed more. ....

....

....

4. The decline in the real value of the US minimum wage is another cause of income inequality. ....

....

....

5. There have been fewer opportunities for employment in production as a result of automation. ....

....

....

6. A cause of income inequality is the loss of bargaining power of US labor unions.

....

....

C. In Exercise 1, Part D, you wrote a paragraph about a cause for income inequality in a country you are familiar with. Write a paragraph about the effects of income inequality for that cause. Use hedges to soften some of your supporting ideas and boosters to strengthen others.

D. PEER REVIEW. Exchange your paragraph with a partner. Respond to the questions to evaluate each other's work. For responses marked No, provide feedback in the Notes column to help your partner revise.

	Yes	No	Notes
Does the paragraph have both hedges and boosters?	☐	☐	
What boosting strategies were used in the paragraph?	☐	☐	
Were they effective in showing the writer's certainty about the statements?	☐	☐	
What hedging language was used in the paragraph?	☐	☐	
Did it effectively soften the statements?	☐	☐	
Is there a place where the writer should have hedged or boosted a statement?	☐	☐	
Was the paragraph credible?	☐	☐	

○ Go to MyEnglishLab to complete a skill practice.

INTEGRATED SKILLS

UNDERSTANDING AND RESPONDING TO IMPLICATION AND INFERENCE

WHY IT'S USEFUL By understanding and responding to implication and inference in the sources you use in your writing, you will be able to accurately incorporate evidence into your paper to support your ideas and fairly represent the meaning intended by the source.

When critically reading source material for evidence to integrate into your writing, it is important to understand the writer's intended meaning. In your sources, you will find direct statements of fact and opinion, as well as ideas that are not stated directly, which can be both **implications** and **inferences**. By reading carefully and developing the ability to understand both implied meaning and inferences you will be able to reach your own conclusions, which will form the basis of the ideas you include as support in your writing.

Critical readers understand that the meaning is not in the text alone, but rather in their relationship to the text. Readers construct meaning based on **evidence in the text** combined with their **knowledge**, **experience**, and **values**. They know that their understanding of the text is often influenced by **assumptions**, or pre-supposed beliefs they accept as true, that influence how they understand the text.

Good readers read ideas as more than just the words on the page. When the writer and reader share knowledge and experience, it is more likely that the reader will understand the text, including the writer's **implications**, and be able to make **strong inferences**— those that are well-supported by the author's ideas and evidence in the text, and by logic. Readers who bring more knowledge and experience depend less on the text for meaning than readers with little or no background on the topic. A reader with less shared knowledge must be aware of this and self-monitor to avoid making weak or inaccurate inferences and assuming that the writer implied an idea when that is not the case, which can lead to misunderstanding.

Making strong inferences will help you understand the ideas presented in a text and choose specific evidence or support for your own ideas when you write. Inferences are educated guesses, so inferring usually brings uncertainty. Consider the intended purpose of the text but also your reason for reading the text. Consider not only what is said, but also what is not said and why. Writers can make implications by what they don't say. Then make inferences consistent with your knowledge and experience, but based on evidence you find in the text.

To understand implications and inferences:

- Consider the author's purpose and intent.
- Consider the evidence in the text.
- Use rhetorical clues in the reading—rhetorical devices and language used to introduce ideas.
- Pay attention to hedges and boosters to determine the writer's attitude toward and degree of certainty about the ideas.
- Consider tone by looking at word choices (positive or negative) and details included.
- Examine your assumptions.
- Apply your knowledge and experience.

When you integrate information that you have inferred from a source into your writing, whether you quote or paraphrase, respond appropriately and fairly by being as accurate and clear as possible in how you represent the original author's intended meaning.

Be cautious when incorporating ideas you have inferred as evidence. Readers can infer things the author did not imply. Writers can imply things the reader does not infer. Consider this statement from the third paragraph in "The Widening Gap in Income Equality":

> While higher education costs have risen, pursuing a degree is worth the investment.

You can infer from this that the writer believes that getting a college education will help a worker get a better salary despite the fact that it is more expensive now than in the past. However, you cannot infer that everyone should get a college education. Not everyone wants or feels the need to earn a high salary and some people simply do not want to pursue a college education. If you incorporated this idea in your paper and stated that the author believes that even though it is expensive, everyone should get a college education, you would <u>not</u> be representing the writer's intent. Additionally, if you stated that having a college education will solve the problem of income inequality or close the income equality gap, this would not be accurate either. That statement would draw a conclusion that the original author did not state or even imply.

For more on identifying reliable sources of information, see Business Ethics, Part 1.

VOCABULARY PREVIEW
Read the vocabulary items. Circle the ones you know. Put a question mark next to the ones you don't know.

capitalism	inspired	dominated	acquisition	subordinated
obligation	imperative	tenets	pursuit	doomed

EXERCISE 4

A. Read the critique of *The Protestant Ethic and the Spirit of Capitalism.*

The Protestant Ethic and the Spirit of Capitalism

reviewed by Jonathan D. Hart

CULTURE NOTE

Max Weber was a 19th century sociologist who is considered one of the founders of modern sociology. Weber was born in Germany in 1864. He was a professor, but suffered from depression and anxiety for much of his life, which eventually ended his teaching career and left him unable to work for five years. His most well-known book, *The Protestant Ethic and the Spirit of Capitalism*, was published in 1905. He later published three additional books about other religions but never completed the series as he intended due to his death in 1920 from the Spanish Influenza.

1   In his 1904 book *The Protestant Ethic and the Spirit of Capitalism*, sociologist Max Weber explores the intersection of capitalism and religion. Weber questioned why people might behave the way they do in a society, and in turn, how the beliefs of a society influence people's behavior. These questions are key in the study of sociology. Weber's focus in this book is on economic sociology, which explores societal behavior and economic structure. In America's capitalistic culture, current business ethics encourage maximization of profits. The roots of this ethic, according to Weber, are in Protestant ethics, which influenced and indeed inspired capitalism.

2   The central claim of Weber's 1904 book is that there is a link between Protestant ethics and the development of Western capitalism. In his book, Weber first defines the "spirit" of capitalism. He believed that Western capitalism had a particular mindset, or attitude, that differed from the type of capitalism that had developed in other parts of the world. In true capitalism— according to Weber—money itself was not the reward. The material items a person could buy with wealth did not matter as much as the actual process of acquiring wealth. In a capitalistic society, Weber writes, "Man is dominated by the making of money, by acquisition as the ultimate purpose of his life. Economic acquisition is no longer subordinated to man as the means for the satisfaction of his material needs." What Weber means by this is that people did not regard making money as something they needed to do simply to pay the bills. Rather, Weber believed individuals felt a moral obligation to work toward acquiring money. This effort to constantly maximize profit is behind the spirit of capitalism.

(Continued)

3   The moral imperative to acquire wealth resulted, at least in part, from Protestant beliefs, according to Weber. Protestantism is a type of Christianity that began in 16th-century Europe after the Middle Ages. Protestant denominations, or religious groups, included Calvinists. At the time, Protestants, and in particular Calvinists, believed that doing their job was a moral and religious duty, unlike in the Middle Ages, when little importance was placed on worldly activities, including work. Calvinists also believed their fate was predestined, and whether they were saved, delivered from sin or evil, or not was decided by God before they were born. Weber suggested that people would, therefore, search for evidence in their lives to try to determine if they had been saved. While Calvinists did not believe that having money and working hard could save them, material wealth that resulted from hard work could be taken as a sign that they would be. Weber believed wealth was evidence, and the ideas he presents in his book about capitalism are based on this belief.

4   Weber argues that Protestant-inspired capitalism arose in contrast to a type of work behavior that he defines as "traditionalism." Traditionalism, according to Weber, occurs among "backward" people, and it is in conflict with capitalism because it is contrary to an ideal work ethic. What Weber means by traditionalism is the idea that a person works only in order to meet their basic needs. Read the passage from Weber's book describing this type of worker. "[The worker] did not ask: how much can I earn in a day if I do as much work as possible? but: how much must I work in order to earn the wage … which takes care of my traditional needs?" Weber saw the move away from traditionalism toward Puritan work ethics as a "favorable foundation" for a capitalistic work ethic.

> **CULTURE NOTE**
>
> The Protestant work ethic, also referred to as the Calvinist or Puritan work ethic, is the concept or idea that hard work, diligence, and attitudes about money come from belief in the values of the Protestant faith, particularly in Calvinism. This is in contrast to the beliefs of the Catholic faith, which does not mention work but rather focuses on confession of sins and forgiveness, as well as living simply and serving the poor and suffering. Nowadays, this work ethic is not always associated with religious beliefs. The phrase "Protestant work ethic" was initially coined by Max Weber in *The Protestant Ethic and the Spirit of Capitalism*.

5   Some modern business ethicists are wary of the ethical implications of Weber's argument. In an early passage in the book, Weber clarifies one of the basic tenets of capitalism, which is to constantly seek profit. "[But] capitalism is identical with the pursuit of profit, and forever renewed profit, by means of continuous, rational, capitalistic enterprise. For it must be so: in a wholly capitalistic order of society, an individual capitalistic enterprise which did not take advantage of its opportunities for profit-making would be doomed to extinction." If pursuing profit is the main goal, ethicists point out, other ethical obligations might be ignored. In fact, the pursuit of wealth without an ethical code may lead to exactly the kind of economic market collapse that occurred in 2008.

6 Weber's conclusions are far from being universally accepted. Many economists and sociologists have argued that Protestantism could not have been the main reason—or even a strong reason—capitalism emerged. Some argue against Weber's cause and effect link between Protestantism and capitalism by pointing to early forms of capitalism that developed before Protestantism existed, such as in the Netherlands, which had a diversified economy based on free markets in both goods and production before other European countries. Some also cite Protestant cultures in which capitalism may not have arisen, such as Scotland in the 17th century. Nevertheless, Weber's hypothesis still has supporters, and his ideas on capitalism are an important topic of discussion in business courses today. Some scholars who adhere to his ideas argue that protestant-inspired ethics may indeed have been a motivating force behind the development of capitalism.

Glossary

Calvinism: the Christian religious teachings of John Calvin, which are based on the idea that events on Earth are controlled by God

Backward: moving away from something; into the past; not making progress

B. Answer the questions.

1. What two topics does Max Weber's economic sociology book explore?

2. What is today's business ethic in US capitalist culture? What does Weber believe are the roots of this ethic?

3. What is the central claim of *The Protestant Ethic and the Spirit of Capitalism*?

4. What is the spirit of capitalism as defined by Max Weber?

5. Where does Weber believe the moral imperative to acquire wealth comes from?

6. What is *fate* for a Calvinist? ....
....
....

7. What was traditionalism according to Weber and how did it differ from Calvinism? ....
....
....
....

8. What do modern business ethicists pose as an ethical concern about Weber's ideas? What example is given as evidence? ....
....
....

9. What do those who disagree with Weber offer as two counterarguments? What is one example they suggest as evidence for each? ....
....
....
....
....

C. Answer the questions. First consider what you bring to the text, and then what is implied or can be inferred from the text based on evidence.

1. What is the author Jonathan D. Hart's purpose? ....
....
....

2. What do you know about Max Weber? What do you know about the book, *The Protestant Ethic and the Spirit of Capitalism*? ....
....
....

3. What is your knowledge or experience of Protestant or Puritan ethics? Calvinism?
....
....

4. What is your knowledge or experience of capitalism? ....
....
....

5. What are your beliefs and values with regard to a work ethic and acquiring wealth?

....

....

6. Weber is quoted as saying, "Man is dominated by the making of money, by acquisition as the ultimate purpose of his life. Economic acquisition is no longer subordinated to man as the means for the satisfaction of his material needs."

   What does the author of the critique infer from this? Find evidence in the critique to support your opinion. ....

   ....

   ....

7. Weber also said, "But capitalism is identical with the pursuit of profit, and forever renewed profit, by means of continuous, rational, capitalistic enterprise. For it must be so: in a wholly capitalistic order of society, an individual capitalistic enterprise which did not take advantage of its opportunities for profit-making would be doomed to extinction."

   What is the implication of this statement? Find evidence in the critique to support your opinion. ....

   ....

   ....

8. What can you infer about the author's opinion of Weber's ideas about capitalism? Support your inference with evidence from the critique. ....

   ....

   ....

D. Compare your answers in Part C with a partner. Discuss the knowledge and experience you brought to the reading and strategies you used to understand the implications and inferences. Then find and discuss at least one other possible inference that the author of the critique made about Weber's ideas.

E. Write a paragraph in which you agree or disagree with Max Weber's ideas about capitalism. Include as support for your position some of the inferences that the author of the critique made about Weber's ideas.

VOCABULARY CHECK

A. Review the vocabulary items in the Vocabulary Preview. Write their definitions and add examples. Use a dictionary if necessary.

B. Choose the sentence that correctly describes the underlined item.

1. Many people believe that <u>capitalism</u> is good for everyone because it gives people more freedom.
   a. Private business owners can make many decisions without government involvement.
   b. Private business owners like to keep their companies small so the companies are easier to manage.

2. The number one priority of our company this year is the <u>pursuit</u> of the top college graduates to staff the new division.
   a. We hired ten people to go to colleges all over the country and interviewed the best students in the five top schools. ˙
   b. We hope that the best students in the top five schools apply for jobs with us because they will help us to make more money this year.

3. Many people were surprised at the company's <u>acquisition</u> of three new factories since business has been bad.
   a. The president is going to make the factories bigger so they can make more products.
   b. The president bought the factories because she wants to start making new products.

4. Companies should have a moral <u>imperative</u> to treat their workers with fairness and respect.
   a. Good company leaders think it is very important to treat people well.
   b. Good company leaders fire people who do not treat them well.

5. Being honest with our customers is a basic <u>tenet</u> of our company's policies.
   a. We strongly believe that honesty is the guiding principle in our company.
   b. We hope that all of our employees will be honest with our customers.

6. Keeping the environment safe should never be <u>subordinated</u> to making a profit in any company.
   a. It is extremely difficult to keep the environment safe. Profit will be lost.
   b. It is extremely important to keep the environment safe. Profit is secondary.

7. The meeting about chemical waste <u>inspired</u> the CEO to change his company's policies to make the policies better for the environment.

   a. It is a complicated subject and he wants to do more research.

   b. He learned a lot and is excited about making positive changes.

8. That department is not running well because it is <u>dominated</u> by Jane and Alex, who are always fighting.

   a. The group doesn't get work done because everybody is worried about the arguments.

   b. The group disagrees with the issues Jane and Alex are fighting about.

9. Managers feel an equal <u>obligation</u> to work hard for their departments and for the company as a whole even if it is difficult.

   a. Managers must do the best thing for everyone even if it is difficult.

   b. Managers have to decide whether to do the best thing for everyone even if it is difficult.

10. The new policies are <u>doomed</u> because they will be very expensive.

   a. The policies will cost a lot of money.

   b. The policies are not going to work.

Go to MyEnglishLab to complete vocabulary and skill practices and to join in collaborative activities.

LANGUAGE SKILL
USING MODALS TO EXPRESS DEGREES OF CERTAINTY

WHY IT'S USEFUL By using modals, you can express degrees of certainty about the evidence you provide in support of your ideas, which can soften or strengthen your views.

Go to MyEnglishLab for the Language Skill presentation and practice.

VOCABULARY STRATEGY
USING A THESAURUS

> **WHY IT'S USEFUL** By using a thesaurus, you learn synonyms, helping you to make more accurate and interesting word choices in your writing. A thesaurus will help you build your vocabulary and achieve a higher quality of writing.

Academic writing can be challenging because the language is more formal and precise than other types of writing and everyday conversation. Word choices must be appropriate for the context, and they should help the reader understand the content as easily as possible. A **thesaurus** is a valuable resource for helping even very advanced or native English speakers choose the best words for expressing ideas clearly and concisely. In a thesaurus, common words are put into groups with other words that have similar meanings, or synonyms. However, words may have slight differences in meaning depending on the context, usage, and how formal or informal the synonym is.

A good English language learner thesaurus can be especially helpful if you know that you are overusing a word, or including too many simple words in your writing. Synonyms typically have slight differences in meaning, and sometimes specific connotations (something a word implies), so it is important that you understand how a word is used in a specific context. A thesaurus shows a list of possible synonyms, their definitions, and example sentences to help you choose the most appropriate word. It may include antonyms (words opposite in meaning) and relevant grammar notes to help you choose the best structure or verb tense so you can use the words correctly. Choosing more precise synonyms will make your descriptions more engaging, explanations more accurate, and ideas more clear.

> **TIP**
>
> Some thesauruses include a topic vocabulary section, which shows all the vocabulary you need to know to write about specific topics such as the Environment, Government and Politics, Jobs and Work, or Science and Technology.

Read the entry for the word *hard-working* in Longman's *Thesaurus of American English.*

---

hard-working /ˌhɑːdˈwɔːkɪŋ/ *adjective*

hard-working
using a lot of effort and spending a lot of time on the work you do: *She is a very hard-working student who gets good grades.*

industrious (formal)
using a lot of energy and effort in your work, spending a lot of time working, and getting a lot of work done: *An industrious couple from Korea run the store by themselves.*

dedicated
working very hard at something because you care about it a lot: *The teachers here are very dedicated, and every one of them wants to help students do their best.*

> **diligent**
> working hard and being very careful to do your work correctly: *Be diligent in doing your exercises, and your muscles will become stronger.*
>
> **disciplined**
> organizing your time and making yourself work even when you do not really want to: *Disciplined students always turn their assignments in on time.*
>
> **productive**
> working hard and producing or achieving a lot: *The workers became more productive when they worked as a team.*

From the entry for *hard-working*, notice the slight differences in meaning for the words *industrious, dedicated, diligent, disciplined,* and *productive*. Which word(s) might you choose if you were writing an academic paper on Weber's Protestant work ethic? Why?

TIP

Always make sure you read the entry for each synonym carefully to understand the subtle differences between words. If you choose too many incorrect synonyms, your writing will be awkward and ineffective.

EXERCISE 5

A. Read the thesaurus entry for the word *basic*. Answer the questions.

> **basic** /'beɪsɪk/ *adjective*
>
> **basic**
> simple and more important or necessary than anything else: *The army is bringing water and other basic supplies to the towns that were destroyed by the flood.* | *One basic rule of English grammar is that an adjective usually goes before a noun: a red car.*
>
> **fundamental** [AWL]
> relating to the most basic and important parts of something, which everything depends on: *Reading is a fundamental skill that children must have in order to succeed in school.*
>
> **essential**
> relating to the most basic part or quality of something, which makes it what it is and makes it different from other things: *The essential difference between the human brain and a computer is the ability to feel emotions.*
>
> • GRAMMAR when used with this meaning, essential is always used before a noun: *Helping children to talk about their feelings is an essential part of what we do.*
>
> **elementary** (formal)
> relating to the most basic ideas in a subject: *Using a computer has become an elementary skill to most jobs.* | *The class was in elementary biology.*
>
> **underlying** [AWL]
> an underlying cause or problem is the basic reason that something happens or exists: *When you are sick, doctors must find the underlying cause for your illness, for example being stressed or not eating well.*
>
> • GRAMMAR: underlying is always used before a noun: *Engineers are working to fix the underlying problem.*

> **inherent** (formal) AWL
> a quality or feature that is inherent in something is a basic and permanent part of it so that it cannot be changed: *One of the dangers inherent in having only one political party is that there is likely to be corruption.*
>
> **intrinsic** (formal) AWL
> an intrinsic quality is part of someone or something's basic character: *Technology has become an intrinsic part of life in the Western world.*

1. Circle the synonyms that are in the Academic Word List. How do you know they are on the list? Why are these words important to learn? ....

   ....

2. What important grammar feature did you learn about the words *essential* and *underlying*? ....

   ....

   ....

3. Which words would you most likely use to describe a value that is part of a specific culture? Why? ....

   ....

4. Which word would you most likely use to talk about the Protestant work ethic that describes US capitalistic culture? Why? ....

   ....

   ....

B. Choose four synonyms for the word *basic* that you could use in the unit assignment. Write an original sentence for each on a topic connected to this unit.

1. ....

   ....

2. ....

   ....

3. ....

   ....

4. ....

   ....

C. Share your sentences with a partner and discuss why the words are appropriate for the context of the assignment. What new information did you learn about the words? In what other contexts might you use them?

⊙ Go to MyEnglishLab to complete a skill practice.

APPLY YOUR SKILLS

WHY IT'S USEFUL By applying the skills you have learned in this unit, you can successfully integrate evidence from sources, use language for hedging and boosting, understand and respond to implications and inferences, use modals to express degrees of certainty, and use a thesaurus to build your vocabulary.

ASSIGNMENT

Write a paper of 800–1000 words that addresses one aspect of culture that influences economies and draw a conclusion about what the effect of that influence is. Support your ideas with evidence from sources. Use boosting as appropriate to strengthen your claims and hedging to avoid overstating or exaggerating them. Use modals to express degrees of certainty about your claims.

BEFORE YOU WRITE

A. Before you begin your assignment, discuss these questions with one or more students.

1. How is culture reflected in the institutions of a society—government, education, and religion? The activities of people—work and leisure?

2. How does culture affect economic growth or development of a country? Are there specific beliefs, values, or attitudes that influence economic outcomes? What are they? How do these aspects influence economies?

3. Which cultural aspect do you think has the greatest influence on an economy in a country you are familiar with? Why?

B. As you consider your writing assignment, complete the tasks. Then share your ideas with another student. Get feedback and revise your ideas if necessary.

1. List the aspect of culture you have chosen to write about. Why did you choose it?

   ....

   ....

2. Describe this aspect and the role it has on economic growth or development. What conclusion can you draw about its effect on an economy?

   ....

   ....

3. What gaps in information do you have about this topic? What do you need to learn more about? Where could you look for more information on this topic?

   ....

   ....

C. Review the Unit Skills Summary. As you begin on the writing task on page 243, apply the skills you learned in this unit.

UNIT SKILLS SUMMARY

Integrate evidence from sources

- State your claim.
- Introduce evidence from sources with signal phrases.
- Explain the significance of the evidence.
- Avoid plagiarism by distinguishing your ideas from the source and citing sources accurately.

Use hedging and boosting language

- Use hedging and boosting to indicate your degree of certainty and attitude about your claims.
- Use hedges to reduce the certainty or soften your claim.
- Use boosters to indicate your level of confidence and strengthen your claims.
- Use adverbs, adjectives, nouns, verbs, and modals to hedge or boost your claims.

Understand and respond to implication and inference

- Make strong inferences by considering the author's purpose, the evidence presented, and the tone of the text.
- Use rhetorical and language clues to understand implications and inferences in a text.
- Examine your assumptions and apply your knowledge and experience.
- Be accurate when you integrate information inferred from sources to represent the original author's intended meaning.

Use modals to express degrees of certainty

- Modals are auxiliaries used with verbs.
- Modals express two types of meaning—personal and logical.
- In academic writing, modals most often express logical meanings.
- Modals are used to express degrees of certainty about ideas in the present, future, and past.

Use a thesaurus

- Identify synonyms to make more appropriate word choices.
- Understand slight differences in meaning between synonyms to make your writing more precise.
- Understand how a word is used in a specific context.

THINKING CRITICALLY

As you consider your writing assignment, discuss the questions with another student. Get feedback and revise your ideas if necessary.

1. Many businesses now operate in many different countries around the world (globalization). With this increase in globalization, is the cultural aspect you are writing about changing? How?

2. What role will this cultural aspect have on economies one year from now? Twenty-five years from now?

3. Is it important to the global economy to lessen the income gap between developed and developing countries? What are the challenges to addressing income inequality in the coming decades?

THINKING VISUALLY

A. Look at this graph showing US trends in family wealth from 1989–2013. Discuss the questions with a partner.

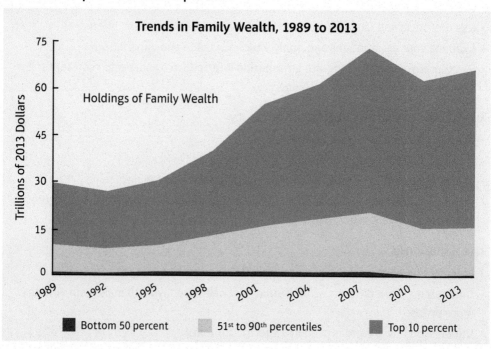

Trends in Family Wealth, 1989 to 2013

Trillions of 2013 Dollars

Holdings of Family Wealth

■ Bottom 50 percent   ■ 51st to 90th percentiles   ■ Top 10 percent

1. What information does this graph give you?
2. Is the graph effective in understanding the difference in wealth distribution between the top 10 percent and families in the 51st to 90th percentiles? The bottom 50 percent?
3. Write two or three sentences describing the graph.

B. Find (or create) a visual that provides information relevant to the cultural aspect you are writing about. For example, a paper on jobs lost to automation might include a visual with the number of workers in different jobs 25 years ago contrasted to the number of workers in the same types of jobs today. Include a citation for this source.

Citation:

THINKING ABOUT LANGUAGE

Write five or more claims for your paper. Use a modal in each statement to hedge or boost the claim by indicating the degree of certainty about the claim.

1. ....
   ....

2. ....
   ....

3. ....
   ....

4. ....
   ....

5. ....
   ....

WRITE

A. Revisit the writing assignment and your answers to the questions in Before You Write, Part B. Make sure all of the evidence you find supports your ideas.

B. Explain the significance of the evidence and cite it correctly to avoid plagiarism. Write the citations here. ....
   ....
   ....
   ....

C. Write your paper. Think about the many ways that culture and economies are connected. Be sure to use boosting, hedging, and modals correctly to accurately state your claims and express degrees of certainty.

BEYOND THE ASSIGNMENT

Write a research paper of 5–8 pages on economic inequality in a country you are familiar with. Include factors that impact economic inequality and ways that it is being addressed. Support your ideas with evidence from sources. Use boosting as appropriate to strengthen your claims and hedging to avoid overstating or exaggerating them. Use modals to express degrees of certainty about your claims.

Go to MyEnglishLab to watch Dr. McLennan's concluding video and to complete a self-assessment.

EARTH SCIENCE

Process Writing

UNIT PROFILE

Having access to sufficient and nutritious food, or food security, is a concern for millions of people worldwide. In this unit, you will read and write about food security and how it is affected by climate change. Specifically, you will learn about vulnerable populations and regions of the world, how extreme weather events lead to food insecurity, and how different strategies can protect against food insecurity.

OUTCOMES

• Organize a process
• Support a process with visuals
• Synthesize information from sources
• Use passive voice in scientific writing
• Build discipline-specific vocabulary

Write a process paper of 800–1000 words explaining one way to lessen food insecurity.
Include a visual as part of your support. Synthesize information from at least two sources. Use appropriate citation format for *all* your sources. Focus attention on the process by using the passive voice.

For more about **EARTH SCIENCE**, see ❶ ❸. See also [R] and [OC] **EARTH SCIENCE** ❶ ❷ ❸.

GETTING STARTED

⬆ Go to My**English**Lab to watch Dr. Osborne's introductory video and to complete
a self-assessment.

Discuss these questions with a partner or group.

1. Do you think we will run out of food at some time in the future? What are some
   contributing factors to food shortages related to climate change? What are some
   factors that are not related to climate change? What can we do as individuals to
   ensure that we all have enough food in the future?

2. How can we feed an ever-growing population on Earth? How can countries
   help each other to deal with this issue? Should there be an effort to create global
   policies on food security?

3. Dr. Osborne suggests that food security rests on three pillars: availability—how
   much food we are producing; access - how much of that food can people get; and
   nutrition—how healthy is the food we are making. Does one seem more important
   than the others? If so, which one and why? Which might be the greatest problem
   in the future?

CRITICAL THINKING SKILL

PROCESS WRITING

> **WHY IT'S USEFUL** By describing a process, presenting the actions in an organized and
> logical order, you give your reader detailed steps showing how to do something.

Process writing explains or describes the series of actions that are required or were
done in order to achieve a particular result. Process writing is an essential organizational
pattern in most academic disciplines, especially in science, technology, and business.

Process writing is used for different purposes.
When the purpose is to **instruct** someone on how to
do something, short clear steps using direct
commands (imperatives) works best. The goal is for
the reader to be able to recreate the steps in the
process to achieve an end result. This might occur in
science or other fields to describe a procedure the
reader must follow to conduct an experiment or
accomplish something in research.

When the purpose is to **inform**, such as what
a writer would do to explain or analyze how
something more complex works or how something

> **TIP**
>
> Process writing is common in many
> areas of academic work. It is used
> in fields like Linguistics to explain
> how new words enter a language.
> In Business, it could suggest how a
> company addresses its responsibility
> to society. In sciences such as Earth
> Science, it can be used to describe
> how climate change affects food
> security, or in Materials Engineering
> to describe how the properties
> of a substance contribute to its
> effectiveness in various applications.

might have happened, more detail is required to fully explain the process. This type of process writing helps the reader learn about the process and understand it, not recreate it. In academic writing, process writing is most often used to inform. Look at the chart.

Process	To instruct	To inform
Description	Clear, easy-to-follow steps Imperatives Illustrations that demonstrate how to do the steps	Clear steps, but with more details and description, examples and analysis 3rd person Illustrations to help explain steps in the process
Purpose	To teach how to do something To recreate process	To describe and explain how something is/was done or happened To understand process
Examples	How to analyze a sample How to map a region	How the 6th mass extinction will happen How drought affects food security

Whether to instruct or to inform, to provide clear and accurate information, including examples, it is important to **organize a process** in a logical order that helps the reader fully understand the series of actions that lead to a particular result. **Supporting a process with visuals** helps the reader see the steps that are required to achieve an end result.

VOCABULARY PREVIEW

Read the vocabulary items. Circle the ones you know. Put a question mark next to the ones you don't know.

fragile	prone	potential	insecurity	malnutrition
vulnerable	livelihood	consumption	susceptible	starvation

EXERCISE 1

A. Read the assignment.

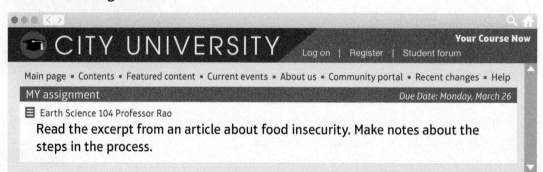

CITY UNIVERSITY

Your Course Now

Log on | Register | Student forum

Main page ▪ Contents ▪ Featured content ▪ Current events ▪ About us ▪ Community portal ▪ Recent changes ▪ Help

MY assignment   Due Date: Monday, March 26

Earth Science 104 Professor Rao

Read the excerpt from an article about food insecurity. Make notes about the steps in the process.

How climate change affects food security

1   Climate change is already putting millions of lives at risk and will continue to do so in the future. People living in fragile environments prone to weather hazards are affected most by climate change. The majority of the world's hungry people live in such areas, with the poor—especially women and children—being the most likely to suffer. When a climate disaster occurs in such an area, it can quickly become a crisis.

2   One of the impacts of more frequent and severe weather due to climate change is a potential increase in food insecurity brought about by a series of steps that result in increasing numbers of people suffering from malnutrition. How does this happen? First, a climate disaster such as severe drought or flooding occurs. We most often see these disasters in areas where the most vulnerable populations, or those least able to adapt, live. The climate disaster then causes loss of life and livelihood and damage to homes, land, crops, and food supplies. Next, as people struggle to just survive, they eat less, lose the tools they need to maintain a livelihood—either because the tools have been lost or have to be sold—and children are not able to attend school. When critical food shortages lead to poor nutrition, the situation becomes a full-blown crisis, with malnutrition becoming widespread as a result of reduced food consumption and less dietary diversity. Children, for example, who are most susceptible to malnutrition, experience stunted growth, a potential for wasting, and even starvation and death. Finally, the disaster results in a population that is much less able to adapt when another climate disaster occurs. The long-term results, in addition to a physically and emotionally weakened population, include having a poorly educated population with a potential loss of a generation or more of the scientists, engineers, and doctors needed to help people deal with the effects of climate change. Look at the graphic.

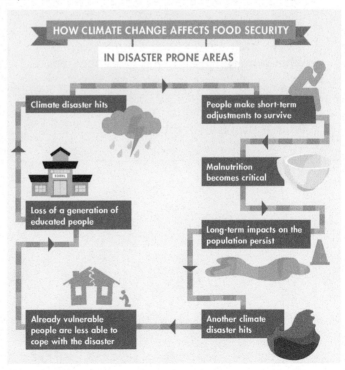

HOW CLIMATE CHANGE AFFECTS FOOD SECURITY

IN DISASTER PRONE AREAS

Climate disaster hits

People make short-term adjustments to survive

Malnutrition becomes critical

Loss of a generation of educated people

Long-term impacts on the population persist

Already vulnerable people are less able to cope with the disaster

Another climate disaster hits

B. Answer the questions.

1. What is the purpose of the first paragraph? ....

....

2. What is the main idea of the second paragraph? ....

....

3. What is the purpose of the second paragraph? ....

....

4. What details are provided to help the reader understand the process? ....

....

5. What example is given? ....

....

6. What words are used to introduce the steps? ....

....

7. What is the result of this process? ....

....

C. List the steps in the process in Paragraph 2 in Part A. Discuss your answers with a partner.

1.	
2.	
3.	
4.	
5.	
6.	

D. Look at the illustration of the process described in Part A and answer the questions.

1. Does the illustration fit your steps in Part C?

2. Are the illustrations in the visual effective in showing the steps?

3. Is the visual helpful in understanding the process?

4. Is there anything you would add to the visual to make it more effective?

5. Is there a better visual to accomplish this?

E. Find a process describing how a climate change event has affected an area. Explain the process and discuss it with your partner. Write notes to guide the discussion. Include a list of the steps in the process and a brief explanation of each step.

VOCABULARY CHECK

A. Review the vocabulary items in the Vocabulary Preview. Write their definitions and add examples. Use a dictionary if necessary.

B. Choose the sentence that correctly describes the underlined item.

1. We have to do all we can to protect fragile environments. Pollution, climate change, and other problems can have deadly effects.

   a. People, animals, and plants are at risk if there isn't enough space around them.

   b. People, animals, and plants are at risk if the space around them is unhealthy.

(Continued)

2. Some areas are more <u>prone</u> than others to be affected by major changes in weather patterns.

   a. The people who live in these areas are always surprised by the problems caused by the changes in weather.

   b. The people who live in these areas are usually prepared for the problems caused by the changes in weather.

3. Scientists are carefully watching the <u>potential</u> problems caused by climate events, including issues with food, water, and housing.

   a. Thankfully, many areas have solutions in place in case the problems start.

   b. Thankfully, many problems are minor, so people don't have to worry.

4. People have feelings of <u>insecurity</u> about things that can be affected by climate change, including food, living situations, and health and well-being.

   a. Because weather changes are out of our control, people feel nervous and unsure about how their lives may be affected.

   b. Because weather changes are out of our control, people feel that scientists need to do more to make sure their lives are not affected.

5. One of the worst problems that is partially caused by climate change is <u>malnutrition</u>.

   a. People getting weak and sick from not having enough food is tragic.

   b. People getting weak and sick from not having a safe place to live is tragic.

6. Children living in areas that are likely to experience food shortages are always more <u>vulnerable</u>.

   a. Because their bodies are not fully developed, they are more upset or sad about not getting enough to eat.

   b. Because their bodies are not fully developed, they are more easily harmed or hurt by not getting enough to eat.

7. Many people would find it difficult to find a new <u>livelihood</u> if theirs were suddenly taken away from them by a major event.

   a. Finding a new way to earn money is hard, even under good circumstances.

   b. Finding a new place to live is hard, even under good circumstances.

8. Sudden changes in food <u>consumption</u> can be very dangerous, especially for children and older people.

    a. Having new types of food to eat is critical to maintaining good health.

    b. Having enough food to eat is critical to maintaining good health.

9. If you don't have enough food and water and don't have a safe place to live, you are more <u>susceptible</u> to disease and injury, which could result in early death.

    a. Living under difficult conditions can make people angry in many different ways.

    b. Living under difficult conditions can make people weaker, both physically and emotionally.

10. Climate-related severe food shortages have resulted in death from <u>starvation</u>.

    a. No one should suffer and die from lack of food.

    b. No one should suffer and die from weather extremes.

🔾 Go to MyEnglishLab to complete vocabulary and skill practices and to join in collaborative activities.

SUPPORTING SKILL 1
ORGANIZING A PROCESS

> **WHY IT'S USEFUL** By organizing a process, you ensure that your reader can understand the series of actions in the process and see the result of those actions.

Organizing a process requires breaking it down into enough steps to fully explain the process in a way that helps the reader understand it. Make sure the steps are in a logical order so that the reader will clearly see the relationship of each step to the process. Provide sufficient description and add examples to the steps when needed.

Consider your audience—who your reader is and how much or how little the reader knows about the topic. The amount of detailed information you provide depends on what the reader brings to the topic. The less the reader knows, the more explicit the information needs to be, including providing definitions of terms.

To organize a process, first, **introduce the process**, making the purpose clear, and convincing the reader of the importance of the process. You can also offer a reason for its importance or state the effect or result of the process. Your introduction should include a thesis statement that names the process and states the main idea.

Here is an example of a possible thesis statement for a paper on climate change-induced severe weather's effect on food security:

> One of the impacts of more frequent and severe weather due to climate change is a potential increase in food insecurity brought about by a series of steps that result in increasing numbers of people suffering from malnutrition.

For more on writing a thesis statement, see Linguistics, Part 2.

Second, **arrange the steps in a logical order;** typically, this is **chronological** with the steps explained in the order they occur in time. You can also arrange the steps in a **sequential** order with each step following the preceding one in a series of actions that end in a stated result.

Use transition signals to show the relationship of the steps–*first, second, third, last* and adverb clauses with *before, after, once, as soon as* that indicate order, and *while, during, over* (+ time), and *between* that indicate duration. Use adverbs such as *then* and *next* for a sequence of actions or events.

> First, a climate disaster such as severe drought or flooding occurs. The climate disaster then causes loss of life and damage to homes, land, crops, and food supplies. Next, as critical food shortages lead to poor nutrition, the situation becomes a full-blown crisis.

Include sufficiently detailed description supported by examples or illustrations to fully explain each step in the process, but do not include unnecessary information that is not relevant to the process.

> The result of reduced food consumption and less dietary diversity is malnutrition. Children, for example, who are most susceptible, experience stunted growth, a potential for wasting away, and even starvation and death.

For more on developing your ideas, see Business Ethics, Part 1.

Support the process with illustrations and other **visuals** to help the reader see the process.

Finally add a **conclusion**. The conclusion might summarize the process or discuss results.

Look at the chart to see how the language used in a process paper helps your reader understand the process and your purpose.

Language to Organize a Process Paper			
To instruct	**Examples**	**To inform**	**Examples**
• Imperatives • 2nd person— *you*	First [you] **promote** farming	• 3rd person— *he/she; they* • Passive voice	People living in fragile environments prone to weather hazards **are affected** most by climate change.
Use verbs that are specific and clearly explain or describe the actions performed in the particular process, including: *identify, support, create, cause, develop, propose, promote, plan, use,* and *offer,* among others.			

Look back at the paragraphs in the Critical Thinking Skill, page 175. What person is used? Find other examples of transition signals and verbs to describe the actions. Circle the transition words and underline the verbs.

VOCABULARY PREVIEW

Read the vocabulary items. Circle the ones you know. Put a question mark next to the ones you don't know.

integrate	nutrient	sustainable	innovation
initiative	neglected	relevant	breed

EXERCISE 2

A. Read the process. Pay attention to how it is organized.

How to integrate biodiversity into small-scale agriculture to address food insecurity

As a means to address malnutrition and food insecurity, the goal of these guidelines is to outline a process to integrate biodiversity into the activities of small-scale farming through support, education, and resources that enable farmers to produce nutrient-rich foods locally and in a sustainable way.

- First, support services and agricultural innovation research to provide small-scale producers of local foods with useful nutrient information, and technical and production support.

- Second, promote backyard/homestead gardening of local fruits and vegetables.

- Next, encourage urban agriculture and the growing of local vegetables by providing easy access to interested groups to obtain seeds for a variety of plants with high nutritional value.

- Then offer technical and production support to these small-scale producers to help them use the seeds successfully.

- At the same time, develop and institutionalize initiatives such as school and community gardens/farms as ways to educate young people about the benefit of foods from specific varieties that contribute to health and good nutrition to ensure sustainability of the efforts to improve local agriculture.

- While supporting the efforts of the small-scale producers, continue to educate them on the incorporation of healthy nutritional foods from specific varieties of plants, as well as wild, neglected, and less used species, into relevant agricultural activities (e.g. research, breeding, seed selection and production). *(Continued)*

- Finally, create or establish the market infrastructure for these plant varieties and breeds with appropriate nutrient profiles, in order to enable market access for these foods and easy availability to local consumers.

It is our hope that these guidelines will help communities become more food secure. Through local means, communities will be able to contribute to conserving species and maintaining biodiversity while addressing hunger and malnutrition.

CULTURE NOTE

Biodiversity refers to all the variety of life that exists on Earth—species, genetic diversity, and ecosystems. One of the goals of the US National Park Service, founded over 100 years ago, is to preserve the biodiversity of a region, which it believes is vital to the future well-being of Earth.

B. Answer the questions.

1. How does the introduction convince the reader of the importance of understanding the process? Is the introduction effective? Can you think of a better way to introduce the topic? ....

....

....

....

2. Is the purpose of the process to instruct or to inform? ....

....

....

3. Write the thesis statement. Underline the process and put the purpose in brackets.

....

....

4. How is the paper organized? Circle the transition signals in the text. ....

....

....

5. How is the reader addressed? ....

....

6. List the verbs that are used to explain or describe the process. ....

....

7. How does the writer conclude the process? ....

....

C. With a partner, discuss your answers to the questions about how the process is organized.

D. Rewrite the process in Part A as a paragraph informing the reader of how one community addressed the needs of local small-scale producers. Begin your paragraph with a thesis statement. Use appropriate language. Include enough detail to fully explain the process. Add a conclusion.

E. PEER REVIEW. Share your process paragraph with a partner. Use the peer review questions to evaluate each other's work and to offer suggestions. For responses marked No, provide feedback in the Notes column to help your partner revise.

	Yes	No	Notes
Is there a thesis statement that clearly states the purpose of the process?	☐	☐	
Does the thesis statement convince you of the importance of the process?	☐	☐	
Are all the steps in the process included?	☐	☐	
Are there transition signals to introduce the steps?	☐	☐	
Is each step fully explained and understandable for the reader?	☐	☐	
Is the language used appropriate to inform the reader about the process?	☐	☐	
Does the writer conclude effectively?	☐	☐	

VOCABULARY CHECK

A. Review the vocabulary items in the Vocabulary Preview. Write their definitions and add examples. Use a dictionary if necessary.

B. Write the correct vocabulary item next to each definition.

breed	initiative	innovation	integrate
neglect	nutrient	relevant	sustainable

1. .... to not pay attention to someone or something

2. .... able to continue or last for a long time

3. .... to keep animals or plants in order to produce babies or new plants

4. .... to combine two or more things in order to make an effective system

5. .... a chemical or food that provides what is needed for plants or animals to live and grow

6. .... directly related to the subject or problem being discussed

7. .... a new idea, method, or invention

8. .... the ability to make decisions and take action without waiting for someone to tell you what to do

Go to MyEnglishLab to complete vocabulary and skill practices and to join in collaborative activities.

SUPPORTING SKILL 2

SUPPORTING A PROCESS WITH VISUALS

WHY IT'S USEFUL By supporting a process with visuals, you can help your reader better understand and remember complex ideas, steps, sequences, or variables that relate to the process. Well-chosen visuals can replace lengthy explanations or descriptions.

Visuals provide additional support for an idea and are often more effective at communicating certain types of information than text alone. While visuals can be used in all types of writing, they are especially useful in technical and scientific writing to illustrate numerical data, spatial information, trends, processes and procedures.

By **supporting a process with visuals**, writers will:

- clarify or simplify complex ideas.
- show relationships between different variables.
- emphasize important points.
- provide additional information or details.
- demonstrate the steps or sequence in a process.
- communicate visually how something happens.

Choose the best visual for the task

Always consider your audience and purpose before deciding which visual to include in your paper. Ask questions to help you choose the right visual.

- What is the purpose of the visual?
- What is the best visual format to communicate the information?
- How does the visual support my thesis or main idea?

Maps show information or variable conditions about different geographic areas. Figure 1 shows the most vulnerable countries to extreme weather events. In which regions or countries would you expect drought to have the greatest impact on food security?

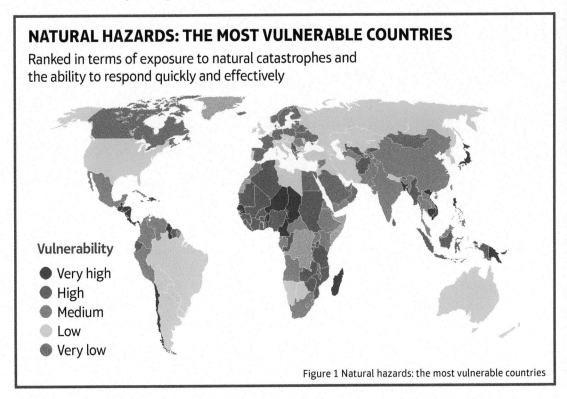

NATURAL HAZARDS: THE MOST VULNERABLE COUNTRIES

Ranked in terms of exposure to natural catastrophes and the ability to respond quickly and effectively

Vulnerability
- Very high
- High
- Medium
- Low
- Very low

Figure 1 Natural hazards: the most vulnerable countries

Graphs show trends over time or make comparisons. Graphs show relationships between different variables in a clear and concise way. Compare the **line graph** and the **bar graph**. Which graph accommodates more information?

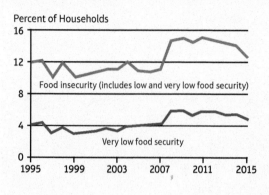

Figure 2 Trends of food insecurity in the US 1995–2015

Figure 3 Food insecurity in the US 2015

Pie charts show the percentage of the whole each part represents. Pie charts are often used to emphasize a point. In Figure 4, is there anything that surprises you about food security in the US?

US HOUSEHOLDS BY FOOD SECURITY STATUS, 2015

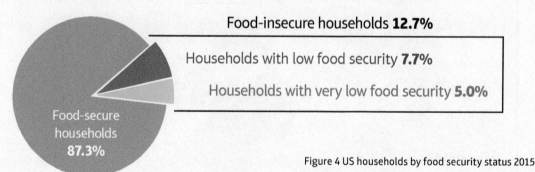

Figure 4 US households by food security status 2015

Source: Calculated by ERS, USDA, using data from the December 2015 Current Population Survey Food Security Supplement.

Tables organize and display large quantities of numerical data. Tables consist of rows and columns, with clear labels for each. A reader can quickly find specific data in a table.

BUREAU FOR FOOD SECURITY	$146,400
Advanced Approaches to Combat Pests and Diseases	$15,461
Markets and Policy Research and Support	$16,307
Climate Resilient Cereals	$26,318
Legume Productivity	$20,867
Nutritious and Safe Foods	$20,282
Sustainable Intensification	$28,887
Scaling Seeds and Other Technologies	$9,805
Other Science and Tech Partnerships	$8,473

Table 1 USAID Research and Development Activities for Food Security 2015

Diagrams are simplified drawings that often depict systems or structures. They frequently have lines or arrows showing stages or steps in a process.

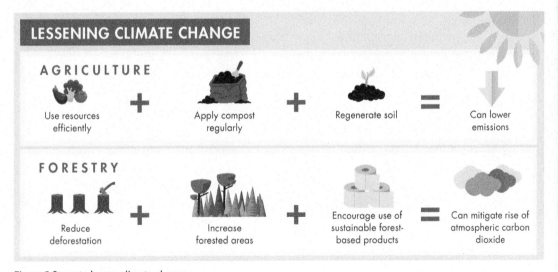

Figure 5 Steps to lessen climate change

Creating effective visuals

When you create a visual, make sure the main idea is clear and the information well organized.

- Keep it simple. Including too much information will make the visual difficult to understand.
- Label different parts of the visual, such as the vertical and horizontal axes, columns, and units of measurement. Include a title and a key if necessary.

- Use reliable sources and accurate data.
- Cite your sources. If you are not conducting original research, you will most likely be using visuals from published sources. Visuals are copyright protected, so always include a citation in the caption. If you modify a published visual, you must still cite the source.

Integrating visuals into the text

If you include a visual in your paper, you must refer to it in the actual text of your paper. This will help your reader understand the purpose for including the visual.

- Number your visuals so you can introduce them in your text (e.g., *As Figure 3 shows* …).
- Keep the visual as close as possible to the text.
- Always make sure you explain the visual in your text. If the information is complicated, you might need to interpret the visual for the reader.

As Earth's temperatures continue to rise, the number of people experiencing food insecurity is expected to rise as well. One way to lessen climate change is to change current agricultural practices that produce significant amounts of global greenhouse emissions. Expanding farmland for crop production and livestock requires clearing forests and using large quantities of fossil fuels, which increases global greenhouse emissions. However, as Figure 5 shows, by carefully managing deforestation and agricultural resources, levels of carbon dioxide, methane, and nitrous oxide, all greenhouse gases, will decrease. Part of ensuring global food security lies in applying both new and traditional agricultural practices that have less of an impact on global warming.

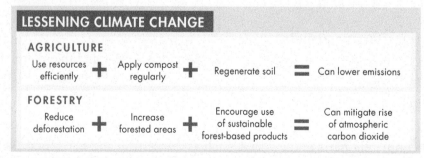

Figure 5 Steps to lessen climate change

EXERCISE 3

A. Read and analyze the visual about climate change and food insecurity. Then discuss the questions with one or more students.

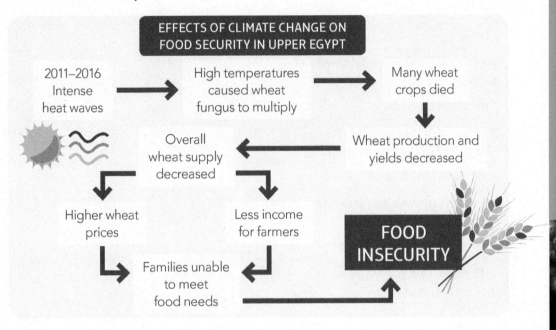

1. How is the visual labeled? ....

2. What is the visual communicating? ....

3. How does the visual help you understand the process? Is the explanation clear?

....

4. Is there anything you would do to improve the visual? Or is there a better type of visual to communicate this information? Explain. ....

....

B. Write a short paragraph introducing the visual in Part A in a paper discussing climate change and food insecurity. Interpret and explain the process in the visual. Be sure to paraphrase and appropriately cite the information.

C. Research an event or process that relates to climate change and food insecurity. For example, this could be an extreme weather event in a specific region, or a government response to that event. Then create a visual to explain the event or process. Make sure your source is reliable and include a citation. Give your visual a title and label it appropriately. Write a brief introduction to the visual.

D. PEER REVIEW. Exchange your visual and introduction with a partner. Respond to the questions to evaluate each other's work. For responses marked No, provide feedback in the Notes column to help your partner revise.

	Yes	No	Notes
Does the title indicate what the visual is about?	☐	☐	
Is the visual labeled?	☐	☐	
Is the visual appropriate for the information the writer is presenting?	☐	☐	
Is the visual easy to understand?	☐	☐	
Does the visual help you understand the process? How?	☐	☐	
Does the visual include a citation?	☐	☐	
Is there anything you would do to improve the visual?	☐	☐	

◐ Go to MyEnglishLab to complete a skill practice.

INTEGRATED SKILLS

SYNTHESIZING INFORMATION FROM SOURCES

WHY IT'S USEFUL By synthesizing information from a variety of sources, you will add credibility to your main idea and make stronger claims, as well as show that you are not simply presenting your own unsupported ideas. Synthesizing allows you to make connections with source material and expand ideas about a topic.

At the university level, you will be expected to **synthesize information from sources** to demonstrate that you have done sufficient research, analysis, and reflection on a writing topic. When you synthesize, you combine different ideas or information from multiple sources together with your own ideas to present something new. Synthesizing ideas in writing can be compared to having an active discussion with people.

> **TIP**
>
> Make sure you develop an accurate system for taking notes. Always include the author and page number with each quote, paraphrase, and statistic. Remember to document all the information you will need to write a citation and Reference or Works Cited page when you are finished.

As the writer, you will "lead" the discussion by presenting your ideas and then integrating source ideas and evidence that contribute to the discussion. While the focus of the paper will be on your original ideas, you must include expert opinion or evidence to broaden the discussion.

A well-written paper includes summaries, paraphrases, and quotes from credible and reliable sources to support the points you are making. When synthesizing, you combine and integrate source material related to your topic and explain how the information connects to the topic. It is important that your ideas and the source ideas build on each other. You can help the reader understand how the ideas are connected from one sentence to the next by providing an interpretation, analysis, or explanation for each source. It is helpful to repeat key words and phrases to connect and integrate ideas. This will ensure that your argument is **coherent.**

For more on identifying reliable sources of information, see Business Ethics, Part 1.

For more on coherence, see Medieval Culture, Part 1.

Here are steps for synthesizing information:

- Present your idea.

- Summarize, paraphrase, or quote from source material.

- Integrate source information (summary, paraphrase, or quote) to support your idea. Use signal phrases with reporting verbs to identify source material and differentiate ideas unless the context is clear. Common signal phrases are:
  - According to [author],
  - [Author] states… (suggests, claims, explains, says, argues)
  - In [title of article], [author] states…

- Provide explanation, analysis, or interpretation of the source information before and/or after the source information.

- Repeat key words and phrases for coherence.

- Cite sources accurately.

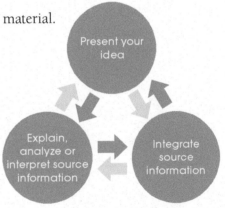

TIP

Whenever possible, include summaries or paraphrases when you synthesize information from sources instead of direct quotations. This will help your writing flow more smoothly because it will be written in your voice.

For more on reporting verbs, see Earth Science, Part 1.

Look at this excerpt from a paper on food insecurity. Notice how the writer has synthesized two sources.

As the world population continues to grow, countries around the world will need to increase their <u>agricultural production</u> to ensure global <u>food security</u>. This will be a challenging goal given the adverse impact of rising global temperatures in the last few decades. Climate change has already caused significant disruptions in <u>agricultural production</u> and is expected to have even more severe impacts on the productivity of most crops after 2050 (US Department of Agriculture, 2014). <u>Extreme weather events</u>, such as floods and droughts, make it difficult for crops to mature or grow at all. Changing temperature patterns can alter growing seasons or <u>make plants</u> more susceptible to <u>diseases and pests.</u> The United Nations' World Food Programme (WFP) claims that these disruptions to <u>agricultural production</u> will disproportionately affect those who are most vulnerable to <u>food insecurity</u>—people who live in environmentally sensitive areas impacted by <u>extreme weather events</u>. In fact, by 2050, the WFP estimates that <u>agricultural</u> output will decrease by up to 30% in parts of Africa, and over 20% in parts of Asia, increasing <u>food insecurity</u> by up to 20% (2016). To address this decline in overall food production, governments around the world will need to focus resources on changing existing <u>agricultural</u> practices. Practices could include developing new seed varieties resistant to pests and disease, implementing new planting schedules based on changing growing seasons, and re-introducing traditional farming techniques that can increase <u>agricultural</u> output in hard-to-farm areas.

writer's argument

source #1 paraphrase provides additional explanation

writer interprets source #1

source #2 paraphrase adds details and statistics

writer makes connections with sources and presents something new

Key:
student writer
paraphrase of source material #1.
paraphrase of source material #2.

In this excerpt, the writer repeats key words and phrases (underlined) to connect and integrate ideas smoothly. Notice how the writer uses a signal phrase to differentiate the writer's ideas from those of the source. The writer also cites the information in the paper and will include full citations in a Works Cited or Reference page at the end of the paper.

For more on paraphrasing, see Business Ethics, Part 1.

For more on summarizing, see Earth Science, Part 1.

VOCABULARY PREVIEW

Read the vocabulary items. Circle the ones you know. Put a question mark next to the ones you don't know.

project (v)	disproportionately	mitigation	emission	efficiency
yield (n)	livestock	deforestation	plague (v)	

EXERCISE 4

A. Read the scientific journal article.

Mitigation Strategies to Protect against Food Insecurity

1   In the coming decades, millions of people worldwide will be at risk of starvation as a result of global warming and population increases. Heat stress, droughts, ocean acidification, and other environmental disasters that already cause food shortages will be exacerbated, or worsened, by climate change. In addition, the demand for food will increase substantially. The global population is projected to rise from 7.3 billion people to upward of 11 billion people by 2100. People in low-income nations are already disproportionately being affected by extreme weather events, and low-income nations that lie in regions affected by storm surges, sea level rises, and drought will be even more susceptible to food shortages in the coming decades. Experts agree that if steps are not taken to address food shortage predictions, hunger will increase substantially by 2050 (IPCC, 2014).

2   There are several mitigation strategies that could protect against food insecurity. One such strategy is to reduce food waste in wealthy countries. Americans waste approximately 70 million metric tons of edible food annually (Dou et al., 2016). According to the Natural Resources Defense Council, 40 percent of food in America is wasted, which amounts to more than 20 pounds of food per person every month. To tackle this enormous waste problem, the public must be educated on how to reduce food waste, and businesses must use reduction measures like waste evaluations. A secondary step is to donate extra food to charities like shelters and soup kitchens. Finally, surplus food may be gathered for animal food, industrial uses, and recycling. Cutting surpluses would save resources that go into producing food, including water, nutrients, and fossil fuels. Scientists agree that producing food creates enormous amounts of greenhouse gas emissions, which in turn contributes to global warming. Reducing food waste would improve efficiency of food systems and reduce global fossil fuel emissions spent on agriculture in developed nations.

(Continued)

3   Part of ending global food insecurity lies in improving the quality of farming rather than increasing the quantity of farming land. Farmers and agricultural partners are increasingly focused on "sustainable intensification," of agriculture, which is making enough food on land already

Food Recovery Hierarchy

Most preferred

Source Reduction
Reduce the volume of surplus food generated

Feed Hungry People
Donate extra food to food banks, soup kitchens, and shelters

Feed Animals
Divert food scraps to animal food

Industrial Uses
Provide waste oil for rendering and fuel conversion and food scraps for digestion to recover energy

Composting
Create a nutrient-rich soil amendment

Least preferred

Landfill/Incineration
Last resort to disposal

https://www.epa.gov/sustainable-management-

available while using practices that are environmentally sustainable. Expanding farmland would require clearing forests, wetlands, and other natural environments. When these environments are destroyed for farming, it increases global greenhouse emissions and reduces biodiversity (Garnett, et al., 2013). To improve the quality of food production, farmers must increase yields on existing land through environmentally friendly land management methods such as adding mulch to the land to retain soil moisture. Another sustainable intensification tool in farming is diversifying the types of crops planted on a given parcel of land. Ecologist Brenda Lin has claimed that doing so will help decrease pest outbreaks in crops in addition to being a good land management practice (Lin, 2011).

4   Yet another method for helping reduce food scarcity in the coming decades is shifting the way livestock is farmed. Scientists point out that about 70 percent of all grains that are being produced by developed nations currently go to feed animals (Eisler, et al., 2014). Grazing animals like cattle and sheep are able to eat crops that are inedible to humans, such as hay. In addition, they can feed in areas that are unsuitable to farming, like hillsides. Rather than feeding cattle in this way, however, cattle in developed nations are often fed corn and other grains from prime farmland. Scientists argue that the 1 billion tons of grains —including barley, oats, corn, and millet—that goes to cattle could feed 3.5 billion humans. (Eisler, 2014). In a double blow for the environment, cattle farming has also contributed significantly to deforestation. Approximately three-fourths of all rainforests have been cleared for cattle production (Nepstad, et. all, 2009). While the deforestation of tropical rainforest land has slowed, the impact of cattle on the environment is clear. Environmentalists argue that consumers can make an impact on both food supplies and the environment by choosing cattle that are grass-fed and by eating less beef in general.

5　Hunger prevention is not a one-step solution. Multiple methods will need to be utilized to avoid widespread malnutrition, particularly in the face of environmental disasters as a result of climate change. Humanity has been plagued by hunger since the beginning of time, and modern agricultural practices have not eliminated food insecurity in the most vulnerable population groups. In the coming decades, farmers and policymakers must work together to find new and innovative strategies to help reduce food insecurity.

References

Intergovernmental Panel on Climate Change. (2014). *Climate Change 2014: Synthesis Report Summary for Policymakers.* Retrieved from IPCC website: https://www.ipcc.ch/pdf/assessment-report/ar5/syr/AR5_SYR_FINAL_SPM.pdf.

Dou, Zhengxia, & Ferguson, James D., & Galligan, David T., & Kelly, Alan M., & Finn, Steven M. (2016). Assessing US food wastage and opportunities for reduction. *Global Food Security, volume 8, p. 19–26.* doi: http://dx.doi.org/10.1016/j.gfs.2016.02.001.

Garnett, T., & Appleby, M.C., & Balmford, A., & Bateman, I.J., & Benton, T.G., & Bloomer, P., & Burlingame, B., & Dawkins, M., & Dolan, L. & Fraser, D., & Herrero, M., & Hoffmann, I., & Smith, P., & Thornton, K., & Toulmin, C., & Vermeulen, S.J., & Godfray, H.C.J. (2013). Sustainable Intensification in Agriculture: Premises and Policies. *Science, volume 341, issue 6141.* p.33–34. doi: 10.1126/science.123448 http://users.ox.ac.uk/~snikwad/resources/Science-2013-Garnett-33–4.pdf.

Lin, Brenda. (2011). Resilience in Agriculture through Crop Diversification: Adaptive Management for Environmental Change. *BioScience Journal, volume 61, issue 3.* p. 183–193. doi: 10.1525/bio.2011.61.3.4 http://bioscience.oxfordjournals.org/content/61/3/183.short.

Eisler, Mark C., & Lee, Michael R.F., & Tarlton, John F., & Martin, Graeme B., & Beddington, John., & Dungait, Jennifer A.J., & Greathead, Henry, & Liu, Jianxin, & Mathew, Stephen, & Miller, Helen, & Misselbrook, Tom, & Murray, Phil, & Vinod, Valil K., & Van Saun, Robert, & Winter, Michael. (2014). Agriculture: Steps to sustainable livestock. *Nature, volume 507, issue 7490, p.32–34.* doi:10.1038/507032a http://www.nature.com/news/agriculture-steps-to-sustainable-livestock-1.14796.

Nepstad, Daniel Curtis, & Filho, Britaldo Silveira Soares, & Merry, Frank, & Osvaldo, Stella. (2009). The End of Deforestation in the Brazilian Amazon. *Science, volume 326, issue 5958, p.1350–1351.* doi: 10.1126/science.1182108 https://www.researchgate.net/publication/40452711_The_End_of_Deforestation_in_the_Brazilian_Amazon.

Natural Resources Defense Council https://www.epa.gov/sustainable-management-food/food-recovery-hierarchy.

EPA Food Recovery Graph https://www.epa.gov/sustainable-management-food/how-prevent-wasted-food-through-source-reduction.

B. Answer the questions.

1. What is the main idea of this article? ....

....

2. Why do experts agree that it is important to address future food shortages now? Include some relevant examples in your response. ....

....

....

....

3. What are three ways food waste can be reduced in wealthy countries? How would reducing food waste protect against food insecurity? ....

....

....

4. What is "sustainable intensification" of agriculture? How can improving the quality of food production reduce food insecurity? ....

....

....

5. Why would shifting the way livestock is farmed improve food security?

....

....

C. Read the article again. Notice how the writer synthesized sources of information. For each paragraph:

1. Underline the topic sentence
2. Put brackets around quoted, summarized, or paraphrased information

D. Choose Paragraph 2, 3, or 4 from the article. Answer the questions and discuss your ideas with a partner or in a small group.

1. Why did the writer include the source? ....

....

2. How was the source introduced? Was it necessary to use a signal phrase? Why or why not? ....

....

3. Did the writer explain, analyze, or interpret the source information? If so, where?

....

4. How effective was the writer in helping you as the reader connect sources of information to the topic? ....

....

E. Write a paragraph in which you synthesize sources of information from two articles that focus on a theme related to climate change and food security. Choose an idea related to this topic and integrate two sources using two or more paraphrases. Use the steps for synthesizing information from sources on page 263.

VOCABULARY CHECK

A. Review the vocabulary items in the Vocabulary Preview. Write their definitions and add examples. Use a dictionary if necessary.

B. Complete each sentence with the correct vocabulary item.

deforestation	disproportionately	efficiency	emissions	livestock
mitigation	plague	project	yield	

1. In areas with unstable and dangerous weather, ... with food production and distribution can be hard to maintain.

2. Scientists .... that climate change will have a major impact on most parts of the world in both the near and distant future.

3. Farmers who don't make enough money may need to sell their .... because they can't afford to feed the animals.

4. The farm's .... on vegetable crops was very low last year because there was not enough rain.

5. People living in areas that have had major problems with weather events .... suffer more with emotional, economic, and physical problems than those that live in safer areas.

6. Both natural and man-made problems .... many developing countries. Scientists and governments must work to protect people who are affected by challenging conditions.

7. Having trees makes the air cleaner, so governments should limit .... to help keep their citizens healthy.

8. People should avoid coming in contact with chemical .... as much as possible. Breathing clean air is essential to good health.

9. Scientists are working with the government to develop ideas that will help in .... of the major problems caused by severe weather.

Go to MyEnglishLab to complete vocabulary and skill practices and to join in collaborative activities.

LANGUAGE SKILL
USING PASSIVE VOICE IN SCIENTIFIC WRITING

> **WHY IT'S USEFUL** By using passive voice in scientific writing, you shift the focus from the performer to the process, which helps the reader concentrate on and understand that process.

◊ Go to MyEnglishLab for the Language Skill presentation and practice.

VOCABULARY STRATEGY
BUILDING DISCIPLINE-SPECIFIC VOCABULARY

> **WHY IT'S USEFUL** By developing strategies to increase discipline-specific vocabulary, you will become more aware of terms and concepts that are important in your field of study and be able to understand and use them in your writing.

All academic disciplines have unique vocabulary that is used by members of that community. These terms, concepts, and key words are necessary to communicate in a given field. It is important to **increase your discipline-specific vocabulary** in your own field of study, as you will more easily understand what you read and hear. It is also critical to go beyond simply understanding these terms and concepts to be able to accurately use them in your own writing.

Learning new words takes effort and attention. It is an incremental process, meaning that it takes place in steps over time. Vocabulary research shows that in order for you to use a word actively and correctly, you must encounter it at least 10 times in a variety of contexts and ways. There are many aspects of a word that you will need to know—its meanings, collocations, grammatical usage, prefixes and suffixes, and its level of formality. It is important to be aware of all of this as you work to increase your vocabulary and to consider using these words in the work you do to build your discipline-specific vocabulary.

Discipline-specific words are the key words in a field of study. They are frequently identified in the abstract of an academic article. They include nouns, verbs, and adjectives that tend to be used over others, as well as abstract concepts that are important to the discipline. You will often find that discipline-specific words have a common meaning as well as their discipline-specific meaning.

> **de·scrip·tive** /dɪˈskrɪptɪv/ ●○○ adjective
> **1 giving a description of something**
> ◄) *the descriptive passages in the novel*
> **2** *technical* **describing how the words of a language are actually used, rather than saying how they ought to be used** OPP **PRESCRIPTIVE**

The first entry gives the common meaning; the second entry gives the technical meaning, as used in Linguistics.

Knowing **affixes**—roots, prefixes, and suffixes—can help you build your discipline-specific vocabulary. Look at these examples:

| Science | **micro**biology   geo**logist** |
| Business | **micro**manage   econo**mist** |

For more on roots, see Earth Science, Part 1.

For more on prefixes, see Materials Engineering, Part 1.

Pay attention to nouns, verbs, and adjectives commonly used in the discipline you are studying. Here are some discipline-specific words from this unit and previous units. Can you think of others?

For more on suffixes, see Materials Engineering, Part 2.

Earth Science	emission, mitigate, biodiverse
Linguistics	lexicographer, prescriptive, descriptive
Business	shareholders, stockholders, stock

Paying attention when you encounter discipline-specific words and recording their meaning and use is essential to the process of adding them to your active vocabulary. Noticing how often a word is used in academic texts and lectures can help you identify critical key words, terms, and concepts. Many words that you find in your discipline may also be used frequently in other disciplines. Be careful, however, because a word can have different meanings in different disciplines.

Creating your own glossary of discipline-specific words is an effective way to build your vocabulary in your field. Here are some tips for creating a glossary:

- Devise a system for recording words. You can take notes on notecards, in a notebook, or on your computer or other electronic device.
- Organize words according to themes or disciplines.
- When you encounter a word that seems to be specific to a discipline, or that you see frequently in your studies, record it.
- Consider the context in which the word is used. Does this help you understand the word?
- Use a dictionary to learn more about the word and write a meaning for the word.
- Include usage notes. Ask yourself, Do I know any word parts? Do other words occur with this word? Are there collocations or grammatical patterns that the word requires?
- Write a sentence with the word. It can be a sentence you have read or one you create yourself.
- Review the words in your glossary and continue to add new words.

TIP

Devise a way to mark in your glossary each time you read or hear a word that is included there. Keeping track of the number of times you read or hear it will give you a quick idea about the word's frequency.

EXERCISE 5

A. Complete the chart with the discipline-specific words used in this unit.

Word + part of speech	Discipline-specific meaning	Notes	Sample sentences

B. Share your chart in Part A with a partner.

C. Complete the chart with five words that are specific to your discipline.

Word + part of speech	Meaning	Notes	Sample sentences

● Go to MyEnglishLab to complete a skill practice.

APPLY YOUR SKILLS

WHY IT'S USEFUL By applying the skills you have learned in this unit, you can successfully organize a process, support a process with visuals, synthesize information from sources, and use passive voice effectively in scientific and technical writing.

ASSIGNMENT
Write a process paper of 800–1000 words explaining one way to lessen food insecurity. Include a visual as part of your support. Synthesize information from at least two sources. Use appropriate citation format for *all* your sources. Focus attention on the process by using passive voice.

BEFORE YOU WRITE

A. Before you begin your assignment, discuss these questions with one or more students.

1. What are the main causes of food insecurity?

2. What are some ways people are addressing these causes?

3. What do you think has been most effective in addressing the causes of food insecurity? Why? What has not been effective? Why?

B. As you consider your writing assignment, complete the tasks. Then share your ideas with another student. Get feedback and revise your ideas if necessary.

1. Which strategy to mitigate food insecurity have you chosen to write about?

....

....

2. List some steps or sequences for the mitigation strategy you are writing about, an explanation, and some results of implementing the strategy.

Food Insecurity Mitigation Strategy		
	Step	**Explanation**
1.		
2.		
3.		
4.		
5.		
	Results	

3. What visual will you use to provide additional support to your ideas?

C. Review the Unit Skills Summary. As you begin the writing task on page 277, apply the skills you learned in this unit.

UNIT SKILLS SUMMARY

Organize a process

- Describe the process in enough steps so the reader can understand it.
- Use a logical order to the steps—chronological or sequential—so the reader can see the relationship between the steps.
- Provide sufficient explanation and add examples as necessary for your purpose and audience.
- Use appropriate language and transitions.

Support a process with visuals

- Consider your audience and purpose before choosing a visual.
- Keep visuals simple.
- Use reliable sources and accurate data.
- Integrate visuals into the text.

Synthesize information from sources

- Present your original ideas.
- Combine and integrate source material by summarizing, paraphrasing, or quoting.
- Include interpretation, analysis, or explanation of the sources.
- Cite sources accurately.

Use passive voice in scientific writing

- Focus attention on the process rather than the performer.
- Provide cohesion by putting the process in the subject position.
- Contribute to the smooth flow of information presenting new information at the end of the sentence.

Build discipline-specific vocabulary

- Notice discipline-specific words and use a dictionary to understand their meaning.
- Create your own glossary of discipline-specific words.

THINKING CRITICALLY

As you consider your writing assignment, discuss the questions with another student. Get feedback and revise your ideas if necessary.

1. Do you think it is possible to live in a world in which all people achieve food security? Why or why not?

2. What role should governments play in ensuring that people are food secure? What should happen at a country-wide level? Local level?

3. What do you think will be the biggest challenges to achieving global food security in the next few decades? Why?

THINKING VISUALLY

A. Look at the visual showing the four food security dimensions that are impacted by climate change. Discuss the questions with a partner.

1. What information does this visual give you?

2. Is the visual effective in understanding the relationship between food security and climate change? If so, how? If not, how could it be improved?

3. Write 2–3 sentences describing the visual.

B. Find (or create) another visual of any type that provides information relevant to the mitigation strategy that you are writing about. Write a citation for this source.

Food Security Dimensions Impacted by Climate Change

FOOD PRODUCTION AND TRADE

ACCESS TO FOOD

CLIMATE CHANGE

STABILITY OF FOOD SUPPLIES

FOOD SAFETY

Source

Rewrite each sentence in the passive voice. Do not change the verb tense. Use the agent in a *by* phrase only if it is necessary.

1. As the world population continues to grow, countries must increase agricultural production. ....

....

....

2. Climate change has already caused significant disruptions in agricultural production. ....

....

....

3. Scientists expect climate change to have even more severe impacts on productivity of most crops after 2050. ....

....

....

4. Changing temperature patterns have altered growing seasons.

....

....

5. In the past, disruptions in agricultural production affected fewer areas.

....

....

6. Now, disruptions in agriculture are affecting those who are most vulnerable to food insecurity. ....

....

....

7. Governments will need to focus resources on changing existing agricultural patterns. ....

....

....

8. Scientists must develop new seed varieties that are resistant to pests and disease.

....

....

9. Farmers should re-introduce traditional farming techniques.

....

....

WRITE

A. Revisit the writing assignment and your answers to the questions in Before You Write Part B. Why did you choose this strategy? ....

....

....

....

B. Organize your process. Choose at least two sources to support your ideas. Write your sources here. ....

....

....

....

C. Write your process paper including a visual. Make sure your visual clearly represents the information that is your focus.

BEYOND THE ASSIGNMENT

Write a research paper of 5–8 pages on biodiversity and its effect on food security. Discuss ways to mitigate loss of biodiversity in the future. Include one or more diagrams in your paper and synthesize information from multiple sources.

🔊 Go to MyEnglishLab to watch Dr. Osborne's concluding video and to complete a self-assessment.

Present times are connected to the past

MEDIEVAL CULTURE

Style and Genre

UNIT PROFILE

Folklore is the traditional customs, rituals, and stories that bind people in a particular culture together. In this unit, you will read and write about topics related to folklore and the stories that are a part of the folklore of several cultures. Specifically, you will learn about the different genres of folktales common in medieval literature that are still being told today.

Research a folklore story that ends with a moral or lesson. Identify the genre, briefly summarize the story, and write an essay of 500–800 words analyzing the style and appeal. Report on how description and figurative language, including symbolism and imagery, were used in telling the story.

OUTCOMES

• Use figurative language
• Appeal to ethos, pathos, and logos
• Analyze descriptive writing
• Vary description
• Use a corpus to expand word knowledge

For more about **MEDIEVAL CULTURE**, see ❶ ❸.
See also R and OC **MEDIEVAL CULTURE** ❶ ❷ ❸.

GETTING STARTED

⏵ Go to MyEnglishLab to watch Professor Galvez's introductory video and to complete a self-assessment.

Discuss these questions with a partner or group.

1. All cultures tell stories and often use those stories to teach lessons and persuade others to behave in certain ways. We typically begin to hear and read these stories in childhood. What stories do you remember from your childhood? What kinds of lessons were they teaching? Do you have a favorite story? Share it with your group.

2. What types of stories or books appeal to you? Why? Do you prefer fiction or nonfiction? Do these stories or texts appeal to your emotions? How? What other reasons do they appeal to you?

3. Professor Galvez suggests that images were used by medieval people to represent or symbolize certain values or virtues, such as honor and love. She says images were a way for people to think through problems. In modern culture, music videos may serve the same function. What images come to mind when you think of love? Life? Virtue? Death? Do you agree that images can help us in our lives? Why or why not?

CRITICAL THINKING SKILL

STYLE AND GENRE

> **WHY IT'S USEFUL** By understanding the connection between style and genre, you will recognize the rhetorical devices that writers use to create a style that fits the genre and meets the expectations of their readers, and you will be able to choose the appropriate style for your purpose in your own writing.

Style and genre are closely connected. As a reminder, **style** is how a writer expresses ideas and is achieved through word choice and sentence structure as well as point of view and register. These give the writer a voice and contribute to the tone of the writing. The style must fit the **genre,** the type of text, in order to help the reader understand the text and its rhetorical purpose.

Particularly in literature and the arts, style affects how the reader perceives ideas. Often, the purpose in literature is to entertain and inform. Style that fits this purpose is achieved through the use of **descriptive** and **figurative language**. When the author wants to evoke an emotional response, the more vivid the images are and the more connections the writer can make through symbolism and other figurative language, the more likely the reader is to respond to the writing.

Literature also often has as a purpose to persuade others to behave in a particular way or accept particular ideas as true. To do this, the writer must appeal to the audience, which involves making style choices to accomplish the purpose. Style is achieved through the specific language that is used to appeal to **ethos** (the reader's belief in the credibility and trustworthiness of the writer), **pathos** (the writer's appeal to the reader's emotions), and **logos** (the writer's use of evidence and logic to convince the reader).

A final style consideration in literature is the appearance of the text and use of visuals to support the narrative. Often, stylized script or fonts are used to create the sense of the stories as being historic or from long ago. Many medieval texts were illuminated, handwritten and decorated with stylized borders and ornate chapter letters in bright colors. **Illustrations** were used to support the

Detail of an illuminated manuscript containing a portion of the *Magnificat*, an ancient Christian hymn

story and its message and to trigger emotions in the reader. Today, we still see carefully-chosen illustrations in folktales, especially in children's literature, and graphic novels, which rely more heavily on visuals than text to communicate their story.

As we saw in Medieval Culture Part 1, **genre** is a way to classify by form, content, and style. In writing, it means using particular features and functions to help guide the audience. Knowing the genre helps readers to understand the writer's message and purpose. Other areas of culture have distinct genres. Can you think of different genres of music? Art? Media?

In the rhetorical context of literature, looking at more narrowed genres can help you understand how style affects the reader. Genre in literature is divided to classify types of literature, typically drama, poetry, and **prose**. Drama includes stories and plays, written in verse or prose that are typically designed for performance, with conflict and emotions expressed in dialogue and action. Poetry, written in verse, often with rhythm and rhyme, uses imagery to create an emotional response in the audience, whether presented orally or in writing.

Prose, unlike poetry and drama, is the ordinary form of language, written in complete sentences organized into paragraphs. There are two types of prose. **Fiction** is narrative writing that comes from the writer's imagination. The characters, settings, and stories are not real, though they may be based on real people, places, and events. The primary rhetorical purpose of fiction is to entertain, but it can also inform, persuade, or inspire. **Nonfiction** is fact-based text about real events, people, or places. Its purpose is primarily to inform and persuade, but it also can inspire and entertain.

Look at the chart listing fiction and nonfiction genres of prose. Does it help you to understand the connection of style and genres in literature? Can you add other genres?

PROSE			
Fiction			
Folklore Story (Folktale)	**Short Story**	Novel	Graphic Novel
fable, fairy tale, legend, parable, proverb, myth, tall tale	fantasy, horror, mystery, romance, science fiction		
Nonfiction			
biography, diary, essay, history, journal, letter			

Each genre has its own style and readers have expectations about how the genre will look and what rhetorical devices will be used. For example, a reader of a mystery novel expects to find clues throughout the text but to only learn the answer or truth at the end of the novel. A reader of fiction has different expectations than a reader of nonfiction. An appeal to logic may fit better in nonfiction, whereas an appeal to emotion suits fiction better. In prose writing, use of description, including figurative language to create mental pictures, helps to engage the reader. Descriptive writing makes a story more believable and draws the reader into that world.

TIP

When reading literature, take time to identify the genre and consider the style conventions of that genre. Knowing what to expect of the genre will help you to better understand the meaning of what you are reading.

VOCABULARY PREVIEW

Read the vocabulary items. Circle the ones you know. Put a question mark next to the ones you don't know.

ritual	conservative	convention	dynamic
anonymous	consistent	generic	intensify
resemble	phenomenon	exaggerated	

EXERCISE 1

A. Read the essay about folklore.

1 Folklore is the culture of the everyday people of a particular community. Early scholars looked at traditional societies and studied folklore through the specific items of the communities such as stories, proverbs, songs, jokes, games, dances, and artifacts. Now, however, the study of folklore examines a group's shared beliefs, values, concerns, customs, and rituals, along with the items. Folklore is handed down from generation to generation, usually face-to-face and through word of mouth. Cultures maintain themselves through folklore, even as folklore changes with the context and over time. It is both conservative, conforming to expectations and conventions, and dynamic, changing with each retelling of a story or creation of a new object.

> **CULTURE NOTE**
>
> The term *folklore* was coined in 1846 by William John Thoms who wanted a term to express customs, beliefs, stories, and artifacts of what he called "old-fashioned and poorer segments" in society. Today, folklore is considered the culture of any group.

2 Folklore stories, or folktales, are a genre of literature, primarily oral prose narratives, shared by a community. Countless folktales were only written down many years after people began telling them. Folktales may have their basis in historical events, but they are fiction and based on the beliefs of a people rather than on strictly factual information. Particularly in the Middle Ages, folktales were often anonymous. They had consistent plots, but varied with each telling to suit the rhetorical purpose of the teller and the local people hearing them.

3 There are many genres of folklore stories going back to medieval literature. All cultures have folktales, and each genre follows certain conventions of style, which can be looked at from three perspectives: generic, cultural, and individual. All genres follow rules found in most cultures so they share a generic style. However, there are many traditions that make folktales from each culture unique. The stories from each tradition were intensified by localizing them, creating a sense in those listening that they belonged to that particular group. The time and place of the telling created a cultural style. Finally, as most folktales were oral, each individual storyteller brought a unique style to the telling. Thus, every folktale genre follows a generic style, but each varies culturally from group to group, time to time, and place to place, and each telling includes individual differences.

4 Folktales are told to entertain and educate. Though we cannot hear the voices of the medieval storytellers, the plots and styles help researchers to see the worldviews of the tellers and their audiences during that time period. Understanding the style of a particular genre requires taking into account variations of plot (storyline), theme, context, and purpose of other texts in the genre. While the plots of many folktales

have been stable over time, they are also fluid. The current tales resemble those told in the past, but since they were spread from oral teller to teller, the oral, and later written, texts influenced each other with style and structure shifts that were affected by culture, social class, and time.

5 Look at these descriptions of folktale genres, common in the Middle Ages and still relevant today. Note the generic style characteristics of each.

Fables are short fictional narratives which often feature animal characters or supernatural phenomena that are given human qualities, including language. They end with a moral lesson. Medieval fables came through Latin prose, but were also influenced by Indian and Arabic/Persian traditions. Fables were popular because they were short, developed characters and action rapidly with twists of plot, and ended with folk wisdom, which was sometimes amusing.

Parables are short narratives that illustrate a lesson, similar to fables. Unlike fables, they do not give animals or natural phenomena human qualities. Parables often have a central character who faces a moral dilemma or makes a bad decision.

Legends are narratives about local traditions, usually presented as true, and centering around a supernatural or extraordinary occurrence. They express the group's collective values and beliefs, but don't often represent accurate recording of historical events. Their value is in reflecting the social and cultural environment of the teller and community. There is often a hero related to the particular place.

Myths are narratives, usually featuring divine beings (gods), which explain natural phenomena or the structure and rituals of a society or group. Myths are about a timeless past. The term is most often applied to the beliefs of groups whose religious beliefs differ from the greater society.

Fairy tales are narratives with characters that have magical qualities. They are usually anonymous and are often the first stories for children. Many scholars believe that the most familiar ones today originated in Germany around the year 1800. They typically use formulaic language such as, "Once upon a time" to begin the story and end with, "They lived happily ever after."

Tall tales are stories with unbelievable elements told as if they were true. They are highly exaggerated. Tall tales are typically told by a narrator who seems to have witnessed the events or been a part of the story, and they are usually humorous.

Glossary

Artifacts: objects created and used by the people in a particular community in the past

Supernatural: impossible to explain by natural causes and therefore seeming to involve the powers of gods or magic

B. Answer the questions

1. What specific items did early researchers examine in studying folklore?

   ....

2. How is folklore studied today? ....

   ....

3. What are folktales and what are they based on? ....

   ....

   ....

4. What are three perspectives for considering style in folktales? Explain each.

   ....

   ....

5. What is the purpose of folktales and how do researchers learn about folktales
   since the oral presentation isn't available to them? ....

   ....

   ....

6. What are some genres of folktales? Pick one and describe it. ....

   ....

   ....

C. Read the short folktales. Identify the genre from the list in Part A and explain how the style fits the genre.

1. One day an older man named Juha went to the public bath. The attendants paid
   little attention to him and the service was poor. When he left, he tipped them with
   a gold coin which pleased them. The next time Juha went to the public bath, the
   attendants were very helpful and treated him well. He tipped them with only a
   small silver coin which made them exclaim angrily at him and say he hadn't paid
   enough. He told them that they were mistaken, that the tip was correct as the gold
   coin was for today's excellent service while the silver coin was for the poor service
   he had received on his first visit. (Arabic/Persian)

   ....

   ....

   ....

2. A raven with feathers as black as coal, was envious of the swan because of her snow-white feathers. He decided that if he lived in the pond, like a swan, he would have white feathers like her. So he left his home in the forest and went to the live in the pond. Instead of flying and eating insects as ravens should do, he swam and ate plants and weeds like the swan. However, instead of becoming white, he became weak. He eventually died from lack of proper food and exercise. Changing your habits will not alter nature. (Greek)

....

....

....

3. Paul Bunyon was a man famous for his size and strength. He worked as a lumberjack, travelling the woods cutting down trees with his large blue ox named Babe. Paul Bunyon was so strong, I once saw him clear a whole forest with one swipe of his ax. He made his way from the east coast to the west clearing forests. Along the way, he dug out the Great Lakes so Babe would have enough water to drink. (American)

....

....

....

4. According to Chinese folklore, life began when the god Pangu, the first living being, emerged from the egg that he was sleeping in. This egg contained Yin and Yang, which then separated. The lighter Yang rose to create the sky. Yin formed Earth, and Pangu stood between them and made sure both were held in place with his hands and feet. (Chinese)

....

....

....

5. A young princess, playing with her favorite toy, a golden ball, drops it into a deep well and to get it back makes a promise to a frog who retrieves it for her. She does not keep her promise to take him back to the palace with her and she runs away. When the frog shows up at the door, her father the king makes her let him in and orders her to keep her promise. She is reluctant but takes him. This breaks the spell, put on him by a wicked witch, and he turns into a handsome prince. They live happily ever after. (Germanic)

....

....

....

D. In a group of three or four students, take turns each telling a familiar folklore story.

E. In your group, summarize each folklore story and decide the genre. Discuss style characteristics from the three perspectives: generic, cultural, and individual, that support your opinion about the genre of each story.

VOCABULARY CHECK

A. Review the vocabulary items in the Vocabulary Preview. Write their definitions and add examples. Use a dictionary if necessary.

B. Write the correct vocabulary item next to each definition.

anonymous	conservative	consistent	conventions
dynamic	exaggerated	generic	intensify
phenomenon	resemble	ritual	

.... 1. a ceremony that is always performed in the same way, in order to mark an important religious or social occasion

.... 2. preferring to continue doing things the way they are being done or have been proven to work, rather than risking changes; not liking new ideas

.... 3. behavior and attitudes that most people in a society consider to be normal and right

.... 4. continuously moving or changing

.... 5. not known by name; done, sent, or given by someone who does not want their name known

.... 6. always having the same beliefs, behavior, attitudes, quality, etc.

.... 7. relating to a whole group of things rather than to one thing in particular

.... 8. to increase in strength, size, amount, etc.

.... 9. to look like, or be similar to someone or something

.... 10. something that happens or exists in society, science, or nature, that people discuss or study because it is difficult to understand

.... 11. described as better, more important, etc., than is really true

⬆ Go to MyEnglishLab to complete vocabulary and skill practices and to join in collaborative activities.

SUPPORTING SKILL 1

USING FIGURATIVE LANGUAGE

WHY IT'S USEFUL By using figurative language, you create mental images that help your reader understand the ideas you are trying to convey.

Figurative language uses words or phrases that create mental images that help readers "experience" events in a story or understand complex concepts in a text. These expressions are called figures of speech and do not have a literal meaning. (Literal meaning is the basic or original meaning.) Instead, they express ideas using comparisons, exaggerations, and symbols to imply different meanings. For example, figures of speech with comparisons like "feathers as white as snow" or "as black as coal" help the reader visualize the objects in a story using familiar objects typically associated with a characteristic such as its color. The reader understands that the writer is not saying that feathers actually are snow or coal.

Figurative language is used in all types of writing. Creating mental images helps the reader to understand concepts, but also to recall the ideas later. Mental images are more likely to evoke emotion as well. The more vivid the picture and the stronger our connection to it, the better we are at keeping it in our memory and later associating it with the concepts. Symbols, such as a rose to represent romance and love, convey meaning through associations and are more memorable.

To create mental images, you must show rather than tell, so that your readers can feel as if they are having the experience firsthand. Telling is vague whereas showing is specific. Good use of figurative language conveys a mood that your reader senses. Exaggeration like "It's so hot you could fry an egg on the sidewalk!" helps the reader feel the heat more than simply saying, "It is hot."

There are different types of figurative language, and like other style elements, writers need to make careful choices to suit the rhetorical context. Comparisons to and associations with familiar objects also aid in understanding and recall.

Look at these types of figurative language. Can you add other examples?

Type of Figurative Language	Examples
Simile: A direct comparison of two things using *like* or *as*. The two things are often very different. Similes help readers visualize by making a comparison to something familiar or common to them.	It was as dark as night in the room. She sang like a bird. Electrons move along a wire like water flowing through a pipe.
Metaphor: A comparison, also of two things that are not alike, but without using a linking word. This can make it harder for readers to see what is being compared. Use of metaphors is common in written and spoken language and in academic writing.	The brain is a machine. The extinction of a species is a wake-up call to humans.
Personification: Giving an animal or inanimate (not living) object human qualities or characteristics.	Fox told Crow that she was lovely. The waves called to her.
Hyperbole: Exaggerating ideas beyond what is believable. Hyperbole is often used to provide humor or evoke a strong emotion in readers.	That superhero is faster than a speeding train. He thinks he is smarter than Einstein! That was the easiest test in the world.
Symbolism: Expressions or words that are used to represent a concept or broader category of people, objects, places, or situations with a deeper meaning. Symbols can be difficult to recognize or understand so readers have to consider the context carefully and may need to have cultural knowledge.	After her husband died, she wore black the rest of her life. [The color black symbolizes death and/or mourning in many cultures.] Defeated, they waved the white flag and the battle was over. [A white flag symbolizes surrender.]
Imagery: Using description that creates a mental image for readers. Adjectives, especially those that appeal to our senses—sight, smell, sound, taste, and touch—help readers experience the ideas and evoke emotions that make the event or concept more memorable.	The waterfall, cascading down from the cliff high above, created rainbows in the mist that swirled up as the water hit the smooth round stones in the shallow pool below.

To use figurative language effectively, choose the type by considering:

- your rhetorical purpose
- your audience
- the genre
- the mood you want to create

When using figurative language:

- Use similes and metaphors that tie the new concept to a familiar one.
- Make original comparisons.
- Visualize the image you want to create for your reader.
- Create unique images.
- Use specific adjectives, nouns, and verbs to create clear and precise images.
- Personify or exaggerate when it helps your reader to visualize a concept.

EXERCISE 2

A. Read the fable and find examples of the six types of figurative language.

One sunny morning the fox was walking through the woods searching for food when he spotted a large black crow perched on a sturdy tree branch out of reach with a piece of cheese in her beak. Smelling the sweet cheese, the fox decided that it would be the perfect food for his breakfast. The fox approached the tree, looked up and said, "Madam Crow! You are the most beautiful bird I have ever seen! Your feathers are so glossy and your eyes are as bright as the stars!" The crow looked down suspiciously at the fox, turned her head to the side to listen more, but firmly held on to the cheese. Licking his lips, the sly fox continued, "Surely, your voice must be as pleasing to hear as you are to see. If you sing just one song for me, I will be able to call you Queen of Birds." The crow was delighted by the fox's flattering words; she very much wanted to be known as the queen of all birds. Raising her head high, she opened her beak, and began to caw loudly. Down fell the cheese to the ground. The fox gobbled up the thick, tasty cheese then said, "You do have quite a voice Madam Crow, but you certainly do not have any good sense!" The vain crow realized her mistake, but it was too late.

Do not trust flatterers!

1. Simile ....
2. Metaphor ....
3. Personification ....
4. Hyperbole ....
5. Symbolism ....
6. Imagery ....

Glossary

Flatter: to praise someone in order to please them even though you don't mean it

Flatterer: someone who flatters people

B. Read the fable. Rewrite it using different types of figurative language that show rather than tell the story. Use figurative language at least five times.

The Raven and the Swan

A raven with black feathers was envious of the swan because of her white feathers. He decided that if he lived in the water and ate plants like a swan, he would have white feathers like her. So he left his home in the forest and went to the live in the pond. Instead of flying and eating insects as ravens should do, he swam and ate plants. However, instead of becoming white, he became weak. He eventually died from lack of proper food and exercise.

Changing your habits will not alter nature.

C. Tell your version of the fable in Part B to a partner. Listen to your partner's version. How were they similar? How were they different?

D. PEER REVIEW. Exchange your fable with a partner. Underline and label the figurative language in your partner's fable. Respond to the questions to evaluate each other's fable. For responses marked No, give feedback in the Notes column to help your partner revise.

	Yes	No	Notes
Does the fable have similes or metaphors that tie new concepts to familiar ones?	☐	☐	
Are the comparisons original?	☐	☐	
Are the images unique?	☐	☐	
Were specific adjectives, nouns, and verbs used to create clear, precise images?	☐	☐	
Was personification or hyperbole used?	☐	☐	
Were clichés used or was figurative language overused?	☐	☐	
Does the fable show rather than tell the story?	☐	☐	

🔊 Go to MyEnglishLab to complete a skill practice.

SUPPORTING SKILL 2

APPEALING TO ETHOS, PATHOS, AND LOGOS

WHY IT'S USEFUL By appealing to ethos, pathos, and logos, you demonstrate that you have considered the rhetorical context for writing and how best to engage your audience. Understanding ethos, pathos, and logos will ensure that your writing is credible, convincing, and logical.

Once you have identified your audience and purpose for a writing assignment, consider how you will engage your readers and persuade, or convince, them of your ideas. What makes a writer persuasive? Depending on the rhetorical context (purpose, audience, genre), there are one or more reasons that readers will be persuaded by a writer:

They see the writer as being trustworthy and credible. – ethos

They are emotionally influenced by the writer's ideas. – pathos

They perceive the text as logical and are convinced by the writer's evidence. – logos

Ethos, pathos, and **logos** are three modes of persuasion that are used to appeal to, or engage, readers. There are different ways you can incorporate these modes of persuasion into your writing to build your credibility, appeal to your audience's emotions and values, or support your ideas with evidence. Academic writing usually requires that you rely more on your credibility (ethos) and logic (logos), although it can be appropriate to appeal to the audience's emotions and values (pathos) depending on the purpose for writing.

Your writing will be most persuasive when you have considered the rhetorical context and an effective combination of ethos, pathos, and logos. A technical report on an engineering process, for example, will rely mostly on appeals to logic and credibility because emotional language would be inappropriate, unprofessional, or distracting. On the other hand, a newspaper editorial arguing for universal health care may rely on a balance of all three appeals if it is written by a medical doctor who has witnessed how patients with no health insurance have suffered. When combined effectively, these appeals work together to create a clear, logical, and persuasive message.

Which appeals would be included in a legal case study? A student's expository essay? A political blog post?

Ethos: Credibility

MODES OF PERSUASION

Pathos: Emotion

Logos: Logic

Readers will be willing to "listen" to you if you use **ethos** to establish your character and expertise. By doing so, you will demonstrate that you are ethical, well-informed on the topic, and present yourself in a professional way. There are several ways to build your credibility:

- Include your title, position, and/or affiliated institution or organization when appropriate.
- Use accurate and reliable sources.
- Use up-to-date research.
- Present both sides of an argument fairly.
- Use accurate grammar and spelling.
- Use the appropriate style for the rhetorical context:
  - word choice
  - sentence structure
  - register and point of view

Consider the publication *Songbook: How Lyrics Became Poetry in Medieval Europe* by Professor Marisa Galvez. What are some ways the author most likely established her credibility?

While **pathos**, or emotional appeals, should never be used as the only mode of persuasion in academic writing, it can be effective to have your audience respond to your ideas with emotions such as happiness, sadness, fear, pride, sympathy, or guilt. If used appropriately and ethically, and in combination with sound logic, your argument can be made more persuasive if it connects with the reader's beliefs and values. You can appeal to your audience's emotions with:

- words with positive or negative connotations
- vivid stories or examples

For more on connotations, refer to Medieval Culture, Part 1.

- figurative or descriptive language
- an emotional tone

Consider a scientific paper on mitigating food insecurity. What are some ways the author most likely would include emotional appeals?

TIP

Never use emotional appeals as a substitute for credible evidence or expert opinion. When you include emotional appeals, make sure they are balanced with ethical and rational ideas and arguments so that readers will take you seriously.

Logos, or the appeal to logic, is critical for any type of academic work. Although you may have sufficient and convincing evidence to support your ideas, if your work is not presented logically, you will not be able to persuade your readers. Use sound reasoning, carefully considering the evidence before reaching conclusions, so that you can persuade your readers to agree with you. A paper with sound reasoning will include:

- clear and rational ideas and arguments
- appropriate organizational patterns to show logical connections between ideas
- cited evidence that supports your claims (facts and statistics, examples, expert opinion)
- reasonable counter arguments to opposing views that make your argument stronger

Think about an article you have read that used sound reasoning. What was the article about? Why were you persuaded by the ideas?

CULTURE NOTE

The words *ethos*, *pathos*, and *logos* come from the teachings of the Greek philosopher Aristotle (384–322 BCE). In *The Art of Rhetoric*, Aristotle emphasized that all three persuasive appeals are needed to construct and deliver an effective argument.

EXERCISE 3

A. Read the five excerpts from different types of academic texts and choose the mode(s) of persuasion—ethos, pathos, or logos—that best fit each example. Support your answer with a brief explanation. Compare your answers with a partner. Did you agree?

1. While climate is the typical weather condition of a particular area, climate change is a long-term change in Earth's climate, or in the climate of a region. Climate change refers to changes in precipitation or typical temperature patterns in specific areas or regions, as well as to long-term changes to global temperatures and weather patterns. The Earth has always experienced climate change, but it has usually happened over the course of hundreds, thousands, or even millions of years. Regions undergoing climate change experience extreme weather events such as hurricanes, or severe droughts and heat waves. These weather events are becoming increasingly more common, creating consensus among climatologists that Earth is experiencing the most rapid climate change ever. The Earth's surface temperature has increased 1.8°F in the last century, with all but one of the 15 warmest years occurring since the year 2001 (NASA 2016).

2. Scientists estimate that by the year 2050, most coral reefs will no longer exist, contributing to a mass extinction of tropical marine species. It is unimaginable to think that future generations won't experience the beauty of a living coral reef.

   ....

   ....

3. The songs of the troubadours were wildly popular. In books that have survived from the time period, the same song lyrics can be found in multiple places, which means they were well-known enough to be performed over and over by different troubadours, and they were likely recognizable by audience members, too. It makes me wonder if the audience ever broke into song as they listened to the troubadours perform, as we so often see at concerts today when musicians perform their fans' favorites.

   ....

   ....

4. Stakeholder theory, in contrast to shareholder theory, proposes that a corporation should have an equal responsibility to all "stakeholders," that is, those who are affected by the corporation's practices and policies. Stakeholders could include employees, customers, the outside community, and even the environment. Many business leaders today argue that businesses must have more of a stakeholder approach in order to be successful and to avoid corporate scandals. Critics of stakeholder theory argue, however, that stakeholders are not always clearly identifiable, nor do corporations have any reason to put the interests of stakeholders above that of shareholders. Moreover, business leaders making decisions on behalf of stakeholders may be making decisions about matters in which they are not experts. There are also cases of businesses that fail in today's economy because they choose to focus too much on stakeholders and not enough on maximizing shareholder wealth.

   ....

   ....

5. Bill Gates, the founder and CEO of Microsoft®, is viewed by most people as the person in charge, but even someone as famous as Bill Gates, who would seem to control his company, understands that a public company answers to its shareholders. He has said, "No one person controls Microsoft. The board and the shareholders decide whether they want to have me as CEO." Clearly, the decision to go public, no matter the size of the business, means giving up the control of a business.

   ....

   ....

B. Persuade someone to take an environmental action that addresses climate change (e.g., driving an electric car or recycling), protest a business practice you think is unethical (e.g., employing children or overcharging customers), or read a classic work of fiction or poetry. Write three short arguments, one that appeals to ethos, one to pathos, and one to logos, for the topic you choose.

1. Appeal to ethos: ....

....

....

....

2. Appeal to pathos: ....

....

....

....

3. Appeal to logos: ....

....

....

....

C. Combine the three arguments in Part B into one persuasive paragraph that appeals to ethos, pathos, and logos.

D. Exchange your paragraphs from Part C with a partner. Use different color highlighters to identify the three appeals in your partner's argument. Discuss the effectiveness of the appeals. Do you have suggestions for making the appeals stronger?

◆ Go to MyEnglishLab to complete a skill practice and to join in collaborative activities.

INTEGRATED SKILLS

ANALYZING DESCRIPTIVE WRITING

WHY IT'S USEFUL By analyzing descriptive writing, you will have a deeper understanding of how writers use language to engage with the reader, and you will be able to effectively use description for different purposes in your own writing.

Writers use descriptive language to give readers a better understanding of people, places, objects, or processes. Descriptive writing gives details and characteristics or describes features or functions of something and is used in all genres for different purposes. In narrative and persuasive writing, including stories and argumentative essays, description is often used to emotionally engage readers. In informative writing such as scientific, medical, or technical texts, description is used to present factual information more clearly. The type of description or how much description to include depends on the rhetorical context for writing. Description is sometimes accompanied by visuals, like pictures, graphs, or flowcharts, to help the reader understand what is being described.

Descriptive writing often emphasizes the sensory details—sight, sound, touch, smell, and taste—and is accomplished through the use of adjectives or other parts of speech that help the reader visualize how something looks, behaves, or even thinks. In **literature**, vivid descriptions with numerous sensory details create mental images that bring stories and characters to life. Note the descriptive language in the fable *The Fox and the Crow*. Is the writer successful in creating a mental picture of the characters for you?

Illuminated manuscript in the medieval library of Strahov Monastery, Prague, Czech Republic

Sight: *Your feathers are so glossy …*

Sound: Raising her head high, she opened her beak, and began to *caw loudly*.

Touch: *Licking his lips*, the sly fox continued …

Smell: *Smelling the sweet cheese*, the fox decided that it would be the perfect meal …

Taste: The fox *gobbled up the thick, tasty cheese …*

In **expository** writing, description is usually a part of a longer explanation or example to help the reader gain a broader understanding of a topic. Note in this excerpt how the writer of an essay on medieval poetry uses description. How do the descriptive details help you understand who the troubadours were?

> One of the most famous types of medieval poetry came from the troubadours, who were poets and singers of the 12th and 13th centuries in southern France. Like all traveling singers common in the Middle Ages, troubadours performed for others. The troubadours differed from other singers, however, because they were of higher status in society. Troubadours were noblemen or noblewomen who performed for the upper classes.

In **persuasive** writing, vivid description can persuade readers to agree with you or compel them to act. Look at this example from a much different type of writing. The writer uses a descriptive example to evoke an emotion in an argumentative paper on climate change. What emotions do you have after reading this description?

> For instance, warmer sea surface temperatures in tropical regions have resulted in significant die-off of coral reefs which are home to 25% of marine species. Snorkeling on a colorful, vibrant, and healthy coral reef was the highlight of a trip to Australia. Now seeing pictures of completely white coral, which has been bleached by warming seas, is shocking.

Scientific and technical texts describe things like biological life, natural phenomena, events, objects, materials, and processes. Depending on its purpose, **descriptive** writing can include definitions; details about the size, shape, or appearance of people and objects; details about how something works; or the steps in a process. Note in this excerpt how the writer uses language to describe one of Earth's mass extinctions. What type of details are used in describing the extinction? What figurative language is used? How does this description help you to understand this event?

> The single deadliest mass extinction in history took place 250 million years ago. Nicknamed "The Great Dying," the Permian–Triassic extinction resulted in the loss of 90 percent of all living species. Marine species were abundant during the Permian period, as were land animals like synapsids, which were mammal-like reptiles. Some geologists point to a catastrophic event, like an asteroid impact, as a cause for such a huge loss of species. To support the theory, geologists offer evidence: "shocked" quartz crystal, which is defined as quartz with microscopic fractures caused by powerful explosions, such as asteroid impacts. Geologists discovered an enormous crater in Antarctica in 2006 that they say may be the footprint of such an impact. If such an explosion took place, carbon dioxide levels would spike, contributing to a warming of the planet.

To **analyze descriptive writing**, first consider the overall purpose of the text. Then analyze the descriptive language and details and why they are included. Doing this will help you understand the impact the writing has on you.

- What is the purpose of the text? To Explain? Persuade? Describe?
- What sensory details does the writer include? Why?
- What figurative language is used in the description?
- What descriptive details are included?
- What is the purpose of any visual included with the descriptive text?
- How is the description used? To create a mental image? Make ideas more vivid or clear? Is it effective?

- How does the descriptive language contribute to the mood or tone of the text?
- How does the description affect you and/or what emotions does it evoke?

EXERCISE 4

A. Read the essay.

The Symbol of the Fox in Medieval Culture

1   European literature in the Middle Ages was rich with animal symbolism. A white dove, for example, symbolized peace and love, and for Christians, the Holy Spirit. Another animal, the dog, often represented loyalty. Some of the most popular stories in medieval times were fables, which are stories that communicate a moral message and have animal characters that speak, wear clothes, walk on two legs, and otherwise behave just like humans. While many animals appear in medieval fables, the fox is the animal that takes the spotlight as a "trickster." A trickster is a character who uses dishonest methods like lying and cheating to succeed. At times, the fox's trickiness is meant to be admired. At other times, it is simply used as a warning to people to be careful of evil, deceptive behavior.

2   Medieval fables about foxes are based on the red fox, which is native to parts of Europe and Asia. The red fox has vibrant, fiery-orange fur and intelligent, catlike eyes. The red fox, a clever hunter of small animals like mice and birds, excels at adapting to its environment. Like wolves, foxes sometimes kill more than they need, which gives them the reputation of being cruel. The fox has a long history of appearing as a wise, sly character. For example, in a vase from Ancient Greece that dates back to the 5th century BCE, a fox can be seen talking to Aesop, who is a legendary author of fables. On the richly-painted black vase, the red figure of the fox amuses Aesop with his clever stories.

3   Aesop's fables were, in fact, quite popular in medieval times. Several of the most famous of these fables feature the fox. One in particular, called *The Fox and the Crow*, is depicted in many art works and story collections from the medieval period. In the story, the fox wants a piece of cheese that the crow is eating. However, the crow is

high up the tree, where the fox cannot reach. From below, the fox begins to praise the crow's appearance and its beautiful song. The reader is immediately in on the joke, which is that the crow, with its plain black feathers, is not considered beautiful among birds, and even less beautiful is its call, which is harsh and unpleasant. In the story, however, the foolish crow believes the fox's flattery. The bird opens its mouth to sing to the fox, and when it does, the cheese falls from its mouth to the ground. The moral of the story, of course, is that a person should not always trust flatterers.

Illustration from Goethe's *The Story of Reynard the Fox*

4   The trickster fox went on to become a well-developed character in European medieval literature. A large collection of stories about a fox named Reynard became immensely popular in France, and they spread to other European countries. The stories were so beloved that the name of the fox in the stories became a synonym for "fox" in French. Even today, *renard* means "fox" in French. Reynard stories are much longer and more elaborate than the simple fable about the fox and the crow. They are also political satires, meaning they make powerful people look foolish. For example, in the stories, Reynard often tricks the king and other men at court by lying to them and stealing from them. Reynard wins through trickery, and though the reader might admire his success, his behavior is not meant to be imitated. Sometimes the fox is called the "antihero" in stories, meaning that he is a hero who succeeds because of his negative characteristics.

5   In medieval times, the stories of the fox were a way for people to explain human nature and to express how they understood the world. Some books at that time portrayed the fox as an evil character. The fox is drawn lying on its back, its tongue hanging out of its mouth, pretending to be dead. In reality, it is waiting for birds to come close enough to catch and eat. The moral lesson in these stories is that the fox, like the devil, is deceptive and encourages people to sin. The fox's reputation as a cunning, tricky, or even evil character is found in many Asian countries, as well. In Japan and Korea, for example, the fox is an intelligent, powerful, often evil character with ability to change form or identity and have influence over others. In Chinese mythology, the fox has supernatural or magical powers and it is sometimes considered to be a spiritual or enlightened being.

6   The fox's infamous reputation has remained surprisingly unchanged over the centuries. Today, stories in which the fox symbolizes some of the negative qualities of humanity are still common. These stories, while modern, are not so different from the tales told in the Middle Ages of the clever fox with the highly questionable behavior.

Glossary

Sly: clever

Cunning: using clever, but unfair or dishonest ways of getting what you want, especially ways that involve deceiving people

B. Answer the questions.

1. How does the essay define fables? ....
   ....
   ....

2. Why is the fox often featured in medieval fables? ....
   ....
   ....

3. What is the moral of Aesop's fable *The Fox and the Crow*? How is the fox used to deliver this moral? ....
   ....
   ....

4. How are the French stories about Reynard similar to Aesop's fables? How are they different? ....
   ....
   ....

5. How is the fox described in medieval stories? Who is the fox compared to? Why?
   ....
   ....

6. What unique characteristics does the fox have in Asian cultures? ....
   ....

7. How is the fox portrayed in modern culture? ....
   ....
   ....

C. Analyze the descriptive writing in the essay by answering the questions.

1. What is the purpose of the text? To Explain? Persuade? Describe? ....
....
....

2. What sensory details does the writer include (sight, sound, touch, smell, and taste) to describe the fox? Why? ....
....
....

3. What figurative language is used in the description? ....
....
....

4. What descriptive details are included? ....
....
....

5. What is the mood or tone of the text? ....
....
....

6. Do the descriptive passages help you create a mental image? Which image is most vivid for you? Why? Is there any part of the essay where more description would help you understand the character of the fox? Explain. ....
....
....

7. Is description used to make ideas clearer? If so, how? ....
....
....

8. Which descriptions in the text evoke specific emotions? What emotions are evoked? Why? ....
....
....

9. How does the visual add to the description in the text? ....
....
....

10. How effective is the essay in accomplishing its purpose? Use specific examples from the text to support your answer. ....
....
....

D. Compare your answers in Part C with a partner. Discuss the descriptive language and details used in the essay. Do you agree with your partner? Why or why not?

E. Write one or two paragraphs in which you analyze the descriptive writing in the essay in Part A. Include examples from the essay to support your analysis.

VOCABULARY CHECK

A. Review the vocabulary items in the Vocabulary Preview. Write their definitions and add examples. Use a dictionary if necessary.

B. Choose the sentence that correctly describes the underlined item.

1. The lesson behind the story seems simple, but that is <u>deceptive</u> because it is actually complicated.

   a. I was very surprised because I thought I understood the story.
   b. I didn't like the story because it was complicated.

2. Professor Blake is <u>infamous</u> for giving unfair grades, but I was happy with the A- I got in her class.

   a. I heard that she doesn't know much about the subject she teaches.
   b. I heard that she is very unpopular with most of her students.

3. That story <u>depicted</u> medieval York in such an interesting way.

   a. I loved all of the descriptions of the city and now I want to visit there!
   b. I didn't understand what the writer was trying to say about York's history.

4. I do a lot of reading during the <u>harsh</u> winters in Alberta.

   a. It is hard to be outside in the bad weather, so I stay home as much as possible.
   b. It is expensive to travel outside of Alberta, so I stay home as much as possible.

5. Lena's mother was upset because Lena wore a <u>plain</u> dress for her wedding.

    a. Lena didn't want to buy a new dress because the wedding cost a lot of money.

    b. Lena always dresses in simple clothing and she wanted to be comfortable.

6. Professor Rogers <u>excels</u> at writing poetry in a medieval style even though many of the words are different than those we use today.

    a. He has learned a lot about medieval history by traveling to England and he is now writing a book.

    b. He has won many awards and is the chair of medieval studies at a prestigious university.

7. Troubadours helped <u>spread</u> information about different towns and cities since they traveled a lot.

    a. People thought the troubadours' stories were interesting, but they didn't always believe them.

    b. People liked to hear the troubadours' news and then tell other people what they learned.

8. Many people <u>praised</u> the exhibit about the history of illuminated manuscripts.

    a. The newspaper review said it was the best exhibit about illuminated manuscripts in New York.

    b. The newspaper review said most people in New York don't know much about illuminated manuscripts.

9. Illuminated manuscripts often used <u>vibrant</u> colors because it helped people understand the stories more easily.

    a. It is helpful to use similar colors to describe wars and other important events.

    b. It is helpful to use bright, strong colors to describe wars and other important events.

10. Artists today <u>imitate</u> the work of medieval illustrators by creating illuminated manuscript pages using similar techniques and styles.

    a. Reproducing these pages helps to preserve the art form.

    b. Preserving these pages is important to saving this art form.

◐ Go to MyEnglishLab to complete vocabulary and skill practices and to join in collaborative activities.

LANGUAGE SKILL

VARYING DESCRIPTION

> **WHY IT'S USEFUL** By varying description using effective and expressive language, your writing will be more vivid for your reader. Well-chosen adjectives, strong nouns, and specific action verbs along with different sentence structures help you create images that your reader will remember.

🔊 Go to MyEnglishLab for the Language Skill presentation and practice.

VOCABULARY STRATEGY

USING A CORPUS TO EXPAND WORD KNOWLEDGE

> **WHY IT'S USEFUL** By using a corpus, you can see how language is actually used in professional, academic, or social settings. This will broaden and deepen your understanding of vocabulary and help you use language the way native speakers do.

A **corpus** is a large collection of samples of written or spoken texts used for studying the English language. Because of today's technology, an online corpus can have millions of language samples created from actual conversations, newspaper articles, business letters, academic texts, and other contexts. A corpus will help you gain a broader understanding of how a word is used in different situations and real-world contexts, and a deeper understanding of the variations possible in the meaning and use of the word. By conducting quick, online searches, you will be exposed to numerous examples of how words or phrases are used in authentic, real-world contexts. Using a corpus can be an efficient way to analyze and notice different uses of a word, such as:

- common collocations
  - verbs commonly used with certain nouns
  - prepositions commonly used with certain verbs
  - typical word combinations like phrasal verbs and compound nouns
- idiomatic phrases in which a word frequently occurs
- grammatical patterns associated with a word
- registers, or language used in professional, academic, or social contexts

One of the biggest challenges for learners is having enough language exposure to develop a deep understanding of a word. For idioms or field-specific vocabulary, a corpus helps you increase your awareness and in-depth knowledge of vocabulary because you will see different ways words are used. Traditional dictionaries often present words in isolation and sometimes only provide thin definitions for specialized vocabulary or idiomatic phrases. An online corpus complements your dictionary learning by providing exposure to numerous example sentences for each entry.

Many online dictionaries now incorporate corpus sentences to help learners gain more exposure to words and broaden their word knowledge from naturally occurring texts. These dictionaries often highlight different uses of a word to make it easier for learners to conduct language analysis.

Read the *Longman Dictionary of Contemporary English Online* definitions for the word *plain* along with its examples from the Longman Corpus Network. Notice how the word *plain* is used in different contexts to refer to food, people, and other objects. An interesting grammatical pattern is that it often precedes other adjectives (e.g., *plain and simple* or *plain brown* [or any color]). The corpus shows the phrase *it is plain (that)* as a common grammatical pattern. Also, the phrase *the plain truth* is a common idiomatic phrase. After analyzing the sentences, what new insights do you have about this word? How might you use this word in your writing or speaking today?

> **TIP**
>
> There are many websites that use corpus tools for language learning. To find a reputable and free corpus, do an online search for "English corpus." Choose a corpus that has millions of samples and that is associated with a reputable school or company.

---

plain¹ /pleɪn/ ••• [SW] [W3] adjective

1   [CLEAR] **very clear, and easy to understand or recognize**
2   [SIMPLE] **without anything added or without decoration**
3   [HONEST] **showing clearly and honestly what is true or what you think about something**
4   [NOT BEAUTIFUL] **not beautiful or attractive; often used because you want to avoid saying this directly**

[EXAMPLES FROM THE CORPUS]

plain

- The company makes **plain** and sweet biscuits and sodacrackers.
- Catherine, who had been rather **plain** as a child, was now an attractive young woman.
- He put the letter in a **plain** brown envelope.
- The document is written in **plain** English.
- Miles was the **plain** one in an otherwise good-looking family.
- Stuffed hardboiled eggs, most often called deviled eggs, can be spicy, **plain**, or very exotic.
- She spoke slowly and carefully, using **plain**, simple language.
- Do you have any **plain** white shirts?
- The chapel was a small, **plain**, white-washed building.

(Continued)

it is plain (that)

- From what I have heard of you, **it is plain** you have fled from somewhere.
- However this may be, **it is plain** that the district judge must have tacitly rejected the argument.
- Yet **it is plain** that the selfishness of a gene can have nothing whatever in common with human egoism.

the plain truth

- I've never seen her before in my life, and that's **the plain truth**.
- That is not a metaphor, it is **the plain truth**.
- But **the plain truth** is that we cannot say what was really done for the children or what the results were.

EXERCISE 5

A. Read the definitions and the corpus sentences for the adjective *harsh*. **Answer the questions.**

---

harsh /hɑːʃ/ ●●○ **adjective**

1 CONDITIONS **harsh conditions are difficult to live in and very uncomfortable**
2 TREATMENT/CRITICISM **severe, cruel, or unkind**
harsh criticism/treatment/punishment etc.
3 SOUND **unpleasantly loud and rough**
4 LIGHT/COLOR **unpleasantly bright**

EXAMPLES FROM THE CORPUS

harsh

.... • The stage lighting is **harsh**.
.... • They suspended him? That seems pretty **harsh**.
.... • Her reaction to the child's bad behaviour was unnecessarily **harsh**.
.... • It revived concern over the **harsh** army round-ups in captured towns and villages.
.... • Since the building of that dam this terrain had been **harsh**, brutal, and bad.
.... • The movie has received **harsh** criticism from the press.
.... • "You'll do what I tell you," he said, his voice **harsh** in her ear.
.... • The lighting in these offices is so **harsh**, it gives me a headache.
.... • The refugees stumbled toward military buses, blinking at the **harsh** lights.

---

harsh realities

- One of the **harsh realities** about the electronic media is that it chews up its stars as fast as it creates them.
- The cold, **harsh realities** of life are for other people to worry about.
- Acknowledging the sometimes **harsh realities** of our own history should not be cause for self-flagellation and blame.

harsh words

- It may mean heated arguments, **harsh words**, and hurt feelings, but once the air is cleared everyone will feel better.
- She had only a few **harsh words**, mostly for Hollywood and its residents.
- I should put aside the **harsh words** that had been said; I should try to make the best of everything.

---

1. Which definition matches each sentence? Write the number of the corpus definition for each sentence.

2. Why do *harsh realities* and *harsh words* have their own entries? Write an original sentence for each phrase. ....

   ....

   ....

3. In what contexts is *harsh* used? Using the information from the corpus sentences, is it appropriate to use in an academic paper? Why or why not? ....

   ....

   ....

4. What else do you notice about how *harsh* is used? ....

   ....

   ....

B. Choose three words from this unit that you want to learn more about. Go to *Longman Dictionary of Contemporary English Online* **(or an online corpus) and enter the word. Analyze the words by answering the questions and writing your responses in the chart.**

1. What is the word and definition?
2. What recurring patterns in the corpus sentences indicate a collocation or idiomatic phrase?
3. What grammatical patterns, if any, are associated with the word?
4. In what contexts are these words used? Are the words appropriate for professional, academic, and/or social settings?
5. What other features do you notice about how this word is used?

Word and Definition	Recurring Patterns	Grammatical Patterns	Contexts	Other Features

C. Share your analysis with a partner and discuss what you have learned about the words. How has this analysis deepened your understanding of the words? How do you expect to use the words in your own writing? Add this vocabulary to your vocabulary flashcards, journal, or study list.

⊙ Go to MyEnglishLab to complete a skill practice.

APPLY YOUR SKILLS

WHY IT'S USEFUL By applying the skills you have learned in this unit, you can successfully use figurative language; appeal to ethos, pathos, and logos; analyze descriptive writing; vary description; and use a corpus to expand your understanding of words.

ASSIGNMENT
Research a folklore story that ends with a moral or lesson. Identify the genre, briefly summarize the story, and write an essay of 500–800 words analyzing the style and appeal. Report on how description and figurative language, including symbolism and imagery, were used in telling the story.

BEFORE YOU WRITE

A. Before you begin your assignment, discuss these questions with one or more students.

1. What genres of fiction, art, and music do you like? Think about the differences between the genres and then focus on one. What style characteristics does it have? Why do these style characteristics appeal to you?

2. What are some common figures of speech from a language you are familiar with? Are there similar expressions in other languages? Ask your classmates or someone you know who speaks another language.

3. What makes an image memorable? Describe a vivid image that you remember from a book, movie, or play, and explain why it is memorable.

B. As you consider your writing assignment, complete the tasks. Then share your ideas with another student. Get feedback and revise your ideas if necessary.

1. Write the name of the story you have chosen to write about. Why did you choose it? Briefly summarize the story orally to another student.

   ....

   ....

2. List the genre, the audience, and the purpose of the story. What appeal is used to persuade the reader that the lesson is valuable? ....

   ....

   ....

3. How is description and figurative language used in telling the story? Why is description and figurative language used? Does the story have an image? If so, describe the image and explain why it was included. If not, describe an image that you would include.

C. Review the Unit Skills Summary. As you begin the writing task on page 313, apply the skills you learned in this unit.

UNIT SKILLS SUMMARY

Use figurative language

- Use figurative language to create vivid mental images for the reader.
- Use mental images to help the reader experience events in a story and understand concepts.
- Use similes, metaphors, personification, hyperbole, imagery, and symbolism to create vivid and memorable images.

Appeal to ethos, pathos, logos

- Identify your audience and purpose for writing.
- Consider how to engage and persuade your readers.
- Use ethos to build your credibility.
- Use pathos to present emotional appeals.
- Use logos to appeal to logic.

Analyze descriptive writing

- Consider the overall purpose of the text.
- Analyze the descriptive language and details.
- Analyze why the writer includes description in the text.

Vary description

- Vary description, through word choice and sentence structure.
- Use specific adjectives, concrete nouns, and action verbs in description.
- Vary sentence structure by using adjective clauses and embedded phrases to describe.
- Combine sentences in both compound and complex sentences to vary sentence structure.

Use a corpus to expand word knowledge

- Analyze and notice different uses of words such as:
  - common collocations
  - idiomatic phrases
  - grammatical patterns
  - registers
- Gain more exposure to words in naturally occurring texts.

THINKING CRITICALLY

As you consider your writing assignment, discuss the questions with another student. Get feedback and revise your ideas if necessary.

1. Experts disagree on a definition of folklore. An early folklore definition looked only at what the expert called "traditional and poorer segments of society" and examined items only from these groups, while folklorists now consider all cultures and groups within a culture to have folklore. Modern definitions include how the community interacts as well as at the items it produces. Which definition do you agree with and why?

2. Psycholinguists, experts who study the brain and language, suggest that we remember strong mental images, especially ones that we have an emotional connection to, better than abstract concepts. This is a strong argument for including description in writing. Do you agree or disagree? Give reasons for your answer.

3. Which type of appeal do you think has the most influence on you, ethos, pathos, or logos? Some people think that the appeal has to be to our emotions to be effective. Do you agree with this?

THINKING VISUALLY

A. Look at the illustration for "The Princess and the Frog," one of the stories you read in Exercise 1, Part A. Answer the questions.

1. What information does this illustration give you about the story?

2. Is the visual effective in understanding the story?

3. Write two or three sentences describing the illustration.

B. Find or create a visual for the folklore story for your writing assignment. Explain how it helps the reader understand the story.

....

....

THINKING ABOUT LANGUAGE

Write six descriptive sentences for your assignment using adjectives, nouns, and action verbs. Vary sentence structure. Include an adjective clause, an embedded phrase, and at least one compound or complex sentence.

1. ....

....

2. ....

....

3. ....

....

4. ....

....

5. ....

....

6. ....

....

WRITE

A. Revisit the writing assignment and your answers to the questions in Before You Write, Part B.

B. Write a summary of the folklore story. Be sure to restate the story in your own words.

C. Consider the use of descriptive language as you analyze the style and appeal of the story. Vary description in your own writing to create images that your reader will remember.

BEYOND THE ASSIGNMENT

Write a paper of 800–1000 words analyzing the style and appeal of a work of fiction or nonfiction. Consider the rhetorical context and how the author engages the reader. What types of appeals does the author use? How is description and figurative language used?

◊ Go to MyEnglishLab to watch Professor Galvez's concluding video and to complete a self-assessment.

MATERIALS ENGINEERING

Research Writing

UNIT PROFILE

Elastomers are elastic materials that are essential for use in applications that support space exploration missions to Earth's orbit, the Moon, and Mars. In this unit, you will read and write about topics related to selecting the right material for a task by evaluating its different properties, and how the wrong decision can lead to a tragedy like the 1986 explosion of the Space Shuttle Challenger.

Write a 1000–1200 word section of a Materials Engineering research paper on polymeric materials. Choose one synthetic polymeric (plastic) material and analyze its properties, characteristics, and processing techniques, focusing on how these enable the polymer to work in various applications. Prepare notes for an oral presentation on that section.

For more about **MATERIALS ENGINEERING**, see ❶❸.

See also ⟦R⟧ and ⟦OC⟧ **MATERIALS ENGINEERING** ❶❷❸.

OUTCOMES

- Develop a research summary
- Develop a strong conclusion
- Present a research paper
- Use parallel structure
- Understand suffixes

GETTING STARTED

🔊 Go to MyEnglishLab to watch Professor Heilshorn's introductory video and to complete a self-assessment.

Discuss these questions with a partner or group.

1. Plastics consist of synthetic polymers, and we see them everywhere. What are some common uses of plastics? How have these materials changed the world we live in, for example, everyday items, technology, and transportation?

2. What types of materials are used in the aerospace industry? Why are these materials useful in space exploration? What properties seem important in materials used in space?

3. Professor Heilshorn suggests that polymers are a class of material that is all around us, including in our bodies. What natural polymers might be in our bodies? What are other natural polymers in the environment, including in your own body?

CRITICAL THINKING SKILL

RESEARCH WRITING

WHY IT'S USEFUL By becoming proficient at research writing, you will gain a deeper understanding of the topics you are studying in your courses. You will also ensure that your original ideas and perspectives are supported and validated by credible sources, which is critical in both your educational and professional pursuits.

Research is the foundation of most types of academic writing, including essays, analyses, research papers, and lab reports. **Research writing** assignments must be informed by established facts and ideas from experts in the discipline and must go beyond the writer's personal experience or observations, often while discovering new facts or testing new ideas.

Professors expect students to demonstrate thoughtful analyses and understanding of topics that are informed by research. Conducting research extends the information from your textbooks and classroom lectures, and allows you to analyze or apply that information in real-world contexts. The research will help you understand various viewpoints of an issue and will provide facts, opinions, or ideas to include in your writing. As you write, you will formulate original ideas, perspectives, or interpretations and use the research to effectively support your ideas.

A critical component to research writing is an understanding of what research already exists on your topic. Listening to experts will help you understand the

> **TIP**
>
> Scientific and medical journals typically organize abstracts into these sections: background, objective, method, results, and conclusions. Often, however, abstracts will consist of just one cohesive paragraph.

subject and give you ideas for research. Reading both primary, or original, research and secondary research articles will give you a more comprehensive foundation on a topic. Many research articles include an **abstract**, which is a 150–200 word summary containing the most important ideas in the larger work. Reading abstracts will help you quickly identify the purpose of the research and decide whether the complete article is relevant to your topic. In some classes, you may be required to **develop a research summary** for one or more research articles or studies. You may also be asked to evaluate the articles.

After listening to, reading, and summarizing research—extending your knowledge of a topic and demonstrating that you are familiar with the literature by including well-developed ideas supported by the research—you will be prepared to **develop a strong conclusion** that emphasizes your original ideas and the importance of the topic and includes implications and possible suggestions for future research.

> For more on primary and secondary sources, see Business Ethics, Part 1.

> **TIP**
>
> Reading a wide range of abstracts online can help you find ideas for a research topic, develop a research question, and/or narrow your topic.

VOCABULARY PREVIEW

Read the vocabulary items. Circle the ones you know. Put a question mark next to the ones you don't know.

monitor (v)	seal (n)	component	rehabilitation	conventional
chronic	traumatic	investigation	compression	quantify

EXERCISE 1

A. Read the writing assignment.

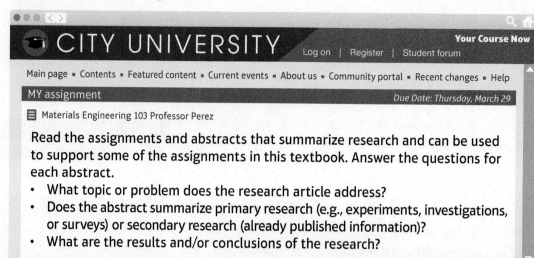

Log on | Register | Student forum

Main page • Contents • Featured content • Current events • About us • Community portal • Recent changes • Help

MY assignment   Due Date: Thursday, March 29

Materials Engineering 103 Professor Perez

Read the assignments and abstracts that summarize research and can be used to support some of the assignments in this textbook. Answer the questions for each abstract.

• What topic or problem does the research article address?
• Does the abstract summarize primary research (e.g., experiments, investigations, or surveys) or secondary research (already published information)?
• What are the results and/or conclusions of the research?

ASSIGNMENT: Write a research paper on food security. Include factors that impact food security and ways to mitigate them in the future.

Abstract

Climate Change and Food Security: Health Impacts in Developed Countries

Background: Climate change will affect global food production, with uncertain consequences for human health in developed countries.

Objectives: We investigated the potential impact of climate change on food security (nutrition and food safety) and the implications for human health in developed countries.

Methods: Literature searches were conducted and synthesized to produce comprehensive assessments of the likely impacts of climate change on global food production and recommendations for future research and policy changes.

Results: Rising food prices may lower the nutritional quality of dietary intakes and increase health inequalities. Altered conditions for food production may result in emerging pathogens, new crop and livestock species, and different use of pesticides, and may also affect how contaminants move from the environment into food. All these have implications for food safety and the nutritional content of food. People may address climate change by increasing consumption of foods whose production reduces greenhouse gas emissions. Impacts may include reduced red meat consumption and reduced winter fruit and vegetable consumption. Developed countries have complex structures in place that may be used to adapt to the food safety consequences of climate change, although their effectiveness will vary between countries, and the ability to respond to nutritional challenges is less certain.

Conclusions: Climate change will have notable impacts upon nutrition and food safety in developed countries, but further research is necessary to accurately quantify these impacts. Evidence that climate change may lead to more variable food quality emphasizes the need to maintain and strengthen existing structures and policies to regulate food production, monitor food quality and safety, and respond to nutritional and safety issues that arise.

Glossary

Pathogen: bacteria or organism that causes disease

ASSIGNMENT: Write about the use of regenerative treatment for one specific injury or illness. What materials are used? Discuss types and their advantages and disadvantages. What is the role of stem cells?

Tissue Engineering and Regenerative Medicine Applications in the Ankle Joint

Abstract

Tissue engineering and regenerative medicine (TERM) have caused a revolution in present and future trends of medicine and surgery. In different tissues, advanced TERM approaches bring new therapeutic possibilities in the general population as well as in young patients and high-level athletes, improving restoration of biological functions and rehabilitation. The mainstream components required for regeneration of tissues may include biodegradable scaffolds, drugs or growth factors, and different cell types that can be cultured *in vitro* before implantation into the patient. Particularly in the ankle, which is subject to a wide range of injuries (e.g., chronic, traumatic, and degenerative), there is still no definitive answer to conventional methods. This literature review aims to provide current concepts of TERM applications to ankle injuries under research applied to skin, tendon, bone, and cartilage problems. Particular attention has been given to biomaterial design and scaffold processing.

Glossary

Cartilage: a strong substance that can bend and stretch, which is around the joints in a person's or animal's body and in places such as the outer ear and the end of the nose

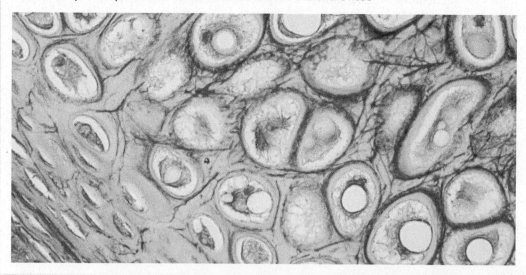

ASSIGNMENT: Write a research paper on one polymeric material used in space applications and analyze its properties, characteristics, and/or processing techniques.

Material Properties of Three Candidate Elastomers for Space Applications

Abstract

A next-generation docking system is being developed by the National Aeronautics and Space Administration (NASA) to support Space Exploration Missions to Earth's orbit, the Moon, and Mars. A number of investigations were carried out to quantify the properties of three candidate silicone elastomer materials for use in the main seal of the Low Impact Docking System. This seal forms the gas pressure seal between two mating spacecraft. All three materials were characterized as low-outgassing compounds, per industry standards, so as to minimize the contamination of optical and solar components. Critical seal properties such as outgas levels, hardness, tensile strength, elongation, glass transition temperature, permeability, compression set, and thermal expansion were measured and are documented in this study.

Glossary

Silicone: a chemical that is not changed by heat or cold, does not let water through, and is used in making artificial body parts, paint, and rubber

Elastomer: natural or artificial polymer having elastic properties

Tensile strength: the ability of a material to bear pressure or weight without breaking

Outgassing: releasing of gas from a material

Glass transition temperature: the temperature region where a polymer changes from a hard, glassy material to a soft, rubbery material

Permeability: a quality that allows water or gas to pass through a material

CULTURE NOTE

In the early 20th century, scientists learned how to create synthetic polymers, or modern plastics, from petroleum. However, the plastics industry did not become widely popular until World War II, when the demand increased for plastics in vehicles, weapons, and other military applications.

B. What type of evidence would you expect to find in the original research studies of the abstracts in Part A that could support your ideas for the writing assignments? What types of visuals might be included? Discuss your answers with a partner.

C. Find an abstract on an academic topic you are interested in. Answer the questions in Part A. How is the format similar to or different from the ones in this exercise?

VOCABULARY CHECK

A. Review the vocabulary items in the Vocabulary Preview. Write their definitions and add examples. Use a dictionary if necessary.

B. Complete each sentence with the correct vocabulary item.

chronic	components	compression	conventional	investigation
monitor	quantify	rehabilitation	seals	traumatic

1. Air that is under .... often helps machines work, but it can also be dangerous.

2. .... injuries can be easier to treat when the patient was healthy before being hurt.

3. .... are very important to connect parts of any machine; parts need to stay together so that machines work properly.

4. There are so many types of .... , such as learning to walk, talk, or even breathe again after an illness or injury.

5. Some doctors always use .... methods to treat their patients; others like to try something new in the hope of finding a better way.

6. After the fire in the university's chemistry lab, there was a long and careful .... to learn how it got started.

7. Good scientists are always able to .... their research findings; seeing numbers helps to simplify complex ideas.

8. It is critical that scientists .... air, water, and food over time and check in different ways to make sure they stay safe.

9. Treating .... pain is very difficult because doctors have to consider their patients' daily routines and all the factors that affect their lives.

10. Most machines have many .... and if one of these parts breaks, the whole machine will often stop working.

🔊 Go to MyEnglishLab to complete vocabulary and skill practices and to join in collaborative activities.

SUPPORTING SKILL 1

DEVELOPING A RESEARCH SUMMARY

WHY IT'S USEFUL By developing a research summary, you will be able to better understand the current and relevant research in a discipline. You will later be able to incorporate the results of the research into your work to effectively support your own ideas in writing.

As part of your academic experience, you will read and discuss scholarly journal articles that present scientific research supported by data. The information in research articles will give you an in-depth understanding of current issues that scholars are studying and investigating in a discipline. You may be asked to summarize the information in one or more research articles as part of a course requirement.

A **research summary** presents a description of what a study is about, the methods used, the study's results, and their significance. A research summary is longer than the abstract at the beginning of a research article because it provides a comprehensive description of the study by including more details and discussion.

To **develop a research summary**, you must first read a research article critically, then plan an outline, write the summary, and finally review it.

Understanding the format of a research article is helpful as you prepare to develop the summary. A research article usually includes these sections:

Abstract	Summarizes the research study; typically includes goals, results, and/or conclusions
Introduction	Provides background information and a rationale for the study; often includes a literature review of other research related to the topic
Methods	Describes how the research was conducted; includes information on materials, participants, procedures, and data
Results	Describes and analyzes the data and the results of the study; typically contains charts and graphs to present the results
Discussion/ Conclusion	Interprets the data and explains the significance of the study; often concludes with suggestions for further research
References	Includes a list of all sources used for the research study

Reading a research article can be challenging because the topics are often complex and include highly technical or discipline-specific vocabulary. Thoroughly understanding the ideas presented in a research article often takes time because you will probably need to read the article several times to fully understand it. Use a variety of reading strategies to boost your comprehension:

- Read the abstract first to give you an overview.

- Read the conclusion before reading the full article. The authors will restate the purpose of the study and the key findings in the conclusion so you can later identify them in the article.

- Identify key ideas and information. Annotate the text and paraphrase ideas in the margin.

- Analyze and take notes on the graphs, tables, and charts to understand how the data supports the conclusions.

For more on annotating research, see Linguistics, Part 1.

After you have read and understood the research article, take time to **plan**, by identifying and organizing the most important points.

- Review your notes to decide what information should be included in the summary.

- Make a list of key words and technical or discipline-specific vocabulary to include.

For more on outlining, see Linguistics, Part 1.

- Create an outline that includes the rationale for the study, the methods, results, and discussion/conclusion.

As you **write** your summary of the research article, include all the main ideas in the research article and present them in the same order as the original research. You do not need to summarize the abstract, literature review, or raw data information. Unlike a paper or essay, you do not need to use reminder phrases to refer back to the source or include direct quotes.

- Include a citation using the style guidelines you have been told to follow.

For more on summarizing, see Earth Science, Part 1.

- Paraphrase the ideas from the original text.

- Use discipline-specific, technical, or scientific vocabulary as needed.

For more on paraphrasing, see Business Ethics, Part 1.

- Use concise language.

As with all academic writing, it is essential that you **review** your work by revising, editing, and proofreading your writing before submission. While your summary will include important details and discussion presented in the research, and the length may vary depending on your purpose, it should be written as concisely as possible and will be shorter than the original article.

TIP

Like all summaries, do not offer your opinion unless your professor requires this as part of the assignment. Sometimes students will be asked to include a critical analysis or short evaluation describing the relevance of the research to their own work and their reaction to it as part of an annotated bibliography.

VOCABULARY PREVIEW

Read the vocabulary items. Circle the ones you know. Put a question mark next to the ones you don't know.

exploration	evaluate	debris	simulated
expose	property	elastic	brittleness

EXERCISE 2

A. Read the summary of the research article *Material Properties of Three Candidate Elastomers for Space Seals Applications.*

1 The National Aeronautics and Space Administration (NASA) is developing a Low Impact Docking System for use in future space explorations of Earth's orbit, the Moon, and Mars. The docking system includes a main gas pressure seal that must prevent breathable air from escaping into space while two mating spacecraft vehicles are docked. This seal will be exposed to a variety of space elements, such as atomic oxygen, ultraviolet radiation, extreme temperatures, small meteoroids, and other space debris, when spacecraft are not docked. The goal of this research study is to summarize and evaluate the properties of three elastomers (Silicone A, Silicone B, and Silicone C) as possible materials in the design of the gas pressure seal.

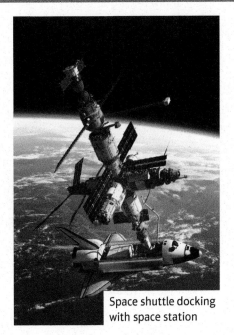

Space shuttle docking with space station

2 A variety of material properties were evaluated under a simulated space environment. Because the seals will be impacted by meteoroids and space debris, the elastomers were measured for their different values of hardness. In addition, tensile strength and elongation were measured to determine the ability to withstand potential damage caused by repeated docking and undocking of spacecraft. Brittleness and glass transition temperature properties were also measured to determine how well the elastomers would perform across large temperature ranges (−58° to 122° F) [−50° to 50° C]. The elastomers were tested for permeability at three different temperatures to measure the amount of air

(Continued)

and helium that leaked through the material. Finally, compression and thermal expansion tests were performed to evaluate how well the elastomers keep their elastic properties after being compressed for long periods of time. Several compression sets were performed at −58°, 77°, 122°, and 257° F (−50°, 25°, 50° and 125° C) for 70-hour periods of time.

3 The report includes a table summarizing and comparing the general material properties of the elastomers. All three silicone elastomers met NASA standards for low gas permeability; however, Silicone B was the least permeable, suggesting that a seal made from this elastomer would be the most effective at preventing oxygen from escaping. Compression set values remained relatively unchanged at room and refrigerated temperatures for all three elastomers. However, as temperatures increased to 257° F (125° C), the compression set values increased more significantly for both Silicone A and Silicone B than for Silicone C. The results from this study are a preliminary evaluation of possible elastomers for making the gas pressure seal; more testing and data collection will be required before a final selection is made.

Glossary

Meteoroid: a small piece of rock or metal that travels through space, but that has not entered Earth's atmosphere

CULTURE NOTE

Docking systems are used to join two separate spacecraft together in space. After launching, the space shuttle will dock with the International Space Station using a docking system.

B. Answer the questions.

1. What is the main purpose of the gas pressure seal for the Low Impact Docking System?

....

....

2. What type of space elements will the seal be exposed to? ....

....

3. What is the purpose of this research study? ....

....

4. What are the material properties that were evaluated? ....

....

5. Explain why the elastomers were evaluated for two of the material properties in Question 4.

....

....

6. What was the result of the permeability test for the three silicone elastomers?

....

....

C. Read the research summary again and answer the questions. Compare your answers with a partner.

1. What information does Paragraph 1 tell you about research? ....

....

2. What is the focus of Paragraph 2? How do you know? ....

....

3. What is the focus of Paragraph 3? How do you know? ....

....

4. What are some key words and discipline-specific vocabulary that the writer identified before writing the summary? ....

....

5. What are the strengths of this summary? ....

....

6. Is there anything you would change or improve? Explain. ....

....

....

D. Read and annotate the full research article for the abstract you read in Exercise 1 Part C. Use your notes to create an outline. Follow the guidelines to write a summary of the research article.

E. SELF-REVIEW. Evaluate your summary. For responses marked No, give feedback in the Notes column.

	Yes	No	Notes
Does the research summary give a description of what a study is about?	☐	☐	
Does the research summary describe the methods used?	☐	☐	
Does the research summary include the results and their significance?	☐	☐	
Are technical or discipline-specific vocabulary words included?	☐	☐	
Are the ideas paraphrased?	☐	☐	
Is the language concise?	☐	☐	
Is an academic citation included?	☐	☐	

VOCABULARY CHECK

A. Review the vocabulary items in the Vocabulary Preview. Write their definitions and add examples. Use a dictionary if necessary.

B. Choose the sentence that correctly describes the underlined item.

1. Products developed for use in space <u>exploration</u> resulted in scientists' inventing things that are now used all over the world.

   a. Products developed to help build space crafts are now used by people all over the world.
   b. Products developed for use in space travel resulted in scientists inventing things that are now used all over the world.

2. Scientists will continue to <u>evaluate</u> many of the products used in space travel to see which ones will be useful for people.

   a. They will test the best products to make sure they are safe for everyday use.
   b. They will buy the best products to make sure they are safe for everyday use.

3. Most people might be surprised to hear that there is a lot of <u>debris</u> in space.

   a. Scientists carefully watch this waste material because it could cause problems for spacecrafts.
   b. Scientists don't worry about watching spacecrafts from other countries because they don't cause problems with other spacecrafts.

4. Professor Wells used a <u>simulated</u> environment to test his invention before allowing it to be used in a hospital.

   a. It was safer to try the invention in a smaller hospital before allowing doctors to use it in bigger hospitals on people.
   b. It was safer to try the invention in a place that was just like a hospital before allowing doctors to use it on people.

5. Dr. Frio tested the highest air pressure that the new part for the spacecraft could be <u>exposed</u> to.

   a. Spacecraft are sometimes not protected from high air pressure, so she needs to calculate the highest pressure that is safe.
   b. Spacecraft sometimes need to have high air pressure, so she needs to calculate the highest pressure that is safe.

6. Scientists need to understand every <u>property</u> of the materials they use for building spacecrafts.

   a. There are many qualities that are safe for use in everyday life, but would be very dangerous in space.
   b. There are many machine parts that are safe for use in everyday life, but would be very dangerous in space.

7. It is best if materials used for building spacecrafts are <u>elastic</u> so they can be used in different ways.

   a. Spacecrafts often need materials to be able to be cut up so they can be used even if there are changes in the spacecraft,
   b. Spacecrafts often need materials to be able to stretch so they can be used even if there are changes in the spacecraft.

8. Scientists don't usually like to use <u>brittle</u> materials in spacecrafts.

   a. They don't want to use something that breaks easily.
   b. They don't want to use something that is very expensive.

🔘 Go to MyEnglishLab to complete vocabulary and skill practices and to join in collaborative activities.

SUPPORTING SKILL 2
DEVELOPING A STRONG CONCLUSION

WHY IT'S USEFUL By developing a strong conclusion, you remind your reader of your main points, demonstrate the importance of your ideas, and leave your reader with a positive final impression of your work.

The final section of an academic essay or research paper is the conclusion. This is a critical part of any paper as it is your final opportunity to address your reader, make an impression that will stay with your reader, and express how your ideas matter. A **strong conclusion** demonstrates the importance of your ideas and offers something interesting, meaningful, or useful to take away.

An effective conclusion goes beyond the paper and considers broader issues. It should do more than simply restate your thesis or summarize your points. It should synthesize your ideas and elaborate on the significance of your claims or the result of your findings. It should make new connections or comparisons to other situations, offer solutions or warn of consequences, provide new perspectives, or convince your reader to consider—or even accept—a new point of view on the topic.

Before beginning to write your conclusion, consider your purpose again and what you want to leave your reader with. Once you are ready to begin writing, combine one or more of these techniques with one or more of the strategies listed.

Conclusion Writing Techniques
Restate the thesis.
Summarize the main points.
Ask a thought-provoking question.
Add an appropriate quotation.
Create a vivid image.
Propose a solution or warn of consequences.
Make a call for further study, investigation, or action.

Conclusion Writing Strategies

Echo your introduction to bring your reader full circle by paralleling the ideas, images, key words, or scenarios you began with to demonstrate how your paper helped increase the reader's understanding.

Show how your main points, support, and examples fit together as a whole to create new meaning or fresh perspectives about the topic.

Broaden your specific topic to the general one to help your reader see the issue more globally and put your ideas in a larger context.

Consider style and tone to create a memorable ending using, for example, simple language for an understated effect or parallel structure for a balanced effect.

Use descriptive language and imagery to paint a picture that leaves a memorable and lasting impression on your reader.

Suggest a new direction or a different way to apply the information to challenge your reader to consider the implications of your ideas and look to the future.

Convey a sense of completeness and closure, but don't close off the discussion. This will allow for possibilities to further develop the topic.

Knowing what **not** to write in a conclusion is as important as knowing what **to** write:

Conclusion Writing Don'ts

✗ Don't simply restate the thesis.

✗ Don't use only a summary of your paper.

✗ Don't use emotional language that doesn't fit the style and tone of the paper.

✗ Don't add new information in support of your ideas.

✗ Don't introduce a new topic.

✗ Don't overuse transition words such as, "In conclusion," "To conclude," "In summary," and "To sum up".

✗ Don't apologize for your ideas or the depth of your study of the topic or suggest that there are others with better ideas.

TIP

Noticing and annotating how proficient writers use techniques and strategies in their conclusion is a good way to improve your own writing skills.

EXERCISE 3

A. Read the conclusions from two research papers. The first, about climate change, includes an excerpt from the introduction. The second, about tissue engineering, includes an excerpt from the abstract. Work with a partner to answer the questions. What techniques and strategies were used in the conclusion? Are there others that would be as effective or more effective?

Climate Change and Food Security: Health Impacts in Developed Countries

In developed countries, food shortages are uncommon and shortage of energy is not a major problem, although micronutrient deficiencies and overnutrition are prevalent. The nutritional quality and safety of food are the primary concerns related to food in these areas. In addition, climate change is likely to have a number of consequences for food security in developed countries. This review aims to investigate the possible impact of climate change on nutrition and food safety and on the subsequent consequences for health in developed countries.

Conclusion

Climate change will have notable impacts upon nutrition and food safety in developed countries, but further research is necessary to accurately quantify these impacts. Uncertainty about future impacts, coupled with evidence that climate change may lead to more variable food quality, emphasizes the need to maintain and strengthen existing means to monitor food quality and safety and governmental policies to regulate food production and respond to nutritional and safety issues that arise.

Tissue engineering and regenerative medicine applications in the ankle joint

This review aims to provide current concepts of tissue engineering and regenerative medicine research into applications to repair injuries to skin, tendon, bone, and cartilage problems of the ankle. Particular attention has been given to biomaterial design and scaffold processing.

Conclusion

The appropriate treatment for ankle injury repair is still controversial. The ideal technique would regenerate a tissue with biomechanical properties similar to normal cartilage. A variety of biomaterials including polymers and ceramics have been proposed for regeneration of the cartilage. Tissue engineering and regenerative medicine approaches are dramatically changing medicine and surgical practice. However, the success of these technologies at present and in the future requires deep knowledge of native tissue biology and understanding of its repair mechanisms and response to injury, as well as the new biomaterials under consideration. These approaches have proven to be effective in clinical cases and problems not previously solved by conventional therapeutic repair and/or replacement options. However, careful study and use of any promising new technique is important to avoid impairing or even blocking its proper development.

B. Read the summary of *Material Properties of Three Candidate Elastomers for Space Seal Applications* in Exercise 2, Part A and its abstract below. Suggest at least two techniques and two strategies for a strong conclusion. Which techniques and strategies would not work? Discuss your suggestions with a partner.

Material Properties of Three Candidate Elastomers for Space Seals Applications

A next-generation docking system is being developed by the National Aeronautics and Space Administration (NASA) to support Space Exploration Missions to low Earth orbit, to the Moon, and to Mars. A number of investigations were carried out to quantify the properties of three candidate silicone elastomer materials for use in the main seal of the Low Impact Docking System. This seal forms the gas pressure seal between two mating spacecraft. All three materials were characterized as low-outgassing compounds, per industry standards, so as to minimize the contamination of optical and solar components. Critical seal properties such as outgas levels, hardness, tensile strength, elongation, glass transition temperature, permeability, compression set, and thermal expansion were measured and are documented in this study.

C. Write a conclusion for one of the final assignments from a previous unit. Use at least two techniques and two strategies.

D. SELF-REVIEW. Evaluate your conclusion. Answer the questions.

	Response
What techniques and strategies were used in the conclusion?	
Why was each technique or strategy effective?	
Which other strategies would be effective?	
What was the reader left with? (something interesting, meaningful, or useful)	

Go to MyEnglishLab to complete a skill practice.

INTEGRATED SKILLS

PRESENTING A RESEARCH PAPER

WHY IT'S USEFUL By preparing a research paper for presentation, you will be able to take the ideas in research writing and organize and deliver them orally in a clear, concise, and comprehensible manner.

It is common for university students to be asked to present their ideas to class members, individually and in groups. Often students are expected to **give a presentation based on a research paper** they have written for the class.

There are differences in how ideas are developed and organized for writing versus oral presentations. Research papers are usually extended writing assignments that allow for ample length to fully develop and support ideas, whereas oral presentations are usually time limited and require that ideas be presented more concisely. The cohesion and coherence devices that are essential to good academic writing may become a hindrance to presenting ideas clearly in speaking. Embedded phrases and adjectives and intensifiers, common in academic writing for adding detail to supporting ideas, may be difficult for an audience to absorb while listening to a presentation. Finally, visuals like tables used in research writing to show data are usually too complex to use in an oral presentation. However, other types of visuals, such as pie charts, are helpful to quickly show or illustrate a point.

Presenting research requires that the information in a research paper be condensed and formatted differently so that the points can be presented in a way that is clear and understandable. Consider the differences between written texts, which are designed to be read, and notes for oral presentations, where the audience must listen and understand.

To condense and format the ideas in a research paper for an oral presentation:

- Identify the key points that you want to make.
- Rephrase the ideas into shorter, simpler phrases.
- Reorganize the ideas to most effectively present and support points.
- Eliminate transitions, connectors, lengthy embedded phrases, and unnecessary articles, adjectives, and intensifiers.
- Mark your text or notes for pauses and important words to emphasize.
- Replace complex visuals with visuals that can be understood quickly.

Look at the differences between written text and oral text.

Written text		Oral text or notes	
Embedded phrases to add detail Transition words and connectors for cohesion Intensifiers for emphasis Unnecessary adjectives and articles	Natural rubber material, a white liquid called latex, is taken out of rubber trees and processed to make a raw rubber product. This rubber product is then combined with sulfur and other additives and heated to a very carefully-controlled temperature that transforms the natural rubber into an elastomer material which is much stronger and more rigid. This vulcanized rubber is suitable for tires and many other products.	Concise text Pauses between phrases for cohesion [Marked with a /] Words to emphasize **nouns** verbs	**Latex** natural rubber **material**/ white **liquid**/ combined with **sulfur**/ other **additives**/ Heated to controlled **temperature**/ transforms into **elastomer**/ stronger/ more rigid/ suitable for **tires**/ other **products**/

When giving an oral presentation, visual presentation aids such as PowerPoint® or Prezi® are excellent tools to help you highlight your key points in a professional-looking way. Presentation slides, when done well and used effectively, enhance your presentation and help your audience remember and distinguish your main

TIP

Don't try to put everything you plan to say in your presentation on your slides. Use slides to support your ideas and help you emphasize key points.

and supporting ideas. However, when the slides are of poor quality, the opposite is true, and they may detract from your ideas or confuse your audience.

When preparing a presentation, carefully consider the appearance of the slides, the number of slides you use, and how you use them. Here are some useful preparation tips:

DO	DON'T
✓ Keep slides simple, uncluttered, and easy to read.	✗ Avoid putting too much text or too many points on a slide.
✓ Limit the number of points per slide to 4–6 points.	✗ Avoid using too many visuals, ones that are too complicated, or that present too much data.
✓ Use clear and visible images that explain your points.	
✓ Use a large enough font that everyone in your audience can read; consider varying the font size for effect.	✗ Do not use a font that is too small or overly stylized so that it is hard to read.
	✗ Do not use all capital letters or too many exclamation points!
✓ Proofread your slides and punctuate appropriately.	✗ Avoid colors or background designs that make text hard to read.
✓ Use colors that will enhance the content of your slides.	✗ Do not use full sentences, especially complex ones.
✓ Use concise phrases to organize text.	✗ Do not use unnecessary or filler slides that don't add information.
✓ Limit the number of slides to fit the length of the presentation.	✗ Do not provide a long or annotated bibliography.
✓ Include citations of sources.	
✓ End with a presentation slide thanking your audience and/or providing your contact information.	✗ Avoid ending with a content slide.

Look at the slide on the next page. Notice that there are a limited number of points on the slide, and they are laid out to help the reader see the steps in the process. The illustrations are easy to understand and help the reader. What else do you notice about the slide? Can you suggest any improvements?

Elastomers

Natural latex is processed into raw rubber → Raw rubber is combined with sulfur and other additives to make a product → Rubber product is heated to controlled temperatures → Product is transformed into strong, rigid elastomer

Natural latex

Vulcanized rubber

TIP

Don't flip through slides too quickly. The audience should have sufficient time to read and understand each slide as you speak, and the slide should fit what you are saying.

Once you have written your notes and prepared your slides, you are ready to make your presentation. Here are some useful **presentation tips:**

DO	DON'T
✓ Prepare and practice, speaking out loud, including pronouncing unfamiliar words.	✗ Do not read.
	✗ Do not mumble or swallow your words.
✓ Use a marked presentation text (notes).	✗ Avoid turning away from your audience to look at your presentation slides or looking down at your notes to read from them.
✓ Speak clearly at an appropriate volume and speed.	
✓ Vary tone and intonation to maintain attention and interest.	✗ Do not lean or sit on anything.
✓ Face your audience, maintain eye contact, and have good posture.	✗ Avoid using repetitive hand gestures or body movements that detract from what you are saying.
✓ Cite sources both in your presentation aid and orally.	
✓ End with a strong conclusion and thank your audience.	

Can you think of other presentation tips? Would the tips be the same for all subject matters and all audiences? Explain your answer.

Good speakers demonstrate enthusiasm for their topic that helps them maintain the interest of their audience.

VOCABULARY PREVIEW

Read the vocabulary items. Circle the ones you know. Put a question mark next to the ones you don't know.

flexible	durability	rigid	resistance
abrasion	versatile	malfunction (n)	withstand

EXERCISE 4

A. Read the section of a research paper on elastomers and answer the comprehension questions.

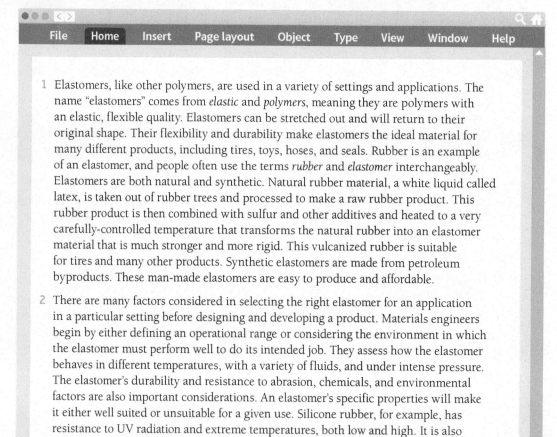

File　Home　Insert　Page layout　Object　Type　View　Window　Help

1　Elastomers, like other polymers, are used in a variety of settings and applications. The name "elastomers" comes from *elastic* and *polymers*, meaning they are polymers with an elastic, flexible quality. Elastomers can be stretched out and will return to their original shape. Their flexibility and durability make elastomers the ideal material for many different products, including tires, toys, hoses, and seals. Rubber is an example of an elastomer, and people often use the terms *rubber* and *elastomer* interchangeably. Elastomers are both natural and synthetic. Natural rubber material, a white liquid called latex, is taken out of rubber trees and processed to make a raw rubber product. This rubber product is then combined with sulfur and other additives and heated to a very carefully-controlled temperature that transforms the natural rubber into an elastomer material that is much stronger and more rigid. This vulcanized rubber is suitable for tires and many other products. Synthetic elastomers are made from petroleum byproducts. These man-made elastomers are easy to produce and affordable.

2　There are many factors considered in selecting the right elastomer for an application in a particular setting before designing and developing a product. Materials engineers begin by either defining an operational range or considering the environment in which the elastomer must perform well to do its intended job. They assess how the elastomer behaves in different temperatures, with a variety of fluids, and under intense pressure. The elastomer's durability and resistance to abrasion, chemicals, and environmental factors are also important considerations. An elastomer's specific properties will make it either well suited or unsuitable for a given use. Silicone rubber, for example, has resistance to UV radiation and extreme temperatures, both low and high. It is also easy to shape and produce. For this reason, silicone rubber is a very versatile material used not only in spacecraft, but also bakeware and clothing. Fluorocarbon elastomers are often selected for seals and other machine parts because they resist extreme heat and chemicals. Ethylene propylene rubber has resistance to oxidation, ozone, weather, and cold temperatures, so it is a good material to insulate high-voltage cables. Another synthetic elastomer, styrene-butadiene, is affordable, durable, and easy to produce, so it is an ideal choice for tires.

3   To understand why some materials are better than others, understanding how elastomers react to temperature is helpful. Elastomers have a temperature point at which they change from a soft, rubbery material into a brittle material with less elasticity. This is called the glass transition temperature, and it is abbreviated Tg. An elastomer's glass transition temperature ranges from below -100° F (-73° C) in flexible elastomers like silicone rubber to higher temperatures in other elastomers. Polychloroprene, for example, which is used in hoses and belts, has a glass transition temperature of -50° F (10° C). When elastomers get too cold and approach their individual glass transition temperature points, they lose their elasticity and become rigid. This effect in elastomers is easy to see in a simple home experiment with a rubber band. If the rubber band is placed in a glass of ice water for a period of time, it will become significantly less elastic, and eventually when stretched repeatedly, may snap. Because elastomers become brittle and lose some or all of their ability to return to their original shape when too cold, they must be used with caution in applications that might be outside their operational temperature range. Under certain weather conditions, elastomers are more susceptible to malfunction. If the right elastomer is chosen for a product, the product will succeed. If the wrong elastomer is chosen, the product may fail.

4   In the Challenger explosion that occurred on January 28, 1986, 73 seconds after lift off, the mechanical failure was caused by the malfunction of an elastomer seal on the space shuttle. Parts of the space shuttle were joined with O-rings, which are elastomer seals. O-rings are circular-shaped rings placed between two parts to help seal them securely, and they are used on a wide variety of products. The Challenger had several large O-rings that helped connect and seal the different parts of the space shuttle. At that time, O-rings were made of a type of fluorocarbon elastomer that was not designed to withstand extremely cold temperatures. The temperature on the day of the launch in 1986, while considered at the minimum to launch the shuttle, was not within the operational range for the O-rings, which were probably colder than the air temperature. In the aftermath of the crash, scientists determined that the elastomer seals lost elasticity due to the cold weather overnight. Once the seals had lowered near their glass transition temperature, they were less able to bounce back into shape as they should have, and so, under the extreme pressure, one did not seal properly. When the seal failed, exhaust leaked and resulted in an explosion. O-rings were improved after the explosion and there has not been another O-ring failure like the one that brought down the Challenger.

The crew of the space shuttle, Challenger

Glossary

Hose: a long rubber or plastic tube that can be moved or bent to put water onto things or take air or gas from place to place

Sulfur: an element that is usually in the form of a light yellow powder with a strong unpleasant smell used in industry

Vulcanized: (rubber) made stronger using a special chemical treatment

Fluorocarbon: a compound formed by replacing one or more hydrogen atoms in a hydrocarbon with fluorine atoms

CULTURE NOTE

The Space Shuttle Challenger disaster on January 28, 1986, resulted in the death of the seven crew members—five astronauts, and two specialists—one of whom was to be the first teacher in space. It was witnessed by many people, including many school children, and the aftermath was covered extensively by the media as scientists worked to determine the cause.

B. Answer the questions.

1. What two properties of elastomers make them ideal for many different products?

2. How is natural rubber used to produce the elastomer material suitable for tires?

3. How do materials engineers begin selecting an elastomer when designing a product?

4. What factors are considered when choosing an elastomer for a product?

5. What are the properties of silicone rubber that make it a good elastomer for products such as spacecraft and bakeware?

6. Why is styrene-butadiene rubber a good synthetic elastomer for producing tires?

7. What is the glass transition temperature and why is it important when using elastomers? ....

....

8. What example of severe damage caused by elastomer failure was given?

....

9. What happened in the example in Question 8? ....

....

C. Analyze the presentation notes and slides. Discuss the effectiveness of the two versions of the notes that contain the same information from the research paper. Do they contain enough information for an oral presentation? Why might the Version 2 be more helpful? Now look at the PowerPoint slides with a partner. What problems do you see in Slide 1 and Slide 2? What could be done to improve them? Why is Slide 3 more effective?

Paragraph 2 – Version 1	Paragraph 2 – Version 2
Properties of elastomers	Properties of **elastomers/**
Temperatures—extreme heat and cold	<u>in</u> different **temperatures**/ extreme heat and **cold/**
Fluids	<u>with</u> **fluids/**
Intense pressure	<u>under</u> intense **pressure/**
Durability	also
Resistance to abrasion, chemicals, environment	**durability/**
	<u>resistance</u> to **abrasion/ chemicals/ environment**
Types of elastomers:	Types of **elastomers:/**
1. Silicone—resistance to UV, radiation, and extreme high and low temperature; easy to shape and produce, spacecraft, bakeware, and clothing.	1. **Silicone** /– <u>resistant</u> to UV, radiation, and extreme high and low **temperature/** easy to <u>shape</u> and **produce** Uses: **spacecraft/ bakeware/** and **clothing**.
2. Fluorocarbons—resist extreme heat and chemicals; seals and gaskets	2. **Fluorocarbons/** – <u>resistant</u> to extreme <u>heat</u> and **chemicals/** Uses: <u>seals</u> and **gaskets**
3. Ethylene propylene rubber—resistance to oxidation, ozone, the weather, and cold temperatures—insulation for high-voltage cables	3. **Ethylene propylene rubber/**<u>resistance</u> to <u>oxidation</u>, <u>ozone</u>, the <u>weather</u>, and cold **temperatures/** Uses: **insulation/** for high-voltage **cables**
4. Styrene-butadiene—affordable, durable, and easy to produce—car tires	4. **Styrene-butadiene** –/ <u>affordable</u>, <u>durable</u>, and **easy** to produce Uses: car **tires**

Slide 1

ELASTOMERS

SILICON – RESISTANCE TO UV, RADIATION, AND EXTREME HIGH AND LOW
TEMPERATURE; EASY TO SHAPE AND PRODUCE, SPACECRAFT, BAKEWARE, AND
CLOTHING.

FLUOROCARBONS – RESIST EXTREME HEAT AND CHEMICALS; SEALS AND
GASKETS

ETHYLENE PROPYLENE RUBBER – RESISTANCE TO OXIDATION, OZONE, THE
WEATHER, AND COLD TEMPERATURES – INSULATION FOR HIGH-VOLTAGE
CABLES

STYRENE-BUTADIENE – AFFORDABLE, DURABLE, AND EASY TO PRODUCE – CAR
TIRES

Slide 2

Elastomers

Silicon

Resistance to:
- UV, radiation
- extreme high and low temperature

Easy to shape and produce

Uses: spacecraft, bakeware, and clothing

Flourocarbons

Resistant to:
- extreme heat
- chemicals;

Uses: seals and gaskets

Ethylene propylene rubber

Resistance to:
- Oxidation
- Ozone
- weather
- Cold temperatures –

Uses: insulation for high-voltage cables

Styrene-butadiene

Affordable

durable,

easy to produce –

Uses: car tires

Slide 3

Silicone

- **Resistant to:**
  - Extreme high and low temperatures
  - UV radiation
- **Easy to shape and produce**
- **Uses:**
  - Bakeware
  - Clothing
  - Spacecraft

D. Create presentation notes for Paragraph 3 or Paragraph 4 of the reading in Part A.
Identify main ideas and write concise text for supporting ideas. Mark phrases for
pauses with a slash/and underline or highlight a word to emphasize in each phrase.
Create two or three slides for a presentation based on the paragraph. Suggest a
visual for at least one slide.

E. Give a two- to five-minute oral presentation using your notes and the slides in Part C.

VOCABULARY CHECK

A. Review the vocabulary items in the Vocabulary Preview. Write their definitions and add examples. Use a dictionary if necessary.

B. Write the correct vocabulary item next to each definition.

abrasion	durability	flexible	malfunction
resistance	rigid	versatile	withstand

1. .... to fail to function properly

2. .... stiff and not moving or bending

3. .... an area that has been damaged or injured by being rubbed too hard

4. .... to be strong enough to remain unharmed by something such as great heat or cold, great pressure, etc.

5. .... having the ability to stay in good condition for a long time, even if used a lot

6. .... the act of opposing or withstanding

7. .... having many different uses

8. .... able to bend or be bent easily

⬆ Go to MyEnglishLab to complete vocabulary and skill practices and to join in collaborative activities.

LANGUAGE SKILL

USING PARALLEL STRUCTURE

WHY IT'S USEFUL By using parallel structure, your writing will be clear and cohesive. Your reader will be able to more easily follow and understand your ideas.

⬆ Go to MyEnglishLab for the Language Skill presentation and practice.

VOCABULARY STRATEGY
UNDERSTANDING SUFFIXES

> **WHY IT'S USEFUL** By understanding suffixes, you will make more precise vocabulary choices in your writing. You will expand your vocabulary and be more likely to use accurate grammatical forms and parts of speech.

A **suffix** is a letter or group of letters added to the end of a base or root word to form a new word. There are two different types of suffixes. **Inflectional suffixes** add information about the grammatical form of a word. They do not change the part of speech or meaning of a word. There is only one inflectional suffix on a word, and when one is used, it is always the last suffix.

Word	Suffix	Example
Noun	-s (plural)	elastomer**s**, O-ring**s**
	-'s (possessive)	an elastomer**'s** properties
Verb	-s (3rd person singular)	An elastomer fail**s** when the temperature is too high or too low....
	-ed (past form in past tense and past participle form in perfect and passive tenses)	The O-ring fail**ed** to seal properly. (past tense)
		An O-ring hasn't fail**ed** due to the temperature since then. (past participle)
	-ing (present participle in progressive tenses)	They are choos**ing** an appropriate elastomer for the application....
Adjective	-er (comparative)	The O-rings were cold**er** than the outside temperature.
	-est (superlative)	Temperature was the bigg**est** problem.

Derivational suffixes create a word with new meaning and usually change the part of speech. Words can have more than one derivational suffix. The last suffix on a word determines the part of speech. Note the changes to the meaning of a word when a suffix is changed or added:

Word	Part of speech	Definition and Example
signific**ance**	noun	The importance of an event, action, etc., especially because of the effects or influence it will have in the future *A conclusion will discuss the **significance** of the research results.*
signific**ant**	adjective	Having an important effect or influence, especially on what will happen in the future *The use of polymers in space applications is **significant**.*

Word	Part of speech	Definition and Example
significant**ly**	adverb	In an important way or to a large degree *The compression set values increased* **significantly** *for both polymers.*

Using suffixes will help you to expand your vocabulary and be able determine a word's function in a sentence. Ultimately, this will help you express your ideas more clearly, which is especially useful for discussing abstract or technical ideas.

Use a dictionary to help you understand the meaning of specific suffixes. Suffixes often have more than one meaning. Note the definitions of the suffix -*ize* in the *Longman Advanced American Dictionary*. Which definition applies to the word *summarize*?

-ize (also **-ise** *British English*) /aɪz/ suffix [in verbs]

1 to make something have more of a particular quality
- ◄») *We need to modernize our procedures.* (=make them more modern)
- ◄») *Americanized spelling* (=spelling made more American)
- ◄») *privatized transport* (=bus or train services that are owned and operated by private companies)

2 to change something to something else, or be changed to something else
- ◄») *The liquid crystallized* (=turned into **crystal**s).

3 to speak or think in the way mentioned
- ◄») *to soliloquize* (=speak a **soliloquy**, to yourself)
- ◄») *I sat and listened to him sermonizing* (=speaking solemnly, as if in a **sermon**).

4 to put into a particular place
- ◄») *She was hospitalized after the accident.*

Look at these examples of words with suffixes from this unit. Can you add other words with the suffixes? Can you think of other suffixes that are used to make words in English?

Suffix	Meaning	Examples
Common Suffixes		
Nouns		
-ity -ty (nouns)	the state of having a particular quality, or something that has that quality	ability; permeability; flexibility; durability; elasticity
-ion -tion -sion	the act, state, or result of doing something	exploration; radiation; evaluation; elongation; selection; collection; oxidation; transition; refrigeration; application
-ness	the quality of	brittleness; hardness

Common Suffixes		
Suffix	Meaning	Examples
Verbs		
-ate	to make something have a particular quality	evaluate
-ize	to make or cause to	synthesize
Adjectives		
-ic (adjective)	of, like, or related to a particular thing	elastic; synthetic; polymeric
-able -ible	having a particular quality or condition	breathable; susceptible; affordable; flexible
-al	related to something or being like something	operational
-ary	pertaining to something	primary; secondary
Adverbs		
-ly	in or considered in a particular way	relatively; significantly; eventually; repeatedly

TIP

In your vocabulary journal, include entries for suffixes and define them. Make sure to write down all the word forms used in your field.

EXERCISE 5

A. List as many parts of speech for each word as possible. If there is an X, there is no word for that part of speech. Use a dictionary to help you.

Noun	Verb	Adjective	Adverb
significance	signify	significant	significantly
		flexible	
application			X
	X	conventional	
radiation			
elasticity	X		X
compression			X
	evaluate		X
investigation			X

B. Choose the correct part of speech in each sentence. Pay attention to the word's function to help you choose the correct answer.

1. The polymer has the (flexible, flexibility) needed for a variety of space applications.

2. The elastomer must be (compressed, compression) for 70 hours to make sure it meets standards.

3. Materials engineers must (evaluative, evaluate) the properties of polymers to make sure they can be used for specific purposes.

4. Researchers (investigated, investigative) the potential impacts of climate change on food security.

5. Rubber bands can stretch because of their (elasticity, elastic).

6. Materials used in space must be able to withstand (radioactively, radiation).

7. Regenerative medicine is not a (convention, conventional) medical treatment.

8. New technology is being (applied, applicable) to aerospace processes.

C. Check your answers in Parts A and B with another student and explain what the words mean. Circle words you can use in the unit assignment. Write an original sentence for each word that you will use.

◑ Go to MyEnglishLab to complete a skill practice.

APPLY YOUR SKILLS

WHY IT'S USEFUL By applying the skills you have learned in this unit, you can successfully develop a research summary, develop a strong conclusion, present a research paper, use parallel structure, and understand suffixes.

ASSIGNMENT

Write a 1000–1200 word section of a Materials Engineering research paper on polymeric materials. Choose one synthetic polymeric (plastic) material and analyze its properties, characteristics, and processing techniques, focusing on how these enable the polymer to work in various applications. Prepare notes for an oral presentation on that section.

BEFORE YOU WRITE

A. Before you begin your assignment, discuss these questions with one or more students.

1. What have you learned about polymeric materials? Why are polymeric materials important?

2. What are some properties and characteristics that should be considered when writing about a polymeric material?

3. What do you think is most important in delivering an academic presentation? How will you ensure you achieve this in your own presentation?

4. What is your biggest challenge in reading or writing about scientific or technical research? What strategies and techniques from this unit will help you overcome these challenges?

B. As you consider your writing assignment, complete the tasks. Then share your ideas with another student. Get feedback and revise your ideas if necessary.

1. What polymeric material have you chosen to research? Why?

   ....

   ....

2. List some of the properties and characteristics of this polymeric material. What are the processing techniques and/or applications for this polymer?

   ....

   ....

   ....

3. Design at least two effective slides for a presentation on the polymer you will write about. What will you include in your slides?

   ....

   ....

   ....

C. Review the Unit Skills Summary. As you begin the writing task on page 349, apply the skills you learned in this unit.

UNIT SKILLS SUMMARY

Develop a research summary

- Read a research article critically.
- Plan your summary by making an outline.
- Write a summary that includes a rationale, methods, results, discussion, and/or conclusion.
- Review the summary by revising, editing, and proofreading.

Develop a strong conclusion

- Use more than one technique and strategy.
- Do more than simply summarize or restate ideas.
- Make new connections: solutions, consequences, new perspectives, broader issues, future study, or investigation.
- Bring closure but leave room to go beyond the paper.

Present a research paper

- Condense and reformat a research paper for presentation.
- Identify key points and simplify supporting ideas.
- Prepare a slide presentation that highlights and illustrates key points in the presentation.
- Prepare and practice using notes and slides.

Use parallel structure

- Emphasize that ideas are equal by using parallel structure.
- Use the same grammatical structure to connect two or more ideas.
- Make structures parallel by using the same word form.
- Repeat function words, as needed, for clarity or emphasis.

Understand suffixes

- Study the meaning of suffixes and how they are used to form new words.
- Use a dictionary to help you understand meaning.

THINKING CRITICALLY

As you consider your writing assignment, discuss the questions with another student. Get feedback and revise your ideas if necessary.

1. Many synthetic polymers have properties that cause harm to the environment. What are some environmental concerns with manufacturing and processing polymers? What are some properties of polymers that make them ideal for specific applications but harmful to the environment?

2. What type of polymer do you think has had the most impact on modern society? Why?

3. What do you think will be the role of polymers in the future? Explain.

THINKING VISUALLY

A. Look at this visual showing the service temperatures, meaning the range of temperatures in which the elastomer's qualities remain unchanged. Discuss the questions with a partner.

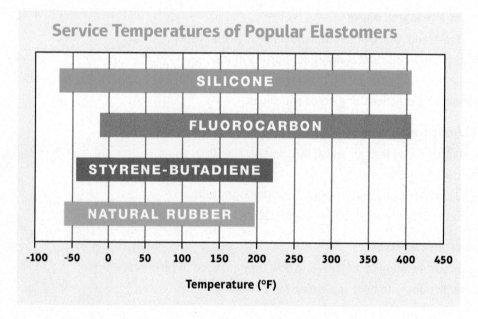

Service Temperatures of Popular Elastomers

SILICONE
FLUOROCARBON
STYRENE-BUTADIENE
NATURAL RUBBER

-100 -50 0 50 100 150 200 250 300 350 400 450

Temperature (°F)

1. How would this information be helpful in writing a paper that addresses the material properties of a polymer?

2. Is the visual effective in presenting the data? Why or why not?

3. What other information would you like to know? Why?

B. Create a visual graph of the different material properties for the polymer you are writing about.

THINKING ABOUT LANGUAGE

Write sentences using parallel structure about the polymer you chose for the assignment.

1. Two or more properties or characteristics of the polymer using nouns. ....

....

2. Two or more adjectives to describe the polymer. ....

....

3. Two or more procedures to test, measure, or evaluate the properties. (Hint: Use passive verbs.) ....

....

4. A sentence about the polymers using two or more prepositional phrases.

....

5. A sentence about applications of the polymers using phrases. ....

....

6. A comparison of the polymer or one of its properties, characteristics, or applications to another polymer. ....

....

7. Two sentences with connected ideas about the polymer. ....

....

WRITE

A. Revisit the writing assignment and your answers to the questions in the Before You Write Part B. What considerations will you take into account as you prepare notes and plan your presentation? ....

....

....

B. Write a few real-life applications of the polymer you chose to keep the reader's interest. ....

....

....

C. Write a section of a research paper and include a strong, well-developed conclusion. Prepare notes for a presentation of your research. Be sure to follow the presentation tips.

> **BEYOND THE ASSIGNMENT**
>
> Write a research paper of 8–10 pages on the environmental impacts of synthetic polymers on the environment. Discuss how the properties and characteristics impact the environment and address current or proposed mitigation efforts. Prepare notes for a presentation on the research paper. Present your research to an audience. Make sure your slides are well designed. Use parallel structure in your paper, notes, and slides.

Go to MyEnglishLab to watch Professor Heilshorn's concluding video again and to complete a self-assessment.

PART

3

Extended Writing

Part 3 presents authentic content written by university professors. Academically rigorous application and assessment activities allow for a synthesis of skills developed in Parts 1 and 2.

Language communicates who we are

LINGUISTICS

Writing as a Linguist

UNIT PROFILE

In this unit, you will watch a video interview with Professor Robert J. Podesva, who will describe in detail his process for finding ideas, planning and organizing his writing, addressing bias, and supporting writing with factual evidence. Have you ever wondered how your professor, or an expert in the field of linguistics, develops a paper? This is your opportunity to find out more about the academic writing process.

You will write an academic paper about the way a particular social group uses language.

For more about **LINGUISTICS**, see ① ②. See also ⓡ and ⓄⒸ **LINGUISTICS** ① ② ③.

EXTENDED WRITING

BEFORE YOU WRITE

Think about these questions before you watch the interview with Professor Podesva. Discuss them with another student.

1. How do you think linguists get their ideas for research or writing? How do you get your own ideas?

2. How do you think a writer balances fact and opinion in an academic paper?

3. What are appropriate sources of evidence in a linguistics paper?

4. What advice might a professor give about avoiding bias?

THE INTERVIEW

Go to MyEnglishLab to watch the interview with Professor Podesva. Take notes while you watch. Then answer the questions in Check What You've Learned.

CHECK WHAT YOU'VE LEARNED

A. Answer the questions based on the interview with Professor Podesva. Refer to your notes to help you answer the questions.

1. How does Professor Podesva get his ideas?

    a. by building off of previous studies
    b. by keeping up with current debates and journals in the field
    c. by picking new questions that arise in doing research
    d. all of the above

2. Why does Professor Podesva start with one main point?

    a. to cut out points he can't support in a paper
    b. to fill an empirical gap
    c. because he doesn't want to waste resources
    d. because you can only make one point well in a paper

3. What brainstorming techniques does Professor Podesva prefer?

    a. talking to colleagues and students
    b. making a list of main points
    c. finding people to feed him ideas
    d. finding empirical and theoretical gaps

4. How does Professor Podesva plan and organize his writing?

    a. He starts with one idea and writes outward.
    b. He uses outlines to plan the full argument.
    c. He uses notecards to fill in the details of the study.
    d. He organizes by the gaps he is trying to fill.

5. Why does Professor Podesva adopt the perspective of people who have opposing views?

    a. to analyze his data from a different perspective
    b. to have more confidence in the validity of his findings
    c. to ensure that his writing is not biased
    d. all of the above

6. What does Professor Podesva believe about factual evidence?

    a. It's not worth as much as opinions.
    b. It's only suitable if it includes empirical observations.
    c. It's important and varies from field to field and over time.
    d. It's better if it's quantitative and statistical.

7. What types of evidence does he recommend using?

    a. He believes it is important for writers to use their own intuitions as evidence.
    b. He believes that qualitative evidence is the most important type to include in a paper.
    c. He believes writers should use a combination of qualitative and quantitative evidence.
    d. He believes empirical observations provide the best support for an argument.

8. Why does Professor Podesva think it is important to know your audience?

    a. It will help you make good points.
    b. You will know how much technical language you can use.
    c. You will understand how much evidence to include.
    d. You can pretend you are teaching them.

9. According to Professor Podesva, what is the best way to learn how to write a good paper in linguistics?

    a. Read good papers in linguistics to understand what makes them effective.
    b. Read books or articles on how to write good linguistics papers.
    c. Ask your professor for advice on how to write a good paper.
    d. Talk to your professor about books and articles about writing.

B. Watch the interview again. Check your answers from Part A with another student.

THINKING CRITICALLY

Think about this situation considering what you have seen in the interview. By yourself or with a partner, use what you know about the writing process to answer the question.

You want to talk to your professor, classmates, or other native speakers about something you have noticed about some English speakers. Sometimes, their voices rise at the end of statements but you learned in your language classes that statements in English have falling intonation. You want to find out why this happens. What is the best way to brainstorm ideas? How will you research this topic? What evidence will you need? How will you avoid bias in formulating an opinion on the topic?

🡒 Go to MyEnglishLab to complete a critical thinking activity.

THINKING ABOUT LANGUAGE

IDENTIFYING PHRASES IN ACADEMIC TEXT

Annotate the sentences to identify the phrases. Highlight the verb phrases. Circle the head nouns and underline the noun phrases. Put the prepositional phrases in brackets. Label adjective and adverb phrases. Compare your annotations with a partner and discuss any differences. Which embedded element(s) are used most often?

1. Strictly speaking, vocal fry refers to a specific type of the more general creaky voice.

2. It is well established in the field of phonetics that speakers of every language use creaky voice from time to time, due to simple aerodynamics.

3. An analysis of the data reveals that, at least in the three California communities under consideration, women do indeed use more creaky voice than men.

4. First, younger men (below age 45) produced similarly strong creaky voice to women of the same age.

5. Additionally, female speakers were more likely to use creak in phrases when they were not smiling.

6. The reproduction of these ideologies is particularly dangerous given the wide reach of most media outlets.

USING ACADEMIC LANGUAGE OF DISAGREEMENT

Connect the claim to the counterargument. Use an appropriate adverbial or coordinating conjunction of concession or contrast. Use each expression only one time.

> Indicate the reason for disagreeing with the claim by writing 1, 2, or 3 in front of each statement.
> 1. The argument ignores or misinterprets a fact, is mistaken, or is wrong.
> 2. The argument exaggerates a claim or is overstated.
> 3. The argument has unsound reasoning.

.... 1. Media coverage of stylistically distinctive elements of language like creaky voice typically implies that young women are using the language differently and are ruining the English language. .... these newscasts have been based on relatively small-scale studies of only a few speakers, or more commonly on opinions.

.... 2. The media claims that creaky voice is new. .... creaky voice has always been used at least from time to time in every language.

.... 3. .... data based on careful reading of scripted sentences is more comparable, when speakers read scripted sentences, they monitor their speech more and this may constrain the extent to which they use new linguistic elements such as creaky voice.

.... 4. .... the media claim that young women creak more than anyone else, young men are producing creak that is nearly as strong as that of young women.

.... 5. It has been suggested that creaky voice serves no useful purpose. .... it appears that speakers systematically use creaky voice to indirectly show a negative stance toward the topic of conversation.

.... 6. .... the fact that the media, like all users of language, are often guided by stereotypes of patterns of language use, care must be taken to not make assumptions about social groups like young women when there is limited empirical support for some claims such as those about creaky voice.

READE

🔘 Go to MyEnglishLab to read "Fact or Fiction: Evaluating Media Coverage of the Vocal Fry Phenomenon" for more practice reading an extended text and using your reading skills. Take notes while you read. Then answer the questions in Check What You've Learned.

CHECK WHAT YOU'VE LEARNED

Answer the questions based on the essay, "Fact or Fiction: Evaluating Media Coverage of the Vocal Fry Phenomenon." Refer to your notes to help you answer the questions.

1. What is the main idea of Professor Podesva's article?

   a. to evaluate why young women use vocal fry, or creaky voice
   b. to evaluate common claims by the media about creaky voice using research
   c. to evaluate why people incorporate uptalk intonation in their speech
   d. to investigate the media's interest in how people use different linguistics features

2. According to Professor Podesva, what flaws did previous studies on creaky voice have?

   a. The studies only address how young women use language.
   b. People monitor their speech during research studies.
   c. The studies have only analyzed the speech of small numbers of speakers.
   d. All of the above.

3. Professor Podesva's research on creaky voice suggests that

   a. Creaky voice is a recent phenomenon in American English.
   b. Creaky voice is not common in older people.
   c. Young speakers are using creaky voice in different positions in a sentence.
   d. All of the above.

4. What did Professor Podesva's research show about who uses creaky voice?

   a. Young women and young men creak about the same amount.
   b. Older women creak more than younger women.
   c. Men tend to minimize their use of creaky voice.
   d. Older men tend to creak the most.

5. What claim does Professor Podesva make on the purpose of creaky voice?

   a. He claims that creaky voice is useless at best, and harmful at worst.
   b. He claims that it is used by speakers to sound less threatening.
   c. He claims that speakers use creaky voice to show they are not engaged in a topic.
   d. He claims that speakers use it when they feel positive about a topic of conversation.

6. When do speakers use more creaky voice?

   a. Speakers use it when they are comfortable during conversations and are smiling
   b. Speakers use it when they are not comfortable during conversations or not smiling
   c. Speakers use it when they are moving around and are smiling
   d. Speakers use it equally when they are comfortable and uncomfortable.

7. Why does Professor Podesva list negative terms such as *vulgar, repulsive,* and *sheer agony* to describe creaky voice?

    a. He is interested in showing that the media dislikes creaky voice.

    b. He wants to present a counterargument to prove that creaky voice serves a purpose.

    c. He agrees that creaky voice can be harmful to people's voices and careers.

    d. He wants to show that creaky voice serves no purpose.

8. Why does Professor Podesva explain how and why he carried out a detailed analysis of creaky voice?

    a. to help the reader understand that his research examined both quantity and quality of creaky voice

    b. to help the reader understand how his research differed from prior research

    c. to show the reader that his research methods are credible and to establish his authority

    d. to show the reader that there weren't enough studies about creaky voice before he did his

9. What can you infer about Professor Podesva?

    a. He uses prior research to guide his own research.

    b. He appreciates the media's attention on different linguistic features of English.

    c. He does not appreciate the work of other researchers.

    d. He doesn't have much interest in creaky voice.

10. According to Professor Podesva, why is empirical evidence important to the study of creaky voice?

    a. It confirms our stereotypes about how people use language.

    b. It ensures that we do not stereotype social groups and their language use.

    c. It helps the media report on how young women use language.

    d. All of the above.

ASSIGNMENT

Write an academic paper of 4–6 pages about the way a particular social group uses language. Consider level of formality and word choice, pronunciation, or grammar. Choose a language you are familiar with and narrow your topic to one specific feature or aspect of the language. Describe the social group that uses this feature. Men or women? Younger or older people? A specific social class? Explain the feature, give examples, and analyze its use. Why do people speak this way? What purpose does it serve?

Be sure to brainstorm and organize your ideas, and support them with facts and expert opinion. Address counterarguments to your claims and include evidence to support your ideas.

RESEARCH

A. Use a brainstorming technique such as mapping to analyze and connect social groups with different features of language use. Narrow the topic appropriately to one you have personal interest in.

B. Brainstorm ideas for your topic, discuss your ideas with a partner, and write a preliminary thesis statement.

C. Conduct research to find information on your topic. Find appropriate sources for the paper.

D. Read and annotate the source materials. Consider how you will use these materials in your paper.

WRITE

A. Read your annotations of the source materials and make notes of ideas to include in your paper to support your claims.

> **TIP**
> Do not try to cover too many points in a paper. Choose one main point and develop it well.

B. Using your graphic organizer and your notes, create a detailed outline of your paper.

C. Write your paper. Support your claims with facts and opinions. Include at least one counterargument.

> **TIP**
> Be flexible and let the argument change and evolve as you are planning and organizing your writing.

🔊 Go to MyEnglishLab to join in a collaborative activity.

How cultural and ethical values define a successful business

BUSINESS ETHICS

Writing as a Business Ethicist

UNIT PROFILE

In this unit, you will watch a video interview with Dr. William "Scotty" McLennan Jr., who will describe in detail how to find reliable sources and integrate them into your own writing, avoiding plagiarism. Have you ever wondered how your professor, or an expert in the field of business ethics, develops a paper? This is your opportunity to find out more about the academic writing process.

You will write an academic paper comparing global business practices of two different countries.

For more about **BUSINESS ETHICS**, see ① ②. See also [R] and [OC] **BUSINESS ETHICS** ① ② ③.

EXTENDED WRITING

BEFORE YOU WRITE

Think about these questions before you watch the interview with Dr. McLennan. Discuss them with another student.

1. How do you think business ethicists get their ideas for research or writing? How do you get your own ideas?

2. What do you think might be the most difficult part of finding reliable sources?

3. What challenges do you think a business ethicist faces in integrating evidence from sources into a paper?

4. What advice might a professor give about plagiarism and how to avoid it?

THE INTERVIEW

Go to MyEnglishLab to watch the interview with Dr. McLennan. Take notes while you watch. Then answer the questions in Check What You've Learned.

CHECK WHAT YOU'VE LEARNED

A. Answer the questions based on the interview with Dr. McLennan. Refer to your notes to help you answer the questions.

1. What is the source of many of Dr. Scotty McLennan's ideas?

   a. everyday news and world events and cultures
   b. the events of the 2008 Great Recession
   c. different religious practices
   d. novels and plays

2. What is important to Dr. McLennan before he organizes his ideas?

   a. to have credible and reliable sources
   b. to understand the key questions that he wants to address
   c. to select the best framework of moral decision-making
   d. to know how he is going to present the material

3. Why does Dr. McLennan use frameworks to organize material?

   a. so it makes sense to other people
   b. to question moral decision-making
   c. to make the writing easier for him
   d. so it is regionally sensitive

4. What types of sources are reliable according to Dr. McLennan?

   a. academic journals, newspapers, Wikipedia
   b. academic journals, fake news, primary sources
   c. peer-reviewed books, academic journals, news sources
   d. peer-reviewed books, encyclopedia sources, primary sources

5. What advice does Dr. McLennan give to students who use Wikipedia?

   a. Use the footnotes to find out where the materials came from.
   b. Check with people who have expertise in those areas.
   c. Go beyond the sources in Wikipedia to the primary sources that they are referring to.
   d. All of the above.

6. What does Dr. McLennan see as the biggest challenge in integrating sources?

   a. taking careful notes and outlining materials
   b. choosing the best quotations for the topic
   c. distinguishing between his ideas and the source's ideas
   d. citing the information correctly

7. What methodology does Dr. McLennan use to integrate sources into his writing?

   a. finding ideas that are correct and interesting
   b. using tone that is not too similar to that of the source
   c. careful note-taking, outlining, and citing accurately
   d. using ideas from many different sources

8. What simple rule for avoiding plagiarism does Dr. McLennan share?

   a. Use many direct quotations.
   b. Remember that nothing comes out of your own head.
   c. Talk to a professor about what to cite.
   d. Cite everything.

9. To prevent a reader from misunderstanding your ideas, he suggests that you:

   a. Be clear and careful in your own writing.
   b. Don't have a political agenda.
   c. Take responsibility if it's your fault.
   d. Expect to be misunderstood.

10. What two pieces of advice does he have for writers?

   a. Write about topics your professor likes and wake up early to write every day.
   b. Make sure you are excited about the topic and find time to write every day.
   c. Write in the morning and only when you have something to say.
   d. Ask lots of questions so you don't get "stuck" and find something to say.

B. Watch the interview again. Check your answers from Part A with another student.

THINKING CRITICALLY

Think about this situation considering what you have seen in the interview. By yourself or with a partner, use what you know about the writing process to answer the questions.

Your assignment in your business ethics class is to write a discussion post on the value of understanding people from other cultures for global business interactions. You need to consider aspects of another culture and whether simple business etiquette is enough to do well. How will you get and develop your ideas so that they are clear and will not be misinterpreted by your classmates reading the post? How will you identify sources for evidence to support your ideas and ensure your sources are reliable?

🔊 **Go to MyEnglishLab to complete a critical thinking activity.**

THINKING ABOUT LANGUAGE

USING DIRECT QUOTATIONS AND REPORTED SPEECH

Paraphrase the excerpts from Dr. McLennan's essay using reported speech. Use reporting verbs from the chart for the purpose described in the brackets at the end of each item below. Introduce the noun clauses in different ways. Circle the subject and underline the reporting verbs.

Reporting Verbs

Indicate strong degree of certainty – *argue, state, explain, claim*

Make a neutral observation – *mention, observe, point out*

Give an opinion – *believe, think, agree, disagree*

Show specific meaning – *suggest, recommend, conclude*

Introduce information or findings from a study – *find, show, demonstrate, report, provide*

---

1. Etiquette and ethos are ultimately grounded in millennia-old religious traditions, although they may be operating unconsciously. Understanding the influence of religion from area to area in the world is a key to making one an interculturally successful businessperson. [Express certainty.] ....

   ....

   ....

   ....

2. A cultural framework provides an important tool in making sense of cultural ethos and the experiential and cognitive differences that one encounters when doing business across borders. ...general cultural frameworks can be a very helpful starting place in alerting one to fundamental differences between people that not only come out in more superficial business etiquette but also affect the very way people think, react, feel, and understand their business relations. [Make a suggestion.] ....

   ....

   ....

   ....

3. Another framework is that of Angela Leung and Dov Cohen from the University of Illinois, who have researched differences between countries based on whether they have dignity, honor, or face cultures. … The research seems to indicate that, in business negotiations, people in dignity cultures pursue information rationally while those in face and honor cultures try to influence others by appealing to their emotions. [Introduce information from a study.] ....

....

....

....

4. Americans assume people are free individuals, rather than embedded in families and other collectives which determine their life circumstances. Americans value personal growth and change rather than following time-tested community traditions as some societies do. Equality is a fundamental value for Americans, while many other societies assume hierarchical ranking of people in society. [Report findings from a study.] ....

....

....

....

5. The deepest level of the cultural iceberg, though—responsible for generating many of the most important values, beliefs, attitudes, and ways of thinking that affect business—is religion. One cannot understand cultural ethos in a profound way without understanding the religion that has created and maintained it. [Give an opinion.] ....

....

....

....

6. Religion should never be neglected when doing global business. [Make a recommendation.] In fact, religion could be the most important factor in coming to know one's business partners, understanding cultural ethos, and even grasping business etiquette. [Draw a conclusion.] ....

....

....

....

USING MODALS TO EXPRESS DEGREES OF CERTAINTY

Read the sentences from the essay. Add a sentence that provides additional support using the degree of certainty indicated. Use some sentences in the negative.

Degrees of Certainty – present and future	
Affirmative	**Negative**
(Strong – Probable) must	(Strong – Improbable) couldn't/can't must not (rarely contracted)
(Likely) should	(Unlikely) shouldn't
(Weaker – Possible) may might could	(Weaker – Not possible) may not (no contraction) might not

Weaker:

1. Etiquette and ethos are ultimately grounded in millennia-old religious traditions.
   The timing of a business transaction in certain countries might be affected by religious beliefs.

2. Employer and employee in Japan have more mutual loyalty with an almost moral link. ....

   ....

3. European countries are long-term oriented, while the US, African, and Middle Eastern countries are short-term oriented. ....

   ....

4. Dignity cultures have egalitarian systems supported by an effective rule of law.

   ....

5. In a face culture, individuals' worth and dignity come from how they fulfill their role obligations in the social hierarchy. ....

   ....

6. Honor cultures historically have had unsettled and unstable social hierarchies.

   ....

Stronger:

7. A cultural framework provides an important tool in making sense of the experiential and cognitive differences that one encounters when doing business across borders. ....

....

8. ... in Japan people see themselves more defined in terms of the groups, including the business enterprises, of which they are a part. ....

....

9. Americans tend to take pride in competition, a future-orientation, directness in relationships, and acquisitiveness ... .

....

10. One cannot understand cultural ethos in a profound way without understanding the religion that has created and maintained it. ....

....

READE

Go to MyEnglishLab to read "Frameworks of Intercultural Understanding in Global Business" for more practice reading an extended text and using your reading skills. Take notes while you read. Then answer the questions in Check What You've Learned.

CHECK WHAT YOU'VE LEARNED

Answer the questions based on the essay, "Frameworks of Intercultural Understanding in Global Business." Refer to your notes to help you answer the questions.

1. What is the main idea of this essay?
   a. Cultural frameworks are important tools to understand people from other cultures.
   b. Successful businesspeople understand how religion has influenced the way a culture conducts business.
   c. It is critical to understand and practice different forms of business etiquette depending on the country you are conducting business with.
   d. Because so much business occurs in global contexts, it is important to learn about the culture in which one conducts business.

2. According to the essay, what is the best way to learn etiquette in another culture?
   a. exchanging business cards
   b. using a cultural framework
   c. listening and watching
   d. learning greetings and gestures

3. What does the author mean when he writes "below the water line, where they cannot be seen, are many dimensions of cultural ethos: attitudes, ways of thinking, worldviews, and ideologies."
   a. There are many aspects of culture that may not be easily observable.
   b. There are too many aspects of culture, so it is impossible to understand all of them.
   c. There are many cultural differences that affect the way people do business with each other.
   d. People purposely hide many dimensions of cultural ethos because they don't want to be judged.

4. Why are cultural frameworks useful for people who conduct business abroad?
   a. They provide useful tips for how to shake hands and present a business card.
   b. They help people wear the right clothing for business meetings and social occasions.
   c. They contrast US business practices with those in other cultures and make sure the US is represented.
   d. They help people understand the differences in attitudes and ways of thinking of people from different cultures.

5. According to Geert Hofstede's cultural dimensions framework comparing Japan and the US, which statement is true?
   a. The Japanese do not have long-lasting loyalty to the company they work for.
   b. In the US, it is common for people to give family members jobs in the same organization.
   c. People in the US and in Japan differ greatly on how distant they feel from highly influential people.
   d. In Japan individualism is not seen as a source of well-being.

6. Which would be most likely to happen in an honor culture?

    a. A businessperson would analyze information rationally to solve problems during a negotiation.
    b. A businessperson would work hard at maintaining social harmony.
    c. A businessperson would appear strong to negotiate the best deal.
    d. A businessperson would find it is acceptable to lose face during a business negotiation.

7. According to Robert Kohls' theory of contrasting core values, which of these statements is <u>not</u> typically associated with people from the United States?

    a. All people are free to do what they want.
    b. Personal growth and change are important.
    c. It's important to follow community traditions.
    d. People should be treated equally regardless of position.

8. Which statement about the influence of religion on business practices is inaccurate?

    a. A Confucian principle affects the importance of interpersonal networking in China.
    b. Hindu ethical laws affect when it is a good time to do business.
    c. Businesspeople in Japan are samurai, meaning they are "living Buddhas" and serve others.
    d. The Protestant ethic explains money as a symbol and the work ethic in the United States.

9. Which statement best describes Mexican opinions about managers in the United States?

    a. They are relationship-oriented.
    b. They are competitive and aggressive.
    c. They are risk-takers with a poor work ethic.
    d. They are cooperative and pragmatic.

10. Based on the discussion about how religion affects business in different countries, what can we infer about Dr. McLennan's opinion about religion?

    a. He is a very religious person.
    b. Some religions are better than others for business.
    c. Religion is a cultural framework.
    d. Religious traditions are the base of cultural differences.

ASSIGNMENT

Write an academic paper of 4–6 pages comparing the global business practices of two different countries. Compare similarities and differences between the two cultures in how business is conducted such as management, negotiations, marketing, and etiquette. What are the implications for business relations between the two countries? Consider how cultural beliefs, attitudes, and worldviews affect business behaviors and practices.

Be sure to develop and organize ideas, find reliable sources, and integrate evidence into your paper.

RESEARCH

A. Use a brainstorming technique such as listing to generate ideas about cultural beliefs, attitudes, and world views that affect business practices.

....

....

....

....

....

B. Share your list of ideas from Part A with another student. Then discuss similarities and differences of the two cultures that you will write about. Take notes for your paper. Write a preliminary thesis statement.

....

....

....

....

....

C. Conduct research to find appropriate sources on your topic. Evaluate the credibility and reliability of the sources.

D. Read and annotate the source materials for ideas and evidence to integrate into your paper.

WRITE

A. Read your annotations of the source materials and paraphrase ideas to include in your paper.

B. Using your graphic organizer and your notes, create a detailed outline of your paper.

C. Write your paper. Develop your ideas and integrate paraphrased evidence from sources. Cite ideas according to the style chosen by your instructor.

🔊 Go to MyEnglishLab to join in a collaborative activity.

TIP

Be sure to choose a topic that is interesting to you and that you think is of value personally and for your audience.

TIP

Accurately representing the ideas in your sources is essential to ensuring that your reader will not misinterpret your ideas.

Decisions we make today will shape our future

Writing as an Earth Scientist

UNIT PROFILE

In this unit, you will watch a video interview with Dr. Michael C. Osborne, who will describe how to organize ideas and navigate through and understand all the literature. Have you ever wondered how your professor, or an expert in the field of earth science, develops a paper? This is your opportunity to find out more about the academic writing process.

You will write an academic paper on an environmental issue that is of concern to a region of the world, a specific country, or a particular community.

For more about **EARTH SCIENCE**, see ① ②. See also R and OC **EARTH SCIENCE** ① ② ③.

EXTENDED WRITING

BEFORE YOU WRITE

Think about these questions before you watch the interview with Dr. Osborne. Discuss them with another student.

1. What are the challenges in making scientific writing easier for readers to understand, while still including all of the technical material?

2. Is organization important in writing scientific material? Why? What type of organization do you think is helpful to readers?

3. Should scientists try to include examples and evidence that they are already familiar with? Why?

4. What types of visuals do you think earth scientists include in research papers? Why?

THE INTERVIEW

Go to MyEnglishLab to watch the interview with Dr. Osborne. Take notes while you watch. Then answer the questions in Check What You've Learned.

CHECK WHAT YOU'VE LEARNED

A. Answer the questions based on the interview with Dr. Osborne. Refer to your notes to help you answer the questions.

1. What are the broad areas in paleoclimate that scientists research?

   a. the climate of certain regions
   b. studies of tree rings or ice cores
   c. fluctuations in natural cycles of the Earth's climate
   d. the geography of the Earth

2. How does Dr. Osborne typically organize his research papers?

   a. He includes an introduction, methodology, results, discussion, and conclusion.
   b. He organizes by writing a story for each region he studies.
   c. He includes a broad picture of the climate over many time scales.
   d. It depends on the topic and the overall ambition of the research study.

3. What is the purpose of the discussion section of a research paper?

   a. to present the tools and techniques used in the study and how they helped researchers find their results

   b. to present only what is found while conducting the research without looking ahead

   c. to offer interpretations about the meaning of the results and how they relate to other areas

   d. to state what has been learned in the study and what has been left out of the research

4. What does Dr. Osborne say is challenging about scientific writing?

   a. reading all the papers that get published every year

   b. understanding the literature and what is relevant

   c. taking notes on the science that is important

   d. trying not to break flow when reading

5. What advice did a former advisor give Dr. Osborne?

   a. Understand the jargon used in papers.

   b. Read at least one paper every day.

   c. Publish a paper every year.

   d. All of the above.

6. What strategy does Dr. Osborne use to help him analyze scientific literature?

   a. He reads through literature reviews quickly so that they are easier to understand.

   b. He looks up all the new words, which will help him understand the science.

   c. He takes lots of notes while reading a study so he does not have to read it again.

   d. He reads a paper completely before rereading parts that are difficult to understand.

7. What types of examples and evidence does Dr. Osborne include in his writing?

   a. research that uses tools and techniques similar to the ones he uses

   b. examples in which he understands the methodology used

   c. examples that are relevant to his own research

   d. all of the above

8. Why does Dr. Osborne think that it is critical to include visuals to support ideas in writing?

    a. because a visual can tell the entire story of the work that has been done
    b. because visuals make writing more interesting
    c. because a visual supports a well-designed study
    d. because it is important to learn how to interpret a visual

9. Why does he recommend drafting some visuals before you write?

    a. It will help you understand how to frame an issue.
    b. It will help you understand which literature you need to read.
    c. It will help you develop your hypothesis, or research question.
    d. All of the above.

10. What advice does Dr. Osborne give to new writers in the sciences?

    a. Read only scientific literature to support your research.
    b. Read scientific literature, popular magazines, and news articles.
    c. Frame issues the same way others do in their research.
    d. Do a research project by yourself.

B. Watch the interview again. Check your answers from Part A with another student.

THINKING CRITICALLY

Think about this situation considering what you have seen in the interview. By yourself or with a partner, use what you know about the writing process to answer the questions.

Your assignment in your earth science class is to create a visual that will tell a story about the impact of climate change on a community, industry, or country. What type of visual(s) will you use? What story will the visual tell? How will you know others will be able to interpret the visual? What thesis or hypothesis could you develop from this visual?

◉ Go to MyEnglishLab to complete a critical thinking activity.

THINKING ABOUT LANGUAGE

USING ADVERBIALS OF CAUSE AND EFFECT

Connect the clauses or sentences with an adverbial of cause or effect. Use each adverbial only one time.

because	since	because of	due to
a reason for	one reason	as a result of	therefore
consequently	thus	as a result	

1. Many scientists warn that we are on the brink of a sixth mass extinction. .... , we stand to lose more biodiversity on a scale not seen since a meteor killed the dinosaurs 66 million years ago.

2. .... environmental activism, concerns grew throughout the 1960s about ecological destruction, air pollution, noise pollution, and contamination from nuclear waste.

3. In 1980, Congress also passed legislation that paved the way for Superfund sites. .... large sums of money were allocated to clean up environmental catastrophes.

4. What constitutes a healthy ecosystem is not straightforward. .... this, "health" is often intertwined with both cultural and economic goals.

5. .... some business leaders view environmental regulations as standing in the way of economic prosperity, there has been a growing backlash against many forms of environmental regulation.

6. .... that American Millennials don't self-identify as environmentalists is that maybe for them the term "environmentalist" doesn't capture the full scope of concerns and the complexity of environmental issues.

USING PASSIVE VOICE IN SCIENTIFIC WRITING

Rewrite each sentence in the passive voice. If a passive sentence is not possible, write, "No change."

1. The next generation will face many enormous environmental issues. ....

....

2. On the brink of the sixth mass extinction, we may lose a lot of biodiversity.

....

3. Congress enacted important legislations as a result of heightened awareness of environmental issues throughout the 1970s. ....

....

4. Many activists in the environmental movement cite the role of science to support their political views. ....

....

5. There has been a growing backlash against many forms of environmental regulation. ....

....

6. Environmental activists may view certain ecosystems as having intrinsic value.

....

7. The fear is that climate change will fundamentally alter ecosystems and landscapes beloved by outdoor enthusiasts. ....

....

8. Climate change will economically impact communities. ....

....

9. American Millennials see the environmental issue differently than earlier generations. ....

....

READE

⊙ Go to MyEnglishLab to read "Environmentalism in the 21st Century" for more practice reading an extended text and using your reading skills. Take notes while you read. Then answer the questions in Check What You've Learned.

CHECK WHAT YOU'VE LEARNED

Answer the questions based on the essay, "Environmentalism in the 21ˢᵗ Century."
Refer to your notes to help you answer the questions.

1. What is the main idea that Dr. Osborne wants to address in "Environmentalism in the 21ˢᵗ Century"?

   a. He wants to explore the history of environmentalism in the United States.
   b. He wants to address the complexity of environmental issues to understand Millennial engagement.
   c. He wants to explore differences in environmentalism and environmental science.
   d. He wants to address policy issues that impact the environment for Millennials.

2. What can you infer about Millennials from the 2014 Pew Research Center survey?

   a. They think it is important that their political views are known.
   b. They join organizations such as The Nature Conservancy.
   c. They behave in ways that reduce environmental impacts.
   d. They care less about the environment than older generations.

3. Why were the 1960s and 1970s the heyday for environmental activism?

   a. because many books were written as a result of activism
   b. because there were ecological problems
   c. because important legislation was enacted as a result of activism
   d. because Earth Day was established

4. Which statement best describes environmental sciences?

   a. It is a distinct field of scientific investigation.
   b. It is a multidisciplinary blend of fields of science.
   c. It is a field that deals with human issues and politics.
   d. All of the above.

5. What does Dr. Osborne mean when he says the role of environmental science is to be policy relevant without being policy prescriptive?

   a. Environmental science should control and plan policy.
   b. Environmental science should inform policy, not dictate it.
   c. Environmental science should regulate policy and set agendas.
   d. Environmental science has no role in policy.

6. What is one example of a co-benefit of environmental action?

   a. establishing basic health services in a society
   b. monitoring air quality which leads to fewer respiratory infections
   c. opposing environmental regulations for economic reasons
   d. ensuring food security for society

7. Why is Dr. Osborne concerned that some of the benefits of environmental action are unseen?

   a. If people don't see the benefits, they may not care.
   b. People won't benefit from unseen actions.
   c. It is not logical and it is hard to understand.
   d. All of the above.

8. Why does Dr. Osborne ask if climate change is an "environmental" problem?

   a. because there is no clear scientific evidence that it is a problem
   b. because species extinction and habitat destruction is inevitable
   c. because it also has economic, cultural, and political impacts
   d. because Millennials are not concerned about climate change

9. Why do environmentalists think it's misguided to place faith in technology innovations in the future that will mitigate greenhouse warming?

   a. Climate change is a large-scale problem.
   b. We will lose economic productivity.
   c. Studies demonstrate that climate change is costly.
   d. We don't know what future advancements will be.

10. How does Dr. Osborne feel about American Millennials?

   a. They will find their own way to deal with climate change.
   b. They aren't concerned about environmental issues.
   c. They would be environmentalists if the term were different.
   d. They don't understand the complexity of environmental issues.

ASSIGNMENT

Write an academic paper of 4–6 pages on an environmental issue (e.g., global population, toxic waste contamination, resource depletion, species extinction, pollution, etc.) that is of concern to a region of the world, a specific country, or a particular community. Analyze why this issue is particularly relevant to the area. Address the problems and solutions. Consider the economic, cultural, and political impacts of this issue for future generations.

Be sure to use appropriate organizational patterns, select relevant examples, and include a visual to support your ideas.

RESEARCH

A. Use a brainstorming technique to generate several ideas about environmental issues that concern you. Choose one issue you want to write about.

B. Discuss your environmental issue with another student. Then write a few ideas about the problems and solutions that you will be able to research. Write a preliminary thesis statement.

C. Conduct research to find information on your topic. Find appropriate sources of information and visuals on your topic.

D. Read and annotate the source materials for examples and visuals to support your ideas. Consider how you will use these materials in your paper.

WRITE

A. Summarize information from your source materials to include in your paper.

B. Using your graphic organizer and your notes, create a detailed outline of your paper.

C. Write your paper. Use appropriate organizational patterns to develop your ideas and integrate information and visuals from sources. Cite your sources in the style chosen by your instructor.

Go to MyEnglishLab to join in a collaborative activity.

TIP

Read as much as you can on your research topic in scientific literature, popular magazines, or news articles to help you understand how experts think about the issue you are researching, and also to see which issues are important to the general public.

TIP

Choose a visual that can tell a story about your research topic. Remember that different types of visuals present information in different ways.

MEDIEVAL CULTURE

Writing as a Literary Expert

UNIT PROFILE

In this unit, you will watch a video interview with Professor Marisa Galvez, who will describe in detail how to make stylistic choices and revise a paper. Have you ever wondered how your professor, or an expert in the field of humanities, develops a paper? This is your opportunity to find out more about the academic writing process.

You will write an academic paper describing a celebration in a local community you are familiar with.

For more about **MEDIEVAL CULTURE**, see ❶ ❷.

See also ⟦R⟧ and ⟦OC⟧ **MEDIEVAL CULTURE** ❶ ❷ ❸.

EXTENDED WRITING

BEFORE YOU WRITE

Think about these questions before you watch the interview with Professor Galvez. Discuss them with another student.

1. Do writers in the humanities have different challenges concerning style and tone than writers in other fields? What are they?

2. What are some considerations when using descriptive writing? Is using too much description as bad as using too little? Why or why not?

3. What are some considerations when using figurative writing? Is using too much figurative language as bad as using too little? Why or why not?

4. What are some keys to effective persuasive writing?

THE INTERVIEW

◐ Go to MyEnglishLab to watch the interview with Professor Galvez. Take notes while you watch. Then answer the questions in Check What You've Learned.

CHECK WHAT YOU'VE LEARNED

A. Answer the questions based on the interview with Professor Galvez. Refer to your notes to help you answer the questions.

1. What does Professor Galvez like to think about when she considers style and tone in her papers?

   a. if she is addressing the general public
   b. what kind of argument she is making
   c. if she is addressing an academic audience
   d. all of the above

2. How can you practice having a voice and tone according to Professor Galvez?

   a. by writing a lot and reading your drafts out loud to other people
   b. by reading a lot to become aware of voice and tone
   c. by using different tones throughout one piece
   d. by revising content to include voice and tone

3. What is Professor Galvez's process for revising content in her writing?

   a. She writes many drafts on her own before sharing them with an audience.
   b. She reads her drafts to an audience and then incorporates feedback into her paper.
   c. She begins at the sentence level before reading her draft to an audience.
   d. All of the above.

4. What advice does Professor Galvez give for using descriptive language in making arguments?

   a. Understand how descriptive language can explain a quote or a text more effectively.
   b. Use descriptive language only to explain a quote or a text so you can compose quickly.
   c. Understand your purpose for using descriptive language and be concise.
   d. Use descriptive language mainly to interpret or analyze information.

5. What does Professor Galvez recommend writers do to persuade their audiences?

   a. Structure arguments by making clear claims and backing those up with examples.
   b. Persuade as quietly as possible so your argument isn't obvious.
   c. Use descriptive language to make persuasive arguments.
   d. All of the above.

6. Why does Professor Galvez say that she feels like she has conversations with writers who are persuasive?

   a. because persuasive writers are not loud or argumentative
   b. because they don't expect to draw a reader in
   c. because the story is easy to follow and the argument seems evident
   d. because she doesn't have to follow the structure of an argument

7. What tips does Professor Galvez give for using figurative language in writing?

   a. Make figurative language as impactful as you can.
   b. Understand how figurative language relates to the concept you are trying to convey.
   c. Use figurative language concisely and sparingly.
   d. All of the above.

8. What is one piece of advice that Professor Galvez has for new writers?

    a. Find a way to write every day.
    b. Always work alone.
    c. Stay connected online to find new ideas.
    d. Change your routine so you don't get bored.

9. Why does Professor Galvez think it is critical to find someone who reads your writing and gives you specific feedback?

    a. They can tell you if you have a good idea.
    b. They can help you write down your goals and frustrations about writing.
    c. Dialoguing about your writing will get you motivated to write.
    d. All of the above.

B. Watch the interview again. Check your answers from Part A with another student.

THINKING CRITICALLY

Think about this situation considering what you have seen in the interview. By yourself or with a partner, use what you know about the writing process to answer the questions.

Your assignment in your literature class is to write an online discussion post in which you review a medieval book that you have read as an out-of-class assignment. What is the rhetorical purpose and who is your audience for the discussion post? What stylistic choices will you make? What steps will you take to revise your discussion post before you submit it?

◎ Go to MyEnglishLab to complete a critical thinking activity.

THINKING ABOUT LANGUAGE

USING COHESIVE DEVICES FOR REFERENCE AND AGREEMENT

Annotate the sentences for the cohesive devices for reference—demonstrative determiners and pronouns (*this/that/these/those*), pronouns, possessives, relative pronouns (*which, who, that, other,* or *another*), cohesive nouns (*these sentences*), and topic introducers (*such as*). Underline the noun phrases and circle the cohesive devices. Draw an arrow from the cohesive device to the phrase or clause it refers to.

1. Medieval feasts were less about dining than the series of activities in which one participated. These feasts included rituals such as singing courtly or drinking songs, acting in theatrical performances, and dancing.

2. When we think about "medieval feasting" the image that most likely comes to mind is one of aristocrats eating fancy food such as duck and other luxury food items. This is true to a certain extent but leaves out the complexity of how people experienced the food, music, table objects, and performances that went on during a feast, and how they thought of the act of eating.

3. Through various forms of engagement, participants in the feasts could also reflect upon the interests of a ruler who was the host of such an elaborate event that involved many people and much preparation.

4. Maidens performed rounds and other dances, each trying to outdo the other in showing their joy.

5. A culinary or theatrical *entremets* could also play with the boundary between the realms of the Church and the courtly hall with their respective spiritual versus earthly values.

6. Such performances promoted military campaigns and the political power of Duke Philip and his court, as well as the continuity between the realms of the church and the power of the Duke.

7. Decorative table objects could make a diner at the table conscious of the role he or she played in the court, or question the values to which he or she was assumed to be subscribing.

8. The potential for a moral lesson is present in objects such as the aquamanile, as it requires its users to think about how one should guard oneself from overindulging in base pleasures.

9. Rather than just providing a relief from everyday life through ritual, ceremony, song, food, and theater, feasts allowed diners to imagine what could be possible as they were true artistic productions that blurred the boundaries between the real and imagined.

VARYING DESCRIPTION

In "Medieval Feast as Artistic Production" Professor Galvez says that the great medieval feasts appealed to and engaged all the senses. Write sentences that describe these aspects of a medieval feast. Use the reading to help you. Use adjectives that paint a picture, strong nouns, and action verbs. Vary sentence structure with adjective clauses, embedded phrases, and complex and compound sentences.

1. the entertainment

....

2. the music

....

3. the performers

....

4. the food

....

5. the clothing

....

6. the dining hall

....

READ

🔊 Go to MyEnglishLab to read "Medieval Feast as Artistic Production" for more practice reading an extended text and using your reading skills. Take notes while you read. Then answer the questions in Check What You've Learned.

CHECK WHAT YOU'VE LEARNED

Answer the questions based on the essay, "Medieval Feast as Artistic Production." Refer to your notes to help you answer the questions.

1. What is the main purpose of Professor Galvez's essay?

   a. to explain the role of food and dining in medieval celebrations and how it changed over time

   b. to explain how expensive and impressive medieval feasts were for courtly celebrations

   c. to describe how festive dining for an elite audience engaged all the senses and represented the participants' tastes and concerns

   d. to compare and contrast medieval ceremonies and celebrations with those of today

2. Who participated in medieval feasts?

   a. royals and noblemen and women

   b. royals, noblemen and women, and military leaders

   c. royals, noblemen and women, military leaders, and performers

   d. royals, noblemen and women, performers, and common people

3. What was the purpose of the medieval courtly feast?

   a. for participants to show their support of a ruler hosting the event

   b. to reflect upon the interests of a ruler hosting the event

   c. to promote moral behavior of the participants while providing sensual delights

   d. all of the above

4. Why does Professor Galvez say that our mental images about "medieval feasting" leave out the complexity of how people experienced the feast?

   a. She is aware that people may not understand the role of ceremony in medieval feasting.

   b. She doesn't believe people understand how impressive the meals were.

   c. She wants to emphasize that noblemen and women wore fancy clothes and ate luxury food items.

   d. All of the above.

5. Why does Professor Galvez include a reference about the 12ᵗʰ century romance *Erec and Enide*?

   a. to show how medieval feasts appealed to various senses and provided many kinds of entertainment
   b. to give examples of different instruments that were common at wedding celebrations
   c. to demonstrate how expensive and lavish wedding celebrations could be
   d. to give examples of different types of foods and how they were prepared for feasts

6. What can we learn from images in a medieval manuscript that show entertainers at a feast dressed as crusaders capturing Jerusalem?

   a. Charles V participated in the crusades.
   b. Military leaders enjoyed the meals at royal banquets.
   c. The diplomatic or political function of royal banquets was important.
   d. Wealthy people had banquets to show how much money they had.

7. How were medieval meals similar to theatrical performances?

   a. They were designed to appeal to the eyes and imagination and often played with appearances.
   b. They often were accompanied by a musical presentation.
   c. They often were part of the between-course entertainment.
   d. All of the above.

8. What is an example of how between-course entertainment could be provocative?

   a. A peacock might be "dressed" in its original feathers.
   b. A message at the bottom of a drinking cup might remind the drinker of overconsumption.
   c. Music emerged from pastries and other foods served during the feasts.
   d. Mimed performances turned the feast into a theatrical event.

9. Which statement best summarizes Professor Galvez's conclusion?

   a. Feasts engaged all the senses and allowed participants to experience artistic productions.
   b. Feasts engaged all the senses and were a relief from everyday life.
   c. Feasts were entremets with strictly religious or political purposes.
   d. Feasts were artistic productions with song, food, and drink.

ASSIGNMENT

Write an academic paper of 4–6 pages about a traditional celebration of a cultural event such as a birth, a coming-of-age, a wedding, a religious ceremony, a transition, or a death in a particular community. Describe the celebration— who participates and what people eat, wear, and do, including music and entertainment. Consider the symbolism involved in the tradition. Analyze the purpose and significance of activities and rituals and how they address the expectations and concerns of the community.

Be sure to consider style and tone, use vivid images and figurative language to describe the celebration, and use appropriate ways to appeal to your audience.

RESEARCH

A. Use a brainstorming technique to generate ideas about traditional celebrations that you are familiar with. Choose one celebration you want to write about.

B. Describe the traditional celebration to another student. Take notes on any questions your partner raises about the tradition. Write a preliminary thesis statement.

C. Conduct research to find appropriate sources of information on the significance and purpose of the celebration to those involved.

D. Read and annotate the source materials to analyze descriptive language about the topic. Consider how you will use these materials in your paper.

WRITE

A. Read your annotations of the source materials and make notes of descriptive examples to include to support your analysis of the celebration.

B. Using your graphic organizer and your notes, create a detailed outline of your paper.

C. Write your paper. Use appropriate stylistic choices and descriptive language as you develop your ideas and integrate information from sources. Revise your paper to ensure your ideas are developed, organized, and supported in the most effective way.

TIP

Use descriptive language carefully and wisely. Understand your purpose for using descriptive language and be concise.

TIP

Find someone who can give you feedback on your writing by reading line-by-line and letting you know whether your sentences make sense.

🜂 Go to MyEnglishLab to join in a collaborative activity.

How the study of molecules relates to the real world

MATERIALS ENGINEERING

Writing as a Materials Engineer

UNIT PROFILE

In this unit, you will watch a video interview with Professor Sarah Heilshorn, who will describe in detail her process for revising and proofreading a paper. Have you ever wondered how your professor, or an expert in the field of engineering, develops a paper? This is your opportunity to find out more about the academic writing process.

You will write research summaries for two peer-reviewed articles based on your research on an innovative technology that uses polymers to address a particular need or problem.

For more about **MATERIALS ENGINEERING**, see ①②.
See also ⓡ and ⓞⓒ **MATERIALS ENGINEERING** ①②③.

EXTENDED WRITING

BEFORE YOU WRITE

Think about these questions before you watch the interview with Professor Heilshorn. Discuss them with another student.

1. What resources do you think engineers use to help them write their research papers? What resources do you use?

2. What are the different ways to review drafts of an academic paper? Does a scientific paper need a different type of review?

3. What techniques or strategies are helpful for proofreading and finalizing a paper?

4. Do writers need to be both organized and flexible in the writing process? Explain.

THE INTERVIEW

Go to MyEnglishLab to watch the interview with Professor Heilshorn. Take notes while you watch. Then answer the questions in Check What You've Learned.

CHECK WHAT YOU'VE LEARNED

A. Answer the questions based on the interview with Professor Heilshorn. Refer to your notes to help you answer the questions.

1. According to Professor Heilshorn, what are the top resources that she uses for writing scientific manuscripts?
   a. internet research
   b. published, peer-reviewed scientific manuscripts
   c. conclusions from other papers
   d. anything that follows the scientific method

2. How does she find resources?
   a. She uses the internet, scientific journals, and peers' work.
   b. She uses key words in manuscripts of authors she knows.
   c. She uses the internet, other scientific manuscripts, and her coauthors.
   d. She uses the internet, key words, and authors she knows.

3. During the first step of the revision process, what does Professor Heilshorn do?
   a. She analyzes the structure and organization of each paragraph to make sure there is a main idea and supporting ideas and they are in a logical order.
   b. She reads through the paper to make sure that one main idea from a paragraph flows into the next paragraph throughout the paper.
   c. She pays attention to grammatical details, sentence structure, and word choice.
   d. She asks for feedback from her colleagues about the different parts of the paper.

4. During the second step of the revision process, what does Professor Heilshorn do?

   a. She analyzes the structure and organization of each paragraph to make sure there is a main idea and supporting ideas and they are in a logical order.
   b. She reads through the paper to make sure that one main idea from a paragraph flows into the next paragraph throughout the paper.
   c. She pays attention to grammatical details, sentence structure, and word choice.
   d. She asks for feedback from her colleagues about the different parts of the paper.

5. During the third step of the revision process, what does Professor Heilshorn do?

   a. She analyzes the structure and organization of each paragraph to make sure there is a main idea and supporting ideas and they are in a logical order.
   b. She reads through the paper to make sure that one main idea from a paragraph flows into the next paragraph throughout the paper.
   c. She pays attention to grammatical details, sentence structure, and word choice.
   d. She asks for feedback from her colleagues about the different parts of the paper.

6. Whose feedback does Professor Heilshorn get on the content of her papers?

   a. her coauthors on the paper and a committee
   b. scientists and engineers in different fields
   c. only engineers in her field
   d. her coauthors and other experts in her field

7. What techniques does Professor Heilshorn use to proofread her work?

   a. She focuses on sentence structure and asks if there's a simpler way to explain her ideas.
   b. She focuses on word choice and asks herself if there's a more precise word she could use to help the reader understand.
   c. She gives her paper to one of her coauthors to proofread.
   d. All of the above.

8. What does Professor Heilshorn do after she revises, but before she publishes a paper?

   a. She considers the paper from the point of view of her audience to make sure the audience will understand the main idea.
   b. She asks one more person to proofread her paper and makes changes based on that person's comments.
   c. She asks her intended audience if her paper is clear; then asks an expert in the field if they agree with the audience.
   d. All of the above.

9. What tip does Professor Heilshorn share to help new writers be organized?
   a. Think about your main ideas before you write them down.
   b. Think about your intended audience when you begin to structure your ideas.
   c. Structure your ideas and thoughts after writing your first draft.
   d. Structure your ideas to make the language flow.

10. What tip does Professor Heilshorn suggest for writer's block?
   a. It's a good idea to take a break so you can find the right word or right phrase.
   b. Stop and organize ideas to make the language flow better.
   c. Keep writing and don't worry if it's not perfect the first time.
   d. Revise and edit another section of your paper.

B. Watch the interview again. Check your answers from Part A with another student.

THINKING CRITICALLY

Think about this situation considering what you have seen in the interview. By yourself or with a partner, use what you know about the writing process to answer the questions.

Your assignment in your engineering class is to participate in a poster session competition on campus on a topic related to the field of materials engineering. You will be judged solely on the content of the poster. What will you do to make sure your ideas are clear and easily understood? How will you ensure that the text is well-written and that the poster is presented as a professional and polished product?

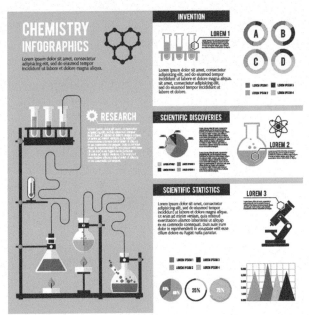

Poster from a chemistry poster session

🌀 Go to MyEnglishLab to complete a critical thinking activity.

IDENTIFYING AND EDITING RUN-ON SENTENCES AND FRAGMENTS

Identify the problems with run-ons, comma splices, and fragments in this paragraph. There are five run-on or comma splice errors and four fragments. Edit the paragraph to correct the problems. There is more than one way to correct each problem. [Hint: annotating each sentence to find the subject and verb and circling the punctuation can help you identify the problems.] Write the problem—run-on, comma-splice, or fragment, no subject, incomplete or no verb, or dependent clause.

A little bit of cornstarch is commonly used in cooking to thicken sauces and soups, however, if you add a lot of cornstarch to water, you will make a goopy substance. If you stir the mixture slowly, it behaves like a liquid. The cornstarch polymers have sufficient time to slide past each other and disentangle, the spoon moves through the mixture easily. If you stir the mixture quickly, it behaves more like a solid. The cornstarch polymers do not have enough time to slide past each other, they get knotted up the spoon gets stuck in the mixture. This high concentration mixture of cornstarch and water is sometimes referred to as "oobleck" in the United States. If you make enough of the cornstarch and water mixture to fill up an entire swimming pool. People can take turns running across the surface of the mixture. The cornstarch polymers, tangled up with each other. Someone deforms the top surface of the mixture with their foot, the polymer chains do not have time to slide past each other. Because they stay entangled together. They act like a net to keep the person suspended on top of the mixture. Stopping halfway across. Will the person sink into the mixture? You can try this experiment for yourself you can do an Internet search to find many entertaining videos that show you the answer.

USING PARALLEL STRUCTURE

Underline the part of each sentence that is not in parallel structure. Complete the sentence that follows to correct the errors in parallel structure.

1. Chewing gum can be used to demonstrate the mechanical properties of polymeric chains, how time affects the properties, and when temperature changes the properties.

   Chewing gum can be used to demonstrate ....

2. Cold chewing gum is hard, brittle, and moves stiffly.

   Cold chewing gum is ....

3. A cold polymer chain requires more time to move apart, remains tangled in a knot, and is being prevented from stretching.

A cold polymer chain ....

4. When a piece of chewing gum is placed into boiling hot water, the molecules in the polymer chain move quickly, slide more smoothly past each other, and it's easy to stretch them.

When a piece of chewing gum is placed into boiling water, the molecules in the polymer chain ....

5. In the first case, the gum stretches out as you pull apart your hands slowly. In the second case, pulling your hands apart quickly makes the gum break into two pieces.

In the second case, ...

6. If you deform a polymeric object slowly, it behaves in a compliant way, but deforming the same polymeric object quickly, it is stiff.

If you deform a polymeric object slowly, it behaves in a compliant way, but

....

7. For polymeric materials, this means that their chainlike molecules can wiggle around more quickly when they are hotter. On the other hand, being cooler, the wiggle of the chains is slower.

On the other hand, ...

8. If the temperature is too hot, the polymer may be too ductile. However, in too cold temperatures, the polymer may be too brittle.

However, ...

READD

READ

Go to MyEnglishLab to read "Why Do Polymers Behave Differently Depending on Their Conditions?" for more practice reading an extended text and using your reading skills. Take notes while you read. Then answer the questions in Check What You've Learned.

CHECK WHAT YOU'VE LEARNED

Answer the questions based on the essay, "Why Do Polymers Behave Differently Depending on Their Conditions?" Refer to your notes to help you answer the questions.

1. What is Professor Heilshorn demonstrating with the chewing gum?
   a. that you can stretch chewing gum
   b. that chewing gum is made of the exact same molecules
   c. that molecules behave differently in different conditions
   d. that molecules have mechanical properties

2. Which is the best definition of a polymer?
   a. long, chainlike molecules tangled together
   b. long, chainlike flexible molecules in constant motion
   c. long, chainlike molecules that form a knot
   d. long, chainlike wiggly molecules

3. What is the key factor that changes the mechanical behavior of polymeric materials that Professor Heilshorn uses cornstarch and water to exemplify?
   a. time
   b. weight
   c. temperature
   d. strength

4. Using the example of ooblek, when does a polymer behave more like a solid?
   a. when molecules slide past each other
   b. when you stir it
   c. when molecules get knotted up and tangled
   d. when you stretch it

5. How does temperature affect the mechanical properties of polymers?
   a. It changes the speed of the movement of the molecules.
   b. It makes the chainlike molecules wiggle more quickly.
   c. It makes the molecules stiffer and more brittle.
   d. It changes the size of the molecules.

6. What does the fact that objects made from polymers change mechanical behavior depending on their temperature mean?

   a. They should be used at high temperatures.
   b. They should never be used when it is cold.
   c. There should be one temperature at which they are used.
   d. There should be a specified temperature range for their use.

7. Why does Professor Heilshorn tell us that there were other engineering and managerial issues that contributed to the space shuttle failure?

   a. She didn't want to blame only the polymers.
   b. She understands that the failure was more complex than having one cause.
   c. She doesn't believe the disaster was caused by the O-rings.
   d. All of the above.

8. What important point has Professor Heilshorn made about polymers with the various examples and explanation?

   a. Time and temperature affect polymers in different ways.
   b. Time and temperature affect polymers in similar ways.
   c. Physical causes are more important than resulting mechanical behaviors.
   d. Polymers must be compliant and ductile.

9. Why is the similarity of effects of time and temperature useful to engineers in designing polymeric objects?

   a. They can do many mechanical tests over a long period of time.
   b. They can design artificial joints to use as orthopaedic implants.
   c. They can test many polymeric designs using mathematical relationships.
   d. They can test for shorter times at higher temperatures and use math to predict mechanical behaviors.

10. What is the essay's main point in the discussion of time and temperature of polymeric materials?

    a. that polymeric objects are interesting, but can be dangerous
    b. that polymeric chains are either ductile or brittle
    c. that molecular motion of polymeric chains affects the mechanical properties of polymers
    d. that everyone should make ooblek to understand polymers

ASSIGNMENT

Research an innovative technology that uses polymers to address a particular need or problem. Examples include affordable 3D printing, material for regenerative medicine, materials for more efficient transportation, or solutions to improve quality of life. Write research summaries of 250–500 words each for two peer-reviewed research articles. Include a brief summary of the study, the methods used, the results, and their significance as reported in the discussion or conclusion of the article.

Be sure to analyze the text, plan and organize your summaries, and edit and proofread for submission.

RESEARCH

A. Use a brainstorming technique to generate ideas about an innovative technology that uses polymers. Choose a technology you want to research.

B. Discuss the innovative technology you chose with a partner and identify key words to use in an internet database search.

C. Conduct research to find two or more peer-reviewed research articles on your topic.

D. Read critically and annotate the source materials to analyze the studies.

WRITE

A. Read your annotations of the articles and make notes for each summary.

B. Using your notes, create a detailed outline for each summary.

C. Write your research summaries. Edit and proofread your summaries to ensure they are well-written, correctly formatted, and error free.

> **TIP**
> Before you publish, consider the paper from the point of view of your audience to make sure your ideas are clear.

> **TIP**
> Don't stop writing if you don't know the right word or phrase to explain an idea or make a point. Keep writing and move on to the next idea, and then go back to revise and edit later.

⊙ Go to MyEnglishLab to join in a collaborative activity.

for research summaries, 326, 326t

for revisions, 127, 128t, 130t–131t

for understanding assignments, 77, 78t

for understanding rhetorical context, 113, 113t

chronological organization of ideas, 48, 252

circling, 24, 24f

citations, using, 219

claims, in integration of evidence, 218–220

clarity, editing for, 156t

classification
  as organizational pattern, 85t, 87t
  signal words and phrases for, 87t

clauses
  adverb, 103(LS)
  dependent vs. independent, 30(LS), 103(LS), 169(LS)
  move in the sentence, 57t
  reduce to a phrase, 57t
  vs. phrases, 30(LS), 169(LS)

clichés, 289

climate change
  abstract on, 317
  academic excerpts on, 264, 330
  and Arctic ice melt, 76, 78t, 89, 91t, 92–93
  and biodiversity, 85, 86, 96–97
  definition of, 293
  descriptive writing on, 297
  and severe weather, 91, 247
  in food security, 247–249, 247f, 261f, 264, 317
  global temperature in, 108, 108f

cluster diagrams
  as brainstorming technique, 14f, 16, 16f, 18f
  in idea development, 41, 43f

codify, definition of, 183

coherence, revising for, 126–130, 126t, 146

cohesive devices
  adverbials as, 103(LS)
  examples of, 126t
  using for reference and agreement, 138, 138(LS), 386–387
  using in revisions, 126–130

collaboration
  as brainstorming technique, 14f, 16
  in extended writing, 74

collocations, 202–204
  in corpus, 304
  definition of, 202
  in dictionaries, 202–204, 203f, 204t
  examples of, 202

commas, in definitions, 65t

comma splices, 169(LS)

community engagement, 79

comparison and contrast
  in language of disagreement, 202(LS)
  as organizational pattern, 85, 85t, 86, 87t
  parallel structure in, 341(LS)
  signal words and phrases for, 87t

complex sentences, 169(LS)

compound sentences, 169(LS)

concessions, to counterarguments, 191, 202(LS)

conciseness, editing for, 155

conclusions
  checklist for, 332, 332t
  examples of, 330–331
  of research articles, 321t
  in research writing, 316, 328–332
  strategies and techniques for writing, 328–329, 328t, 329t

conjunctions
  coordinating, 103(LS), 169(LS), 202(LS), 208, 356
  subordinating, 103(LS)

connotations
  definition of, 139
  vs. definitions, 139
  in dictionaries, 139–141, 140f, 141f
  in style and tone, 132
  understanding, 139–142, 140f

content, revising for, 125

context clues, for in-text definitions, 65–67, 65t, 66t

contrast. see comparison and contrast

conventions
  of folklore, 282
  of genres, 112

coordinating conjunctions, 103(LS), 169(LS), 202(LS), 208, 356

coral reefs, 92, 92f, 294

corporate social responsibility (CSR), 59–61, 63

corpus, 304–309
  definition of, 304
  using, 304–309, 305f–307f, 308t

counterarguments
  checklist for peer review of, 193, 193t
  definition of, 190
  guidelines for, 191t
  language of disagreement in, 202, 202(LS), 356
  presenting, 190–193
  signal phrases indicating, 192, 192t

courtly love, 114, 120, 127, 129

credentials, author, 194

credibility
  appeals to, 280, 291–295, 291f
  and author bias, 194–195
  of sources, 53–55

environmental issues, in-text assignment on, 380
envoi, 146
errors
  in editing stage, 156–159, 156t–157t
  in proofreading stage, 160–162
essay excerpts. *see* academic writing excerpts
ethics. *see* business ethics
ethnic groups, definition of, 183
ethnicity, vs. race, 183
ethos, appeals to, 280, 291–295, 291f. *see also* credibility
etymology, 11
evidence
  integrating, 213, 217–221, 217f, 218t
  types of, 217
evidence-based opinion, 180, 180t, 185t
examples
  definition of, 90–91
  in definitions, 66, 66t
  development of, 91–92
  in extended writing, 73, 85, 85t, 86, 90–94
  peer review of, 94, 94t
  signal words and phrases for, 87t, 91
exemplification, as organizational pattern, 85, 85t, 86, 87t, 90
expert opinion, 180, 180t, 185t
expository writing, description in, 296
extended definition
  as organizational pattern, 85–87, 85t, 87t
  signal words and phrases for, 87t

extended writing, 72–109
  definition of, 73
  examples of, 79–81
  examples used in, 73, 85, 85t, 86, 90–94
  rhetorical modes in, 73
  summaries in, 95–103
  summary of skills for, 107
  understanding assignments in, 74–83, 74t, 78t, 81t, 83t
  using organizational patterns in, 73, 84–90
extinctions, mass
  article excerpt on, 99–101
  descriptive writing on, 297
  and global temperature, 108, 108f
  in-text assignments on, 106, 109

fables, 283
  academic excerpts on, 283, 298–302
  definition of, 283, 298
  descriptive writing in, 296
  examples of, 289–290
fact and opinion, 178–209
  in counterarguments, 190–193
  definition of, 179
  inferences about, 212
  in news articles, 52
  signal phrases indicating, 181, 188t
  types of, 179, 180t, 185t
  using expressions of, 187–190, 188t
fairy tales, 283
family wealth, 242, 242f
Fantastic Mr. Fox (film), 300
feedback
  during editing, 150
  in research writing, 7–9, 8t
  during revisions, 7–9, 127, 128t, 130, 130t–131t

Feuerstein, Aaron, 60–61
fiction, 280–281, 281t
figurative language, 287–290
  checklist for peer review of, 290, 290t
  definition of, 287
  identifying, 289–290
  in literature, 279
  types of, 287–289, 288t
  using, 287–290, 290t
figures of speech, 287, 289
final draft, in research writing, 5t, 9
financial crises, 214
first draft, in research writing, 4, 4t, 7
first person, 132
flash cards, 104
flatter, definition of, 289
flatterers, definition of, 289
flattery, 289
flow, in editing stage, 155
fluorocarbon, definition of, 338
folklore, 278–313
  academic excerpts on, 282–284, 298–302
  conventions of, 282
  definition of, 278, 282, 311
  examples of, 284–285, 289–290
  genres of, 283
  illustrations in, 280, 312
  in-text assignment on, 309
  medieval, 282–283, 298–302
  style of, 282–283
food security, 244–277
  abstract on, 317
  academic excerpts on, 264, 330
  article excerpts on, 246–249, 253–255, 265–268
  biodiversity in, 253–255
  climate change in, 247–249, 247f, 261f, 264, 317

Credits